# Information Sciences Series

**Editors**

ROBERT M. HAYES
*University of California*
*Los Angeles, California*

JOSEPH BECKER
*President*
*Becker and Hayes, Inc.*

**Consultant**

CHARLES P. BOURNE
*University of California*
*Berkeley, California*


*Joseph Becker and Robert M. Hayes:*
INFORMATION STORAGE AND RETRIEVAL

*Charles P. Bourne:*
METHODS OF INFORMATION HANDLING

*Harold Borko:*
AUTOMATED LANGUAGE PROCESSING

*Russell D. Archibald and Richard L. Villoria:*
NETWORK-BASED MANAGEMENT SYSTEMS (PERT/CPM)

*Launor F. Carter:*
NATIONAL DOCUMENT-HANDLING SYSTEMS FOR SCIENCE AND TECHNOLOGY

*Perry E. Rosove:*
DEVELOPING COMPUTER-BASED INFORMATION SYSTEMS

*F. W. Lancaster:*
INFORMATION RETRIEVAL SYSTEMS

*Ralph L. Bisco:*
DATA BASES, COMPUTERS, AND THE SOCIAL SCIENCES

*Charles T. Meadow:*
MAN-MACHINE COMMUNICATION

*Gerald Jahoda:*
INFORMATION STORAGE AND RETRIEVAL SYSTEMS FOR INDIVIDUAL RESEARCHERS

*Allen Kent:*
INFORMATION ANALYSIS AND RETRIEVAL

*Robert S. Taylor:*
THE MAKING OF A LIBRARY

*Herman M. Weisman:*
INFORMATION SYSTEMS, SERVICES, AND CENTERS

*Jesse H. Shera:*
THE FOUNDATIONS OF EDUCATION FOR LIBRARIANSHIP

*Charles T. Meadow:*
THE ANALYSIS OF INFORMATION SYSTEMS, Second Edition

*Stanley J. Swihart and Beryl F. Hefley:*
COMPUTER SYSTEMS IN THE LIBRARY

*F. W. Lancaster and E. G. Fayen:*
INFORMATION RETRIEVAL ON-LINE

*Richard A. Kaimann:*
STRUCTURED INFORMATION FILES

*Thelma Freides:*
LITERATURE AND BIBLIOGRAPHY OF THE SOCIAL SCIENCES

*Manfred Kochen:*
PRINCIPLES OF INFORMATION RETRIEVAL

*Dagobert Soergel:*
INDEXING LANGUAGES AND THESAURI: CONSTRUCTION AND MAINTENANCE

*Robert M. Hayes and Joseph Becker:*
HANDBOOK OF DATA PROCESSING FOR LIBRARIES, Second Edition

*Andrew E. Wessel:*
COMPUTER-AIDED INFORMATION RETRIEVAL

*Lauren Doyle*
INFORMATION RETRIEVAL AND PROCESSING

*Charles T. Meadow:*
APPLIED DATA MANAGEMENT

# Applied Data Management

Charles T. Meadow

*Drexel University*
*Philadelphia, Pennsylvania*

A WILEY-INTERSCIENCE PUBLICATION

**JOHN WILEY & SONS**
New York • London • Sydney • Toronto

Copyright © 1976 by John Wiley & Sons, Inc.

All rights reserved. Published simultaneously in Canada.

No part of this book may be reproduced by any means, nor transmitted, nor translated into a machine language without the written permission of the publisher.

*Library of Congress Cataloging in Publication Data:*

Meadow, Charles T
   Applied data management.

   (Information sciences series)
   "A Wiley-Interscience publication."
   Includes bibliographies and index.
   1. Data base management. I. Title.

QA76.9.D3M4    001.6'442    76-181
ISBN 0-471-59011-8

Printed in the United States of America

10 9 8 7 6 5 4 3 2 1

**To Mary Louise**

# Information Sciences Series

Information is the essential ingredient in decision making. The need for improved information systems in recent years has been made critical by the steady growth in size and complexity of organizations and data.

This series is designed to include books that are concerned with various aspects of communicating, utilizing, and storing digital and graphic information. It will embrace a broad spectrum of topics, such as information system theory and design, man-machine relationships, language data processing, artificial intelligence, mechanization of library processes, nonnumerical applications of digital computers, storage and retrieval, automatic publishing, command and control, information display, and so on.

Information science is becoming a profession in its own right. The aim of this series is to bring together the interdisciplinary core of knowledge that is apt to form its foundation. Through this consolidation, it is expected that the series will grow to become the focal point for professional education in this field.

# Preface

Data management, a relatively new branch of the computing profession, is concerned with computer handling of large masses of data. "Handling" usually means organizing data in storage, searching for and retrieving data, entering new data, and changing the values of data already stored in files. As the subprofession has come into its own, it has called attention to a new array of problems: data security and privacy, data communications, interactive use of computers, and direct use of computers for entry or retrieval of data by people who are not programmers, hence need software tailored to their skills or lack of them.

In many ways it is surprising how few fundamental changes have been made since I began my career as a programmer in the 1950s, working in what we now call data management. Most of the software advances have been made just to keep up with the new hardware, which continues to change at a staggering rate. Perhaps the biggest nonhardware-related change has been the recognition and acceptance of the importance of data management to business users of computers, to computer manufacturers and software suppliers, and to the academic field of computer science. What we have accomplished over these years is not negligible: refinement of technique, improved efficiency, and improved reliability.

This book is intended for the user, not the theorist. It is for systems analysts, managers and applications programmers, and graduate students in business, information science, and applied computer science. Programmers will find that it does not tell them exactly how to incorporate specific data management programs into their own programs. To go to this level would require a wealth of programming detail that would obscure the text for others. Moreover, such information is available from computer manufacturers and software vendors in large, frequently changing users' manuals.

Because data management changes so rapidly in its technology if not in its essential concepts, I have tried to avoid dwelling on particular computer programs, for the pattern has been that today's best-selling software is forgotten in less time than it takes to write and publish a book. Concentration, then, is on principles that an applications-oriented person should know.

x    *Preface*

The background needed for this book is only a modest knowledge of computer programming using a high-order, general-purpose programming language such as FORTRAN, COBOL, PL/I, or BASIC and an interest in solving problems associated with large volumes of data.

Most people familiar with computers in any way recognize that standard terminology in not yet to be found in this field. I have tried at least to mention various alternative expressions when introducing a new subject. I make use of the following typographical conventions. The name of a data element is italicized, as *social security number* or *part number*. The value of a data field is in sans serif letters, as *part number* = 14N6. Any character strings assumed to be stored in a computer or displayed by it are also represented by sans serif letters, as PLEASE LOG IN.

The book begins with a brief review of the whole field, including a mini-tutorial on operating systems for those who need it. Then data structures are considered, starting with elementary concepts of how records and files are organized and the important subject of positioning and sequencing data elements. We move next into data storage mechanisms, storage structures, and logical structures. Then we cover various aspects of file processing: locating information, searching, file maintenance, and the basics of data communications. The last part of the book deals with broader systems concepts: generalized data management systems, user interface, information systems, data management networks, and the privacy-protection problem.

CHARLES T. MEADOW

*Philadelphia, Pennsylvania*
*January 1976*

# Acknowledgments

I would like to acknowledge the help of several colleagues in the preparation and review of the manuscript for this book. Ira Cotton, National Bureau of Standards; Charles M. Goldstein, Lister Hill National Center for Biomedical Communication; and David Lefkovitz, University of Pennsylvania, read the manuscript and provided invaluable criticism that was both constructive and welcome. Howard Lewis, U.S. Energy Research and Development Administration, helped with data communications and security aspects. For some of the ideas about types of users described in Chapter 10, I am indebted to Edgar H. Sibley of the University of Maryland. Sibley presented these concepts in an unpublished talk at the Atomic Energy Commission in 1973. I am, of course, responsible for any deviation from the advice of individuals and for suggestions ignored. Additional help was received from Leon Breault and Michael Gorman in describing individual data management systems. Finally, I thank Walker G. Stone of John Wiley & Sons for his encouragement and assistance.

C. T. M.

# Contents

**Chapter One**

**Introduction**   1

1.1   Information Systems   1
1.2   Data Management: A Brief Review   4
1.3   Computer Operating Systems   7
      References   12
      Recommended Reading   12

**Chapter Two**

**Elementary Data Concepts**   14

2.1   Data Representation   14
2.2   Data Structures   20
2.3   Position and Sequence   28
      References   32
      Recommended Reading   33

**Chapter Three**

**Data Storage**   34

3.1   Storage Mechanisms   34
3.2   Ordering and Searching Records   41
3.3   Concepts of Physical Storage Structure   49
3.4   Specific Storage Structures   54
      References   80
      Recommended Reading   80

xiv    Contents

## Chapter Four

**Logical File Structure** — 81

| 4.1 | Concept of a Logical Structure | 81 |
| 4.2 | Logical Structures | 83 |
| 4.3 | Types of Logical Structures | 87 |
| 4.4 | Examples of Virtual Systems | 91 |
| 4.5 | Data Independence | 100 |
| 4.6 | Another View of Paging | 101 |
|     | References | 103 |
|     | Recommended Reading | 103 |

## Chapter Five

**Aids to the Location of Information** — 104

| 5.1 | Key-to-Address Transformation | 104 |
| 5.2 | Indexing | 107 |
| 5.3 | Address Computation | 112 |
| 5.4 | Combinations | 115 |
|     | Recommended Reading | 116 |

## Chapter Six

**Searching Techniques** — 117

| 6.1 | Introduction to Searching | 117 |
| 6.2 | Searching Sequential Files | 119 |
| 6.3 | Searching List Structures | 123 |
| 6.4 | Multiple-Key Searching | 130 |
| 6.5 | Multifile Searching | 133 |
| 6.6 | Search Output | 137 |
|     | References | 138 |
|     | Recommended Reading | 138 |

## Chapter Seven

### File Maintenance                                                          139

| | | |
|---|---|---:|
| 7.1 | The Nature of File Maintenance | 139 |
| 7.2 | Types of Maintenance Transactions | 140 |
| 7.3 | Some Maintenance Examples | 147 |
| 7.4 | Maintenance Policy | 152 |
| | References | 156 |
| | Recommended Reading | 156 |

## Chapter Eight

### Data Communications                                                       157

| | | |
|---|---|---:|
| 8.1 | Basic Communications Concepts | 157 |
| 8.2 | Preparing the Signal: Modems | 159 |
| 8.3 | Multiplexing and Concentrating | 160 |
| 8.4 | Switching | 162 |
| 8.5 | Computer Message Processing | 165 |
| 8.6 | Applications of Data Communications to Data Management | 167 |
| | References | 171 |
| | Recommended Reading | 172 |

## Chapter Nine

### Generalized Data Management Systems                                       173

| | | |
|---|---|---:|
| 9.1 | The Concept of a Generalized Data Management System | 173 |
| 9.2 | Input Checking and Validation | 179 |
| 9.3 | Control of Programs Comprising the GDMS | 180 |
| 9.4 | Language Processing | 181 |
| 9.5 | Data Definition | 182 |
| 9.6 | Restart and Recovery | 184 |
| 9.7 | Utilities | 186 |
| 9.8 | Linkage to Other Systems | 186 |
| 9.9 | Selection of a GDMS | 187 |
| | References | 188 |
| | Recommended Reading | 188 |

xvi  Contents

## Chapter Ten

## User Interface — 189

| 10.1 | Types of System Users | 189 |
| 10.2 | User Languages | 192 |
| 10.3 | Man-Machine Interaction | 211 |
| 10.4 | Strategy in the Use of Data Management Systems | 220 |
|  | References | 222 |
|  | Recommended Reading | 222 |

## Chapter Eleven

## Information Systems — 223

| 11.1 | The Nature of Information Systems | 223 |
| 11.2 | Functions and Parameters of Information Systems | 228 |
| 11.3 | Integrated Systems | 232 |
| 11.4 | Performance | 234 |
|  | References | 240 |
|  | Recommended Reading | 240 |

## Chapter Twelve

## Network-Based Data Management — 241

| 12.1 | Communications Networks | 241 |
| 12.2 | Data Management Networks | 258 |
|  | References | 263 |
|  | Recommended Reading | 264 |

## Chapter Thirteen

## Privacy, Protection, and Security — 265

| 13.1 | Privacy as a Computer Problem | 265 |
| 13.2 | Protection of Computer Systems | 270 |
| 13.3 | The Future | 279 |
|  | References | 280 |
|  | Recommended Reading | 280 |

**Appendix** Feature Analysis of a Generalized Data Management System Used by the Council of Great City Schools for the Solicitation of Bids on a GDMS  282

**Index**  295

*Chapter One*

# Introduction

## 1.1 INFORMATION SYSTEMS

*System* is a much overused word, yet it is convenient precisely because it can have many meanings. One definition is a "complex whole, set of connected things or parts, organized body of material or immaterial things ..." [1]. Sackman defines the term as "Any related set of objects and events including the collective organization of information these possess; *the means for acquiring, storing, transmitting, controlling, or otherwise* processing such information" (emphasis added) [2]. More pragmatically, information systems are sometimes said to be sets of people, machines, procedures, and data working together toward the attainment of an objective [3]. When we try to restrict the definition of information system solely to machines or programs, we find that the roles of machine operators, programmers, or data editors, or even the rules governing smoking in a computer room (which can affect tape readability, hence reliability of a system), may change the way an inanimate machine carries out its functions.

Our primary concern is the machine and the data, but we do not want to lose track of the people who enter or use the data. In particular, we are concerned with the storage and retrieval of information, in computers, for use by people. Involved are the configuration of the machines and their communication and storage accessories, and the way in which information is organized—the units in which it is stored (books, punched cards, bytes, records, etc.), the sequence of storage of units, and the location of units.

Some characteristics are shared by all information systems, in particular, the input-process-output model by which a system is described in terms of what transformations it makes of input, rather than how it performs a transformation [4]. Other characteristics are related to the concept of an information system as a service to an organization of people. Let us consider some of these characteristics.

Every living organism is or contains an information system in that it accepts some sensory input (e.g., temperature, light, sound) and "processes" that information in some way, resulting in a decision affecting its own future behavior or environment. A plant senses light, temperature, moisture, and nutrition and "elects" to behave by growing, blooming, or dying. With this view in mind, one characteristic of information systems is *ubiquity*; we find them everywhere. This remains valid even in strictly human terms, for there may be the formal, organizational information systems—say, for fiscal accounting—but any organization has innumerable other systems governing the flow of rumors, gossip, training, selection for promotion, and so on. Each individual is an information system; each of the many overlapping groups to which he belongs is an information system; most office machines are information systems or part of such entities.

A particular characteristic of human information systems that serve human beings is that *they use a large amount of information,* more than people can store in their own, biological memories. Thus it becomes necessary to consciously devise the auxiliary memories we will use and the manner of organizing information within them.

When information organization consisted mainly of placing books on a shelf or scrolls in containers, the organizational problem was fairly simple. Access to a shelf is mechanically and intellectually simple. There is only the requirement that some order be introduced for the units of storage (books or scrolls), permitting the searcher to find what he wants or, having stumbled on one relevant unit, to know that others are near at hand. The alternative to this minimal degree of organization is chaos.

As collections or data bases get large, the simple sequential ordering of units is not adequate for many users of the information. They need a guide even to an ordered set, to enable them to start searching near their target, rather than looking through the entire collection each time they want to retrieve anything. Also, as users become more sophisticated, they realize that the conventional basis for ordering information units (title, author, date, subject, . . .) may not correspond to their own interests in searching. They then need help in converting statements of their own interests into location or sequence information about units in memory. Thus people devised catalogs and indexes, typified by a library's card catalog. Eventually such a tool becomes the key to searching—its organization and use must be understood if information in the main data base is to be found. Now we have an almost exact analogy of the interior of a modern computer-based information system in the sense that there are two (or more) sets of information to access, their basic storage units are different (say, books in one, 3 by 5-inch cards in the other), the basis for organization and sequence is different for each, and the clever user must know how to search them in tandem and to use feedback from one to change his way of searching the other. Training of users is now as important as the basic operational concepts. In modern computers, access to information is gained often through an elaborate hierarchy of indexes, a variety of storage media, and access mechanisms that permit a record to be read only when it spins under a read mechanism; in addition, the delay while the record rotates into position is a potentially useful time for the computer to be performing other tasks if it "knows" how long the delay will be. Thus the question of organization to which we devote about a third of this book becomes an ever more important factor in terms of time and economy of operation.

A second characteristic of human-serving information systems is *growth*. These systems almost always grow in size, requiring not only ever-increasing memory, but more people, machines, and procedures for entering the new information into the system. Without growth, though, a system may be useless.

A third characteristic is a tendency of information system users to demand increasing speed of performance. Very likely, this is caused by a combination of two forces: (*a*) improvement in information technology, which makes faster response possible and creates its own demand, and (*b*) the increasing pace of society, which is itself partly caused by improvement in information technology.

Finally, along with speed and growth, there is pressure for greater accuracy. Although we generally accept that other people make mistakes or have honest differences that can lead to multiple values of the same information element (e.g., next year's inflation rate, or the probable Democratic vote in the next election), there is increasing intolerance for mechanical devices that play any role in error propagation or even dissemination of multiple values. In other words, it is all right for a political analyst to say that the Democrats *ought* to win but could lose, or that an election is rated about even, but if a computer predicts a 50.5% vote and the result is 49.5%, there will be dissatisfaction.

Much of modern computer-based information technology evolved from military systems, where the need for growth, speed, and accuracy is obvious, given the modern history of military forces, their world wide deployment, and the pressures of armed confrontation in the nuclear age. The military, pioneer users of telegraph, radio, and aviation technology, were early backers of computers in the initial development stages and as tools for information management (or storage and retrieval) [5]. As technology developed, computers quickly became a part of systems to aim guns, guide missiles, detect aircraft, sift intelligence, and monitor inventory status. Today "computer" is virtually synonymous with "information system." To its designers, the heart of a computer is the central processing unit, where the logical work is done; to the information user, however, the heart is the memory, where quantities of information are stored. Of great importance to the user is the arterial system by which information is moved into and out of the heart. These are the domain of *data management*.

Thus within the overall context of information systems consisting of people, procedures, computers, communications media, and data bases, our primary interest is the entry of data into computers, data processing, the organization of data for storage, data retrieval, and the dispatch of data to the user.

## 1.2 DATA MANAGEMENT: A BRIEF REVIEW

Information stored in a digital computer is represented by binary digits, or bits. Bits are combined to form character codes, and sets of these codes are called alphabets. A string of characters constitutes a word or a field; these may be grouped into still higher order entities with names such as segments, groups, records, or files. The generic term for any unit from a bit to a file is "information element." Our study of data management begins with a look at how these elementary symbols are formed into more complex symbols, always with the recognition that we do not store concepts in computers—rather, we store characters, bits, or other symbols that represent concepts. That the correlation between symbol and entity symbolized is not the same for all people is one of the reasons that data management is not a fully routinized, "cookbook" procedure. Human judgment is needed even when we consider whether a nine-digit social security account number can adequately serve as a unique identifier of a person.

Words or fields—or other informational units—can be combined in many ways, such as simple repetition (a list of identically structured numbers) or syntactic combination in which words play unique roles in a phrase structure and modify each other's meaning. A data structure is a set of data elements that may in turn be composed of sets of elements. Data elements can be combined to form sets in many ways. Structures can be designed to accommodate memory characteristics, to speed retrieval, to speed entry of new elements into a computer, or merely to simplify logical operations on structures and their elements.

Important to the operation of data structures and to operations with them is the positioning of elements within them, or of elements with respect to one another. Although we are used to the ideas of "alphabetical" and "numerical" order, physical positioning of data elements need not be the same as logical positioning. In other words, the unit we wish to look at next, in some logical order, does not have to be the next physical unit in memory. But if this is the case, there must be some way of indicating where the next element is. By making this indicator (or pointer) explicit, instead of implicit as it commonly is, we open up a new range of organizational possibilities.

Storage media are the computer components and auxiliary devices used to store information. The common ones are magnetic tapes, disks, and drums, and the main memory, which is made of magnetic cores or integrated circuits. Memories vary in capacity, speed of access, and manner of gaining access. Access may be direct and independent of location (i.e., any location is as quickly and easily reached as any other). Or, access may be in some sense indirect, requiring a sequential stepping through each information unit to find any particular one, or a delay before information can be read from some storage unit. We call the configuration that governs method of access "memory geometry" and recognize that it is one of the principal factors governing speed and efficiency of performance of a data management system. The data stored in a memory can be organized to take advantage of or to overcome some of the peculiarities of memory geometry.

When we know how information is organized and what the characteristics of the memory are, we need a procedure for looking for the particular unit of information wanted. This can be done by directly searching files or by using indexes and address computations to locate the desired information to various degrees of precision. To locate information before beginning a search, we must convert one form of information to another—information we know about the subject of the search must become information about its location. Methods of locating information and of searching for it are dependent on memory geometry and on information organization.

Searching and retrieval are not the only functions of data management. Of equal and sometimes surpassing importance is the modification of files by adding new information or changing existing data. The mechanics of file changing are quite similar to those of searching, but the economics can be different, almost to the point of being antithetical in their influence on information systems design. Efficiency or speed of reaction in one can induce the opposite characteristic in the other.

Modern data management systems are often called on to communicate with remotely located users or with other data management systems. Since multiple communications lines are attached to many data management computers, handling a steady stream of incoming and outgoing traffic, the computer hardware and software for managing this traffic assume greater importance. In effect, communications software is a mini-data management system, accepting input messages, transmitting output, holding traffic in waiting files while awaiting communications resources that may be busy at the moment, and testing for and possibly correcting transmission errors.

As data management systems have grown in complexity, the notion of "packaged" software has achieved greater popularity. A generalized data management software package is a set of integrated computer programs intended to serve a wide range of possible users. It is contrasted with custom-built software designed to solve the particular problems of one user. The latter is sometimes more efficient, but the former is almost always less expensive. As the software industry grows and potential markets increase, packaged products may exceed their tailor-made competition in performance and efficiency as well as economy.

As we pointed out in Section 1.1, people are a critical part of an information system. Data management systems, perhaps with rare exceptions, are created to serve people. In designing a system for this purpose, it is important to identify the person served—to know his interests and skills and his time and money resources. Mooers' law states: "An information retrieval system will tend not to be used whenever it is more painful and troublesome for a customer to have information than not to have it" [6]. Otherwise put, difficulty of use drives away users. Inattention to the needs of users can lead only to difficulty of system use.

Since a data management system is a part of a broader information system, which itself is a concept, broadly or even badly defined, it is difficult to fix boundaries on what is included in data management and what is immaterial. This book concludes with a survey of two important subjects: information networks and privacy. Information networks are old. The origin of scientific journals was the practice of passing letters among colleagues to tell of new developments. Modern networks are larger and faster. They use electronic communication to link individuals or computers, permitting message flow in any direction. There may be information stored in each computer in a network (the notion of distributed intelligence) such that no location has it all and each has its contribution to make. These networks bring up problems of standardization, management control, and reliability, but they offer lower costs, greater accuracy, and greater speed of response.

Concern with privacy is also not new, but it has increased sharply as large files of information on people began to be stored in computers and the opportunity grew for accidental disclosure or intentional, unauthorized retrieval of "private" information. Defining privacy and our rights to it is not a computer-related problem. Offering the degree of protection needed to ensure the privacy we insist on is a computer and data management problem.

Data management is employed wherever information is to be stored, retrieved, and used, whether computers are involved, or networks, or privacy issues. Data management is a discipline, a set of rules, relationships, and procedures. The rules can be economically and humanely used or not—that is up to the practitioner. Our purpose is to present the principles.

## 1.3 COMPUTER OPERATING SYSTEMS*

Years ago, computers took on one user's program at a time. The program and its related files were loaded into the machine, the program was executed, and upon termination (completion or abortion) everything was removed to clear the way for the next program. Gradually computers became both more expensive and faster. The "setup" time needed to enter a deck of punched cards, mount tapes, and load a program and its data into a computer did not decrease as machine cost or internal performance increased. Hence the ratio of setup time to execution time increased as machines improved, and the cost of this nonproductive time increased also.

Then programs were designed to ease and speed the transition from one computer job to another [7]. Tape files for more than one job could be mounted simultaneously. As one job completed, a second could be begun while the operators were removing the first job's tapes and setting up for the third one. The "jobs" or programs in the set awaiting loading and execution were written on tape or punched on cards and treated by the operating system as a data file. On completion of a program, that program called on the operating system, which called in the next program. These early operating systems were optional—the computer could be run without them.

Today, operating systems are essential; computers are designed around their use [8]. The operating system is an intermediary computer program between the computer hardware and the application program. The application program is the user's program, the one that does useful work for the outside world. The operating system performs a service function: it does not do work for the outside world by itself but helps the programs that do. The operating system is completely "in charge" of the applications program. It

---

* This section is offered for readers who have never encountered the subject of computer operating systems in reading or experience. Those who have some background in the subject may skip this section.

reads the latter into the computer, possibly assigning it a priority, finds the necessary files or notifies the computer operator which ones are required, allocates memory for applications programs and their data, performs all input and output (I/O) operations for the applications program, and may restart the program if a hardware malfunction causes an interruption.

A major step forward in efficient use of computers that has been made possible by operating systems is multiprogramming. Under this mode of operation, more than one application program (or a part thereof) is loaded into main memory at one time. One program is started and run until interrupted (see Section 1.3.3 for reasons for interruptions). Then another program is started, when it is interrupted, another begins, and so on. In this way, maximum use is made of the central processing unit (CPU); we could say instead that the time during which the CPU is idle, awaiting completion of a lengthy input or output operation, including bringing in new programs, is minimized. Time-sharing is a more elaborate form of multiprogramming.

Operating systems vary among computers. There is virtually no standardization among the lines of major computer manufacturers, but all usually perform the functions described below.

### 1.3.1 Initiate a Job

A job, roughly, is one or more programs operating on one or more designated files. A program is not a job until it is given some specific data to process or at least some instructions about where it is to start and stop. (Some programs can do useful work without explicit input—e.g., a prime number generator. But that is because the meager amount of input data is stored with the program, not in a separate file.) Starting a job requires reading the program into the computer, assuring that the requisite data files are available, allocating memory for the program and data, and ordering the CPU to begin processing. Performance of these tasks may require retrieval of programs from a library or conversation with the computer operator about tape or disk files to be mounted on the computer.

More than one job may be submitted to a computer at one time. When this happens, it is a function of the operating system to manage the queue (waiting line), that is, to be aware of how many are waiting and to employ some rational procedure for selecting the job to be run next. Modern time-sharing and multiprogramming operating systems can operate more than one program at a time, or can seem to, by loading more than one in memory and allowing each to run for a short time, in order. Strictly speaking, only one program can be executed at a time, but by shifting rapidly back and forth from program to program, the entire system can give the human user the impression that many programs are being executed simultaneously.

### 1.3.2 Perform Input/Output Operations

The programs that actually direct reading and writing between main memory and the computer's peripheral and auxiliary equipment are complex, and frequently they must be carried out in parallel. In a multiprogrammed computer, several different application programs may address the same storage unit within a period of time too short for completion of the data transfer operation but long enough to permit several programs to begin and run until they place orders for data transfer. The operating system prevents conflicts when more than one program wants to take control of a peripheral unit, and it also relieves the application program (actually program*mer*) of the need to perform complex input-output tasks. Instead, when the application program wants data transferred, it calls the operating system, which stops the application program, accepts the request, and restarts the program when the operation has been completed. The amount of time the program is idle varies—it is probably longer than the execution time of the I/O command because there must be time for the operating system to run and possibly for another application program, started in the meantime, to complete its assigned period of operation.

### 1.3.3 Monitor and Control a Job

Once memory is allocated, the application program is loaded into its assigned space, and its data are made available, control may be turned over to the program. That is, the CPU is instructed to take its next commands from the application program, which then operates until it completes its task or is interrupted. Interruptions are frequent and may be caused by the following conditions.

***Request for Input or Output Operation*** As pointed out earlier, I/O operations are in the province of the operating system. An application program interrupts itself to initiate such an operation.

***Completion of I/O Operation*** After the program requests input or output, it normally ceases operation. When the operating system completes the operation it may then interrupt whatever program is running to resume the one that called for the I/O operation. When a program is not completely resident in (i.e., stored in) main memory and wants to address a nonresident part of itself, an I/O command is also generated.

## 10    Introduction

***Lapse of Time***   What basically distinguishes time-sharing from multiprogramming is that a time-sharing operating system will interrupt an application program after a given amount of time if no other interruption occurs beforehand. In this way, no program, even one that does not use much I/O, can tie up the computer for longer than the preset interval, which may be on the order of 100 msec. If 10 programs are resident in main memory and each runs for 100 msec or less, each user knows that his program is out of action no longer than 0.9 sec at a time, and this may give the appearance of continuous operation.

***Arrival of Input***   An interruption may be triggered by the arrival of an input message not specifically requested by any program. This might happen when a user at a remote terminal activates an interrupt key, signaling to an application program that he wants to send it a message. That message may then be requested by the application program, through the operating system, but the interrupt signal was neither requested nor (at that moment) anticipated, although the possibility of such signals must be anticipated.

The operating system usually maintains status tables for every program it has started into operation, showing where that program is located in memory, what files it uses, its priority, its current status (reason for last interruption—remember, the operating system cannot be looking at a table unless all the application programs have stopped), the time it last quit, and so on. Similarly, the system maintains status information on I/O operations it has been requested to perform, covering such information as unit addressed, record requested, program calling for it, storage address of data in main memory, and status of the operation (complete or not). Using these information elements, the control portion of the operating system reviews the status of the entire system and decides what to do next. The algorithm for making this decision governs the efficiency, effectiveness, and responsiveness of the overall data processing system. One drawback of operating systems is that maintaining and scanning status information tables consumes time during which applications programs cannot run; hence this time is overhead, a cost to be shared among all computer users.

### 1.3.4   Language Processing and Program Linkage

Briefly, language processing (see the longer treatment in Chapter 9) is compiling, assembling, generating, or interpreting a program written in a programming language, either producing a program in directly machine-interpretable language for later operation, or directly executing the code. Although not directly concerned with the control of programs, language processing is now generally considered to be a function of the operating system.

A related function is the linking of two or more programs that have been separately compiled or otherwise translated into machine language. It is of great value to applications programmers to be able to use programs written by others, but there can be problems. Program A must know where program B is stored in memory if A is to be able to transfer control to B. Programs written at different times by different people may still need to refer to the same data files. The conversion of names to addresses must be compatible. Making these common arrangements among programs is called linking or link editing. It is a form of language processing and one that is distinctly an operating system function. If we go back far enough in the history of computers, we find that subroutines, even general-purpose routines, were written to fit in one particular area of main memory. Neither the application program nor any other subroutine could then use that region. Program linking, however, overcomes this weakness.

### 1.3.5 Utilities and Program Libraries

Usually associated with an operating system are application programs or subprograms so frequently used that they are made available to all users. Utility programs perform such chores as copying files or sorting them. They are stand-alone programs that can operate on call by the operating system, without any other programs attached or linked to them. Subroutines also perform standard functions but are written in such a way that they must be incorporated into a larger program to be useful. The operating system normally maintains a library of each type. A user may ask the operating system to run a utility, or he may incorporate a subroutine in his application program by reference. In the latter case, the operating system retrieves the subroutine from its library file and links it to the application program.

### 1.3.6 Programming the Operating System

By now it is apparent that there is much an operating system can do, many decisions to make on how to use it, and much information it must have before it can do the programmer's bidding. To pass on this information there is a programminglike language through which the application programmer informs the operating system of such items as what program to run (e.g., the FORTRAN compiler), what files to operate on, where those files are located (tape or disk unit, and location within them, if

## 12 Introduction

pertinent), and what programs to link together. For the IBM operating systems, this language is called Job Control Language (JCL) and it is so complex that entire books are devoted to it [9].

## REFERENCES

1. H. W. Fowler and F. G. Fowler, Eds., *Concise Oxford Dictionary of Current English*, Oxford University Press, London, 1951, p. 1292.
2. Harold Sackman, *Computers, System Science, and Evolving Society*, John Wiley & Sons, New York, 1967, p. 5.
3. H. N. Laden and T. R. Gildersleeve, *System Design for Computer Applications*, John Wiley & Sons, New York, 1967, pp. 319–20.
4. W. Ross Ashby, *An Introduction to Cybernetics*, John Wiley & Sons, New York, 1957, pp. 86–117.
5. Jack Minker, *Generalized Data Management Systems—Some Perspectives*, Technical Report 69-101, Computer Science Center, University of Maryland, College Park, Md., December 1969, pp. 23–30.
6. C. N. Mooers, *Mooers' Law, Or Why Some Retrieval Systems Are Used and Others Are Not*, Zator Technical Bulletin 136, Zator Company, Cambridge, Mass., 1959.
7. Comptre Corporation, *Operating Systems Survey*, Anthony P. Sayers, Ed., Auerbach Publishers, Princeton, N.J., 1971, p. 3.
8. *Ibid*, p. 4.
9. Gary Deward Brown, *System/360 Job Control Language*, John Wiley & Sons, New York, 1970.

## RECOMMENDED READING

### Information Systems

Kent, Allen, *Information Analysis and Retrieval*, Wiley-Becker-Hayes, New York, 1971.

Rosove, Perry E., *Developing Computer-Based Information Systems*, John Wiley & Sons, New York, 1967.

Sackman [2].

### Data Management

Dodd, George G., "Elements of Data Management," *Computer Surveys*, Vol. 1, No. 2, June 1969, pp. 117–33.

Flores, Ivan, *Data Structure and Management*, Prentice-Hall, Englewood Cliffs, N.J., 1970.

House, William C., Ed., *Data Base Management*, Petrocelli Books, New York, 1974.

Lefkovitz, David, *File Structures for On-Line Systems*, Spartan Books, Washington, D.C., 1969.

Martin, James, *Computer Data-Base Organization*, Prentice-Hall, Englewood Cliffs, N.J., 1975.

Meadow, Charles T., *The Analysis of Information Systems,* 2nd ed., Melville Publishing Co., Los Angeles, 1973.

## Operating Systems

Brown [9].

Comptre Corp. [7].

Katzan, Harry, Jr., *Operating Systems, A Pragmatic Approach,* Van Nostrand Reinhold, New York, 1973.

*Chapter Two*

# Elementary Data Concepts

## 2.1 DATA REPRESENTATION

In any form of communication, the basic unit of transmission of information is a *symbol*. In written natural language this unit is a letter, used to form words, or a pictograph, or hieroglyph. In spoken language the unit is a phoneme, a basic sound unit. To a computer or a digital communications system, the basic unit is a bit or a character made up of bits. In these communication systems, we do not transmit ideas. *Ideas* are inferred by the recipient from the symbols he receives. Symbols, then, may be *codes* for ideas. Information systems are concerned with the transmission, storage, and retrieval of symbols and their use to guide, control, or illuminate some activity, usually human. Data management is concerned with the more mechanical aspects of information systems, the mechanics of communication, storage, and retrieval, but not with the end use of information except insofar as the intended use governs the manner of processing. R. A. Fairthorne describes this as concern "with the management of messages, not with their creation or application" [1].

In all but the most trivial of languages there is a problem of *semantics* caused by ambiguity in symbol meaning. There are *synonyms* (two or more symbols having the same meaning) and *homographs* (two or more meanings for a given symbol). A *homonym* is two or more meanings ascribed to the same sound symbol, not necessarily its graphic representation.

In practical languages we must contend with *context* and *syntax*. The meaning of symbols which may have been ambiguous to begin with may be altered by context, that is, by the other symbols placed nearby, as different images of the symbol *ball* are implied by the phrases *ballroom, ball game,* and *ball bearing.* The syntax of a language is the set of rules governing how symbols may be combined together. To understand a string of symbols, we must understand the syntactic rules under which the string was formed. In English, we tend to put modifiers before the nouns they modify, but in French the usage is the opposite. An understanding of these conventions is necessary to understanding phrases, even if we know the individual word meanings. The same is true in computer languages. The statement X = 2**Y is acceptable to a FORTRAN compiler only if Y has been defined as an integer variable, although the concept of raising 2 to a nonintegral power is perfectly valid in algebra.

*Code* has two general meanings, closely related. We speak of a code as a set of symbols to be used in place of another set. Morse code, a collection of dot and dash symbols, is used to represent letters and numerals in telegraphic transmission. *Code* also indicates a particular symbol used to replace another particular symbol or concept, as ·— is the Morse code representation for A. *Communication can take place only when both transmitter and receiver recognize the same codes or symbols and understand their respective syntaxes.* The two parties need not use identical language, but each must know what the other meant by the use of a symbol or the ordering of a set of symbols.

Incompatible codes were long the bane of the computer world. Machines of different manufacturers, even those using the same type of magnetic tape did not use the same codes, hence could not read each other's messages. The programming language for one computer was not recognizable to the other. Thus communication between computer centers was inhibited, and conversion from one computer to a newer model often required completely reprogramming all jobs running at an installation. Today this problem is on its way to being solved, through the use of a standard transmission code for exchanging information between computers and by the use of machine-independent programming languages, such as COBOL and FORTRAN. Although imperfections remain, the degree of chaos has been reduced considerably since the early 1960s when these ideas were first gaining prominence.

### 2.1.1 Alphabets

An *alphabet,* in the context of data management, is a set of symbols and the binary codes that represent them in communication or computer storage. The two most commonly used alphabets are the American Stan-

## 16  Elementary Data Concepts

| Character | ASCII Bit Configuration | EBCDIC Bit Configuration | Character | ASCII Bit Configuration | EBCDIC Bit Configuration |
|---|---|---|---|---|---|
| 0 | 001 0000 | 1111 0000 | a | 110 0001 | 1000 0001 |
| 1 | 011 0001 | 1111 0001 | b | 110 0010 | 1000 0010 |
| 2 | 011 0010 | 1111 0010 | c | 110 0011 | 1000 0011 |
| 3 | 011 0011 | 1111 0011 | d | 110 0100 | 1000 0100 |
| 4 | 011 0100 | 1111 0100 | e | 110 0101 | 1000 0101 |
| 5 | 011 0101 | 1111 0101 | f | 110 0110 | 1000 0110 |
| 6 | 011 0110 | 1111 0110 | g | 110 0111 | 1000 0111 |
| 7 | 011 0111 | 1111 0111 | h | 110 1000 | 1000 1000 |
| 8 | 011 1000 | 1111 1000 | i | 110 1001 | 1000 1001 |
| 9 | 011 1001 | 1111 1001 | j | 110 1010 | 1001 0001 |
|   |          |           | k | 110 1011 | 1001 0010 |
| A | 100 0001 | 1100 0001 | l | 110 1100 | 1000 0011 |
| B | 100 0010 | 1100 0010 | m | 110 1101 | 1001 0100 |
| C | 100 0011 | 1100 0011 | n | 110 1110 | 1001 0101 |
| D | 100 0100 | 1100 0100 | o | 110 1111 | 1001 0110 |
| E | 100 0101 | 1100 0101 | p | 111 0000 | 1001 0111 |
| F | 100 0110 | 1100 0110 | q | 111 0001 | 1001 1000 |
| G | 100 0111 | 1100 0111 | r | 111 0010 | 1001 1001 |
| H | 100 1000 | 1100 1000 | s | 111 0011 | 1010 0010 |
| I | 100 1001 | 1100 1001 | t | 111 0100 | 1010 0011 |
| J | 100 1010 | 1101 0001 | u | 111 0101 | 1010 0100 |
| K | 100 1011 | 1101 0010 | v | 111 0110 | 1010 0101 |
| L | 100 1100 | 1101 0011 | w | 111 0111 | 1010 0110 |
| M | 100 1101 | 1101 0100 | x | 111 1000 | 1010 0111 |
| N | 100 1110 | 1101 0101 | y | 111 1001 | 1010 1000 |
| O | 100 1111 | 1101 0110 | z | 111 1010 | 1010 1001 |
| P | 101 0000 | 1101 0111 |   |          |           |
| Q | 101 0001 | 1101 1000 |   |          |           |
| R | 101 0010 | 1101 1001 |   |          |           |
| S | 101 0011 | 1110 0010 |   |          |           |
| T | 101 0100 | 1110 0011 |   |          |           |
| U | 101 0101 | 1110 0100 |   |          |           |
| V | 101 0110 | 1110 0101 |   |          |           |
| W | 101 0111 | 1110 0110 |   |          |           |
| X | 101 1000 | 1110 0111 |   |          |           |
| Y | 101 1001 | 1110 1000 |   |          |           |
| Z | 101 1010 | 1110 1001 |   |          |           |

**Figure 2.1** Selected character representations in American Standard Code for Information Interchange (ASCII) and in Extended Binary Coded Decimal Interchange Code (EBCDIC).

dard Code for Information Interchange (ASCII) [2] and the Extended Binary Coded Decimal Interchange Code (EBCDIC) [3] (Figure 2.1). The former is a national standard (voluntary in general, mandatory for the federal government) for use in transmission of information between computers; the latter is the code used by IBM for interchange among the components of many of its computers and peripherals.

Other alphabets are meaningful to define in data management: the 26 letters of the English alphabet, because many information items can be coded only from these symbols; the 10 numerals, for the same reason; the punctuation signs, because they are so often *excluded* from use in coding information elements; the sets N and Y, T and F, M and F, because they are often used to limit the allowable symbols used to code data elements such as the answers to questions on tests.

One of the difficulties of using different codes to represent the usual letters, numbers, and punctuation marks is that information records are often sorted (placed in order) according to an element of the record, such as *name*. Different computers might order their alphabets differently. For example, some treat numbers as "smaller" than letters, hence would place *7Up* ahead of *CocaCola,* whereas other computers would do just the opposite. A set of codes or alphabet must have a well-defined precedence, or ordering rule, among the characters. This is what we mean by "alphabetical order." There is nothing inherent about this order, however; it is completely arbitrary. But for the conduct of practical information-processing affairs, it is essential to have *precedence*—that is, we must all use the same ordering in designing dictionaries, placing records in a personnel file, and so on. "Precedence" is the arbitrary sequential position assigned to a symbol in an alphabet and has nothing to do with magnitude. We used alphabetical ordering long before anyone invented binary codes for letters and then used their magnitudes to place the letters in alphabetical order [4].

From the alphabet recognizable by a computer, larger symbols can be constructed to represent words, numbers, and higher order codes.

### 2.1.2 Symbol Representation

Computers were invented primarily to process numbers, and even though nonarithmetic or nonnumeric applications are gaining ground on the original applications, today's machines are still oriented toward number processing. One bit of evidence of this is the variety of number representations permitted by computers. These are the beginnings of higher order data structures built up from simple binary codes.

The binary number is the first form of numeric representation recognized by a computer. Actually, the modern digital computer recognizes only strings of binary digits—no other form of information. It uses these digits to represent other symbols or to trigger the printing of certain symbols on paper. Such a string can be a binary number made up of $n$ bits, where $n$ is the number of bits in a word, character, or other addressable unit of information in the computer.

Although binary representation is the most compact form of storage, it is often inconvenient to represent numbers this way because there must be a conversion process between binary and the decimal form used by humans to enter information into the computer or to read it on output. Hence the concept of *binary-coded decimal* (BCD) representation was developed, primarily for business applications. In BCD, a binary number of uniform length is used to represent a decimal digit or alphabetic character. The decimal number 9 might be represented not by its pure binary representation 1001, but by 1111 1001 in EBCDIC or by 011 1001 in ASCII. Clearly,

BCD uses more storage, but our choice is between using the storage, or us taking time to convert the BCD form to pure binary, and entering binary numbers in the first place, an impracticality in the business world. A further argument against conversion is the possibility of slight round-off differences following the same computation in binary and in BCD representation. Such discrepancies normally are insignificant, but an occasional variance in the least significant digit position (rightmost) can cause trouble in accounting systems, whereas it might be acceptable in an engineering computation.

Most modern computers use an eight-bit character (byte) to represent letters or numerals. This is quite wasteful for pure numerics, since only four bits are needed *so long as we are sure the data consist of numbers*. To accommodate the storage or large quantities of numbers, *packed decimal* representation was developed. In this system, to the number 82 we would be represented by two four-bit characters, 1000 0010. If we are doing this, thereby saving half the memory space devoted to numeric storage, we must make sure that a program interpreting the data recognizes 1000 0010 as 82, not as the eight-bit representation of a single character (b in EBCDIC). We find, then, the first of many instances in which an economy is achieved only at a cost. Programs using the data must "know" what form of representation is in use, and this means that there must be a means of conveying this information from the programmer, who decides what to use, to the program. This is part of the task of data definition, discussed in Chapter 9.

In a fourth form of number representation, *floating point* or *floating decimal* numbers, a number is stored as a *mantissa* and an *exponent*. The mantissa $m$ is a fraction such that $1 > m \geq 0$, and it is understood by programs using the data that there is a *radix* that is to be raised to the power indicated by the exponent, then miltiplied by the mantissa. For example, 12 may be represented as $.12 \times 10^2$. If we agree always to use 10 as the radix, it may be omitted from the notation and all that is stored is one continuous string of numbers, 1202; the mantissa being .120 and the exponent 2. The decimal point, mathematical operation signs, and radix may be omitted because they are understood. Again, we have a compact form of data storage requiring that any interpreting program or hardware understand the "syntax" by which the elementary symbols are combined.

Other variations on number representation include *fixed point* numbers and *multiple precision* numbers. In a fixed point representation a scaling factor is assumed by the programmer, and a number such as 30,000 might be stored as the binary or BCD equivalent of 30, or 112.87 as 11287. This is the most common form of number storage for business applications.

Many mathematical programs call for more precision in representing numbers than is available using the usual four-byte computer word (4 digits, 8 packed decimal digits, or 32 bits). In this case two (or more) words can be concatenated. In modern computers the machine can recognize this requirement and do double-precision arithmetic automatically. Extra-length numbers were possible in earlier machines, but a program had to carry out the additional steps involved in multiple-precision arithmetic. Using two-digit words, for example, $02 \times 03 = 0006$, which would have to be stored as 00 and 06. To add this result to 0297 one must compute $06 + 97 = 103$, stored as 03 with a carry of 1, then compute $00 + 02 = 02$ plus the carry $= 03$. Therefore, $0006 + 0297 = 0303$, but two additions, or three when there is a carry, are required to reach the result.

### 2.1.3 Codes and Identifiers

It is an ancient and fundamental step in any information system to assign an easily manipulable symbol to a thing, entity, or concept that cannot itself be easily manipulated. The standard examples are serial numbers assigned to people or machines, a classification code for the subject of a book or the nature of a person's occupation. More errors or misuses of information systems are probably due to misunderstanding of the relationship between the symbol and the thing symbolized than to any other single cause.

Is a United States social security number, the "standard" identifier for people in many information systems, unique? It is intended to be by the Social Security Administration, but unhappily for many system designers, this is not necessarily the case. A simple error in keypunching can equate two numbers with no means at hand for detecting and correcting the error until the error is propagated farther into an information system, causing, for example, the two people represented to receive each other's paychecks. In 1938 a manufacturer of wallets included a facsimile of a Social Security card in their product, and in 1943 there were 5755 people who reported the number thereon as their own [5].

Also, since one person can acquire two numbers, there is no guarantee that knowing the number that person supplies will give access to all information about him. The Social Security Administration reports that 4.2 million persons have two or more numbers [6]. It is far more obvious that a library's subject classification code does not uniquely identify a book, for this was never intended. What is not always recognized is that the classification code does not necessarily identify the subject matter, either. It represents one person's *opinion* of the most important subject of the book; but if this opinion does not match that of the searcher looking for information, he may never find what he wants. Here, then, is a code for an idea (subject) which not all readers will recognize as having the same meaning. Finally, does the amount represented by the term "balance" tell how much money is actually on deposit in a bank account? Not necessarily, for a balance can have meaning only if modified by a date and time.

It is a basic principle of communications that both transmitter and receiver must understand the same thing by a message. This remains true when the message is a single code used for computer storage of data. The assumptions made when designing the code must match the assumptions made when using the code.

## 2.2  DATA STRUCTURES

A *data structure* or *data organization* is a method of organizing a collection of one or more symbols. It is analogous to the syntax of a natural language plus the rules for grouping sentences into higher structures, such as paragraphs, articles, or chapters. Packed decimal notation for numbers is a data structure, as is the plan for organizing books and catalogs in a library. A *data element* is any component of a data structure.

The most elementary concept of data structures is *repetition,* the generalization from a single symbol to a set of similarly defined symbols. More formally, a *vector* is a set of *n* symbols having the same definition (Figure 2.2). Thus we may have a vector consisting of a set of distances

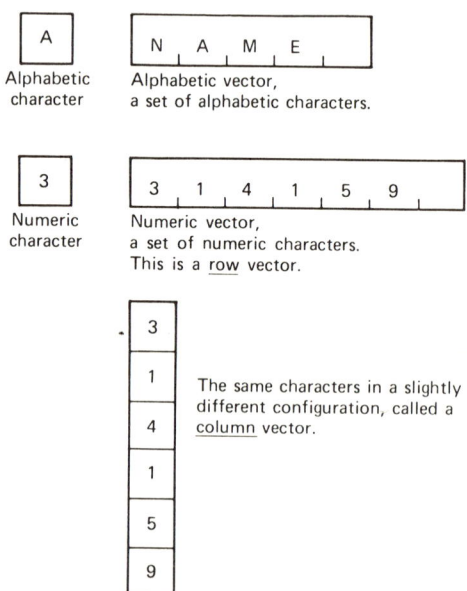

**Figure 2.2**   Vectors.

along an axis (the most common mathematical meaning), scores on a battery of tests, letters comprising a word, or relevant subject-defining terms for a book. The vector itself is unidimensional. It has only length. It may be descriptive of $n$ dimensions, as a three-element vector may define a point in three-dimensional space. The vector can be further generalized into an *array* (Figure 2.3). A two-dimensional array is a rectangular organization of data, consisting of $m$ rows and $n$ columns. In these terms, the vector consists of either one row of $n$ columns or one column of $n$ rows. A two-dimensional array may represent the grades of all students in a class, over a series of tests. Each row might hold data for one student, each column representing the score on a particular test. Such arrangements have been used in teachers' grade books from time immemorial. An organization's budget (Figure 2.4) also can be represented as an array in which the rows stand for projects or classes of work to be undertaken and the columns are organizational components. The data element represented at each position is the amount of money assigned to organization $j$ to work on project $i$. Algebraically, the array is represented by the notation $A_{ij}$ where $A$ represents the amount of money and $i$ and $j$ denote a row and a column, respectively, of the array.

Arrays are not confined to two dimensions only. A three-dimensional array is represented by $A_{i,j,k}$, where $i, j,$ and $k$ designate distance along each of three axes. The concept may be generalized indefinitely.

We have said that each element of an array represents the same kind of information—test scores, amount of funds, and so on. But our need for storing information is not so conveniently restricted. A more general set of symbols allows for members to have different definitions: a name, an address, and a telephone number; a time, a temperature, and a pressure reading; a student's name, a course number, and a grade (Figure 2.5). Such a set of possibly dissimilar symbols is called a *group*.

A collection of one or more groups may be called a *record*. This term was first used in a computer context to indicate a unit of information, usually a collection of elements all concerned with a single subject or entity. It also designated a unit of data storage or transmission, such as a punched card or magnetic tape record. Today the unit of transmission and the logical unit of associated information need not be coextensive. In particular, a *physical* or *machine record* often contains more than one *logical record* but also might contain a portion of a logical record, or portions of two or more of them (Figure 2.6). We still encounter the term *unit record* to refer to the punched card, and we still find many data records designed to accommodate the limit of 80 characters that can be represented on such a card, even though computers have long been freed of the restriction of treating their internally stored and processed records as if they were punched cards.

ARRAY

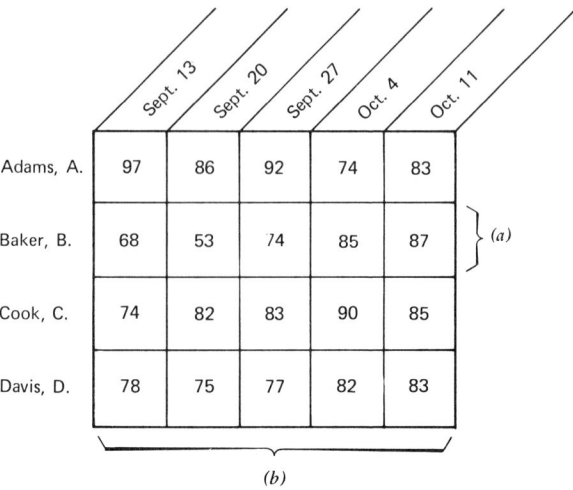

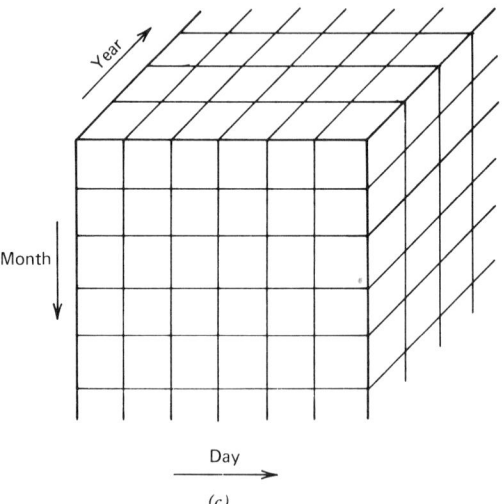

**Figure 2.3** Arrays. (*a*) A one-dimensional array of characters (vector). (*b*) A two-dimensional array; rows represent students, columns represent dates of tests, and entries represent test scores. (*c*) A three-dimensional array; the cell identification is a date (*day, month, year*). The item stored in a cell might be a measurement or observation made on that date, such as *sales*.

## Data Structures 23

Organization

| Project | Laboratory | Engineering | Factory | Sales |
|---|---|---|---|---|
| Support of Product A | 1012 | 483 | 2500 | 750 |
| " " B | 300 | 0 | 0 | 0 |
| " " C | 0 | 0 | 8750 | 1200 |
| " " D | 275 | 250 | 100 | 50 |

An array of amounts of money to be allocated
to an organization for a given project.

**Figure 2.4** A budget as an array.

We shall find it convenient to discuss data organization within the logical record separately from that concerned with how records are themselves grouped into larger units, called *files*.

### 2.2.1 Record Organization

A *field* is the basic semantic unit of a record. Made up of other symbols, characters, or bits, it is not necessarily subdivisible to produce a meaningful symbol. For example, if *name* is a field, there may be no subdivision of *name* that necessarily has any independent meaning. A *group* is a set of fields having some common referent, perhaps identifying a person or specifying the dimensions of a machine part. An element of a group may also be a group or an array. Thus one group may be an address (number, street, city), another group the list (array) of people living at that address, and the encompassing group is descriptive of a dwelling place and its inhabitants.

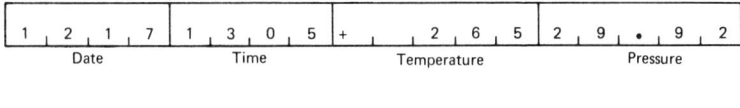

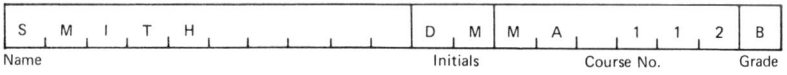

**Figure 2.5** Groups.

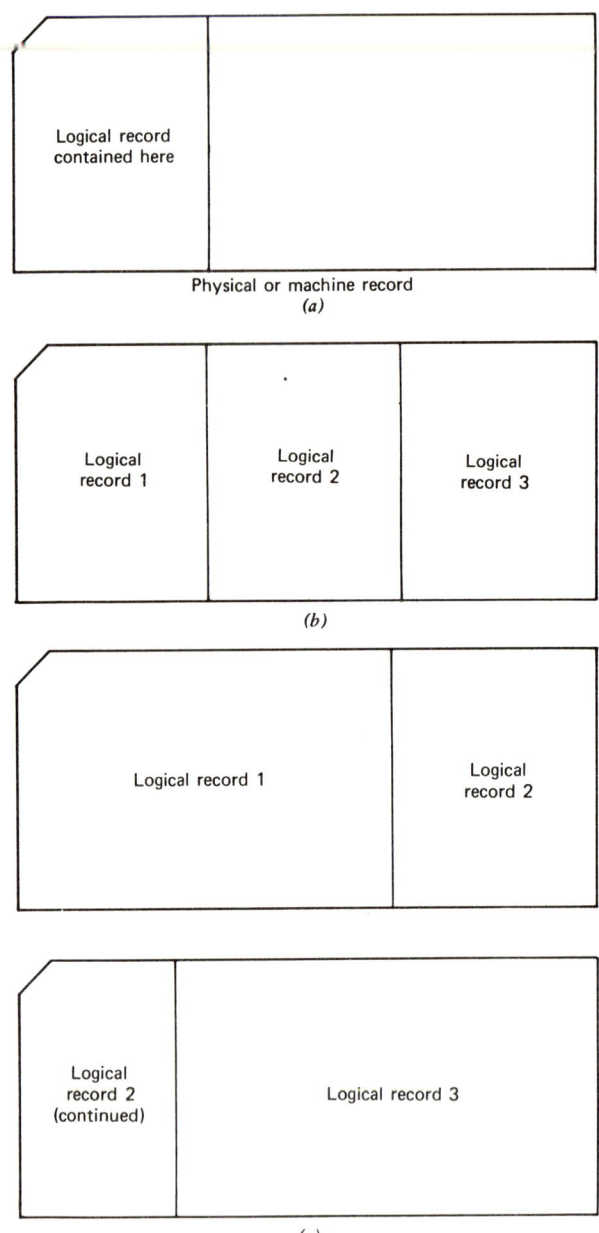

**Figure 2.6** Logical and machine records. (*a*) One logical record in one machine record, (*b*) three logical records in one physical record, (*c*) part of a logical record in two machine records.

Occasionally an addressable *subfield* makes it possible to extract, for example, *month* from a *date* field (Figure 2.7). A field name can be used in program commands such as A = B + C or IF A > 12 GO TO. . . . Normally, however, a group cannot be used as an arithmetic command address or argument. That is why the subfield is used rather than calling the field a group and the smaller elements fields.

An array can be an element of a group. But an array can also have a group as an element (Figure 2.8). We can define the group *address,* consisting of *number, street, city.* We can then form the array *previous addresses* consisting of a set of these address groups. We would normally use such a notation as ADDRESS$_i$ or ADDRESS(I) to identify one array element or STREET(I) to identify a particular value of the field *street.*

A record (Figure 2.9) is a set of groups that is not contained in any other group. A record, or any of its constituent groups, can consist of as little as a single field; but because of the physical implications of a record as a unit of transmission or storage, we rarely define records to be so small. The kind of record organizational structure permitted in a computer is a function of the application program or programming language, not the computer hardware. Computers can address characters or words (uniformly long sets of characters or bits) but leave it to programmers to ascribe meaning and structure to data. File organization, on the other hand, is governed both by the computer hardware and the programs. Different programming languages, even if allowing the same logical structure, may impose a different terminology on the user. Table 2.1 compares the terminology introduced here with that of COBOL and PL/I, the principal high-order languages for nonnumeric information processing. Also listed are terms in common use but not tied to a specific language.

### 2.2.2 File Organization

A *file* or *data set* is an array of records. Files are generally too large to be stored entirely in main memory; hence they must be placed on magnetic

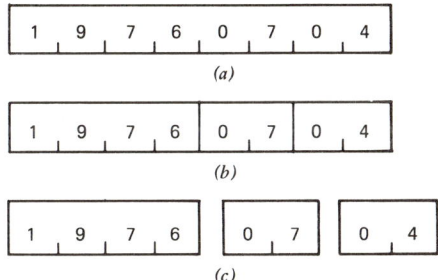

**Figure 2.7** Subfields. (*a*) *Date* as a single field, (*b*) *date* as a set of three subfields (*year, month, day*), (*c*) *date* as a group of three fields.

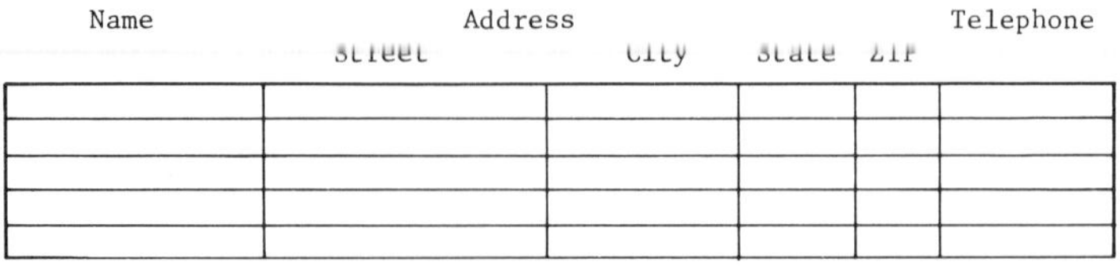

## 26  *Elementary Data Concepts*

| Name | Address | | | | Telephone |
|---|---|---|---|---|---|
| | Street | | City | State  ZIP | |
| | | | | | |
| | | | | | |
| | | | | | |
| | | | | | |

**Figure 2.8** An array of groups.

tape, disks, drums, or other auxiliary memory units. The characteristics of these devices, in regard to where records can be written or found for retrieval, how long a read or write operation takes, and how subdivision is ordered, are major factors in determining how data are to be organized into files.

File organization is largely concerned with how records are sequenced on a memory unit and that, in turn, determines how rapidly and efficiently records can be accessed for retrieval or modification. On a magnetic tape, for example, file organization is rather limited. Records must be written in the order received and can only be recovered by reading each record in sequence until the desired one is found. Inserts can be made only by copying the entire tape and making the insertion during the copy operation. Disks and drums, on the other hand, permit records to be inserted at any desired location where there is room in an existing file or data set. Similarly, individual records can be addressed directly and recovered without reading all other or all preceding records in the file.

Computer manufacturers usually provide with their equipment programs that create, maintain, and search files. These programs, as a rule, are unconcerned with record structure. They treat the record as the smallest

*Table 2.1  Equivalent Terms for Data Elements*

| Term as used herein | COBOL equivalent | PL/I equivalent | Other synonyms |
|---|---|---|---|
| Field | Item, or elementary item | Variable | Datum, or descriptor |
| Group | Group, or group of items | Structure, or minor structure | Set of fields, or data set[a] |
| Array | Repeated items | Array | List, or table |
| Record | Record | Major structure | |

[a] Section 2.2.2 gives another meaning of this term.

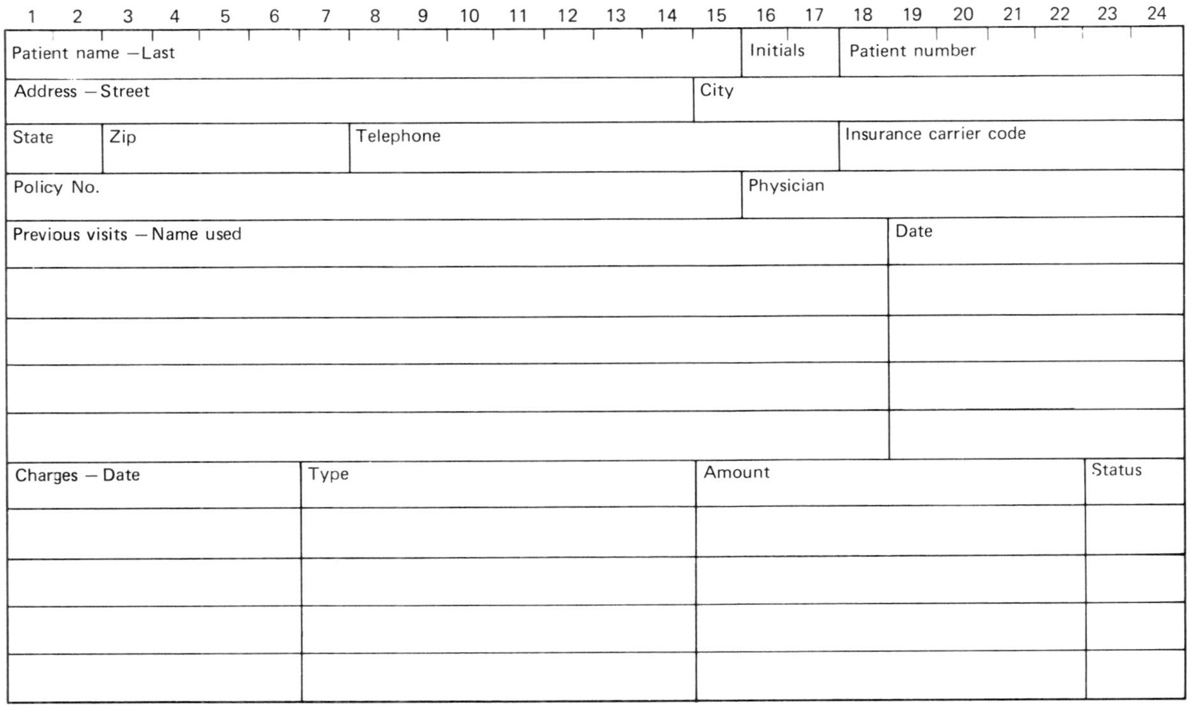

| 1 | 2 | 3 | 4 | 5 | 6 | 7 | 8 | 9 | 10 | 11 | 12 | 13 | 14 | 15 | 16 | 17 | 18 | 19 | 20 | 21 | 22 | 23 | 24 |
|---|---|---|---|---|---|---|---|---|---|---|---|---|---|---|---|---|---|---|---|---|---|---|---|
| Patient name — Last ||||||||||||||| Initials || Patient number |||||||
| Address — Street ||||||||||||||| City |||||||||
| State || Zip || Telephone |||||||||| Insurance carrier code ||||||||
| Policy No. ||||| Physician |||||||||||||||||
| Previous visits — Name used |||||||||||||||| Date ||||||||
| |||||||||||||||||||||||
| |||||||||||||||||||||||
| |||||||||||||||||||||||
| Charges — Date |||||| Type |||||||| Amount ||||| Status |||
| |||||||||||||||||||||||
| |||||||||||||||||||||||
| |||||||||||||||||||||||

**Figure 2.9** A record.

## 28    Elementary Data Concepts

unit of information and leave it to the user's program to examine and process the interior of a record. Since records are then usually examined only within main memory, after having been retrieved by a file handling program, it is of far less consequence how the record is structured with respect to speed of operation or efficiency, since there is relatively little loss of time in searching at main memory speeds.

## 2.3  POSITION AND SEQUENCE

In storing or organizing almost anything—data records, objects, even people—we like to put the units in some neat order, to facilitate finding them again or remembering who or what is stored. This requires selecting a basis for positioning things in a file (title, subject, height, ...) and creates the habit of assuming that the "next" physical element in the file is the "next" in terms of the ordering criterion. In a data file, the basis for ordering is usually the value of one or more fields in each record, such as *name, serial number,* or *subject classification* and *author name.*

In data management we can separate the physical position from the logical position, with the result that the next physical element is not necessarily the next logical element. For example, library books are normally arranged by subject and author, but they may be organized by size for reasons of storage economy (Figure 2.10). Then the "next" book on the shelf is not the "next" one in subject matter. Having found any one book on a subject gives no clue whatever to the location of the next one, unless some special arrangement is made to provide this information. Positioning by size

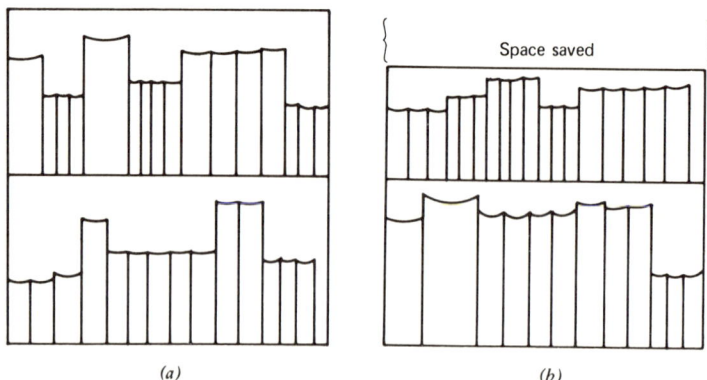

**Figure 2.10**   Organization of books for storage economy. (*a*) Organization by subject, (*b*) organization by size, to save space.

is still positioning by something, but this not uncommon practice serves to illustrate that the order of items in a file does not necessarily have to conform to the most obvious basis for searching. The parameters of the individual system—the composite of file elements, organizational method, and nature and frequency of search—all must be taken into consideration.

When searching a file, it is clearly useful, to know where the next logical record is. But insisting that the next logical record be the next physical record restricts us to considering only one meaning of "next" for each file. It is often useful to be able to make simultaneous use of more than one concept of "next" for any given file. For example, in searching bibliographic records, we might be interested in the next book on the same subject, the next book by the same author, or even the next book of the same size. In business files, we might be interested in the inventory status of the article having the next higher part number, the next item supplied by company X, or the next higher selling item.

The process of placing records physically in sequence is called *sorting*. Because physical order is so important to efficient searching, sorting plays a large role in the economics of data management. It has been estimated that 30% of computer time devoted to business applications is consumed by sorting [7]. There are many different techniques, another indication of the importance of the process. We review a number of them in Chapter 3.

We have now introduced the concepts of logical and physical ordering of records, pointing out that the basis for ordering, either logical or physical, normally is a field or element within the record. In the files we most often encounter, especially *outside* computers, the next physical record is also the next logical record.

Complete separation of logical and physical positioning can be achieved by use of a device called the *pointer*. A pointer is a field of information in a record that indicates the location of the logically next record. It is not a datum descriptive of the subject of the record, it is an address telling where related information is to be found. The nature of the relation may vary; hence the meaning of a pointer must be clearly understood between the file designer and the programmer who tries to make use of it. A pointer is an overhead item, carrying no substantive information about the record or its subject. However, pointers simplify the task of file management by permitting records to be added and deleted randomly, and they permit the nature of "next" to be generalized—there may be different "nexts" for different classes of data.

In a sense, all records have pointers (Figure 2.11), but in our most common, sequentially ordered files, the pointer is understood. It is sufficient to tell a library user that the catalog is in alphabetical order; it is not necessary to explain where the successor to each card is to be found. The

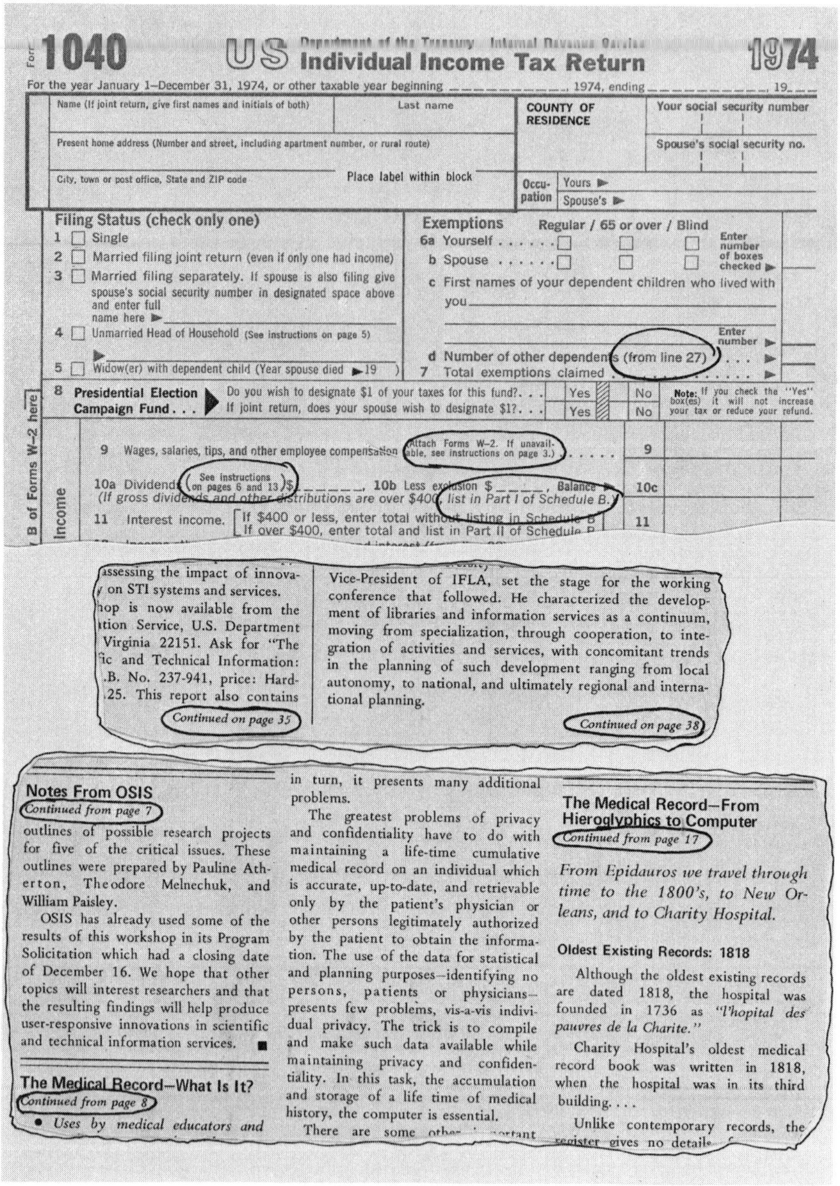

Form 1040 US Individual Income Tax Return 1974

For the year January 1–December 31, 1974, or other taxable year beginning ............, 1974, ending ............, 19..

Name (If joint return, give first names and initials of both) | Last name | COUNTY OF RESIDENCE | Your social security number

Present home address (Number and street, including apartment number, or rural route) | Spouse's social security no.

City, town or post office, State and ZIP code | Place label within block | Occupation | Yours ▶ | Spouse's ▶

Filing Status (check only one)
1 ☐ Single
2 ☐ Married filing joint return (even if only one had income)
3 ☐ Married filing separately. If spouse is also filing give spouse's social security number in designated space above and enter full name here ▶
4 ☐ Unmarried Head of Household (See instructions on page 5)
5 ☐ Widow(er) with dependent child (Year spouse died ▶19 )

Exemptions Regular / 65 or over / Blind
6a Yourself ☐ ☐ ☐
b Spouse ☐ ☐ ☐ Enter number of boxes checked ▶
c First names of your dependent children who lived with you ............ Enter number ▶
d Number of other dependents (from line 27) ... ▶
7 Total exemptions claimed ... ▶

8 Presidential Election Campaign Fund... ▶ Do you wish to designate $1 of your taxes for this fund?... Yes No. If joint return, does your spouse wish to designate $1?... Yes No. Note: If you check the "Yes" box(es) it will not increase your tax or reduce your refund.

B of Forms W-2 here

Income
9 Wages, salaries, tips, and other employee compensation (Attach Forms W-2. If unavailable, see instructions on page 3.) ..... 9
10a Dividends (See instructions on pages 6 and 13) $............, 10b Less exclusion $........, Balance ▶ 10c
(If gross dividends and other distributions are over $400, list in Part I of Schedule B.)
11 Interest income. [If $400 or less, enter total without listing in Schedule B. If over $400, enter total and list in Part II of Schedule B.] 11

assessing the impact of innova-
/ on STI systems and services.
hop is now available from the
ition Service, U.S. Department
Virginia 22151. Ask for "The
ic and Technical Information:
.B. No. 237-941, price: Hard-
.25. This report also contains

Continued on page 35

Vice-President of IFLA, set the stage for the working conference that followed. He characterized the development of libraries and information services as a continuum, moving from specialization, through cooperation, to integration of activities and services, with concomitant trends in the planning of such development ranging from local autonomy, to national, and ultimately regional and international planning.

Continued on page 38

**Notes From OSIS**

Continued from page 7

outlines of possible research projects for five of the critical issues. These outlines were prepared by Pauline Atherton, Theodore Melnechuk, and William Paisley.

OSIS has already used some of the results of this workshop in its Program Solicitation which had a closing date of December 16. We hope that other topics will interest researchers and that the resulting findings will help produce user-responsive innovations in scientific and technical information services. ■

**The Medical Record—What Is It?**

Continued from page 8

• *Uses by medical educators and*

in turn, it presents many additional problems.

The greatest problems of privacy and confidentiality have to do with maintaining a life-time cumulative medical record on an individual which is accurate, up-to-date, and retrievable only by the patient's physician or other persons legitimately authorized by the patient to obtain the information. The use of the data for statistical and planning purposes—identifying no persons, patients or physicians—presents few problems, vis-a-vis individual privacy. The trick is to compile and make such data available while maintaining privacy and confidentiality. In this task, the accumulation and storage of a life time of medical history, the computer is essential.

There are some other important

**The Medical Record—From Hieroglyphics to Computer**

Continued from page 17

*From Epidauros we travel through time to the 1800's, to New Orleans, and to Charity Hospital.*

**Oldest Existing Records: 1818**

Although the oldest existing records are dated 1818, the hospital was founded in 1736 as *"l'hopital des pauvres de la Charite."*

Charity Hospital's oldest medical record book was written in 1818, when the hospital was in its third building....

Unlike contemporary records, the register gives no details

**Figure 2.11** Everyday uses of the pointer concept. (*a*) Magazine article continued on another page. (*b*) Federal income tax form, showing references from line to line and form to form.

## Position and Sequence 31

page numbers of a book are intended to help readers find information, not to indicate where the next page is. Book manufacturers expect readers to know the logical organization of the book. If written in English, the flow of symbols is from left to right in a line, from top to bottom on a page, and the next page is the one on the right if there is one, or on the back, if there is one, or to the right of the back of the current page. A book printed in Hebrew is just the opposite: right to left on a line, still top to bottom, but again right to left between pages. In the absence of these conventions, it would be necessary (Figure 2.12) to follow each letter with a pointer to the next one, each word, each line and each page with its pointer, for the direction of *next* is not fixed. This would be space-consuming to a computer, but it may yet turn out to be the most efficient way to organize information. One reason for this is that information in a computer file, unlike information in a book, is subject to change, often frequent and rapid change, and explicit pointers permit the storage of new information anywhere, without loss of logical sequencing. In searching, pointers permit rapid access to information by several criteria, while the book reader is normally only going to access information in normal reading sequence. For example, a concordance to a book is the alphabetized list of words used, with locations in the text.

Pointers are useful and economical only if it is reasonably easy to follow them. Their utility, then, may be a function of memory configuration. In main computer memory, pointers are highly useful, because we can jump around at random without adding to access time. On magnetic tape, pointers are of little value because records must be read sequentially regardless of whether we know where they are, thus knowing the location of information is of little value.

Use of explicit pointers has led to the development of a special method of organizing information called *list structures*. Briefly, a list is a file whose records contain explicit pointers, permitting complete freedom from physical positioning constraints except for the requirement to stay within bounds of assigned memory areas. Use of a list saves the programmer the

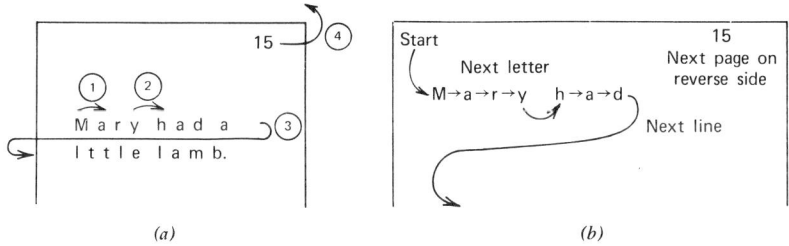

**Figure 2.12** Pointers on a book page. (*a*) Implicit pointers on a book page show transitions from letter to letter (1), word to word (2), line to line (3), and page to page (4). (*b*) Book page with pointers made explicit.

## 32 Elementary Data Concepts

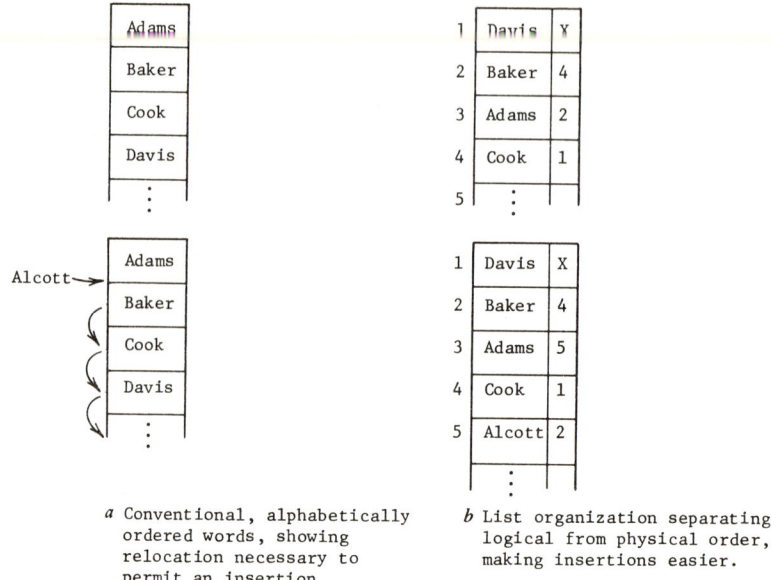

*a* Conventional, alphabetically ordered words, showing relocation necessary to permit an insertion.

*b* List organization separating logical from physical order, making insertions easier.

**Figure 2.13** Lists. (*a*) Conventional, alphabetically ordered words, showing relocation necessary to permit an insertion. (*b*) List organization separating logical from physical order, making insertions easier.

trouble of repositioning records when he wishes to make an insertion into a file and allows him to locate data within the file conveniently (Figure 2.13). List structures are described more completely in Chapter 3.

We have now discussed the role of symbols in information transfer and storage, as well as the grouping of symbols into syntactic units and higher entities. Sequence has been shown to be a critical factor in data organization, and we have introduced two meanings of sequence: logical and physical. Logical sequences is a chain of relatedness of information elements, regardless of physical positioning. Physical sequence is the order of physical placement of elements on some storage medium. The speed and economics of information processing depend very heavily on physical structuring of data. In the next chapter we describe in some detail the principal physical organizational methods.

## REFERENCES

1. R. A. Fairthorne, "Problems of Data Retrieval and Dependent Techniques." In *Problems of Information Science,* A. I. Charnyi, Ed., All-Union Institute for Scientific and Technical Information, Moscow, 1972.

2. *USA Standard Code for Information Interchange,* X3.4-1967, United States of America Standards Institute, New York, 1967, p. 6.
3. *Introduction to IBM Data Processing Systems,* GC20-1684-2, IBM Corp., Poughkeepsie, N.Y., 1972, pp. 18–19.
4. Donald E. Knuth, *Sorting and Searching. The Art of Computer Programming,* Vol. 3, Addison-Wesley Publishing Co., Reading, Mass., 1973, pp. 379–88, 417–19.
5. *Records, Computers and the Rights of Citizens,* Report of the Secretary's Advisory Committee on Automated Personal Data Systems, U.S. Department of Health, Education, and Welfare, Washington, D.C., 1973, p. 112.
6. *Ibid.*
7. C. C. Gottlieb, "General Purpose Programming for Business Applications." In *Advances in Computers,* Vol. 1, F. L. Alt, Ed., Academic Press, New York, 1960, p. 17.

## RECOMMENDED READING

Cherry, Colin, *On Human Communication,* 2nd ed., M.I.T. Press, Cambridge, Mass., 1966.

Flores, Ivan, *Computer Software,* Prentice-Hall, Englewood Cliffs, N.J., 1965.

McCracken, D. D., and U. Garbassi, *A Guide to COBOL Programming,* 2nd ed., Wiley-Interscience, New York, 1970.

Pierce, J. R., *Symbols, Signals and Noise: The Nature and Process of Communication,* Harper & Row, New York, 1961.

Pollack, S. V., and T. D. Sterling, *A Guide to PL/I,* Holt, Rinehart and Winston, New York, 1969.

Reference 5, Chapter I, "Records and Record Keepers," pp. 1–10, and Chapter VII, "The Social Security Number as a Universal Identifier," pp. 109–22.

*Chapter Three*

# Data Storage

### 3.1 STORAGE MECHANISMS

The characteristics of the media on which symbols are recorded are the dominant factors in determining what data organizations are possible which ones are best under various circumstances. Each medium and the corresponding recording and reading device has what amounts to a geometry that limits the path and time of access to information stored on the medium, or access to unused areas in which new information is to be recorded.

#### 3.1.1 Memory Geometry

A memory can be characterized by the relative speed at which an associated reading or writing device "moves" from one position to another to read or record information. For example, after a record has been written at location $x$, it may be desirable to write another record at location $y$. A magnetic tape characteristic permits reading or writing of the adjacent (usually following, sometimes preceding) physical record only, regardless of what may be known about the actual location of the information wanted. Furthermore, the time required to reach a given point in this memory is a linear function of the number of intervening records. On the other hand, magnetic core memory has the characteristic that regardless of where the last memory accession occurred, the next location accessed can be any in the memory, so long as the address is known. The time to reach the information stored at the new location is independent of the addresses involved. Time to reach a given location in memory is called *access time* and is a function of hardware limitations and starting point of the accession. Much of file organization is concerned with ways of placing records in memory to minimize access time.

When using magnetic tape that can only read in the forward direction, the worst possible case of search timing is that of having just read the last record in the file and then wanting to reread it, for this requires that the tape be rewound, then read, sequentially, through $n$ records. Some tapes can be read backward, in which case this example becomes one of minimum timing. In effect, the geometry of a backward-readable tape is different. In one case the read mechanism must go only forward, then rewind to get to the beginning again, then read the entire file to reach record $n$ again. In the other there is a direct path from the position of the read mechanism after reading record $n$ back to $n$ again. In designing a file organization, it is sometimes very important to avoid having a record in a forward-only tape memory contain references to the preceding record, whereas this arrangement might prove quite economical when the use of a backward-read tape is contemplated.

Disks, drums, and the many varieties of memory using tape strips or cards fall between the extremes of core and tape. Access time for these devices is not uniform, nor is it a linear function of distance away from the previously accessed location. Generally, the time consists of a major delay (e.g., traversing across several disk tracks or bringing a data cell to the read station) and a minor delay, such as the rotation time for a disk or drum. These delays, together, bring us to the record, which then may require further search for the specific information wanted. However, memory geometry and delay calculations are generally based on record accession only.

It may be that neither time constituent is a constant or a linear function of distance (difference in address values). For example, for disks having a single read/write head, it takes less than half the time to move the read mechanism from one track to the adjacent one than it does to move from one track to another two tracks away. Also, careful programming can minimize rotational delays, as can new hardware design concepts that permit use for other purposes of a communications channel between disk and computer during much of the rotation delay time. Although this does not actually shorten the total time, it reduces the cost of the time and changes the effective geometry.

The essential point is that delays do exist. Reliance on popular conceptions or hasty reading of computer manuals can give the impression, for example, that because average access time to a record on a disk is 50 msec, it will take 50 msec, on the average, to retrieve information from a file. But this is not necessarily true. The average figure is computed by assuming some typical path of a read device (or the memory past the device), such as across two tracks, then waiting for one-half a rotation. But whether a user can achieve that average value (or perhaps better it) depends on how he has organized his data relative to the demands placed on it. If access is always sequential, the user may consistently beat the advertised average time. If access is truly random, he may do much worse. One of the purposes of file design, then, is to reduce access time to records, particularly to reduce the number or length of the major delays that will occur in the execution of a given application.

The early model magnetic disk units had a single read/write head for each set of disks. The arm on which the disks were mounted had to move from surface to surface from and track to track. A change to a new surface took a large amount of time, to a new track less, and to a record within a track still less. Later models had a read/write head for each surface, and all moved together from track to track. This eliminated the surface-to-surface delay. Still later models have a head for each track, and on some several heads are mounted around each track to reduce rotational delay. Because of the variety of design of units still in use, it is important to know the geometry of the particular unit to be used for a given file and file processing program.

Let us consider three examples (Figure 3.1) to show the interrelation of memory geometry and file design. In each case, assume we are using a magnetic disk with one read/write head per surface which must then be moved from track to track. Assume the file is a sequentially organized inventory file containing a large number of part records. In case I we want to read each record of the file and compile a report showing the number of sales of each part during this reporting period. In case II we want to respond to random inquiries concerning stock levels of parts, assuming we can calculate the address of a record from the part number. In Case III we again want to access records at random, but we maintain an index of part numbers in the same auxiliary memory in which the file is stored. Each time we search for a record, we look up the part number in an index, retrieve the address, then access the record. We are concerned with average access time to any record, rather than total elapsed time to complete a task. This is because the first case, involving all records of the file, could take tens of minutes or hours, whereas the latter two cases, involving only one or a few records at a time, will take only fractions of seconds for each search. Since,

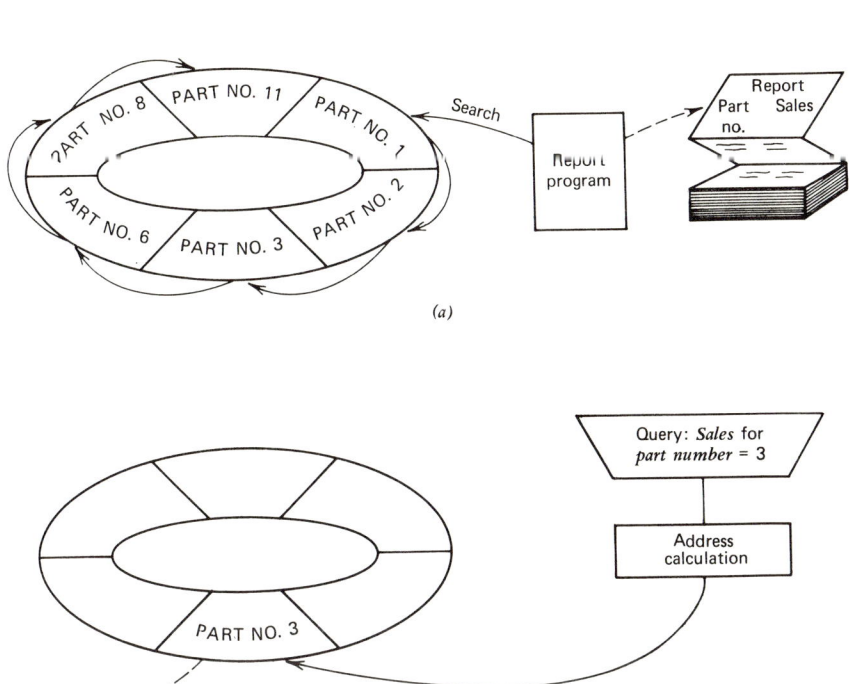

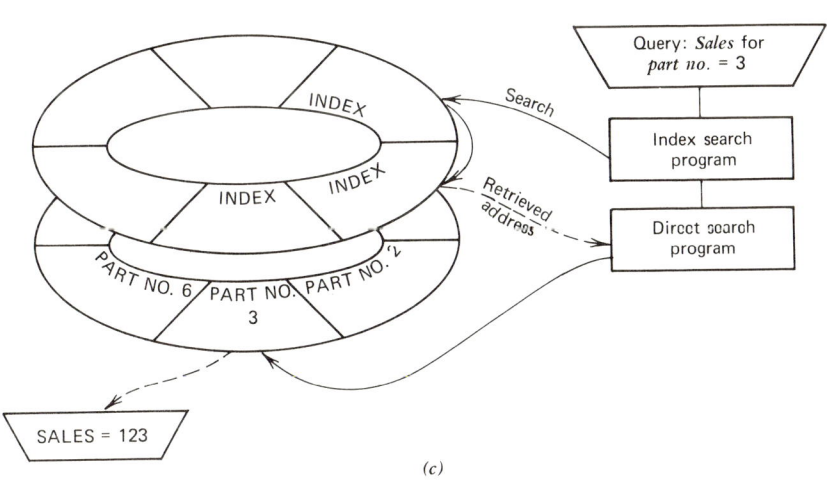

**Figure 3.1** Interaction of memory geometry and file design. (*a*) Case I, sequential search; (*b*) case II, direct search; (*c*) case III, index search.

38  Data Storage

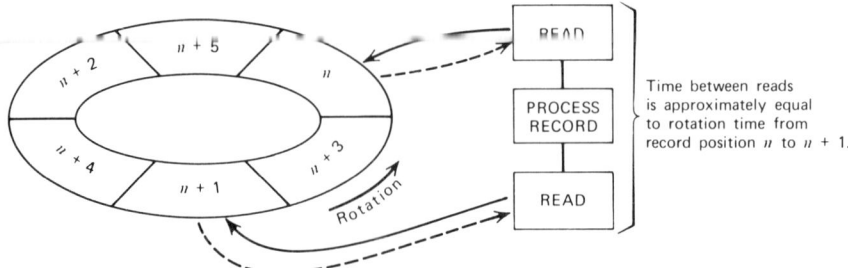

**Figure 3.2** Case I: Distributing records in sequential storage.

moreover, the searches are called for only one at a time, total time may be a misleading statistic here.

In case I (Figure 3.2) the access time for each record is at or near the absolute minimum. We are always looking for the next sequential record, which usually is on the same track and necessitates only a rotational delay. By distributing the records around the track, it might be possible to minimize even rotational delay; that is, we would place record $i + 1$ not next to record $i$ but far enough away that the time taken to process record $i$ internally is the same as that required to bring record $i + 1$ under the read head. When all records in a track have been read, we always want to go to the next track. Average time is, at worst, average rotational delay (half the total rotation time) plus some small amount for the occasional head movement. The fact that rotational delay can be brought to near zero indicates that the sequential method of file organization is still often useful and efficient, even in the day of direct access memories.

In case II (Figure 3.3) the average access time is probably close to the

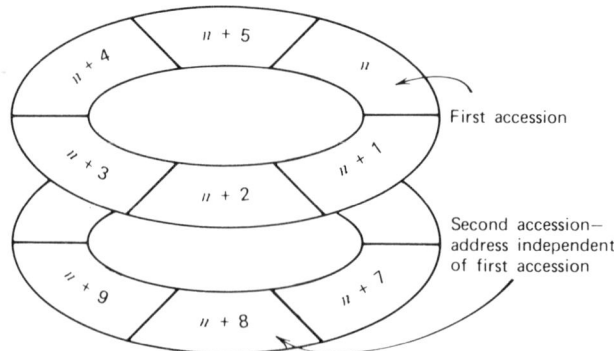

**Figure 3.3** Case II: random accession of records.

*Table 3.1  Some Representative Memory Measurements*

| Device | Access time (msec) | | | Rotational period (msec) | Data transfer rate (1000 bytes/sec) |
| --- | --- | --- | --- | --- | --- |
| | Minimum | Maximum | Average | | |
| IBM 2321 data cell | 95 | 600 | 350 | 50 | 55 |
| IBM 2314 disk | 25 | 130 | 60 | 25 | 312 |
| IBM 3330 disk | 10 | 55 | 30 | 16.7 | 806 |
| UNIVAC Fastrand III drum | 30 | 86 | 57 | 68.2 | 236 |
| UNIVAC FH 1782 drum | 0.12 | 17 | 34 | 33.3 | 90–1440 |
| UNIVAC FH 432 drum | 0.12 | 8.5 | 4.3 | 8.4 | 1440 |

average stated in the computer manual, for we assume no logical connection between the location of the last accession and the next. This time will be some number of track traverses plus an average rotational delay.

In case III (Figure 3.4) we have two file accessions for each request, one for the index and one for the data. If the index is stored at the beginning of the disk and the data are placed beyond that, each retrieval operation involves one accession in the index area and one in the data area. On average, the first accession is in the middle of the index and the second in the middle of the data area. If the index takes up one-tenth of the file, we always have one accession in the first tenth, then one in the next nine-tenths, making for two accessions of about the average "distance" used in case II.

Table 3.1 compares the speed of several representative memory units. Access times are to physical records of known location. Note that in addition to access time there is a data transfer rate for each device. The total time to transfer a record is, of course, a function of read rate and record size.

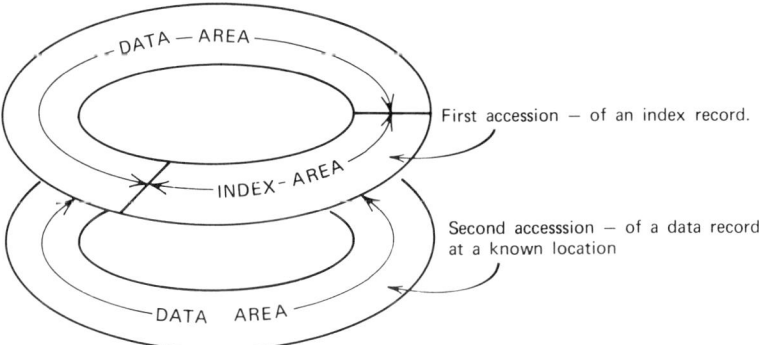

**Figure 3.4**  Case III: use of an index.

40  *Data Storage*

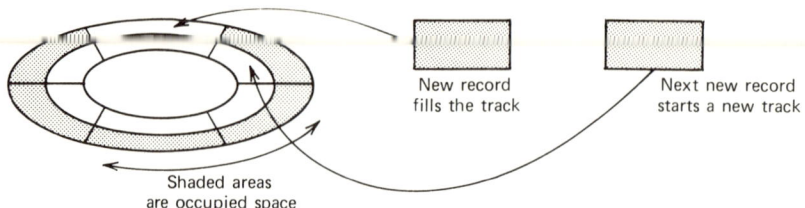

**Figure 3.5**  Track mode of disk storage.

### 3.1.2  The Cylinder Concept of Disk Storage

When data are stored on a disk with a read/write head for each disk surface, there are two choices open to the hardware designer in sequencing data. One possibility is to begin using track 2 on any surface as soon as track 1 is full. Then, upon filling the last track of a surface, move to the first track of the next surface (Figure 3.5). This requires an arm motion between each track, although each motion except the last is minimal.

A second method puts succeeding records one below the other in corresponding positions on adjacent surfaces (Figure 3.6). When a column thus formed fills, the next record to arrive starts a new column. In this method, since there is an arm positioned at the same track of each disk, no arm motion is required to move from surface 1, track 1, to surface 2, track 1, and so on. No such motion is needed until an entire set of tracks has been spanned. This set of tracks constitutes something of a cylindrical shell (Figure 3.7); hence the name of this method is the *cylinder mode*. The formal definition of a *cylinder of data* is that which can be accessed with one positioning of the access mechanism [1].

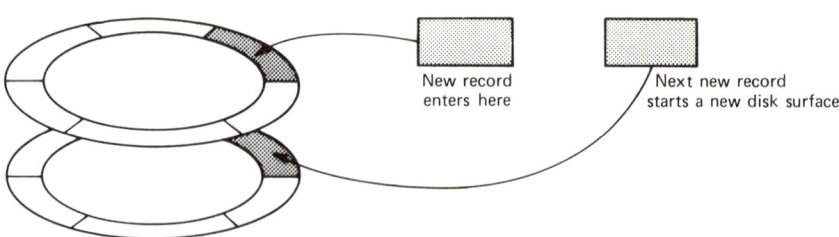

**Figure 3.6**  Cylinder mode of disk storage.

*Ordering and Searching Records* 41

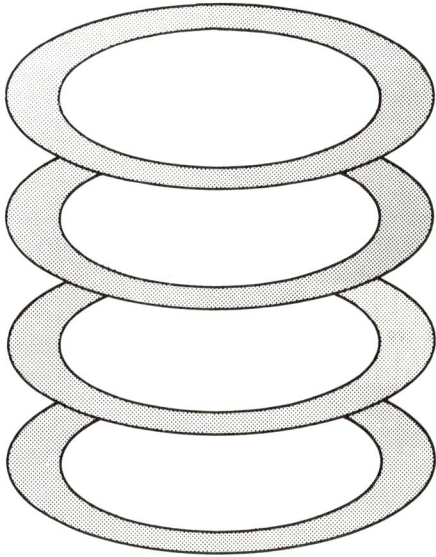

**Figure 3.7** A cylinder of data.

## 3.2 ORDERING AND SEARCHING RECORDS

The importance of control of sequence has been stressed in several of the foregoing organizational descriptions. The process of physically arranging records in a prescribed sequence, based on the value of one or more fields within the records, is called *sorting*. With the newer organizational methods, records often can be accessed in whatever sequence is desired without their actually being stored in that sequence, and as a result, the criticality of sorting has abated somewhat.

### 3.2.1 Sorting

A *sort key* is the field of a record on which record order is based. Order can be *ascending* or *descending* (keys increase or decrease in value or precedence as record follows record in sequence). A file whose records are in order based on some key is called an *ordered file*. It is possible for two or more records to have the same value of the key. In such a case either these records will be in random order with respect to each other (but properly in prescribed order with respect to records having other keys), or some other field must be used to determine the relative positions of the records.

Fields used for this secondary decision making are called *secondary sort fields* (or *tertiary*, etc.). If there is a secondary field, the original one is called the *primary sort field* or *key* (Figure 3.8). If key values are unique—that is, if only one record in a file may have any given value for a sort key—there is no need for secondary keys.

It happens that there are file organizations in which records are not ordered in our sense. One such organization has records in order of arrival in the file. Another involves purposely randomizing storage location to evenly distribute records in available storage space. These alternatives are considered later.

Because of the importance of sorting, an entire literature has developed on different methods [2-4]. We mention only a few approaches here, and these the more simple ones. The essence of most methods is to create, among the set of records to be sorted, strings of records that are in sequence, then to gradually combine these strings into ever larger ones, until the entire file is a single, sorted string.

The process of combining strings is called *merging*. Input to a merge is two or more strings of ordered records (sorted on the same keys), and the output is a single, ordered string. Each string can be an entire file. Figure 3.9 illustrates how two input strings are merged into one output string.

In the general sorting problem we face a set of unordered records, and our objective is to form them into a single, ordered string. This can be accomplished by treating the file or record set as a set of strings of length 1 and successively merging the strings of length 1 into strings of length 2, these into strings of length 4, and so on. Obviously, as the length of the strings doubles, the number of strings is cut in half, until there is a single string containing the full set of records. This method of sorting is workable, but it has two weaknesses: (*a*) there are faster ways, and (*b*) the method

| Sort keys: | Primary | Secondary | Tertiary | |
|---|---|---|---|---|
| | MANUFACTURER | MODEL NO. | COLOR | ... other information ... |
| | FILCO | A-7 | GREEN | |
| | FILCO | A-7 | WHITE | |
| | FILCO | AF-7 | GREEN | |
| | GECO | A6 | YELLOW | |
| | GECO | A8 | WHITE | |
| | WEST | W-13 | GREEN | |
| | WEST | W-13 | YELLOW | |

**Figure 3.8** Sort keys.

*Ordering and Searching Records*  43

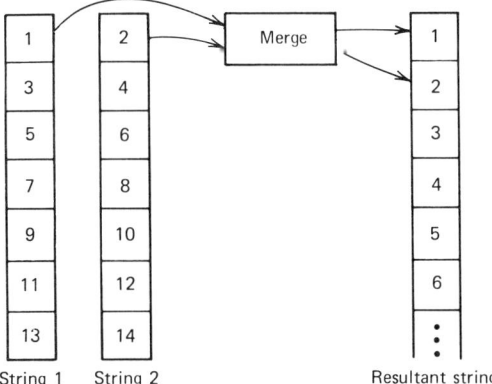

**Figure 3.9** Merging.

assumes that the complete set of records can fit into core memory. If the latter assumption is not valid, memory access time must be considered as well as program logic in evaluating this approach to sorting.

The usual approach for sorting large files, or sets of records too large to fit in core memory, is to read as many records as can fit into core memory, sort these into a single string, write the string on an auxiliary memory, and repeat until the entire file has been so processed (Figure 3.10). Then the strings are merged into successively longer strings, until a single one survives. If this is done, the sort operation is performed in two separate steps, whose methodology may be different. The first reads a set of records into main memory and sorts them into a string. The work is entirely performed in main memory, hence access time is of relatively little consequence. This is called *internal sorting*. The second step consists of repeated merge operations on the strings. The internal computer work in merging is trivial; it involves issuing read and write commands and making decisions regarding the order of writing, based on a given sort key. Hence the timing of this operation, called *external sorting,* is almost entirely determined by auxiliary memory access and read/write times.

Among the many methods of performing internal sorting is the successive merge method just described. Its weakness is that it requires moving every record in every *pass* through the data; that is, all records are moved in going from strings of length 1 to strings of length 2; then all are moved again in going to strings of length 4, and so on.

In the *exchange* or *bubble sorting* alternative (Figure 3.11), records 1 and 2 in the set are compared and their positions exchanged if record 1 has the larger key (or smaller if sorting is to be in descending order). Records 2

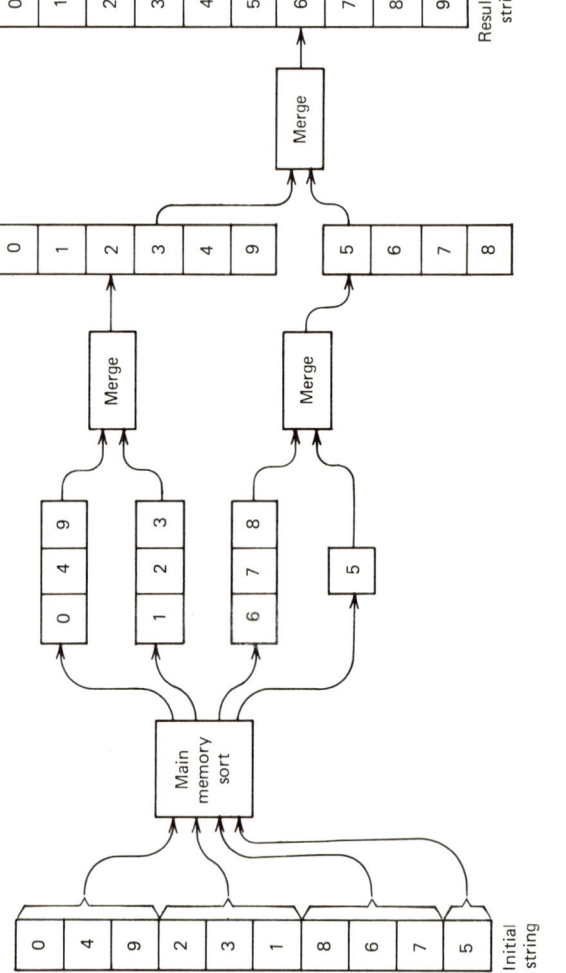

**Figure 3.10** Sorting.

44

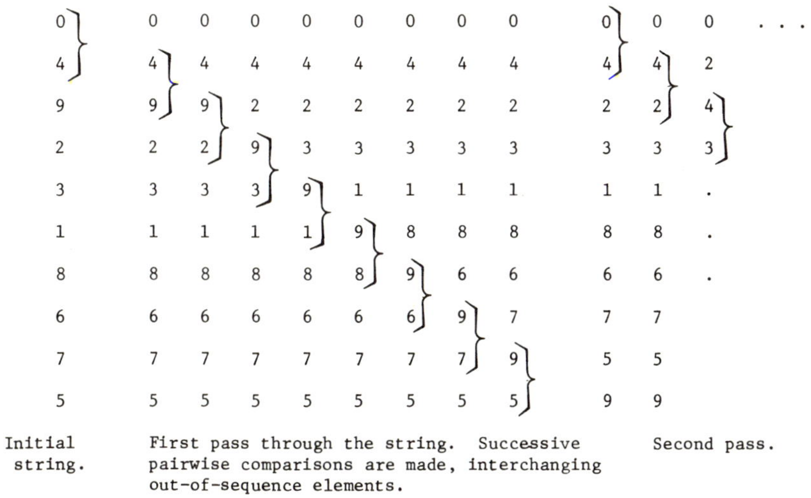

*Ordering and Searching Records*    45

```
0⎫      0   0   0   0   0   0   0   0      0⎫     0   0   ...
4⎬      4⎫  4   4   4   4   4   4   4      4⎬     4⎫  2
9⎭      9⎭  9⎫  2   2   2   2   2   2      2      2⎭  4⎫
2       2   2⎭  9⎫  3   3   3   3   3      3      3   3⎭
3       3   3   3⎭  9⎫  1   1   1   1      1      1   .
1       1   1   1   1⎭  9⎫  8   8   8      8      8   .
8       8   8   8   8   8⎭  9⎫  6   6      6      6   .
6       6   6   6   6   6   6⎭  9⎫  7      7      7
7       7   7   7   7   7   7   7⎭  9⎫     5      5
5       5   5   5   5   5   5   5   5⎭     9      9

Initial    First pass through the string. Successive    Second pass.
string.    pairwise comparisons are made, interchanging
           out-of-sequence elements.
```

**Figure 3.11**  Exchange sorting.

and 3 are compared next, then 3 and 4, and so on. When the last record is reached, the process is repeated, again and again, until there is only one string of sorted records. The advantage of this method is that the only records that are moved are those that are out of sequence. The number of complete passes through the data depends on the degree of ordering that was present in the records at the start (Figure 3.12). If the records were already in sequence, there would still be one complete pass, to verify this. If the records were in exactly inverted order, $n$ passes would be required to sort $n$ records. In practical applications, there is often some degree of ordering of data when they arrive at a computer for processing, introduced by such practices as assigning serial numbers to transactions depending on arrival sequence, or using the originator's identification number to sequence records (e.g., teacher's identification numbers to sort student grade records).

A second alternative is not to move any records, but to scan the set for the smallest (highest) key, recording the location of the record containing it, then scanning again for the next key in sequence, recording its location, and so on (Figure 3.13). This method requires as much scanning as does the worst case of exchange sorting, but it never moves any records. When the order has been fully recorded, the records are written onto auxiliary memory in the order specified. Since the write operation would be required in any case, the method avoids all unnecessary movement of records.

Other sorting methods may be chosen to take advantage of different attributes of the data set being sorted or the machinery and memory employed. There are methods to make use of prior ordering in data or of extra memory availability. Another approach involves special-purpose hardware. A small processor, attachable as a peripheral device to an early Sperry Univac machine, the UNIVAC File Computer, sorted a file without tying up the main computer.

Sorting is not logically difficult in concept, but it is difficult to program because of the need for high performance, imposed in turn because of the frequency of use of sorting and the amount of computer time consumed. Computer manufacturers usually supply a sort program as one of the utility programs accompanying the computer's operating system. These programs are generalized to permit the handling of different sizes and organizations of records. Typically, when a programmer wants to incorporate one of these sort programs into his own program system, he provides it with a list of parameters describing his file and the file he wishes to produce. He describes or specifies the input file organization, its size and location, the keys and their location within the record, whether sorting is to be in ascending or descending order, and where the output file is to be stored. Given these parameters, the prewritten program takes over and

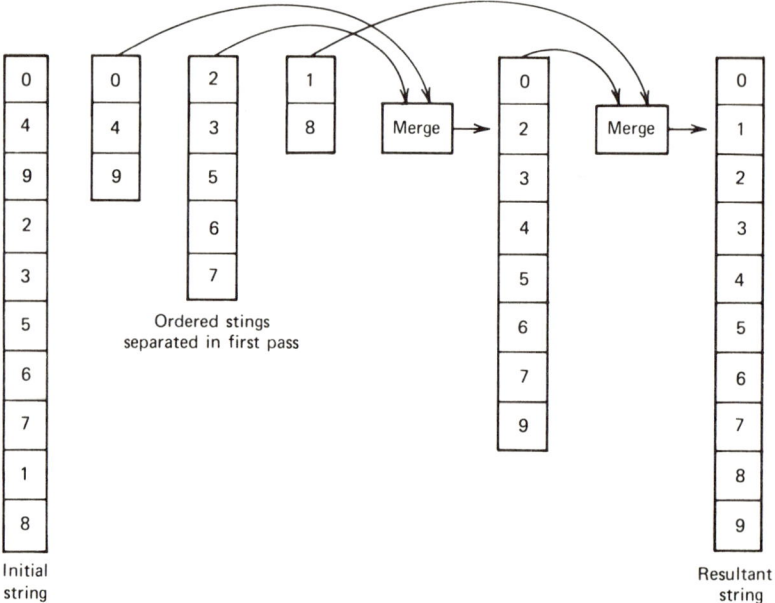

**Figure 3.12** Taking advantage of order in sorting.

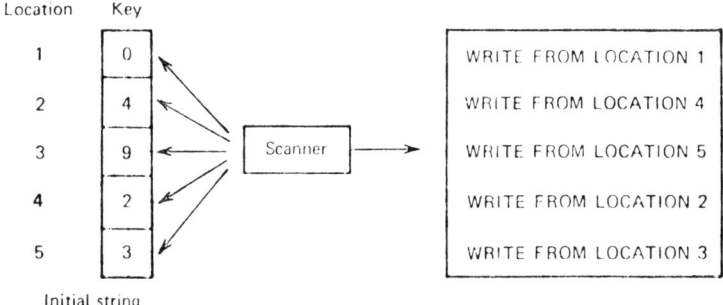

**Figure 3.13** Sorting by computing of location.

performs the work. If there is a disadvantage to this approach to sorting, it is that no single program is likely to be efficient for all the many conditions in which sorting is to be performed.

In data management, sorting is often the first and the next-to-last process on a file. On input to the computer, records may be sorted to create an ordered file for listing in a report. On output, records are often put into sequential order before being processed by a report program. Users of information frequently want reports in several different sequences, and each may require a complete re-sort of the basic file. For example, a hospital may want one report on its patients ordered by patient identification number (say, for billing purposes), another by room number (as the most convenient way to pass information to nurses and dieticians), and another by attending physician, to better enable doctors to keep up to date with their patients.

### 3.2.2 Searching

A *search* is a systematic accessing of data elements performed to locate those meeting stated criteria. A *match* is the process of examining a data element to determine whether it meets the criteria. The word "match" is also used to indicate an affirmative result, as in "The record matches the search criteria." Chapter 6 is devoted entirely to searching. We introduce the subject briefly here to make the discussion of data structures more meaningful.

*Search criteria* consist of any logical statements about record attributes whose truth can be evaluated. Typically, they are statements of relationships of elements in the data to be searched to other data elements or constants, for example: *age* > 25 or *color* = GREEN. A *search key* or *search field* is a single field used, together with a relationship and value for the field, as a search criterion. In the examples just given, the search keys are *age* and *color*.

The amount of searching required (in number of records accessed) and the length of a search (in time) are functions of memory configuration, file structure, and knowledge of file structure.

In the worst case of searching, nothing is known of record sequence or uniqueness of key values, although it must be known where the file is and how to access individual records of it. Because of the lack of information, we must allow for the possibility that the file is not ordered and has nonunique keys. This would require examining every record in the file, and if done in the most efficient way, sequentially, this procedure is called a *linear* or *sequential search*. In this case the search is also *exhaustive* in that it must examine every record. If the file contains $n$ records, an exhaustive linear search requires $n$ record accessions.

If the file in the previous case were ordered, the records could be examined in sequence until either the desired key is found or a higher (lower, if in descending sequence) one is found, indicating the desired key will not be found. On average, the search key will be found, or found not to exist, in $n/2$ accessions, and the search may be terminated at that time.

A procedure called a *binary search* is employed during searches of an ordered file for a single record when the search key is the file's sort key. On average, records are found with the minimum number of comparisons of search key with record keys. This assumes equal record access time, which in practice is true only in main memory, but the method also is of value in searching auxiliary memory-stored files. The theory is to successively cut in half the portion of the file that might contain the desired record. Each time a cut is made, the remaining portion of the file is cut in half again, until only a single record remains.

To simplify the procedure, assume a file of $m$ records, where $m$ is a power of 2; then $m = 2^n$, for some integer $n$. Make the first test at record number $m/2$. If the key of that record is greater than the search key, the desired record, if it is present in the file, is in the first half of the file. If the key is smaller, the record is in the second half. If equal, a $1/m$ probability, the search is ended.

Now repeat, on half the file. Examine, in the first half, record number $m/4$ and eliminate either the first half or the second half of this half. Continue for at most $n$ matches, at which point there will be only one record left. This procedure is illustrated in Chapter 6 (Figure 6.5).

For large files, even a binary search presents a formidable problem. In such cases it may be preferable to use an index to help locate the physical address of the desired record. An *index* is a table of equivalences of keys to addresses. Searching the table to retrieve the record address can result in finding the record in a single accession. However, the index itself may be a large file, and care must be taken not to simply transfer the search time of the main file to that of an index. Usually, though, far fewer records need be accessed when using an index than if only the main file is accessed.

## 3.3 CONCEPTS OF PHYSICAL STORAGE STRUCTURE

We have described the physical characteristics of the media on which information is stored. Our next concern is the manner in which records are placed on these media and how information about their location is made known. Any given medium presents a range of choices of physical structures. We also find, in the next chapter, that the same physical structure may be made to appear differently to different users. How a structure appears to a user is in the realm of logical structures.

A *storage structure* is a plan for the organization of data in a storage unit or device. Storage structures are generally designed to capitalize on some desirable access features of the memory or to overcome some undesirable features. "Desirable" and "undesirable" are relative terms that may vary for the same memory unit from application to application.

In describing storage structures, we are concerned with *physical location,* expressed in terms of absolute address, a number recognized by the computer as the location of an information record; *relative location,* expressed in terms of an ordinal number ("the $n$th record," "next," or "*previous,*" which are terms having a precise, predetermined meaning); or a *symbolic location,* such as a key, used as the basis for record sequencing, whose value then uniquely identifies a record location. Present-day commercial computers do not directly search memory on the basis of keys. A computer program must convert the key to an address, or it must direct the computer in a search of a set of records until the one containing the desired key is found. Hence when a key is used as the basis for record location, it is a logical structure being addressed, not the physical structure.

A data organization must provide for information to be added to the structure, deleted from it, changed, or retrieved. The first three of these functions are generally grouped together under the term "file maintenance." We often find that an organization may be designed to favor either maintenance or retrieval functions; these tend to be in conflict, however, and both cannot be optimized.

### 3.3.1 Random Structure

The simplest arrangement of information is that often called *random* (Figure 3.14). Records, or input, are placed seemingly at random and may be retrieved at random also. The order of records is not specified by the

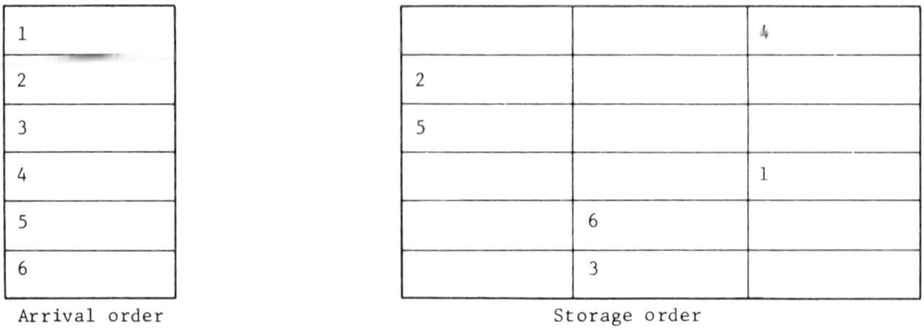

## 50  Data Storage

| Arrival order |
|---|
| 1 |
| 2 |
| 3 |
| 4 |
| 5 |
| 6 |

| | | | Storage order | | |
|---|---|---|---|---|---|
| | | | | | 4 |
| 2 | | | | | |
| 5 | | | | | |
| | | | | | 1 |
| | | | 6 | | |
| | | | 3 | | |

**Figure 3.14**  Storage of records in random order.

method of organization. A record is stored wherever a computer program so directs. The decision on location is external to the organizational method. Thus it may *appear* random to one observer but not to the program assigning addresses. A program wishing to retrieve a record stored under this organization must present the machine address. Again, the organizational method does not determine addresses: they must be externally determined. There are a number of ways of doing this, which we cover in Chapter 5. In effect, the random organization is a no-organization organization. The method may impose limitations on minimum and maximum address only. This organization is also called *direct* because the using program must directly address data—there is no relative or symbolic address.

### 3.3.2  Sequential Structure

The organizational method most commonly used (particularly if noncomputer files are considered) is called *sequential organization* or sequential structure. Records are placed adjacent to each other, in accordance with a predetermined meaning of "next in sequence." On a disk, for example, the sequence will be as follows: records are placed adjacent to each other within a track, then on the beginning of the next track on the same disk surface or the beginning of the corresponding track on the next surface. Record position is a function solely of *arrival sequence. If a user wishes his file to be in order by some key, he must see to it that records arrive in key sequence.* This can be done by sorting or by assigning key values as a function of arrival order. Records may be added to a sequential file only at the end. There can be no insertion within the file. If an insertion must be made, the file must be copied over, and the new record must be copied at the appropriate time (caused to arrive in the output record stream in appropriate sequence; see Figure 3.15).

Retrieval from a sequential file is limited to retrieval on the basis of record adjacency getting the next record, or with some memories, the previous record, and repeating as necessary. It may also be possible to instruct the access program to start at a particular physical location and then get the next record.

### 3.3.3 List Structure

A third organizational mode is the *list*, briefly introduced in the previous chapter. There are three key features of the list organization: (1) records may be physically placed wherever there is available space, (2) the determination of address is the responsibility of the list access program, (3) each record carries a pointer telling where the next logical record is. Inherent in any list organizational method is a method for keeping track of available space and returning unused space to a pool, a process sometimes called "garbage collection" (Figure 3.16). When a new record arrives in the file, space is drawn from the pool (i.e., an address is taken from a list of available addresses); when a record is deleted, its space is returned to the pool by relisting the address as an available one. The user of a list is not concerned with physical placement of records. He addresses them in logical terms by naming a key, asking for the $n$th record or the next record.

A more limited form of list is a *chain*, a set of records linked together by pointers, like the elements of a list. The difference, if any, between a list and a chain lies in lack of formality of definition of the latter. Chains are

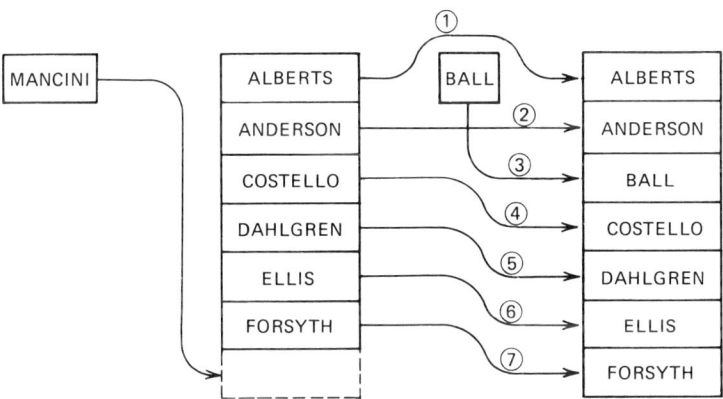

**Figure 3.15** Insertion of records into a sequential file. Records can be added at the end of the file, as on left. To insert a record into the interior of a file, however, the file must be completely copied and the insertion made during the copying process.

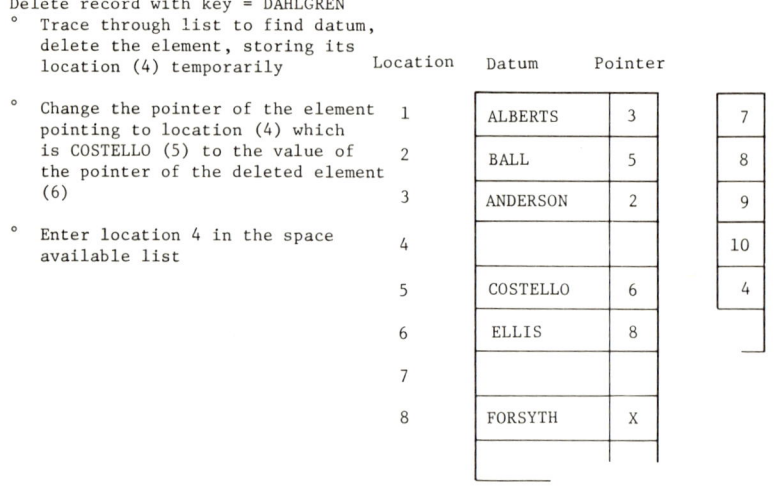

| Transactions | Location | Datum | Pointer |
|---|---|---|---|
| 1. Add record with key = BALL | 1 | ALBERTS | 3 | 2 |
| ° Recover address 2 from space-available list | 2 | | | 7 |
| ° Delete 2 from list | 3 | ANDERSON | 5 | 8 |
| ° Store new record in location 2 | 4 | DAHLGREN | 6 | 9 |
| ° Trace through list for logically preceding datum (ANDERSON), set its pointer to 2 | 5 | COSTELLO | 4 | 19 |
| | 6 | ELLIS | 8 | |
| ° Set pointer of new entry to the location previously pointed to by ANDERSON (5) | 7 | | | |
| | 8 | FORSYTH | X* | |

Initial List   Space-available List

*X denotes end of list

2. Delete record with key = DAHLGREN
   ° Trace through list to find datum, delete the element, storing its location (4) temporarily

| | Location | Datum | Pointer |
|---|---|---|---|
| ° Change the pointer of the element pointing to location (4) which is COSTELLO (5) to the value of the pointer of the deleted element (6) | 1 | ALBERTS | 3 | 7 |
| | 2 | BALL | 5 | 8 |
| | 3 | ANDERSON | 2 | 9 |
| ° Enter location 4 in the space available list | 4 | | | 10 |
| | 5 | COSTELLO | 6 | 4 |
| | 6 | ELLIS | 8 | |
| | 7 | | | |
| | 8 | FORSYTH | X | |

Figure 3.16

List after completion of transactions   Space-available List

**Figure 3.16** The space management function.

often established within other data structures and may not follow all the conventions of a list. A list structure is described in Section 3.4.2.

### 3.3.4 A Unified Definition of Storage Structure

Some writers [5] see the three methods just listed as the basic methods of file organization. There are many others, but all are derived from the first three or a combination of them. This is a useful classification, but there is a unifying principle from which the three are derived. Storing or retrieving records, in any organization, requires that four functions be performed:

1. Determine the address (at which a new record is to be stored or from which one is to be retrieved).
2. Access that location, or order the computer to position its memory device to be able to read (or write) the record at the location.
3. Perform the read or write operation.
4. On storage, establish the logical linkage between the new record and previously stored ones.

The major differences among organizational methods are caused by differences in how addresses are computed and linkages established. For example, if the only address the method is able to compute is "next physical record," we have a sequential data organization. In the direct organization, address determination is external, as is linkage. If the external process for address determination should always assign a new record to the "next" location and retrieve from the "next" location only, it would perform exactly as a sequential organization. In a list, the next available storage address is determined by look-up in a list of available addresses; and retrieval is done by following explicit pointers that are the means of linking records logically. A list can also be made to look like a sequential organization if the assignment of available space is sufficiently constrained.

If a storage structure is an arrangement of data and an addressing procedure for locating data, there must be a program or method for using the organization, performing such functions as additions of records, deletions, changes, or retrieval. This program is a *data manager,* described below. We have seen three organizational methods, how they differ, and their essential unity. In Section 3.4 we describe a number of variations on these three methods.

### 3.3.5 The Data Manager Program

Regardless of the organizational method used, ultimately a computer program is called on to store records in the structure, retrieve them, and delete or rewrite them on command. This program need not be concerned with record *content* except insofar as content determines location. We call such a program a *data manager*. Other terms used include *access method* and *data management support system*. The former term, used by IBM, emphasizes that the principal function is to access data or memory locations. The latter term indicates that a data manager is used only in support of another program: it does not answer questions, compile reports, or edit data, but it serves programs that perform these functions.

The precise set of functions assigned to a data manager varies with individual programs and structural forms. Typically, a using programmer deals with the data manager through a set of high-order or macro commands such as the following, which are not from any particular data manager:

GET NEXT   Retrieves the "next" record using the data manager's definition of next.

GET (*key, loc*)   A value of the key is given. The data manager either finds the corresponding record or sends the using program an error message. When found, the record is stored at the indicated (*loc*) location in main memory.

WRITE (*loc, key*)   Write the record now stored in the indicated location of core memory, placing it at a physical address determined by the key value given.

REWRITE (*loc, key*)   A WRITE may be programmed to refuse to write if a record already exists with the given key. The REWRITE command is the programmer's statement that he *expects* an existing record with this key but that he wishes to overwrite it, probably because he has changed its content. In this case failure to find an existing record may produce the error message.

There are, of course, many more commands and variations on the basic concepts of each. A user must become familiar with the data manager available to him in each case.

## 3.4 SPECIFIC STORAGE STRUCTURES

Some of the more common physical arrangements of data in storage are now presented. We continue to emphasize general method rather than attempting to detail specific organizations or to provide an exhaustive catalog of organizations.

### 3.4.1 Sequential Methods

***Arrays, Tables, and Indexes*** One of the most common data structures is the array or table (Figure 3.17). An array (Section 2.2.1) is a sequential set of fields that are often but not necessarily in order. A table is an array, and it may be an array of groups. An element in an array or table may be addressed by position. In a table, which is usually ordered on one of the fields, addressing may be by ordinal number, or position in the array, or by key—the content of the ordering field. Retrieval yields some other field of the table corresponding to the search argument.

Generally, arrays and tables are data structures that can be stored in main memory. Also, the basic element, a field or a group, is usually small. If the table is too big for main memory storage and the group is large enough to be called a record, however, the table becomes a file. There is no specific point at which this happens. The difference is largely in terminology.

A special case of a table is an *index*. No different in form, an index is a table used to store information about the location of information in another file. It contains one field that is an attribute of a record in the other file (such as the sequencing key) and one or more pointers to the other file, in the form of machine addresses or content keys (Figure 3.18).

***Sequential Files*** A sequential file, as already described, has its records in order based on arrival sequence; alternatively, they may be sorted on a key field. Searching can only be done by moving to the next record, or in some cases the previous one, except that a machine address or ordinal number may be given as a place to start a search. No insertions are possible without recopying the file.

| MONDAY    |
|-----------|
| TUESDAY   |
| WEDNESDAY |
| THURSDAY  |
| FRIDAY    |

a.

| FRIDAY    |
|-----------|
| MONDAY    |
| THURSDAY  |
| TUESDAY   |
| WEDNESDAY |

b.

| 1.00 | .84147 | .54030 |
|------|--------|--------|
| 1.01 | .84683 | .53186 |
| 1.02 | .85211 | .52337 |
| 1.03 | .85730 | .51482 |
| 1.04 | .86240 | .50622 |

Arrays: <u>a</u> not sorted on constituent field, <u>b</u> sorted alphabetically on constitutent field.

Table: an array of groups

**Figure 3.17** Arrays and table.

## 56   Data Storage

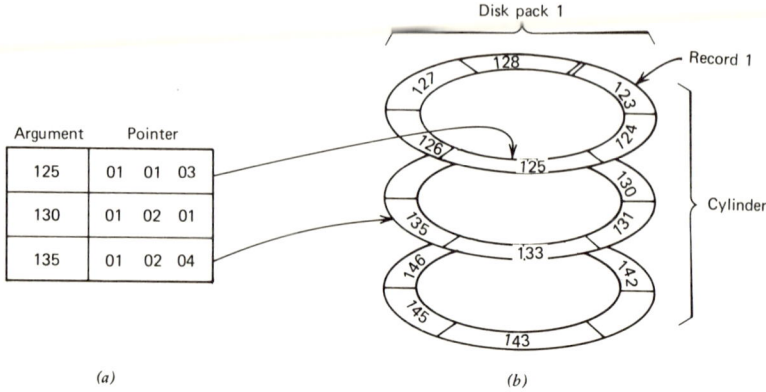

**Figure 3.18**   (a) Index, containing (b) records in storage.

### 3.4.2   List-Type Structures

The essential characteristic of a list-type structure is the independence of the physical location of a data element from its logical relationship to some other data element. An obvious disadvantage occurring when lists are used is that they have their own form of overhead expense. The overhead associated with a sequential file organization is excessive time to insert new records or to search. With lists it is the extra space devoted to pointer storage, the time necessary to interpret pointers, and both the space and time needed to use and maintain space available lists.

*List Structures*   In original concept, a list consisted of a set of elements chained together by pointers (Figure 3.16). The basic element was a *cell* containing a *datum* and a *pointer*. Lists had to be searched from the beginning along the chain of pointers. The address of the logically first element of a list was called its *name*. The name of the list in Figure 3.16 is *l*. The pointer field of the last element contained a special symbol to indicate the end of the list. Any datum of a list could be replaced by a pointer to a sublist (Figure 3.19). The pointer of the element continued to point to the next list element and the datum was used to point to the sublist. The sublist is simply another list, or set of elements, subordinated to the first list, just as a single datum was. The sublist is identically structured. Any element of a sublist, in turn, can be replaced by a sublist, and so on.

The advantage of a list structure is ease of insertion of new elements or change of logical data structure. Physical placement of elements is completely independent of content or hierarchical relationship among elements. When the structure is formed, a certain amount of space is set aside and all unused space is assigned to a *space-available list*. This may be another list of elements, chained together, but containing blank datum fields or having some other indication that they contain no data. When a new insert is made to a list, space for the new element is "drawn" from the space-available list; that list is modified by having one element deleted; and the main list is extended by having appropriate pointers adjusted to accommodate the new element. When an element is deleted, it is returned to the space-available list, by being chained to the last (or some other) element of that list.

The space-available list can be the same list as that containing valid data but using a different chain of pointers. The separate list method and the same information in one list appear in Figures 3.20a and 3.20b, respectively. In the second method, the data manager must keep track of the beginning of the data list *and* of the beginning of the space-available portion of that list.

Once the basic idea of a list structure began to be used, many variations were introduced, and some of them render obsolete certain original, formally defined, attributes of a list. *Backward pointers,* for example, indicate the logically preceding element in the list (Figure 3.21). They enable a search program to move in either direction along a chain. Also, the last element in a chain can be made to point to the first element, and the first to the last, by backward pointers (Figure 3.22). A list or sublist so organized is called a *ring.* From this concept came the more general *ring structure.*

**Ring Structures**  Ring structures arose from the need to have a structure that would permit entry into a list at any point, not just at the "top" or beginning. For example (Figure 3.23), if element *i,* say *physician,* on ring $R_1$ has a logical linkage A. B. SMITH with element *j* on ring $R_2$, it may be desirable to jump from ring 1 directly to element *j* of ring 2 without starting at

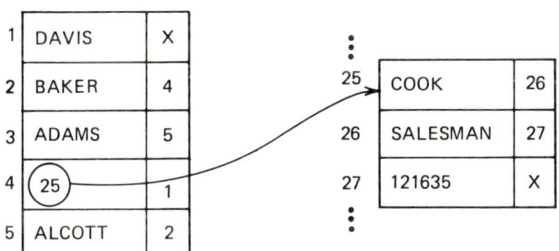

**Figure 3.19**  Sublist. A name in the list has been replaced by a pointer to a sublist that contains more information than was provided for in the original list. In this case the datum in the original list is replaced by the pointer. In other file designs the pointer is a separate field, which permits retaining the *name* in the original list. In either case the 1 in location 4 points to the next logical record in the list. This is not used as the sublist pointer.

Data List

| 1 | ALBERTO | 3 |
| 2 | | |
| 3 | ANDERSON | 5 |
| 4 | DAHLGREN | 6 |
| 5 | COSTELLO | 4 |
| 6 | ELLIS | X |
| 7 | | |

Space Available List

| 21 | 2 | 22 |
| 22 | 7 | 23 |
| 23 | 8 | 24 |
| ⋮ | | |

| 1 | ALBERTS | 3 |
| 2 | BALL | 5 |
| 3 | ANDERSON | 2 |
| 4 | | |
| 5 | COSTELLO | 6 |
| 6 | ELLIS | X |
| 7 | | |

| 21 | | 22 |
| 22 | 7 | 23 |
| 23 | 8 | 24 |
| 24 | ⋮ | |
| 25 | | |
| 26 | 4 | |
| 27 | | |

a. Data and space available lists, separately maintained, before (l.) and after (r.) inserting record with key BALL and deleting record with key DAHLGREN.

| 1 | ALBERTS | 3 |
| 2 | | 7 |
| 3 | ANDERSON | 5 |
| 4 | DAHLGREN | 6 |
| 5 | COSTELLO | 4 |
| 6 | ELLIS | X |
| 7 | | 8 |

| 1 | ALBERTS | 3 |
| 2 | BALL | 5 |
| 3 | ANDERSON | 2 |
| 4 | | 7 |
| 5 | COSTELLO | 6 |
| 6 | ELLIS | X |
| 7 | | 8 |

b. Data and space available lists maintained by two separate pointer systems in the same physical list, before (l.) and after (r.) the same insertion and deletion illustrated in a.

**Figure 3.20** Space-available management. (*a*) Data and space-available lists, separately maintained, before (left) and after (right) inserting record with key BALL and deleting record with key DAHLGREN. (*b*) Data and space-available lists maintained by two separate pointer systems in the same physical list, before (left) and after (right) the same insertion and deletion illustrated in (*a*).

## Specific Storage Structures 59

|   | Datum | Forward Pointer | Backward Pointer |
|---|---|---|---|
| 1 | 7 | X | 5 |
| 2 | 1 | 4 | X |
| 3 | 3 | 6 | 4 |
| 4 | 2 | 3 | 2 |
| 5 | 6 | 1 | 7 |
| 6 | 4 | 7 | 3 |
| 7 | 5 | 5 | 6 |

The highest valued datum is 7 in location 1. It points to the next highest, 6, in location 5, etc. The backward chain ends at value 1 in location 2, the lowest-valued datum.

**Figure 3.21** Backward pointers.

the top of 2 and tracing down the list to element *j*. In this way, a search program could find all patients of Dr. Smith, then scan their rings for other attributes, then go on to the next Smith patient, in an economical way.

A ring structure, then, is a list structure in which the lists have no specially designated starting point. Elements point to their successors and what would have been the last points back to the first. Any list element may point off to a sublist, also in ring form. Available space would be managed in the same fashion as for conventional list structures.

**Multilist** Multilist structures [6], also called *knotted* or *threaded* lists [7], consist of sets of records chained together. A set of records sharing a common attribute, such as having the same value of a given field, would be so linked (Figure 3.24). If one set of records is linked by one attribute (*state* = MD) and another set by a different attribute (*date of birth* = 1931), there

|   |   |   |   |
|---|---|---|---|
| 1 | 7 | 2 | 5 |
| 2 | 1 | 4 | 1 |
| 3 | 3 | 6 | 4 |
| 4 | 2 | 3 | 2 |
| 5 | 6 | 1 | 7 |
| 6 | 4 | 7 | 3 |
| 7 | 5 | 5 | 6 |

A simple ring. The terminator symbol used in Figure 3.21 (X) has been replaced by a pointer from the last element to the first, in the respective chains.

**Figure 3.22** A ring.

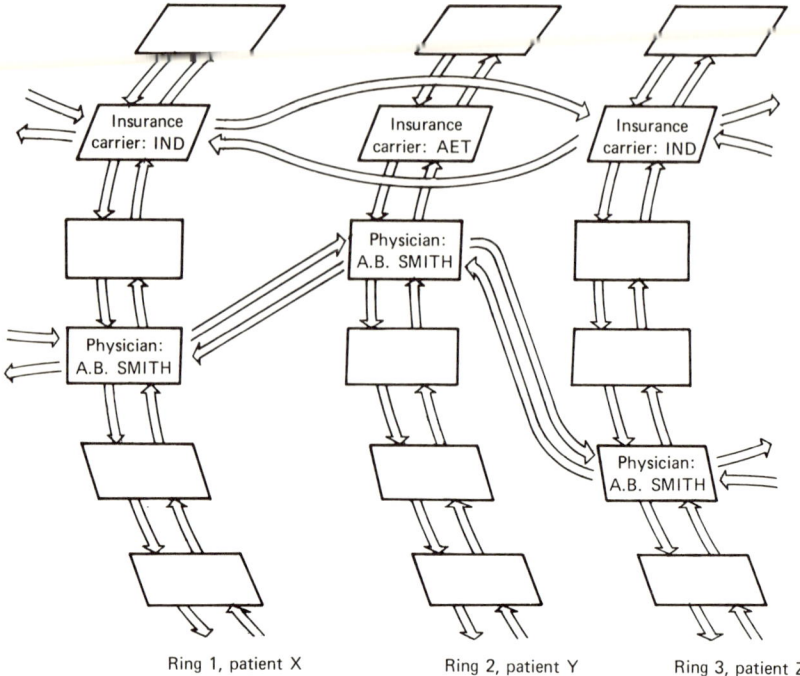

**Figure 3.23** Interlocking rings for *insurance carrier* and *physician* forming a ring structure. Data for each patient are stored as a ring.

may be some records common to both sets. The pointers linking each set would be different fields; hence nothing would prevent any given record from being a member of any number of linked sets, called *threads*. It is the joining together of threads having records in common that gives the structure the name *knotted list structures*.

As in a conventional list, entry to a thread is made at the top, and this, in turn, is located by use of a *directory*. For each thread, the directory lists the attribute that threaded records share, the address of the first record in the thread, and the number of records in the thread. The directory is an index as defined in Section 3.3.1. Directory data appear at the top of Figure 3.24. The first element shows attribute *state* = MD, address of first element 010, and number of elements in the thread 6.

When a new record is added to a thread, it is placed in such a way that a search of the thread will not necessitate a reversal of the search mechanism. A disk read head, for example, should be kept moving continually in one direction until the end of the thread is reached, to help hold access time to a minimum. With such a restriction on the management of

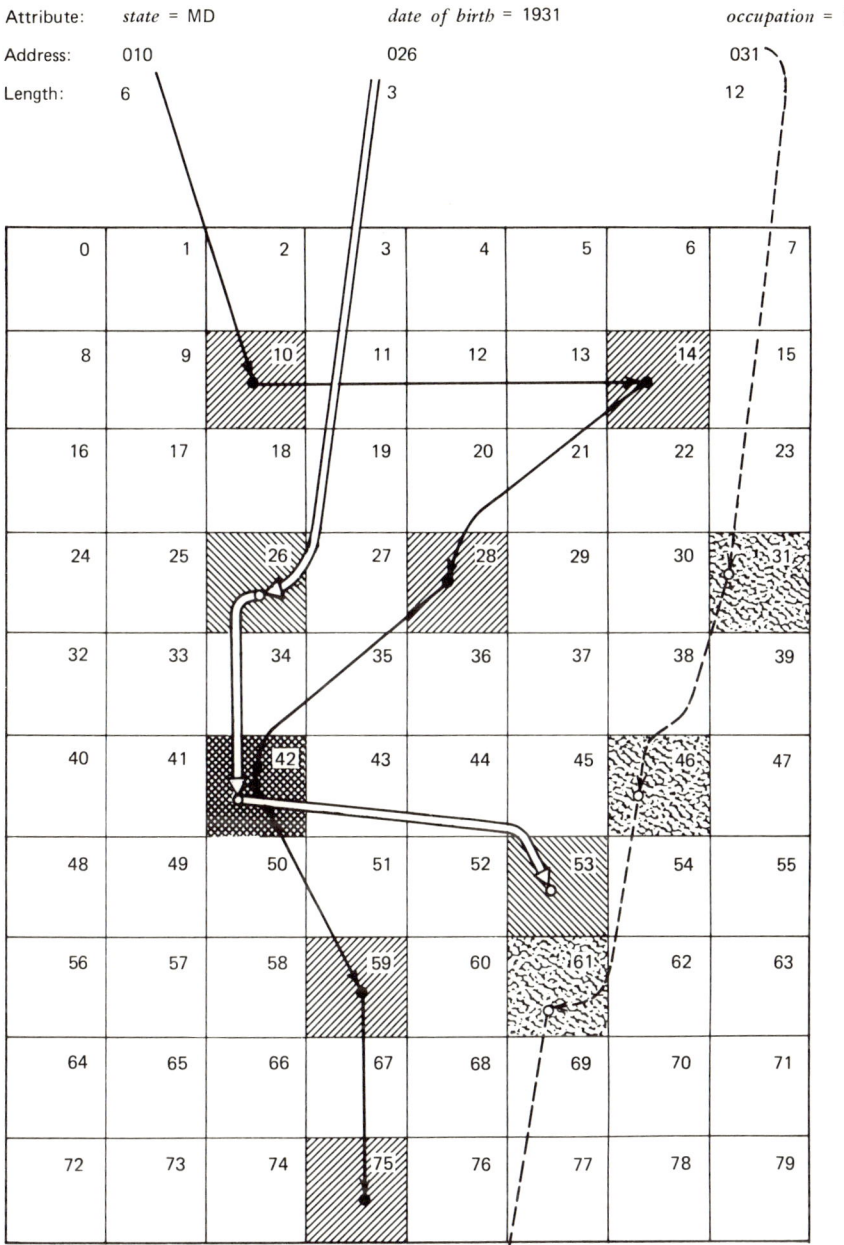

**Figure 3.24** Multilist. The file directory (top) contains a field name and value, the location of the first record in the thread, and the thread length. Record 42 is on both the threads for *state* = MD and *date of birth* = 1931.

available space, empty space would accumulate near the beginning of the file, as records were deleted, and the extent of the file (range of physical addresses) would increase indefinitely. To alleviate this problem, threads may be limited in length (Figure 3.25). When the limit is reached, a new thread is begun for records with the same attribute, and an additional entry must be made in the directory. There is no reason the second thread has to start beyond the first. Thus the space released by deletions from a file may be collected and reused for starting new threads.

Another variation on thread length restricts threads to those records stored on the same major memory subdivision, perhaps a cylinder. In *cellular partitioning* (cell, in this usage, being the major memory partition such as a cylinder) multiple entries in the directory are also required

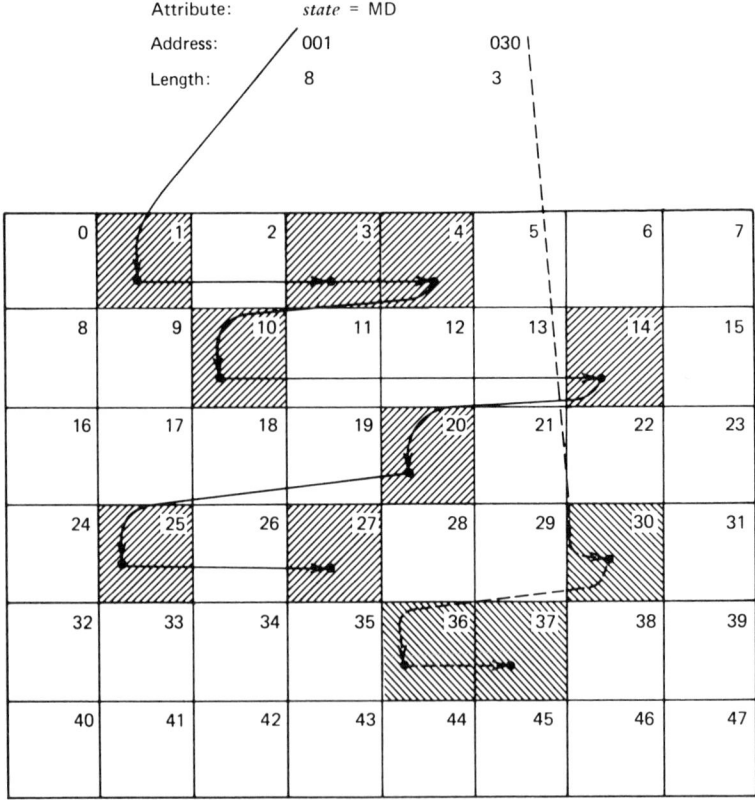

**Figure 3.25** Limited thread length in multilist. Threads can be limited in length, with a new thread for any attribute begun when that length is exceeded. Here a limit of eight records is imposed, the first thread terminating at location 27. The second thread begins at 30.

Specific Storage Structures    63

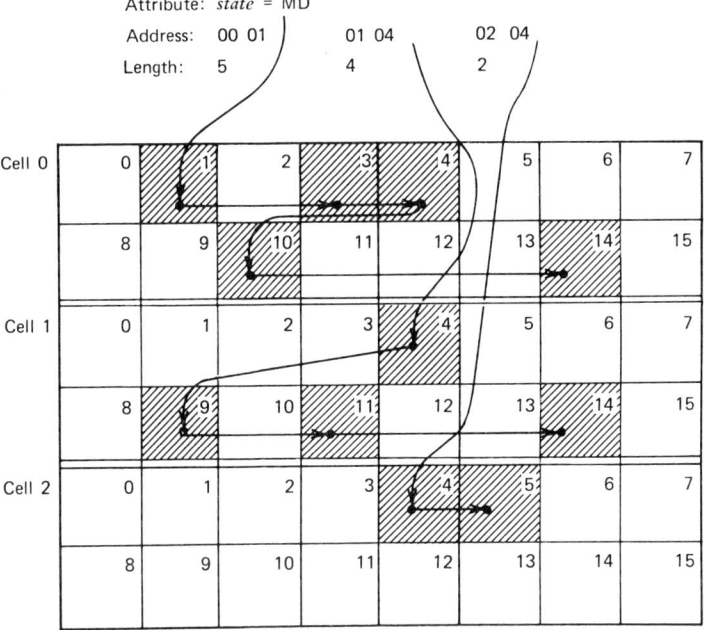

**Figure 3.26** Cellular partitioning. In this variant of multilist threads must begin and end in the same cell or major memory subdivision. A cell might be a cylinder in disk memory.

whenever there are multiple threads formed for the same attribute (Figure 3.26).

*Inverted File Structures*  The variations on the multilist concept are almost endless. One of the most common predates multilist in historical appearance but can be most easily explained as a multilist variant. This is the *inverted file structure*. Consider a multilist structure with threads limited in length. There are, of course, multiple entries in the directory for each attribute, one for each thread segment. Records sharing these attributes are threaded together, but since a thread ends after $n$ records, the $n$th record points nowhere. Now imagine the maximum thread length shrinking to *one* (Figure 3.27). In this case there is a directory entry for each record possessing a given attribute, and no record is chained to any other. The name *inverted file structure* derives from the fact that the main file records themselves might be ordered, as a sequential file; then each directory changes the order of listing of references to these records, or "inverts" the order. An inverted file is an ordered file, in order by attribute and record location.

## 64  Data Storage

Attribute:  state = MD

a. Address: 001 030
   Length:  8   3

b. Address: 001 014 030
   Length:  4   4   3

c. Address: 001 004 014 025 030 037
   Length:  2   2   2   2   2   1

d. Address: 001 003 004 010 014 020 025 027 030 036 037
   Length:  1   1   1   1   1   1   1   1   1   1   1

**Figure 3.27** Inverted index, presenting the evolution of a multilist into an inverted index structure by progressively shortening the thread length of the file in Figure 3.25 until it reaches 1—an index entry for each data record.

For any given file, the number of directories or inverted files is optional. One would not devote storage space and maintenance time to a directory for an attribute unlikely to be used for searching. On the other hand, establishing an inverted file after the multilist structure has been built is cumbersome. Hence users are usually under some pressure to select inverted files beforehand and then live with the choice.

### 3.4.3  Direct Structures

A direct structure is one for which no searching is necessary to access a record. Either the data manager knows or can compute the address, or the address of desired data is presented to the data manager along with the request for data. Put negatively, a direct structure is characterized by the absence of a search for records by the data manager. The application program using the data manager may be conducting a search by asking the data manager for one record at a time. Computation is the most common form of address determination used with direct structures. The computation is performed on the record key and yields the machine address. The computation should be such that if the input keys are evenly distributed over their range, the addresses are evenly distributed over their own range. Obviously, it is important to avoid having a large number of different keys yield the same machine address. The mathematical process is often called

## Specific Storage Structures 65

*randomizing, hashing,* or *hash coding* because a set of random numbers has the same property—even distribution over a range. Computation of addresses is covered in greater detail in Chapter 5.

Once again, the variations on the basic methods are many. Two are presented here.

***Random Structures*** A block of memory is set aside for the storage of records. The location of any record within the block is determined by a randomizing computation. The computation algorithm must be fed the limits (minimum and maximum addresses) and a specific key. It produces an address within the stated limits. Even if the key is alphabetic, an appropriate address can be produced by treating the key as a binary number. Inevitably, unless the expanse is vast with respect to the number of different keys, there will be two or more different keys assigned to the same location. When this happens, a chain is set up (Figure 3.28). The first record assigned to the location has a pointer indicating where the second one assigned that address has been placed instead. Placement of the second record is in a secondary storage area. The second record would point to the third, should it arrive, and so on.

Thus for the example of Figure 3.28 the first three letters of the name are used as the basis of record assignment—a convenience for illustration but not actually an effective randomizing device because the resulting assignments are not evenly distributed. McGinn, McGann, McGonigle, and McGinty all are initially assigned to location 101 in the original data area, by virtue of their first three letters. The first record to arrive is stored in location 101. Other records are put in the first available spaces in the secondary data area, and all are chained together. Alphabetic order is not necessarily followed for records in a chain, or records in the original data area. Records in a chain are not necessarily contiguous to each other. If

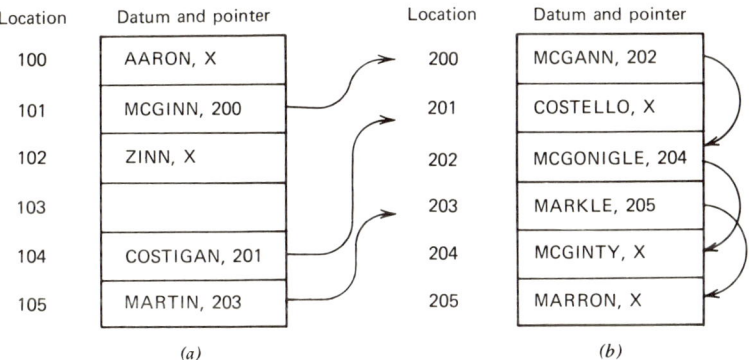

**Figure 3.28** Random data structure. (*a*) Original data area, (*b*) secondary data area.

## 66  Data Storage

Costello arrives before McGonigle, the record for Costello occupies the space next to McGann. The main body of the file is in the sequence determined by the memory assignment algorithm (in this case "random" but actually determined by a computation on the key). In the secondary area, records are in sequence by arrival order. Chaining links those assigned to the same memory location. Keys that yield the same address are called *synonyms*, although they do not necessarily have any semantic resemblance.

Retrieval from this file structure follows the same procedure. The search key is put through the computation and a location is computed at which a record with this key would be stored. That physical location is accessed. If it is null (no data stored), it is immediately clear that nothing will be retrieved. That location, however, might have a record whose key does not match the search key because both keys yielded the same address (Figure 3.29). In this case, the search program must follow the chain until it finds the record desired or comes to the end. We can see that the search efficiency of this method will degrade if there are too many records in chains. In this event, the file would have to be reorganized to have a larger expanse, bringing a greater percentage of the records into the main data area where they can be reached by a direct computation.

To delete a record, the same procedure is followed as for a search (Figure 3.30). When the record is found, it is modified by setting a tag to indicate *deleted*, and the record is *rewritten* in its original place. If it is in a chain, the pointer of the preceding record can be given the pointer of the deleted record and the address of the deleted record reported to the space available program for future use. In the main data area we delete by tag-

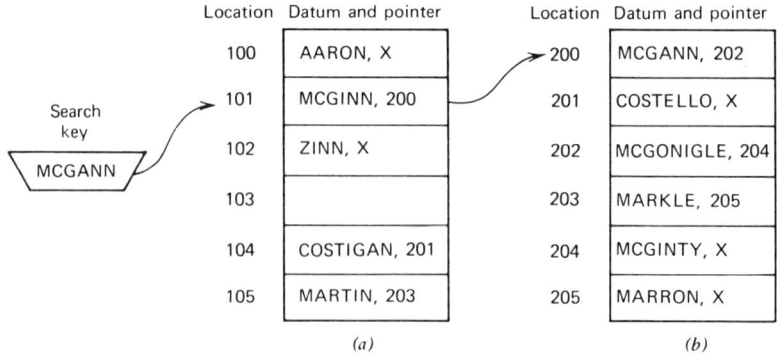

**Figure 3.29** Searching a random data structure. (*a*) Original data area, (*b*) secondary data area. Using data and technique of Figure 3.28, McGann yields an address of 101. A direct access to that location indicates that the key stored there is not equal to the search key. Hence, the chain must be followed until a match occurs.

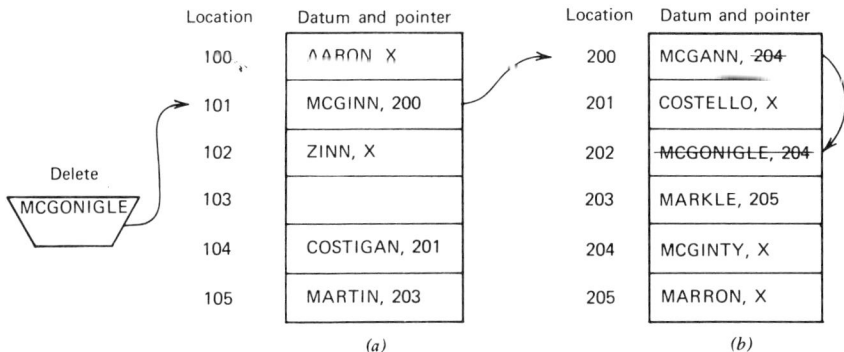

**Figure 3.30** To delete a record from a random structure, it must be searched for as illustrated in Figure 3.29. When found, the record is tagged as deleted or erased, and its pointer is moved to the logically preceding record. (*a*) Original data area, (*b*) secondary data area.

ging. In the secondary area we delete by changing pointers and by reporting to space available.

This basic concept can be combined with other file organizational concepts. The next method combines the basic direct method with inverted files.

***Direct Access to Inverted Files*** When the inverted files or directories or indexes are direct files, searched by a combination of computation and chaining, the inverted file yields the machine address of a record in the main data area (Figure 3.31). Each inverted index is a random data structure searched by doing a computation on the search key, then following a chain of records assigned to the same location. Finally a pointer is reached to a location in the main data file. Note that the inverted index contains a key, a pointer to the main data file, and a pointer to another location in the inverted index. The direct access to inverted files method can be very fast for searching, when the directories are large, so long as the directory chains can be kept relatively small.

The main data area may contain key pointers to inverted files. For example, we may search an inverted file or directory to find the address of a hospital patient's record. Given the address, we can access the record directly. The record may contain the name of the patient's doctor, and if we are so inclined, we can follow this pointer (i.e., *name of physician* is a pointer; it is the key of another inverted file or list) to the next patient of the same physician.

***Indexed Random*** Another variant on direct access to inverted files is the *indexed random* method [8], featuring a *full index*, an index containing

## 68  Data Storage

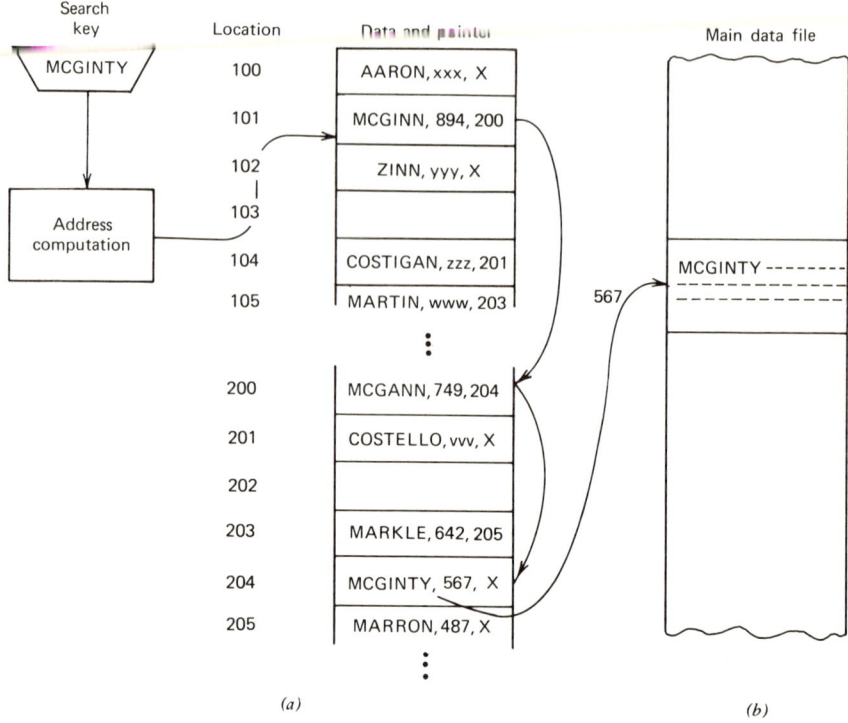

**Figure 3.31**  Direct access to inverted files. (*a*) Inverted index, (*b*) main data file.

an entry for each record in the main file. Because the index is ordered and full, the main data records may be organized in any fashion, perhaps random or sequential (arrival sequence). The index entry gives the machine address of a block in storage containing the desired record. Since the data file may not be in key order, the other records in a block may have no relationship to the indicated one. The advantage of this method is speed; data records can be stored in the most time-efficient manner, and the index search quickly gives a direct machine address of the data.

### 3.4.4  Combinations

The direct access to inverted files and indexed random organizational methods are not pure systems. Both make use of more than one data organizational concept. In this section we describe two major file organizations that combine two or more basic methods.

***Indexed Sequential Files*** An indexed sequential file (usually abbreviated ISAM, after the IBM terminology *indexed sequential access method*) is basically a sequential file to which the user can gain access by key, for either search or insertion [9]. It differs from a sequential file in three ways. (*a*) The key of each record must be made available to the data manager program. Recall that a sequential file is in sequence only if the user sees to it that records arrive in key sequence. Its data manager has neither use for nor knowledge of the key. (*b*) An index or directory is maintained, allowing access to be gained "reasonably" directly. In fact, the access method used is a compromise between sequential and direct. (*c*) Provision is made to allow records to be inserted without recopying the file. This is done by storing inserts in an *overflow area,* a portion of the structure physically separate from that holding the main body of sequentially ordered data. A list is set up linking the main body with the overflow area. The three main portions of an ISAM file—index, data area, and overflow area—are shown in Figure 3.32.

In the main data storage area of an ISAM structure, records are stored sequentially (Figure 3.33), with the key physically separated from the remainder of the data record. This permits the data manager to access the

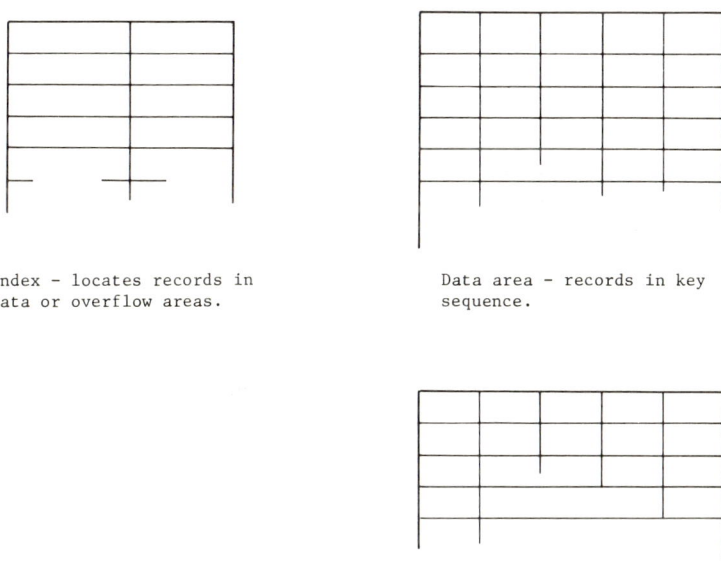

Index - locates records in data or overflow areas.

Data area - records in key sequence.

Overflow area - records in arrival order, placed here when displaced from data area.

**Figure 3.32** Schematic of ISAM file structure.

70  *Data Storage*

| Address | Key | Data | Address | Key | Data | Address | Key |
|---------|-----|------|---------|-----|------|---------|-----|
| 100 | 123 | | 101 | 124 | --- | 102 | 125 |

**Figure 3.33**  Data storage in ISAM.

key without having any knowledge of how the rest of the record is organized. Records are in strict sequential order. In some implementations of ISAM there may not be any blank records (i.e., space set aside in the main data storage area for later insertions), but others may have such blanks. In either case, if a record is deleted, it is tagged as such, but it continues to occupy space except as noted below (Figure 3.34). Several records may be grouped into a block; in this case the highest key in the block is separately recorded, as are the individual keys of each record of the block, and the key of the last record is then recorded twice (Figure 3.35).

The ISAM index or directory is a table containing keys and machine addresses of records corresponding to the keys (Figure 3.36). The lowest level index contains an entry for each track of a cylinder. This entry lists the *machine address of the first record in the track* and the *highest key* in the track (the key of the last record). Thus it tells the manager program that any record containing a key less than the one shown (but higher than keys stored in other tracks) will be found by starting to search at the given location and *searching the track sequentially.* A higher order index contains a similar arrangement of data but tells the search program the highest key in any given cylinder. The data manager starts with the cylinder index, determines the cylinder potentially containing the record sought, then searches the track index to find the track in which to search (Figure 3.37). The index is not exhaustive; it does not contain every key in the file. Hence a search program cannot tell from the index whether a given key will be found in the file. It may be necessary to go all the way through the two indexes, then perform a sequential search within a track to verify that a key is *not* present. If the file is large enough, there may be an index to the cylinder indexes; indeed, there may be an arbitrary number of such nested indexes. The minimum is for the two lower level ones, the track and cylinder indexes.

Since the file we have described so far is sequential, it cannot accom-

| Address | Key | Data | Address | Key | | Address | Key |
|---------|-----|------|---------|-----|---|---------|-----|
| 100 | 123 | ----- | 101 | 124 | DELETED | 102 | 125 |

**Figure 3.34**  Deletion of a record by tagging.

## Specific Storage Structures 71

| Block address | Key | Key | Data | Key | Data | Key | Data |
| 100 | 126 | 123 | ----- | 124 | ------ | 126 | ------ |

| Block address | Key | Key | Data | Key | Data | Key | Data |
| 101 | 131 | 129 | ----- | 130 | ----- | 131 | ----- |

**Figure 3.35** Storage of keys in blocked records.

modate insertions without being recopied. When an insertion is to be made, a record is moved from the primary area where it was initially stored to an *overflow* area (Figure 3.38) to make room for the new record. In one method of handling overflow, some number of tracks (uniform across the entire file) is set aside in each cylinder for overflow from that cylinder. All overflow records are then chained together in the overflow area in key

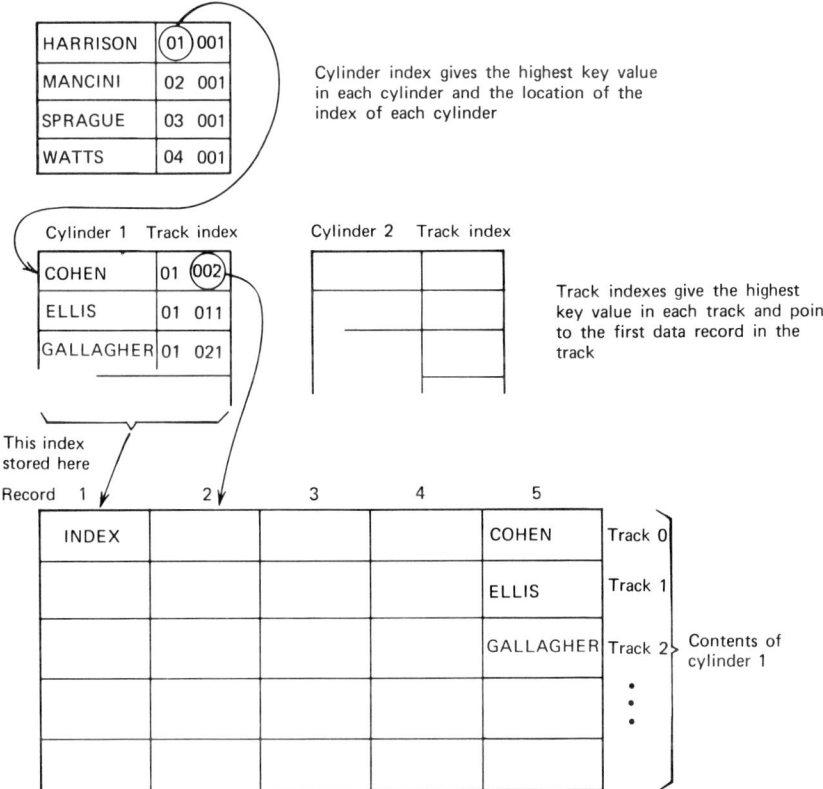

**Figure 3.36** ISAM index structure.

## 72  Data Storage

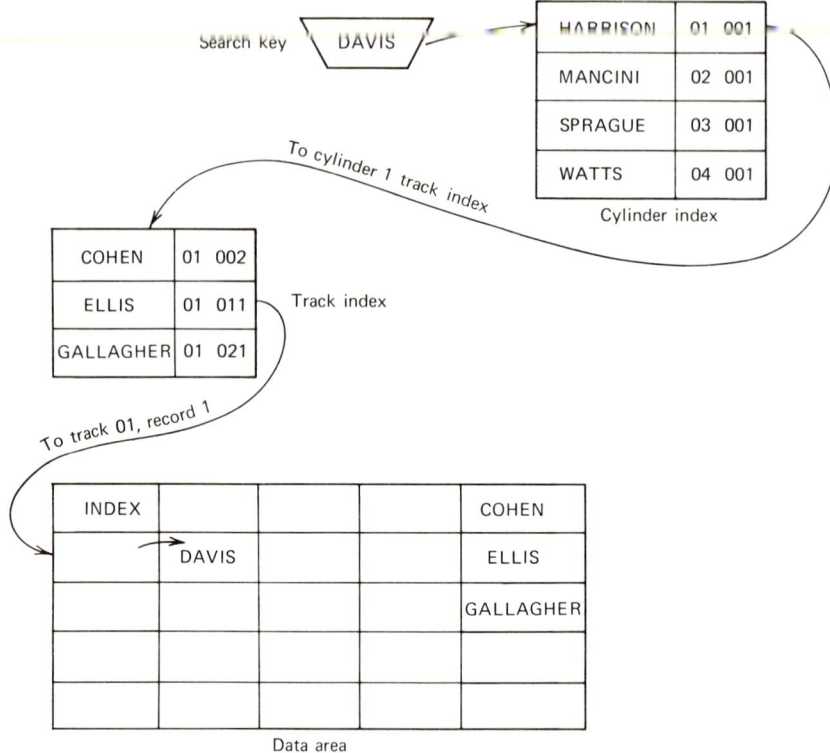

**Figure 3.37** ISAM search. The search key is used to locate the first key in the cylinder index that is *larger than* or equal to itself (here, HARRISON). This leads to the appropriate track index, where once more the first key equal to or higher than the search key is sought (ELLIS). This leads to the first data record in the track potentially containing the search key. Records in the track are sequentially searched.

order, but actual position is independent of key value (Figure 3.39). Sequential order is not preserved. Records are positioned in arrival sequence, but since they may originate in any track in the cylinder, they are not in sequential order. If a large portion of records in a file were placed in the overflow area, most of the records in the file would be in a list structure, and it would be inefficient to search compared with a sequential file.

The records that go into the overflow area are not necessarily the insertions themselves. In any given track, an insertion is placed into its proper sequential position, whereupon the record in that track with the highest key is "bumped" out of the main storage area into the overflow area (Figure

Specific Storage Structures 73

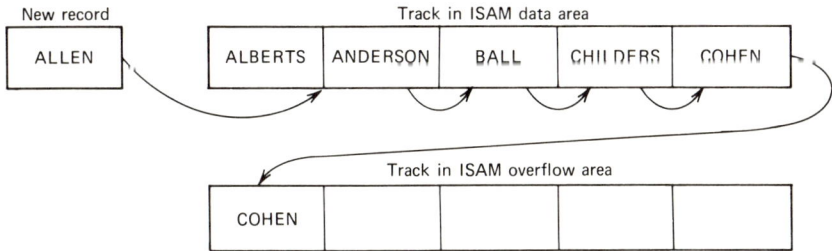

**Figure 3.38** Overflow in ISAM.

3.40). If the record with the highest key had been tagged as deleted, it would not be moved to overflow and its space would therefore be recovered.

Another way to organize the overflow area is to assign a single large overflow area for the entire file (*a* in Figure 3.41). This is called an *independent overflow area* (independent of source) and is organized internally like the cylinder overflow areas (*b* in Figure 3.41), where each cylinder's overflow goes to a reserved area in that cylinder. Yet another possibility is to combine the two methods (*c* in Figure 3.41), using cylinder overflows with an independent area to back up the cylinder areas, in case one or more cylinder areas overflow. Regardless of method, when the last overflow area available to any track overflows, a record is liable to be lost and the data manager may not have all its pointers properly organized. Therefore, the

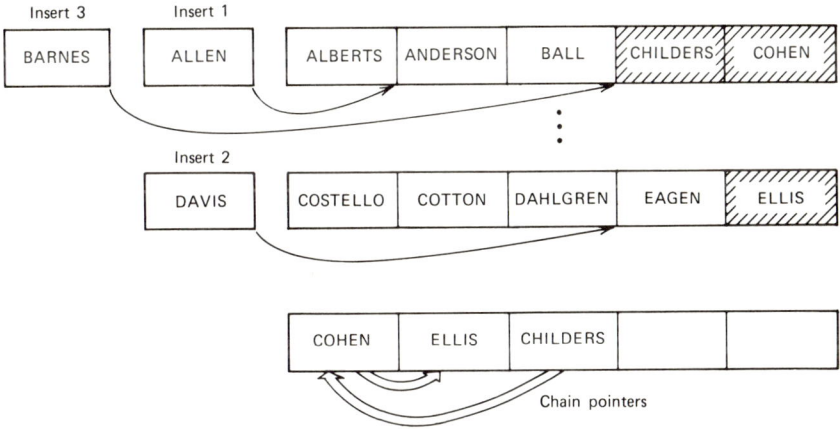

**Figure 3.39** Chaining in an ISAM overflow area. Shaded records are moved to overflow area in the physical order shown, and chained in key order.

74  *Data Storage*

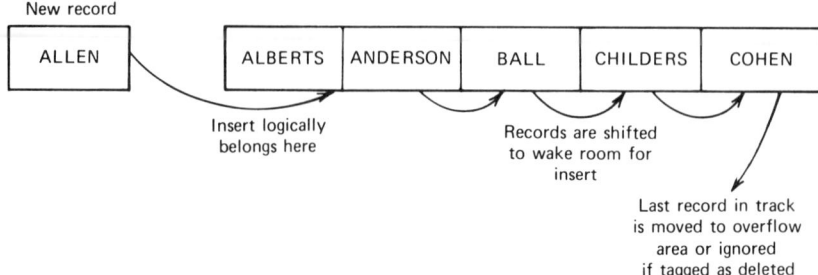

**Figure 3.40** Repositioning of records after insertion in ISAM.

user of an ISAM program must take steps to ensure against overflowing of the overflow areas.

Selection of the size of overflow areas is at the discretion of the using programmer. He must guard against overflowing them, but he must also be careful not to waste too much space merely awaiting overflows. One way of balancing the two requirements is to use a modest amount of space, monitor its use, and *reorganize* the file occasionally. Reorganizing an ISAM file entails copying records out in logical sequence and rebuilding the file in another portion of memory. When rebuilt, the file will have all records in the main data area and all overflow areas will be empty. Logically simple,

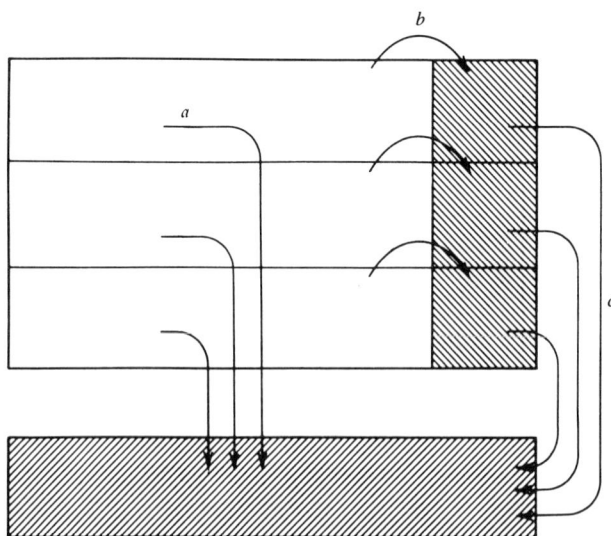

**Figure 3.41** Overflow control in ISAM.

reorganization of a large file can be a very time-consuming process. A file of one million records, stored on an IBM 2314 disk (average access time 60 msec) can take 16 hours to read! By the time a file is ready for reorganization, it may be so badly malorganized, due to excessive numbers of records in overflow chains, that the average time is not attainable.

***Integrated Data Store*** The integrated data store (IDS) has attributes of both a physical and a logical structure [10]. It is a method of organizing records such that related records are chained together and any record within a chain may point to any number of other, subordinate chains. The physical placement of records in auxiliary storage may not be under user control. As a storage method and associated computer software, IDS permits the user to visualize a logical structure different from the physical record chains. One of its benefits is that data elements can be entered only once in a large, diverse data base. For example, an employee's home address may be found in records of a firm's payroll department, its personnel department, and the mail room. If all these files are computer stored, it requires three times the minimum space to store all these addresses and three times the work to collect them and enter them into the computer. With IDS, the payroll, personnel, and locator files each could point to a single chain of home address data.

A data base in which all data items are defined and interconnections established, and in which any given data element appears only once, is called an *integrated data base*; the files contained are said to be *integrated files*. The advantages of integrated files are compactness of storage and ease of determining which, if any, elements are going to satisfy a request for information. We discuss this concept further and present some of its disadvantages in Chapter 11. For now, it is important only to realize that IDS permits integration of a data base and is also useful if that approach to file building is not desirable.

In IDS there may be a *master record* that *owns* any number of *detail records*. Sometimes all the detail records are identically structured; for example, they all may be individual patient records, with the master being a physician's record or a hospital ward record. On the other hand, the detail records may be a series of different kinds of records that, collectively, make up the logical record descriptive of an entity. A patient record, for example, may consist of a small identification record pointing to a series of detail records containing laboratory results, dietary restrictions, and account status. A chain of detail records is a sublist. Any detail record may in turn have detail records, indefinitely, but the master record may not be a detail of itself or any of its progeny.

CHAIN STRUCTURES A *chain type* is a generic designation for all instances of a given type of detail record. If the master record is part of a chain, each record in that chain may have a detail chain of the given type (Figure 3.42). If the master is the patient identification record, there may be a *previous visit* chain type, implying that each master can have a detail chain of this type. Each chain type has a *name,* which in this example might be PREVVISIT. Then, knowing the patient's name and the name of the chain type, reference can be made symbolically to the information about that individual's previous visits.

There may be many chains within a chain type, up to one for each master record in the chain making reference *to* this chain type. There may be as many PREVVISIT chains as there are records in the PATIENT chain. Some chains, of course, may have no members; that is, some patients may have had no previous visits.

Each chain can have only one master record. Any given record within that chain, however, may have more than one master because it may be on more than one chain (Figure 3.43). But there must be a separate set of pointers maintained for each chain, to eliminate confusion about which chain is being followed at any given time. A PREVVISIT record may be linked not only to a patient but perhaps also to a history of bed usage.

There is no limit to the number of records in a chain. Here, however, as with ISAM, the user must add records without precise knowledge of the current file size, and he may inadvertently exceed his reserved file storage limits.

The master record must exist before a detail record can be stored "under" it. For example, it could happen that data enter a computer through two or more streams of manual processing, and this could cause a nurse to create a detail record for a patient assigned to his ward before the patient's identification record has been entered by the admitting office. This becomes a system design problem that can be solved in a number of ways; for example, a simple telephone call from the ward to the admitting office would verify that the patient was indeed admitted properly. Given that information, the ward record can be reentered in a short time, probably successfully. But it can be solved *only* if the system designer knows that this circumstance can arise, why it happens, and what he can do about it. This is an example of the danger of integrated files. If there had been two independent files, one for the admitting office and one for the ward, this particular problem would not have occurred.

When a master record is deleted, its owned chains are deleted; thus there can never be a chain without a master. If a detail record is on more than one chain, and the master for one chain is deleted, only the pointer for that one chain is altered. Other chains remain intact.

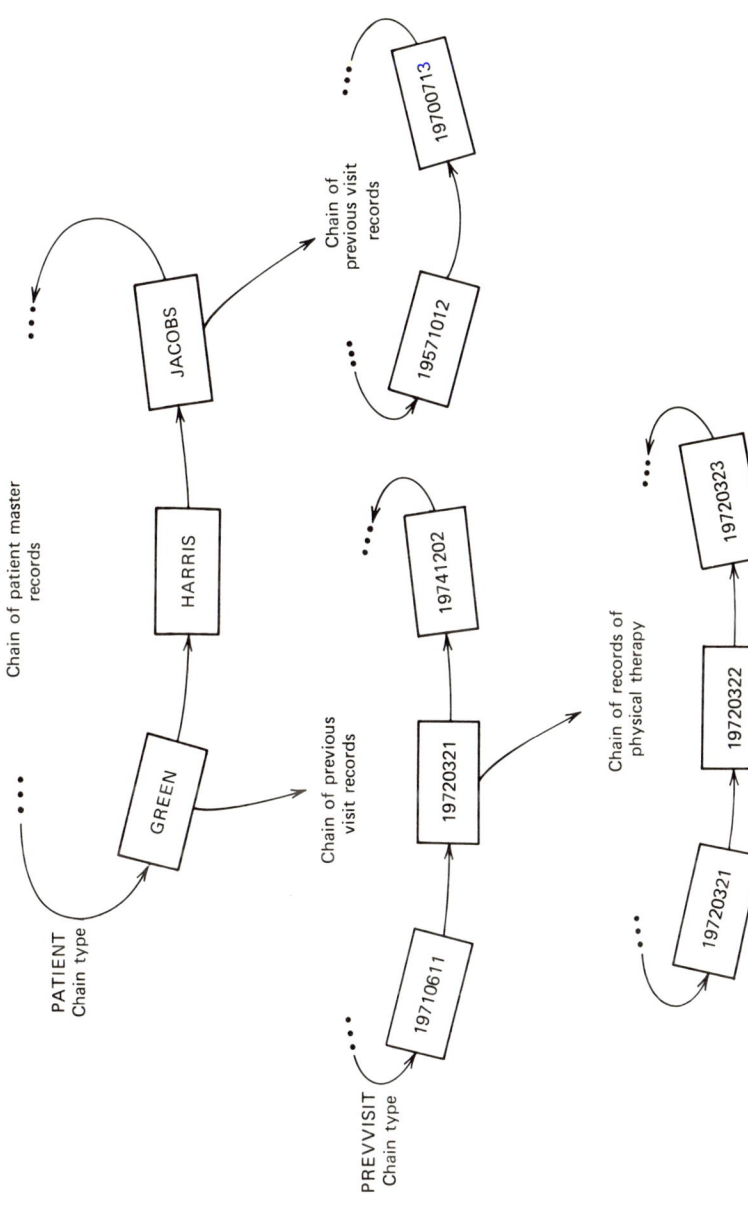

**Figure 3.42** Hierarchy of chains in IDS.

## 78  Data Storage

RECORD ORDER  The logical order of records in a chain can vary at the user's option. There can be a single sequence of records of a given type, say all detail records of whatever type, belonging to a given patient, as shown in Figure 3.44a. Or, the details can be in sequence by type (e.g., all previous visit records in order by date, another chain of all laboratory records by date, etc., such as the chain of Figure 3.44b).

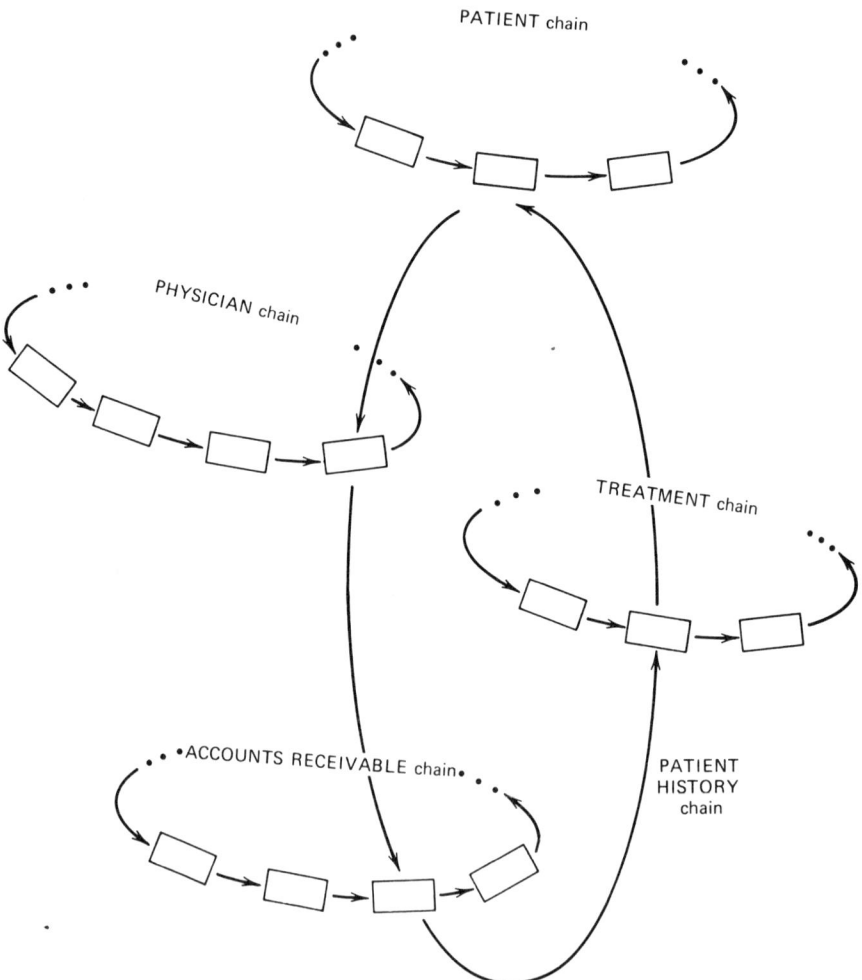

**Figure 3.43**  Multiple chaining in IDS. No chain can have more than one master, but any record in a chain may be on one or more other chains.

## Specific Storage Structures 79

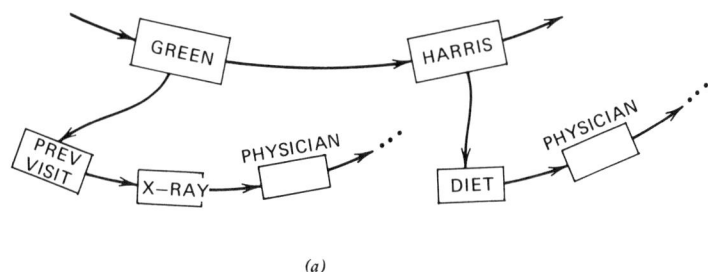

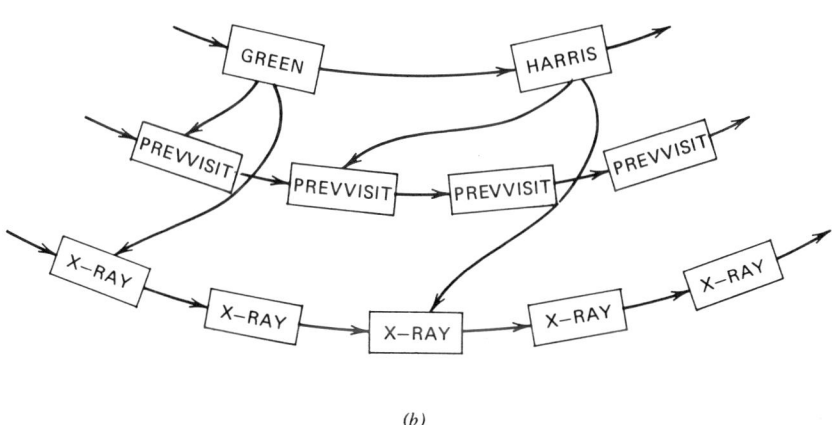

**Figure 3.44** Sequence of IDS records. (*a*) Detail records of all types grouped by master record, (*b*) detail records grouped by type.

When a new record is being inserted into a chain, it can be placed

- *first*—as the first detail record logically following the master record
- *last*—as the last detail record in the chain
- *before*—logically preceding the record of a chain that is currently in use (the last one retrieved)
- *after*—logically following the last record retrieved

RECORD STORAGE  The precise location in storage is not under user control. The IDS attempts to store related data (records on the same chain) close together, but since records can be on more than one chain, there is no

*80    Data Storage*

way to ensure that the "next" record is always physically near the previous one. The programmer does have control over which chain determines record sequence when there are interlocking chains, but as the file grows and changes, the user increasingly deals with a logical structure that may be quite different from the physical one.

In this chapter we have reviewed the storage mechanisms for data and various methods of organizing the data stored on these media. Design decisions on these factors—deciding exactly how data shall be arranged and what storage devices used—may dominate a system's performance and economy. Yet just as many people who drive automobiles have only a vague idea of how they work and what factors are really important to their care and operation, many users of data management systems do not deal with data structure at the level of detail presented here. They tend to view data in terms of how they are to be used, not how they are mechanically organized. In the next chapter we explore *logical* data structure.

## REFERENCES

1. *Introduction to IBM System/360 Direct Access Storage Devices and Organizational Methods,* C20-1649-4, IBM Corp., White Plains, N.Y., 1969, pp. 10–11.
2. Donald E. Knuth, *Sorting and Searching. The Art of Computer Programming,* Vol. 3, Addison-Wesley Publishing Co., Reading, Mass., 1973, pp. 1–388. See, especially, the bibliography.
3. R. L. Rivest, and D. E. Knuth, "Bibliography 26, Computer Sorting," *Computing Reviews,* Vol. 13, No. 6 (June 1972), pp. 283–89.
4. Ivan Flores, *Computer Sorting,* Prentice-Hall, Englewood Cliffs, N.J., 1969.
5. George G. Dodd, "Elements of Data Management Systems," *Computer Surveys* Vol. 1, No. 2 (June 1969), pp. 117–33.
6. David Lefkovitz, *File Structures for On-Line Systems,* Spartan Books, New York, 1969, pp. 126–80.
7. J. Weizenbaum, "Knotted List Structures," *Communications of the ACM,* Vol. 5, No. 3 (March 1962), pp. 161–65.
8. David Lefkovitz, *Data Management for On-Line Systems,* Hayden Book Co., Rochelle Park, N.J., 1974, pp. 56–8.
9. *Introduction to IBM System/360* [1], pp. 32–7.
10. C. W. Bachman, and S. B. Williams, "A General Purpose Programming System for Random Access Memories," *AFIPS Conference Proceedings, 1964 Fall Joint Computer Conference,* Spartan Books, Baltimore, Md., 1964.

## RECOMMENDED READING

Lefkovitz [8].

Martin, James, *Computer Data-Base Organization,* Prentice-Hall, Englewood Cliffs, N.J., 1975.

*Chapter Four*

# Logical File Structure

## 4.1 CONCEPT OF A LOGICAL STRUCTURE

A *logical structure* is the structure a programmer or other computer user assumes when he addresses a file in a program or query language. It may be quite different from the actual, physical data organization, and translation between the two is done by software. A data management programming language or a query language is an interface or communication channel between a user and a physical storage structure, and the language used affects the apparent data structure. This is analogous to a camera lens and filter, which change the appearance of the physical world from the *point of view of the film* or an eye behind the lens. A different camera with a different lens "sees" the same image differently. Similarly, an appropriate language can make almost any physical structure assume any logical form.

An ideal physical structure might be defined in terms of its ability to minimize space utilization, access, or read/write time. A definition of an ideal logical structure, if such could be stated, would probably stress ease of use. For example, a language for use with a list structure should relieve the user of having to set and reset pointers. These should be "transparent" to him. A feature is said to be *transparent* to a computer user if he is not aware of its existence when he communicates with the computer. It may be a function that is carried out automatically or a structural feature he need

## 82  Logical File Structure

not be aware of to use the data, because the programming language in which he is working takes the feature into account automatically. Thus the user of a list structure should be able to use the data contained in it without having to "see" the pointers or to deal with them explicitly. Rather, he could address the file in such terms as *next, first,* or *previous.*

A danger of transparency of physical structure is that the user who is truly unaware of physical constraints may make uneconomical use of his computer. Such might be the case if a user were encouraged to address a sequential file as if it were an ISAM file—to request records by key when the only way to find them is to proceed sequentially through the file, examining every record until the desired one is found. A language can easily

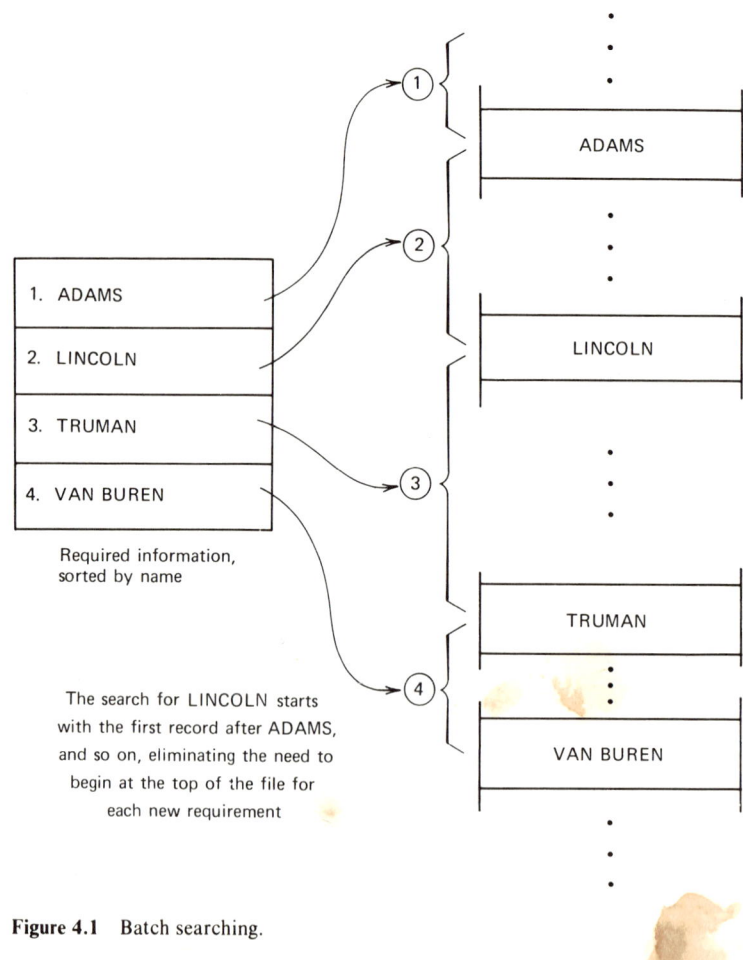

**Figure 4.1**  Batch searching.

be developed to permit this usage, but the user might be better advised to change his method of accessing data to better conform with economic reality. Most likely, he should accumulate all his information requirements, sort them by the search key, and search the sequential file in such a way that having found record *i*, the search for the next desired record begins with record $i + 1$, not back at record 1 again (Figure 4.1). This is a form of batch processing that may be called *batch searching*. A user wholly ignorant of physical data structures may never realize the disadvantages of his search method and may waste a large amount of computer time.

The benefits of dissociating logical and physical structures are as follows: (*a*) the user does not have to program tedious mechanical operations, (*b*) changes can be made in the physical structure of data without affecting the user's program, and (*c*) changes can be made in a program without affecting the structure of the data. As a simple example, when an ISAM file is reorganized, the user may not be aware of it, and his program need not be modified, just as he is unaware when ISAM begins to put records into an overflow area, rather than keeping them in strict sequential order. In brief, tying logical and physical structures closely together enables efficient use to be made of the computer on any given task. Separating the structural concepts simplifies the task of the user, hence permits conservation of *his* time, rather than the machine's. Separation of the concepts may also reduce the total amount of computer time used, when one considers the hours spent debugging complex programs, although it is difficult to estimate how much time might have been used under some organization other than that actually selected. Complete separation of logical and physical structures is called *data independence* [1].

## 4.2 LOGICAL STRUCTURES

A logical structure can be any structure that is definable, implicitly or explicitly, in the user language. It may or may not differ from the physical structure. For example, regardless of the physical structure, if a user addresses a file only in terms of *next*, his logical structure is that of a sequential file. If the physical structure is also sequential, they are the same. The physical structure, however, might have been a list structure. In some user languages, data structures are formally defined, but a user may treat the data as having a structure that is not formally defined, hence is implicit. For example, a user may define a *date* field as consisting of six numeric digits, with no further description. Yet, he may treat it as a group of three subfields, two digits each to specify *year, month,* and *day* or *day, month, and year.* This becomes an implicit structure.

## 84   Logical File Structure

Another form of logical structure is a subset of a file. The subset is defined by specifying attributes of its records. For example, we might wish to define the set of records of patients of Dr. X as a subset of a hospital patient information file. Suppose that from this subset we wish to extract the set of those of Dr. X's patients who are over 21 years of age and to list them sequentially, by *postal zip code* and *name* within zip code. None of these sets or organizations may exist at the time the program is written, yet the programming language may permit them to be logically defined and to have statements made about them.

Here are some other examples of how a user's view of a file may differ from the physical implementation:

1. The physical file is sequential, sorted by *name*. The user requests a count of the number of people represented whose year of birth is 1940 or later. The actual sequence and content of the file are transparent to the user, who might be permitted to specify his requirements in terms such as COUNT YROFBIRTH $\geq$ 1940 and remain unconcerned with physical sequence, access time, or location of the *yrofbirth* field within the record.
2. The user wishes to insert a new record into an ISAM file. He uses a single command to present his record and its key to the ISAM data manager program. As far as he is concerned, the key is the address. He remains unconcerned with conversion of the key to a machine address, overflow control, and index adjustment. To the user, ISAM is a direct logical organization, having key as address.
3. The user of a file wants to expand a record structure by adding a new field (not a new *value*, of an existing field, but an addition to the record structure). An example is expanding a patient information record to accommodate a separate field for *county* in the address group. If we assume the physical structure to be a list structure, a single user command could communicate all the information needed to the system. This could be something such as: ADD COUNTY TO ADDRESS SUBLIST, which would cause a new pointer to be set when the present sublist terminator symbol is reached (Figure 4.2). The new pointer leads to *county,* and the pointer with that datum becomes the sublist terminator. Thereafter, the user of the data structure assumes that the *county* field is in place logically following what was previously the last field in the address group. The user may treat the address sublist as if it were contained in a single physical record.
4. The user of a computer graphics system has sketched a drawing of part of a building. Desiring to rotate the image of the building part on his

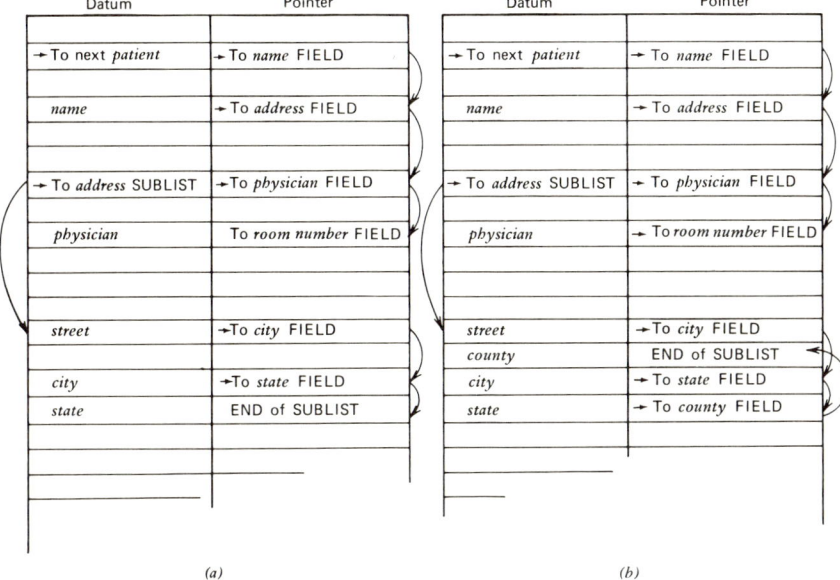

**Figure 4.2** Changing the structure of a list. (*a*) Original list elements, (*b*) modified list elements.

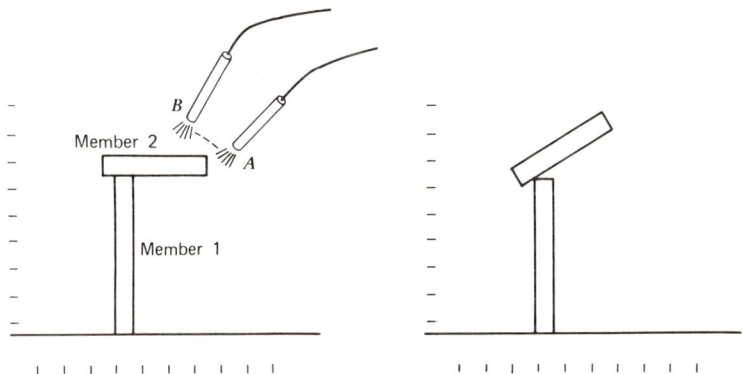

**Figure 4.3** Changing a structural image. Motion of a light pen through arc *AB* can order the computer to rotate a designated part or set of parts through the same arc. Modification of the records descriptive of the individual parts, their positions, and their interconnections becomes transparent to the user.

## 86  Logical File Structure

```
Data in                     Data in                     Data in
Ring for Member 1           Ring for Member 2           Ring for Member 3

type:   IBAR                type:   IBAR                type:   STRUCTURE
position:  4,0;4,8          position:  3.5,8;7,8        contains:   MEMBER 1
attached to:   MEMBER 2     attached to:   MEMBER 1     contains:   MEMBER 2
intersection at:  4,8       intersection at:  4,8
attached to:   MEMBER 3
intersection at:   . . .
```

**Figure 4.4**  Records for individual members and a structure.

screen, he uses a combination of light pen and keyboard to convey to the computer the following message: "move this (displayed) structure by rotating it the number of degrees indicated by the light pen motion" (Figure 4.3). The file containing the information from which the display was formed is a ring structure. There is a set of data elements descriptive of the building part and a list of components (walls, windows, beams, etc.), as in Figure 4.4. For each contained component there is a ring with essentially the same kinds of data. There may also be components of these components. The data elements carried to describe

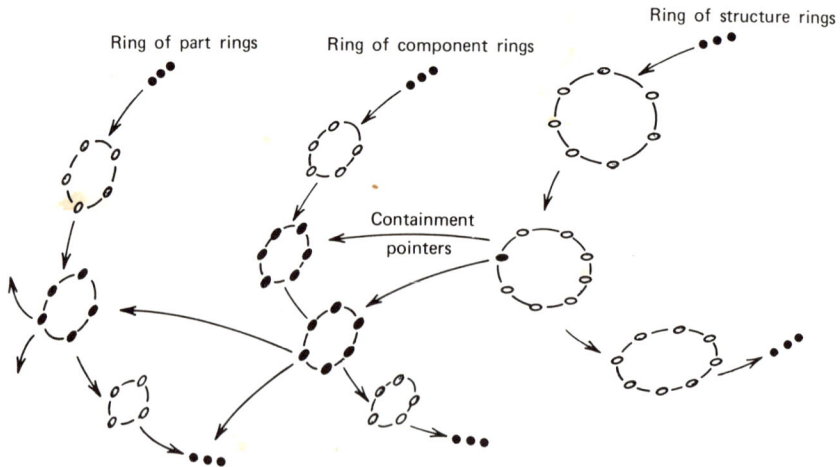

**Figure 4.5**  Propagation of changes in a ring structure for a complex graphic structure. Changing the orientation of a structure may change its component rings and so on.

a typical element are *position on the screen* and *nature of relationship to other elements* (e.g., parallel, perpendicular at point $x, y$). The single command to rotate the overall structure must be propagated (Figure 4.5) to every element in the structure; it cannot be applied only to the ring that is descriptive of the overall structure. The user does not participate in this propagation. He addresses only the structure he wants—the entire figure, one wall, one window, or whatever—and assumes that all subordinate components will be properly taken care of.

## 4.3 TYPES OF LOGICAL STRUCTURES

Storage structures must be constructed by first building often elaborate computer programs to store data. Logical structures exist only in the mind of the beholder. Although the logical structures that may be based on any given physical structure are limited, there may be a great number of such variations for each physical structure. In the representative set of structures described below, addressing method is the principal classification variable. Recall that it is the programming language, which includes the addressing scheme, that is the means of creating a logical structure.

### 4.3.1 Positionally Addressed Structures

The logical equivalent of a sequential or direct file is one that is addressed in terms of record or element position, regardless of whether the data are so stored. A minimum system would allow for two search commands: GET NEXT and GET PREVIOUS (or GET, with NEXT implied, and INITIALIZE—return to the beginning of the file), and one write command: WRITE, with NEXT the implied address. This addressing capability describes a one-dimensional, limited-access array. A sequential access data manager may also permit a positioning command with an absolute machine address (e.g., START AT N) to avoid an exhaustive search when approximate location is known.

A related structure, also visualized as an array, permits access by specifying the ordinal number of the desired record. This is the capability provided for addressing main memory-stored arrays by FORTRAN, BASIC, COBOL, and other high-order programming languages. In these languages $A(I)$ denotes the $I$th element of array $A$. It is not necessary to GET data already in main memory. It can be directly addressed for processing, as X = 2*A(I).

Both the more limited *next* form of addressing and ordinal addressing, while presenting the logical image of a sequential file, may be used with lists as well.

### 4.3.2 Hierarchical Structures

Probably the most common logical record structure is hierarchical, organized as described in Chapter 2 by combining fields into groups and groups into arrays, other groups, or records. The physical representation of this hierarchy may be a sequential arrangement of fields or a list; the programmer "sees" only the hierarchy, however, and he need not be concerned with actual storage implementation. Neither does the storage structure include any indication of logical relationships. The usual way to bridge the gap is to define the hierarchy to the compiler used with the programming language and let it generate the code needed to translate between hierarchical data element names and storage location.

There may be hierarchies above the record level, as well. For example, one may view the personnel records of a corporation as being hierarchically organized according to department or division employing the person. Similarly, part records can be subordinated to assemblies, assemblies to machines, and machines to factories that produce them or warehouses that store them.

Generally, a program or information retrieval system user can address a component of a hierarchy contained in a record directly. COBOL and PL/I permit the programmer to denote *name* as a single entity even though it consists of *family name, first name,* and *initial.* On the other hand, when records are the element of a hierarchy, it is more often necessary to include some physical structure notation. For example, to request that the records of personnel of Department 123 be searched for someone whose occupation is civil engineer, one might like to say

> SEARCH DEPARTMENT 123 PERSONNEL FOR
> OCCUPATION = CIVIL ENGINEER

in which the phrase DEPARTMENT 123 PERSONNEL is the name of a subset of the personnel file. More likely, he would use a notation such as

> FOR DEPARTMENT = 123 AND OCCUPATION =
> CIVIL ENGINEER . . .

or the programmer might have to create a working file of Department 123 records and then query this file, perhaps saying

> PRINT NAME FOR OCCUPATION = 123

The first of these examples is more like programming language notation for within-record hierarchies in that the user can name the logical structure he wishes to work with and does not need to give a procedural statement to find or create the data set before using it.

### 4.3.3 Key-Direct Structures

A key-direct structure is that implied by the term *random access memory,* which in turn implies that a user can "go" directly to the record he wants. Each record desired is separately specified. ISAM, as described earlier, gives this logical capability. Records to be retrieved or written are addressed by key, and the user is unconcerned with the physical mechanics of address transformation or chain following.

An inverted index file structure (Figure 4.6) also provides key-direct access for each key for which there is an inverted index. The user supplies a key name and value, the data manager does a double access—one to the inverted index and one to the main file—but the user treats the process as a direct access based on key value.

### 4.3.4 Content-Addressable Structures

A key-direct structure and a positionally addressed structure differ in that in the former the user addresses the file in *content* terms. He retrieves information by specifying *what he wants,* rather than *where it is.* However, users are not always able to specify their requirements in terms of a single value of a single field, nor is it always possible to restrict search key values to fields used as primary sort keys of files or inverted files. A more generalized concept permits the user to describe a set of records (rather than a single record) by specification of content and then request retrieval of the entire set. Specification of content is done through search criteria that may specify any number of values of any number of fields. The fields named are not necessarily restricted to those for which there is an inverted index.

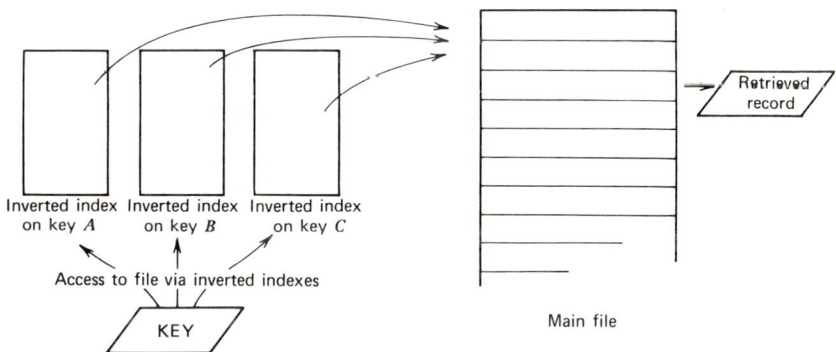

**Figure 4.6** Key-direct access through inverted indexes. The user needs only a key to retrieve a record.

*90   Logical File Structure*

This form of generalized logical access to files is provided by many generalized information retrieval systems or data base management systems designed for use by other than professional programmers. A typical specification may have the following form:

A: AGE ≥ 40 AND MARITAL STATUS = SINGLE OR DIVORCED

This defines a data set *A* consisting of records taken from a file having the stated characteristics. Such a statement, unlike a single key specification, may yield a set of records, a single record, or none. Both the user and the retrieval program must be prepared to deal with a retrieved *file* instead of a single record.

The user may sometimes specify the logical sequence of records in the file of retrieved records. In the example just given he might add ASCENDING BY AGE, which would put the records of set *A* into ascending order on field *age*. Or, the order may be implicit, perhaps preserving the order of the file from which the subset was extracted. DIALOG [2], a bibliographic information retrieval system, puts retrieved records nearly in reverse order of storage. Records are originally stored in order of receipt, which approximates increasing order by date. Retrieved records are displayed in decreasing date order—latest first.

Content addressing is more convenient for the user, but it leaves him completely masked from the realities of access cost. In the long run, this may be a disservice to users. It is a controversial point among designers and users of information systems how much effort should be exerted (and paid for) by the system builder to relieve the system user of the need to learn and use a mechanical language. To many, the ultimate is natural language whose use apparently frees the user from learning any artificial constraints on what he may request, but whose interpretation by a program may be expensive indeed.

### 4.3.5   Virtual Memory

A *virtual memory* falls partially into both the physical and logical realms. It permits a programmer to assume a large memory having the characteristics of main memory, hence he can address any record as if it were stored in main memory. Data are stored in auxiliary memory, and either a program or the hardware must translate the data name or address as it appears in the program into an auxiliary memory address. The unit of transfer of information between memories is often called a *page*.

With virtual memory, the programmer can use the positional notation of his programming language to address data. For example, he may use an expression such as

IF NAME(I) = SMITH, PRINT ADDRESS(I)

to search a file far larger than can fit into main memory. Input commands, bringing segments of the file in from direct access memory, are performed when needed by the virtual memory data manager. The programmer thinks only in terms of scanning a positionally addressed file.

## 4.4 EXAMPLES OF VIRTUAL SYSTEMS

Paging is used with many time-sharing systems to achieve a compromise between speed and efficiency in transfer of data between main and auxiliary memory. IBM's System/370 computers have a hardware feature that speeds address translation in their particular implementation of virtual memory.

### 4.4.1 Paging

Paging is a generalized concept for which there are many individual variations. A *page* is a block of data of uniform size. The page is stored on a disk or other direct access memory and called into main memory when needed and as space is available. It has to be written back onto direct access memory (the original disk location) only when modified or when first created. Areas of main memory reserved for storage of pages are called *page frames*. The particular frame, or location at which a page is stored, is independent of page number or disk location (Figure 4.7).

Paging supports multiprogramming or time-sharing operating systems when there is more than one program placing demands on the operating system for data transfers between main and auxiliary memories and, consequently, contention for core storage space and communications facilities.

A program may need several pages to operate. In fact, the program, as well as its data, may be stored on pages. If a segment of a program is stored in a given page frame, another page is requested, implicitly, when there is a reference to data outside that page frame or to a portion of the program not in that frame. When a page is requested, the operating system or control program first checks whether it is already in main memory. (If it is, it does not need an input command.) Since the program requesting the data has no way of knowing whether the page is there, the paging structure is a logical one; a program addresses data and assumes that the page is available. If the

## 92 Logical File Structure

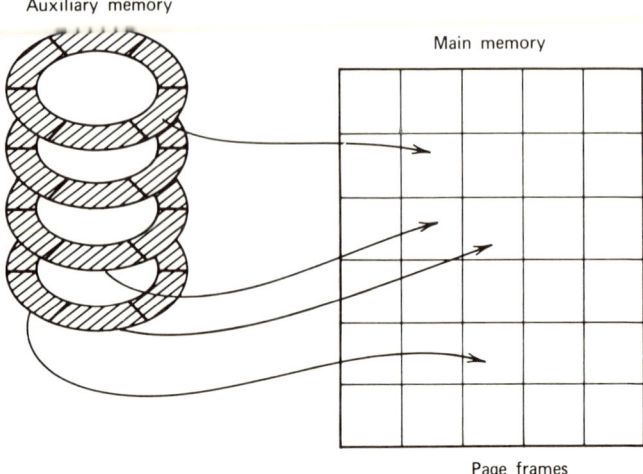

**Figure 4.7** Paging.

page is not physically present, input activity is carried on by the operating system without the "awareness" of the requesting program.

The real problems of page management arise when a page has been requested but there is no space available for it in main memory. Then the only way to bring it in is to delete or overwrite an existing page, and the question becomes one of which page to eliminate to make the space available. The efficiency of the algorithm used to make this decision affects the efficiency of the entire computer system. In what is probably the worst case, the page frame being overwritten would be the one containing the program segment that requested the data. Those data, now, cannot be used unless the program page is brought back in. If the program page were brought back on top of the data page, a condition of stalemate or an endless loop would exist—that is no useful work is being performed, but the operating system is busy moving pages into main memory. Excessive reading and writing of pages is called *thrashing* (Figure 4.8). Ideally the frequently used pages should remain in main memory, but thrashing activity may occur in situations less extreme than that illustrated in Figure 4.8*b* whenever overwritten pages have a high probability of early recall.

More realistically, the decision of which page to overwrite is based on such factors as priority of the program being operated and *age* of the page frame contents (i.e., the time since the page was last used). The tendency is to delete the pages belonging to programs that are inherently of low importance or have not used their data for some time, leading to the assumption that they are not going to use the page in the very near future. Although it might seem that lack of recent use raises the probability of future use, we are concerned with use during a time period of duration on the order of one second or less. Frames that were little used for the past few seconds will probably not be used during the next one. On the other hand, when there is frequent interaction between a program and a page of data, the tendency to leave that data page alone is reinforced.

The storage structure for pages on disk is not determined or limited by the main memory space or structure. Pages have, or can have, a unique number, allowing them to be used with a direct storage structure for fast access. But some other structures may be dictated by other factors, such as the desire to provide for overflow from the disk area set aside for pages, or perhaps the desire to store pages having a higher priority in a more quickly accessible area of disk.

Paging mechanisms are a function of individual operating systems and tend to be highly machine dependent. The CODASYL recommendation [3] provides for a uniform logical page structure, but different computers might still use different physical structures to support it. Section 4.6 contains a whimsical description of paging written by Jeffrey A. Berryman.

### 4.4.2 The Virtual Sequential Access Method

The Virtual Sequential Access Method (VSAM) is an advanced access method produced by IBM for use with its 370 computers. It combines features of ISAM and sequential access with some new characteristics not previously available with either.

VSAM grew out of the need for an access method that allows data to be accessed both directly by key and sequentially in key-defined collating order. Conventional index-sequential access methods that satisfy this need usually use a chaining

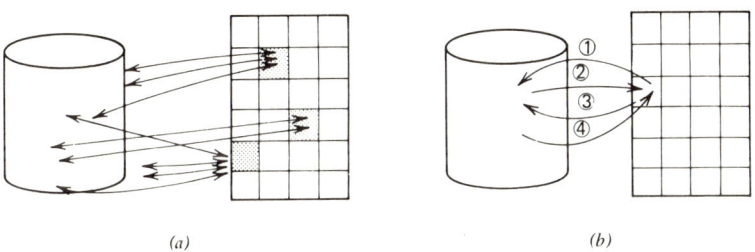

**Figure 4.8** Thrashing (a) General case. (b) Worst case, where a program (1) requests data, the data page is put on top of the program page (2), the operating system requests the program again (3), and the program overwrites its own data (4).

## 94   Logical File Structure

technique to insert additions into a file after it has been initially loaded. With these techniques performance degrades rather substantially as more and more additions are made. VSAM has been designed to avoid performance degradation while retaining the index sequential facility [4].

***File Organization***   As with other access methods, data sets are stored on auxiliary memory and records are transferred to main memory as needed, or transferred from main memory to auxiliary as directed by the using program. Even while in main memory, records are considered in virtual memory and are addressed by virtual address, the using program not being concerned with the actual machine location. Records may be indexed and blocked, but the user is not concerned with these either; all actual storage and retrieval, blocking and deblocking, are done by VSAM.

ORGANIZATION OF RECORDS   Records may be of fixed or variable length. Records in auxiliary storage are blocked into *control intervals* (CINV). These fixed-size blocks (Figure 4.9) become the basic unit of indexing and data transfer between main and auxiliary storage. Data records may not be split over more than one CINV. Hence the CINV must be at least as big as the largest anticipated data record. VSAM's maximum record size is 65,536 bytes.

Records are addressed within VSAM by *relative byte address* (RBA), which is a record's logical displacement from the beginning of the file. In a file of fixed-length records of $b$ bytes each, record $n + 1$ is at RBA $nb + 1$. The RBA is independent of actual sequencing of records which, as in ISAM, may not be physically in key order. When an insertion is made to a file, it may cause the RBA of existing records to change.

A CINV consists of a group of records and some control information. Unlike the ISAM block, the CINV need not be full; it may contain empty space, or it may be entirely empty. A group of CINVs constitute a control area (CA), presented in Figure 4.10.

Records may be stored in key sequence or in arrival sequence. Under the latter option, VSAM performs as a sequential access system or a direct access system, depending on the user. If the programmer arranges for his own index or address computation scheme, an arrival sequence method can be used as a direct access method. Otherwise, the user would have to ensure that records arrived in key sequence.

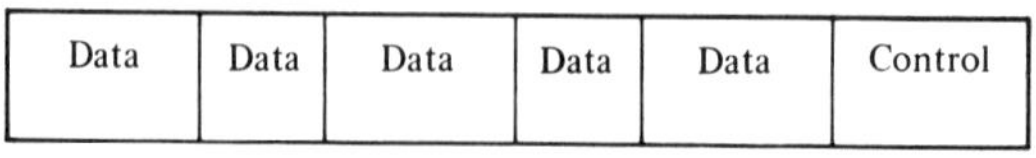

| Data | Data | Data | Data | Data | Control |
|------|------|------|------|------|---------|

**Figure 4.9**   Blocking of records in a control interval (CINV).

*Examples of Virtual Systems* 95

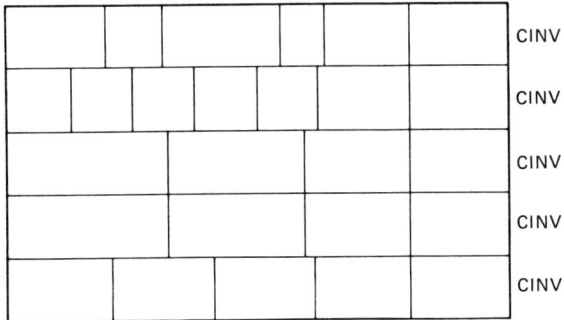

**Figure 4.10** A control area (CA) consists of a set of control intervals.

INDEXES  A key sequenced data set is most like an ISAM data set. Records can arrive in any order and will be inserted in physical order by key. Space must be reserved to allow room for insertion, although VSAM handles insertion space much differently from ISAM, whose overflow areas can become cumbersome to search as they fill.

Indexes are created by VSAM at several levels (Figure 4.11). At the lowest level there is a *sequence set,* consisting of one record for each control area in the data set. Within this record there is an entry for each control in-

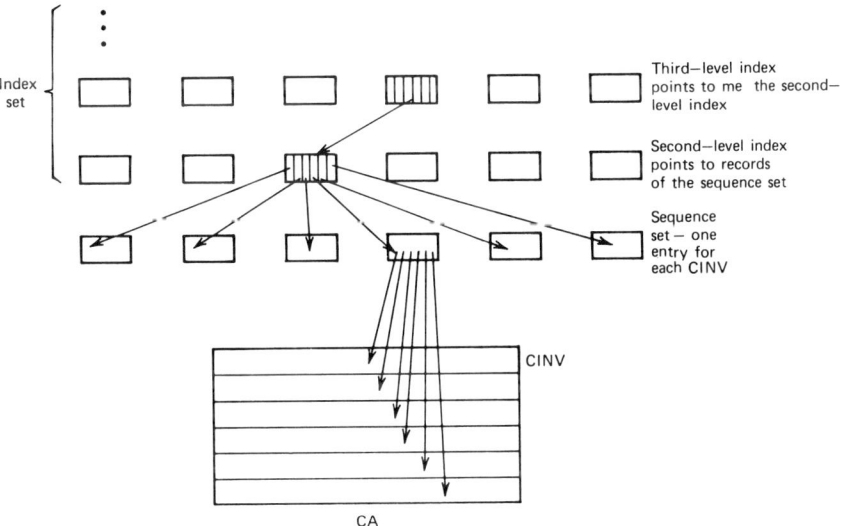

**Figure 4.11** VSAM indexing.

## 96 Logical File Structure

terval. As with ISAM, the entry consists of the highest key in the indicated control interval and a pointer to that CINV. Higher level indexes point to the sequence set. Collectively, these higher indexes are called the *index set*. An entry in an index set record contains the highest key in a lower level index record and a pointer to that record. The sequence set may be stored with the data it controls or separately. If stored together, the sequence set would occupy the first track of a control area and would be replicated the number of times that will fit on that track, to reduce rotational delay in accessing.

FREE SPACE  Rather than setting aside overflow areas for insertions into a key sequence file, VSAM permits unused space to be distributed within control intervals, and it permits free control intervals within a control area (Figure 4.12). This is somewhat similar to track and cylinder overflow areas in ISAM, but when an insertion is made into a CINV that has free space, the record is placed in key order relative to the other records; there is no break in the sequence to consume extra time during a subsequent search.

***Access to Data Sets***  VSAM offers two major access modes: sequential and access by key. The latter mode, has three variants: key direct, key sequential, and generic.

In sequential mode, VSAM operates logically like other sequential access systems. A new record is entered at the end of a data set. A record in a data set may be changed in content and returned to its original position, so long as the change does not extend its length. An application of this form of record modification is to create a file of dummy records and "modify" these with real data as new records arrive, saving the cost of completely copying a file before a few records can be inserted. In this way, a using

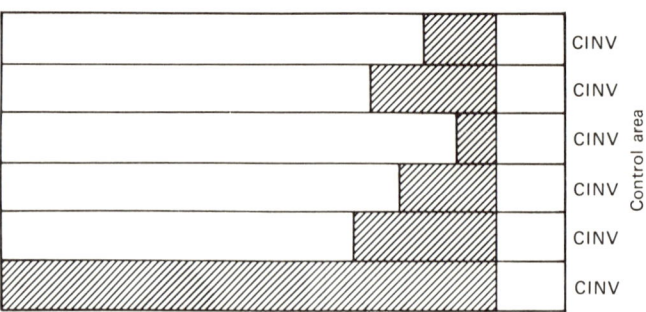

**Figure 4.12**  Distribution of free space in VSAM; shaded areas indicate some free space in each of the top CINVs and a free CINV at the bottom.

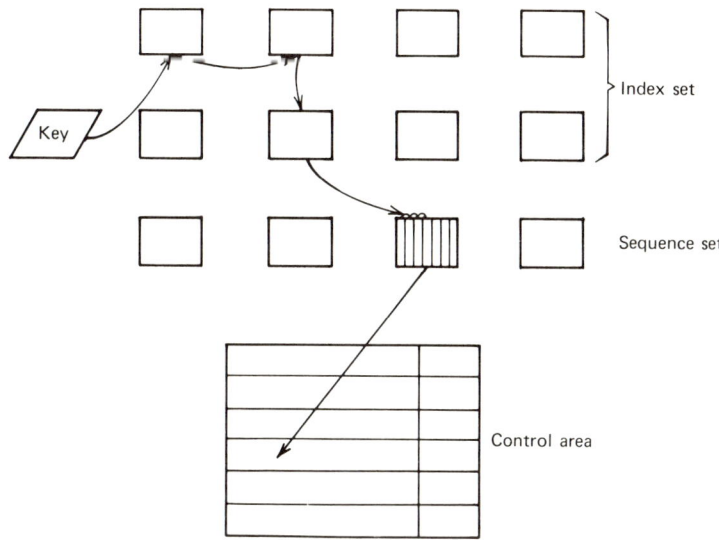

**Figure 4.13** Key-direct searching in VSAM. The user supplies a key; VSAM searches the indexes and recovers the corresponding record.

programmer can maintain a file in any order he wants, using the sequential access mode, provided he maintains an index that will tell him where records are to go. He can, for example, randomize the positioning of records, making the equivalent of a direct access system. In the key sequence mode, records can be accessed in the following ways.

KEY DIRECT  The user (or using program) provides a key, whereupon VSAM uses its nest of indexes to locate the CINV that potentially contains the desired record and extracts the record from the CINV for delivery to the using program. The user is unaware of the use of indexes or of the process of extraction of a record from a CINV (Figure 4.13).

KEY SEQUENTIAL  Once VSAM is "positioned" at a given record (i.e., has a starting address), it can be instructed to retrieve records in key sequence without the user having to supply the keys and without recourse to the full nest of indexes, therefore without the lapse of time needed to search the indexes. VSAM uses only the sequence set to go from one CINV to another (Figure 4.14).

GENERIC SEARCH  The user supplies only the high-order portion of a search key. He might do this if he were, say, uncertain of the exact spelling of a name and wished to check the birth dates of all persons in a file whose

**98**  *Logical File Structure*

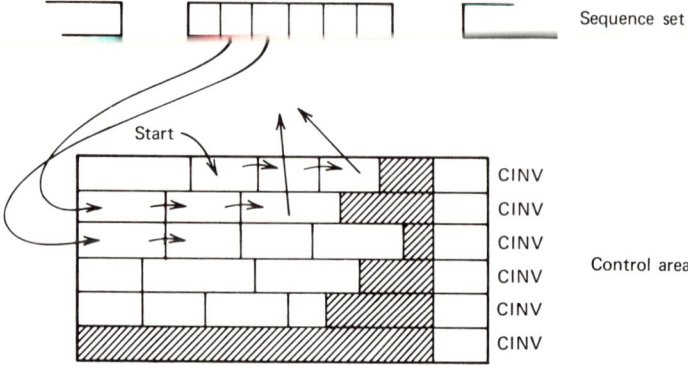

**Figure 4.14** Key sequential search. After initial positioning, VSAM can do a sequential search in key order to the end of a CINV, then refer to the sequence set for location of the next CINV.

names began with a certain string of letters; for example, RODRI might recover such variants as RODRIGUEZ, RODRIQUES, and RODRIGEZ. In this case VSAM finds the first record whose key meets this fragmentary specification. Thereafter, the user would control the search using the key sequential mode (Figure 4.15).

*Free Space Management*   Space is left free in two ways. A user-stated percentage of each CINV is left empty and a user-stated percentage of the CINVs in each CA is left empty. The sequence set contains the locations of the free CINVs. As insertions are made, there is initially always room in a CINV, but eventually one or more intervals fill up. When a CINV is about to overflow, a free CINV is brought into play through a *control interval*

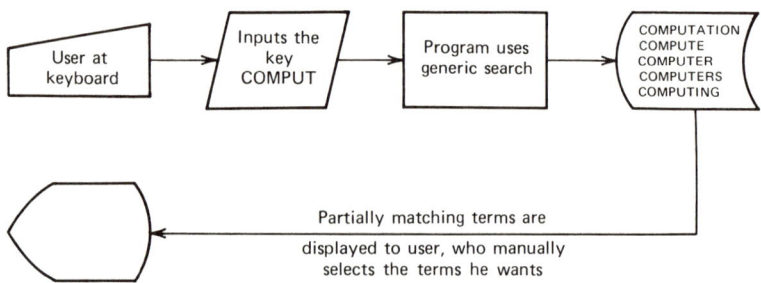

**Figure 4.15** Generic search in VSAM. The user expects more than one stored key to approximately match his search key. He truncates the key, locates the first match, then sequentially searches the remaining nearly equal keys, deciding for himself which is the best match.

*split*. The new record and all following it in key sequence in the CINV in which it logically falls are moved to a free CINV, which need not be adjacent to the original (Figure 4.16). Both the original and the newly used CINV then have some free space. Thus *within* CINVs sequential order is preserved, but *among* CINVs it may be lost. As a result, in a search there can be some hopping about from CINV to CINV, but not from record to record within a CINV. The enlarging of a record may also cause a control interval split, just as an insertion does. In a key sequence data set, the pace of deleted or shortened (modified to have a shorter length) records is recovered by VSAM and used as free space.

***Services and Interprogram Communication*** VSAM operates under IBM's operating system OS/VS (operating system/virtual storage). It is not a stand-alone program but must operate as part of a user program. The user program normally must be in assembler language. Alternatively, a user program written in PL/I or COBOL and originally designed for use with

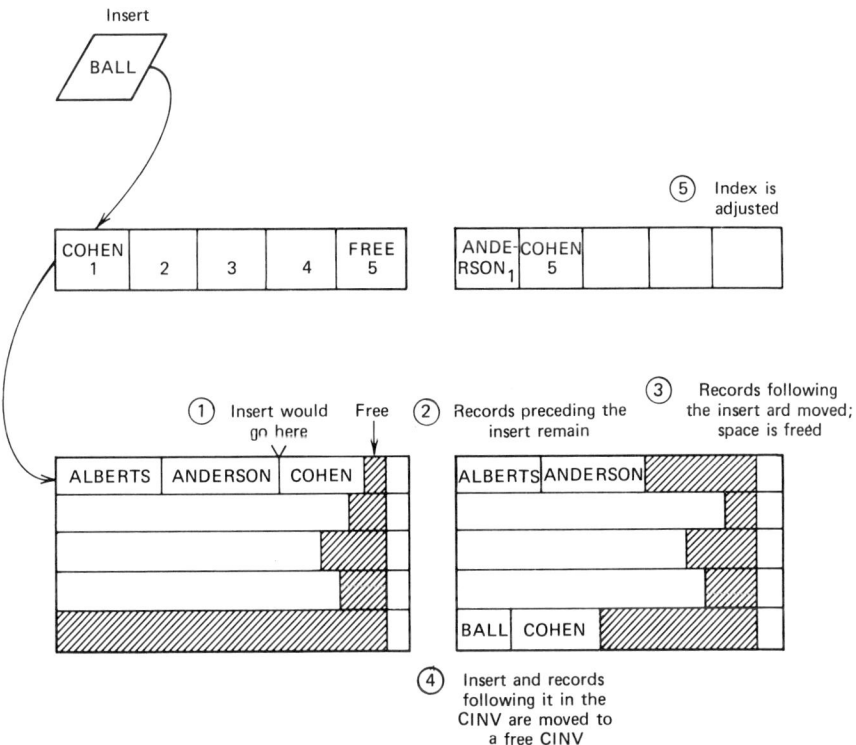

**Figure 4.16** A control interval split to accommodate an insert.

*100    Logical File Structure*

ISAM may access a VSAM data set through an intermediate program called the ISAM Interface and supplied as part of OS/VS.

VSAM offers a variety of *access method services,* which are programs for use in conjunction with VSAM data sets to create, copy, or reorganize a data set. VSAM also makes provision for data set protection by use of a password system that requires the using program or a person accessing a file from a remote terminal to provide an authorized password before a file can be accessed.

VSAM was designed after the experience of using separate systems for sequential access, indexed sequential, and direct access. On this basis alone it ought to outperform the older methods. IBM says "... you can get better performance with VSAM while achieving essentially the same results that you achieve with ISAM; you can also achieve results that you can't achieve with ISAM" [5].

## 4.5   DATA INDEPENDENCE

The history of computer development reveals an increase in both complexity and potential for performing useful work. *Work* may be interpreted as the storage of data, a passive, containing act. It may be the more active process of ordering the computer to store data in, or retrieve data from, a particular physical structure implemented on a particular hardware configuration and perhaps doing some arithmetic operations on the data as well. Although the most common meaning of *work* has to do with the execution of commands, a third meaning involves the generation of computer commands by a high-order language processor. More work is deemed to be performed by the computer if the user can reduce the number of statements *he* writes without reducing the computer's production. This is where logical data structures make their contribution. They permit a user, working in a high-order language, to produce a large number of computer commands by use of a relatively small number of language statements. This makes the computer an amplifier of input effort.

The trend in language development has been to reduce the number of user commands by a combination of high-order languages and logical data structures. As stated at the beginning of this chapter, a high-order language is a vehicle for expressing functions of or processes on logical data structures. Meantime, auxiliary memories have matured from their start as magnetic tape, which was suitable only for sequential files and worked off a single communications channel that did not permit simultaneous operation with either the CPU or another input/output unit. Today a wide variety of memories can be linked to computers through multiple channels; these are suitable for direct as well as sequential access, and simultaneous operations are standard. To take advantage of this hardware, physical data structures such as ISAM or multilist were developed. To write a computer program that can wend its way through indexes and directories, prime data areas and overflow areas, and at the same time handle communications traffic management and rotational delays would be forbidding to most users and time-consuming to all. This led to pressure to simplify the programmer's and others' efforts and eventually to logical structures.

The ultimate in data independence is complete separation of the logical data structure—the structure addressed by the user in a language designed for him—from the physical structure. We might call this a *virtual structure,* by analogy with a virtual memory. A virtual structure is the structure that appears to the user, and it can vary from user to user of the same physical structure and programming language. Like a virtual memory, a virtual structure would permit a user to address any data directly, without the issuance of input or output commands.

## 4.6 ANOTHER VIEW OF PAGING

### THE PAGING GAME*

Jeffrey A. Berryman, University of British Columbia

#### Rules

1. Each player gets several million *things*.
2. Things are kept in *crates* that hold 4096 things each. Things in the same crate are called *crate-mates*.
3. Crates are stored either in the *workshop* or a *warehouse*. The workshop is almost always too small to hold all the crates.
4. There is only one workshop but there may be several warehouses. Everybody shares them.
5. Each thing has its own *thing number.*
6. What you do with a thing is to *zark* it. Everybody takes turns zarking.
7. You can only zark your things, not anybody else's.
8. Things can only be zarked when they are in the workshop.
9. Only the *Thing King* knows whether a thing is in the workshop or in a warehouse.
10. The longer a thing goes without being zarked, the *grubbier* it is said to become.

*Reprinted by permission of the author.

11. The way you get things is to ask the Thing King. He only gives out things in multiples of eight. This is to keep the royal overhead down.
12. The way you zark a thing is to give its thing number. If you give the number of a thing that happens to be in the workshop it gets zarked right away. If it is in a warehouse, the Thing King packs the crate containing your thing back into the workshop. If there is no room in the workshop, he first finds the grubbiest crate in the workshop, whether it be yours or somebody else's, and packs it off with all its crate-mates to a warehouse. In its place he puts the crate containing your thing. Your thing then gets zarked and you never knew that it wasn't in the workshop all along.
13. Each player's stock of things has the same number as everybody else's. The Thing King always knows who owns what thing and whose turn it is, so you can't ever accidentally zark somebody else's thing even if it has the same thing number as one of yours.

## Notes

1. Traditionally the Thing King sits at a large, segmented table and is attended to by pages (the so-called table pages) whose job it is to help the king remember where all the things are and who they belong to.
2. One consequence of rule 13 is that everybody's thing numbers are similar from game to game, regardless of the number of players.
3. The Thing King has a few things of his own, some of which move back and forth between workshop and warehouse just like anybody else's, but some of which are just too heavy to move out of the workshop.
4. With the given set of rules, oft-zarked things tend to get kept mostly in the workshop while little-zarked things stay mostly in a warehouse. This is efficient stock control.
5. Sometimes even the warehouses get full. The Thing King then has to start piling things on the dump out back. This makes the game slower because it takes a long time to get things off the dump when they are needed in the workshop. A forthcoming change in the rules will allow the King to select the grubbiest things in the warehouses and send them to the dump in his spare time, thus keeping the warehouses from getting too full. This means that the most infrequently zarked things will end up in the dump so the Thing King won't have to get things from the dump so often. This should speed up the game when there are a lot of players and the warehouses are getting full.

*Long live the Thing King.*

## REFERENCES

1. Donald A. Jardine, "Principles of Data Independence." In *Data Base Management Systems,* D. A. Jardine, Ed., North Holland Publishing Co., Amsterdam, 1974, pp. 195–205.
2. Roger K. Summit, "DIALOG: An Operational On-Line Reference Retrieval System," *Proceedings of the 22nd National ACM Conference,* Washington, D.C., 1967, pp. 51–6.
3. *Data Base Task Group April 1971 Report,* Committee on Data Systems Languages (CODASYL), Association for Computing Machinery, New York, 1971.
4. D. G. Keehn and J. O. Lacy, "VSAM Data Set Design Parameters," *IBM Systems Journal,* Vol. 13, No. 3, 1974, pp. 186–212.
5. *OS/VS Virtual Storage Access Method (VSAM) Planning Guide,* GC26-3799-0, IBM Corp., White Plains, N.Y., 1972, p. 36.

## RECOMMENDED READING

Chapin, Ned, "A Comparison of File Organization Techniques," *Proceedings of the 24th ACM National Conference,* 1969, pp. 273–84.

*Data Processor,* Vol. 15, No. 4 (September 1972). (Entire issue devoted to virtual storage in IBM System/370.)

Dodd, George G., "Elements of Data Management Systems," *Computer Surveys,* Vol. 1, No. 2 (June 1969), pp. 117–33.

Flores, Ivan, *Data Structure and Management,* Prentice-Hall, Englewood Cliffs, N.J., 1970.

*Introduction to Virtual Storage in System/370,* GR20-4260, IBM Corp., White Plains, N.Y., 1972.

Jardine, Donald A., *Data Base Management Systems,* North Holland Publishing Co., Amsterdam, 1974.

Lefkovitz, David, *File Structures for On-Line Systems,* Spartan Books, Washington, D.C., 1967.

Lefkovitz, David, *Data Management for On-Line Systems,* Hayden Book Co., Rochelle Park, N.J., 1974.

*Chapter Five*

# Aids to the Location of Information

## 5.1 KEY-TO-ADDRESS TRANSFORMATION

To retrieve information, one must first find it. Reducing the cost of finding information or finding the location at which an information element is to be stored is the principal purpose of file organization. It is always possible to store records randomly or in arrival sequence and to retrieve by exhaustive search. The disadvantage is obvious. It is also possible to make all files ordered and to search them sequentially. Indeed, there was little other choice before direct access memory was introduced. The disadvantages of this procedure are clear, too: high cost of inserting a record (done only by recopying a file) and high cost of retrieving small numbers of records (searching for a single record requires a search of, on average, half the file). Under some circumstances, however, this is an efficient approach.

Interactive applications and many batch processes require faster access to the memory location at which a given record is stored or is to be stored. Direct access memories provide the necessary hardware. The next step is to find a faster way than sequential search to locate the information, to take full advantage of the hardware's capability to retrieve or store quickly at any given address.

## Key-to-Address Transformation    105

The logical position of a record of a file or an element of an array is determined by a key, which may or may not be physically present in the data element (Figure 5.1). Arrival position or ordinal number within an array are examples of possible keys not necessarily explicitly present. Searching may be based on record attributes or fields other than the sequencing key. As an example, consider the use of a table whose elements are in order on probability of occurrence of value. Although a search must be programmed to look at every table element, with no index or computation to speed searching, the likelihood is that the value sought will be found near the top of the table. This technique implicitly stores information about the location of field values. For instance (Figure 5.2), if all employees of a firm located in New York City are asked to list their state of residence for tax purposes, it would make sense to test first for New York, New Jersey, or Connecticut,

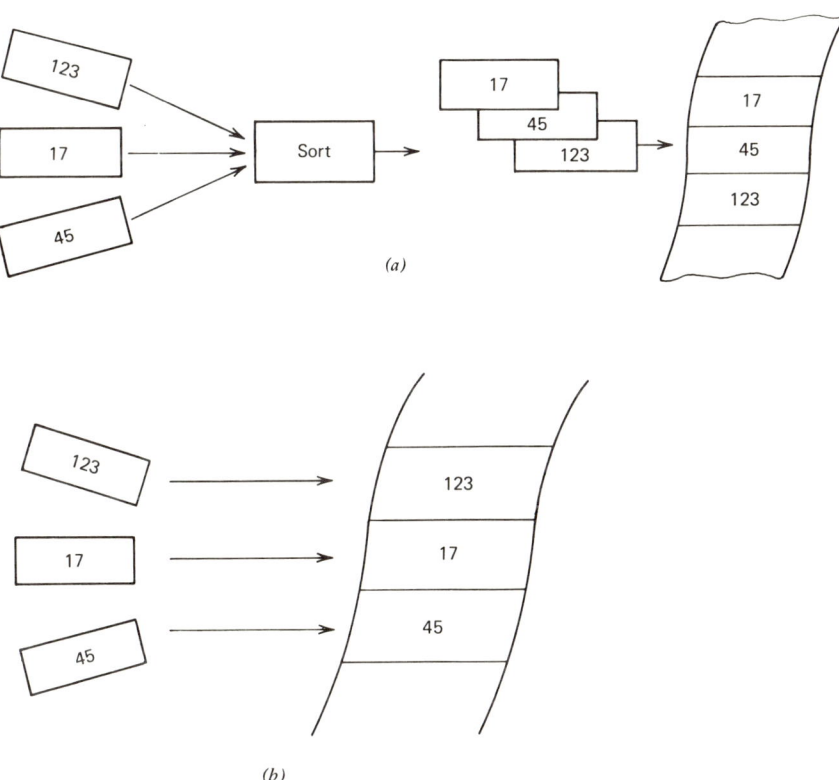

**Figure 5.1** Explicit and implicit keys. (*a*) Records sorted by key and stored in key order. (*b*) Records stored in arrival sequence; order of arrival not explicitly recorded as a key.

106    *Aids to the Location of Information*

in which most employees will reside, rather than search an alphabetically organized table of state names. Even though the record may not be positioned on these fields, they may be the only keys available to locate the records containing them. We use the term *key* to refer both to location-determining fields and to other fields, used only as search criteria.

The conversion of a key to a logical or physical location where information pertaining to this key is stored or is going to be stored is called *key-to-address transformation*. The key is usually stated in user-oriented terms, such as *name* or *social security number*. The address is in computer terms, such as a main memory location or a cylinder-track-record number. Having a means of transforming one to the other provides a form of symbolic addressing of information—the user identifies attributes, the computer uses the attributes to determine location. Addressing an array in a high-order programming language furnishes one of the simplest examples: the user refers, perhaps symbolically, to ordinal number within an array. The computer "sees" this as an address. If a programmer wants to address an array of daily sales figures, he may use an expression such as SALES(MONTH,DAY) (Figure 5.3). If he has provided numeric values for MONTH and DAY, this expression addresses a particular number in a two-di-

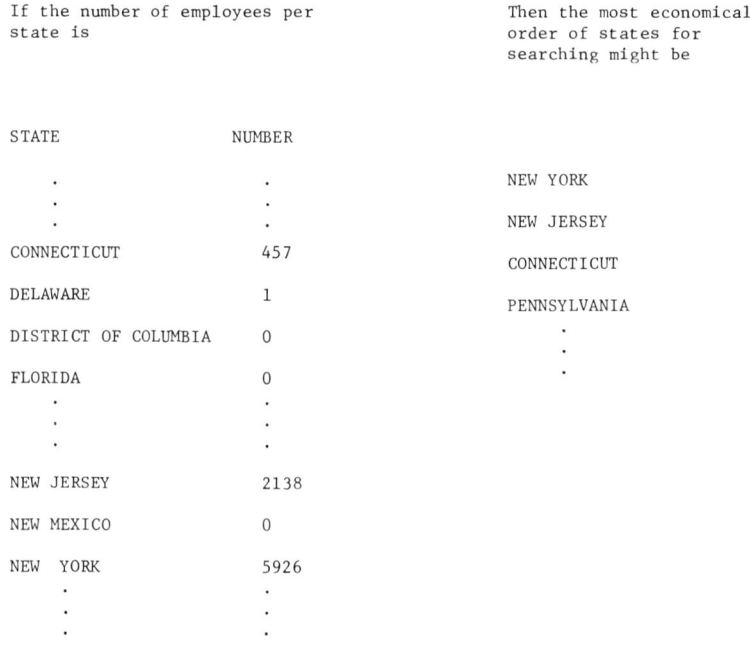

**Figure 5.2**  Probability ordering of records.

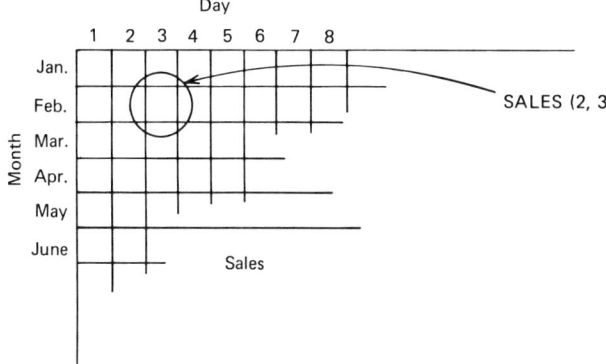

**Figure 5.3** Addressing a two-dimensional array.

mensional array, where the keys are not explicitly stored. The computer computes an address from the values of month and day and the known location of the beginning of the sales array.

Another common form of addressing by key occurs in a key-direct search, which can produce the record for an employee given his social security or other unique identifying number that serves as an explicit record key. Such a key can be transformed into an address in several ways. We describe two classes of methods: the use of a table or index to retrieve a location (covered in Chapters 3 and 4 for ISAM and VSAM) and the computation of the location from the key value. It is possible, of course, to combine methods.

## 5.2 INDEXING

In the first group of methods addresses are stored in tables. When the keys are a number sequence from 1 to $n$ and few if any values are missing from the sequence, the key need not be stored explicitly; otherwise the key is also part of the table. The table is called an *index,* which primarily means a tool for finding something—in this case, an address. Regardless of whether the keys are themselves present, there are two logical elements in an index entry (Figure 5.4), the *argument* or the key to be transformed, and the *address* or reference to another file (i.e., other than the index). We call the other file the *referent file.* If we permit the index itself to be the referent file, we have a means for internal cross-referencing, a necessity in dictionaries and thesauri.

An index is *linear* if the index elements are in the same sequence as ele-

## 108  Aids to the Location of Information

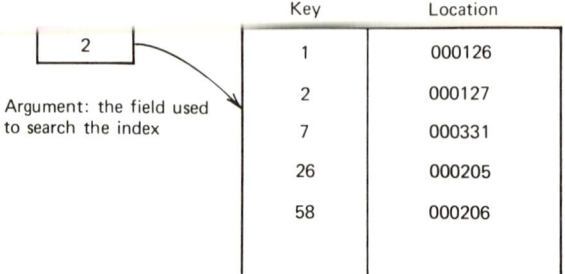

**Figure 5.4** Composition of an index.

ments (records) of the referent file. In other words, the sequence of elements in the index parallels the sequence of elements in the referent file (Figure 5.5). Common linear index examples are the table of contents of a book (Key = chapter title, Address = page number, chapters are listed in increasing page number order) or the thumb index of a dictionary (Key = first letter of a word, Address = page on which that initial letter first appears, letters are listed in order of their appearance on pages). Note that the dictionary thumb-index does not yield a page *number*; it physically points to the page itself. When an index is linear it is not necessary to list every key, because it is possible to interpolate—to locate keys logically preceding and following an argument and to assume that the address corresponding to the argument lies between the addresses of the two keys retrieved. Thus to find in a dictionary a word beginning with the letters *im,* one locates the begin-

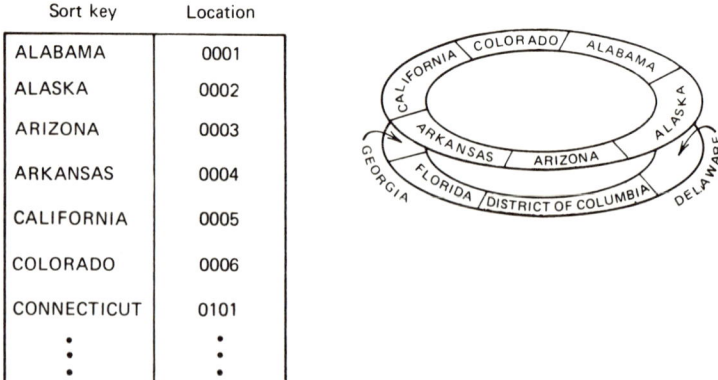

**Figure 5.5** A linear index. The order of entries in the index is the same as the order of storage of referent records.

ning of *i* and the beginning of the next letter, *j,* and starts to look about halfway between them.

An *inverted index* is one in which the key-address elements are in key order but not in referent order. This comes about when the keys used in the index are not the keys used to sequence the referent file. One example is a book index book that is sequenced by work or term, not by number of the page(s) on which the items occur. The term *"inverted index"* is derived from the way the index is usually constructed. Keys and locations are compiled in referent order, perhaps extracted from the referent file; then the elements are sorted (the sequence *inverted*) into key order. Figure 5.6 shows an inverted index for the state records of Figure 5.5. The data records are ordered by *state name.* The inverted index is based on *state capital* and the order of listing is alphabetical by *state capital,* an order different from that of the data records. For any given record there can only be one linear index because the record can only be sequenced on one key; but there can be as many inverted indexes as there are other fields in the record. Note that interpolation is meaningless in an inverted index. If one searches a book index for the word *index,* it may lie between *image* and *input,* but the location in the referent file bears no relationship to the locations of *image* and *input.*

If an index, whether linear or inverted, is large enough, it may be necessary to have an index to *it,* and that index may need an index, and so

| INVERTED INDEX | | LINEAR INDEX | | MAIN FILE |
|---|---|---|---|---|
| Key | Address | Key | Address | |
| ALBANY, NY | | ALABAMA | | ALABAMA |
| ATLANTA, GA | | ALASKA | | ALASKA |
| ANNAPOLIS, MD | | ARIZONA | | ARIZONA |
| AUGUSTA, ME | | ARKANSAS | | ARKANSAS |
| AUSTIN, TX | | CALIFORNIA | | CALIFORNIA |
| BATON ROUGE, LA | | COLORADO | | COLORADO |
| BISMARK, ND | | CONNECTICUT | | CONNECTICUT |
| BOISE, ID | | DELAWARE | | DELAWARE |
| . . . | | . . . | | . . . |

**Figure 5.6** An inverted index. The order of entries in the index is not the same as the order of keys in the linear index or main file.

on. We saw specific instances of this with ISAM and VSAM. Consider a file of $n$ records (Figure 3.7). An inverted index has one entry for each value of the selected key that occurs in the data file. In a personnel file ordered by social security number there might be an inverted index on *name (last, first, middle)*, in which case we would expect nearly $n$ inverted file entries because most names will occur only once. If there were an inverted file on *last name* there would be fewer entries, but more addresses in each, and if there were an index on *first name* there would be far fewer entries, each having many more addresses. If the field used for an index occurs more than once in a data record (e.g., *previous address*) the number of entries in the inverted index could greatly exceed $n$.

In some circumstances it is meaningful to replace the address part of an index entry with a key used in a linear index to a file. This forces a second index search before data records are found, but may cut the cost of maintaining indexes as records in the main file change location because of insertions or reorganization.

An index that is too large for most computer main memories would have to be stored on a direct access device. In such a case access would be enhanced by an index. The second index would be linear (same sequence as the first index), hence it would not be necessary for it to represent all key values. It might contain only one key in 100, then it would have $0.01n$

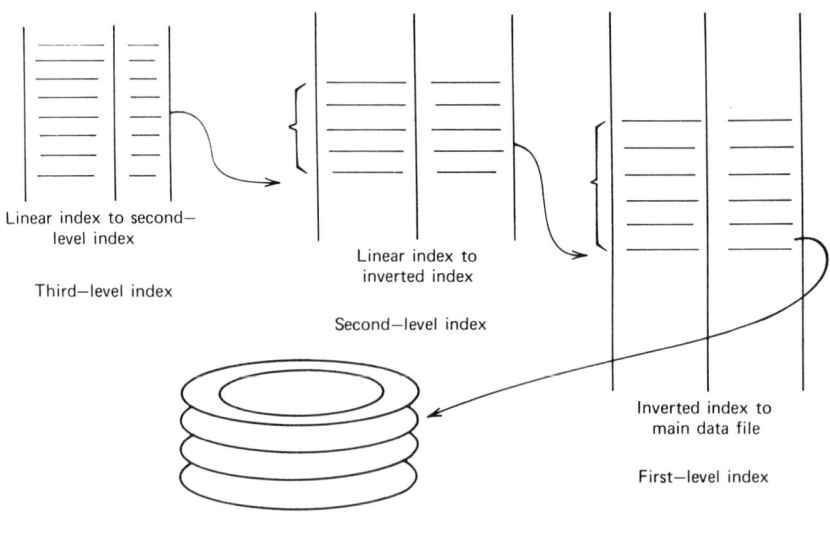

**Figure 5.7** A nested index. The third-level index points to a region of the second level, which points to a region in the first level, which points to a specific record in the file.

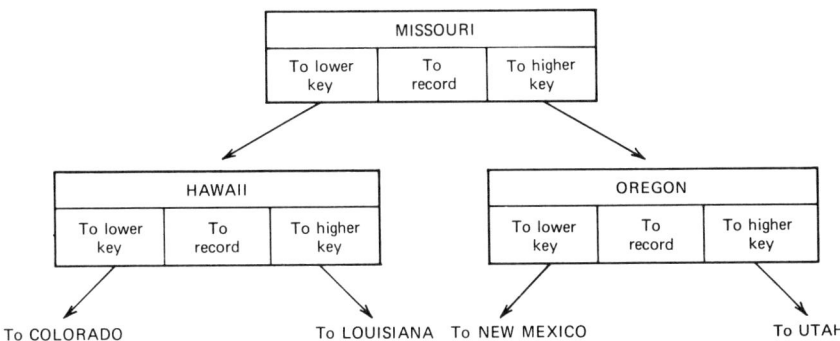

**Figure 5.8** A tree structure as index. Each entry contains a pointer to a record in the main file and to other index entries having keys smaller and larger than its own.

entries, again, possibly of several computer words each, and possibly too big for main storage. A third index to the second index would also be linear and might also represent only one key in 100, reducing its size to $0.0001n$ entries, which, let us assume, would fit in main memory. To find an address in the main referent file, one would search the third-level index, go to disk storage to locate an entry in the second level, and repeat this process for the first-level index. Finally, the first level points directly to the desired record in the main file. This concept is called *nested indexing* and the indexes are called *nested indexes*.

If in this example the number of records $n$ were 1,000,000 (not large at all for, say, an insurance company's policy holder file), the first-level, inverted index would have up to 1,000,000 entries, depending on the repetition rate of key values. Assume an average repetition rate of 2, and the index would have 500,000 entries. Then the second-level index would have 5000 entries and the third level 50. An entry in the second and third levels would consist of a key value and an address, perhaps taking up two computer words per entry. The first-level index would consist of a key value and an average of two addresses per entry.

The ISAM hierarchy of indexes (track, cylinder, master) is an example of nested indexing, as is the VSAM index set and sequence set.

A nested index is close to being an example of a *tree structure,* whose name derives from the graphic representation of the relationship of the elements (Figure 5.8). If we start with the middle term in the highest order index and search for the location of a record containing a given key, we make a series of decisions on where to look next if we do not find the key immediately. The decision is made at each node of the tree structure, until the desired key is found or determined not to be in the file. The difference

*112  Aids to the Location of Information*

between the tree form of the index and the conventional nested index is that the entries in the former may point either to a referent file location or to another index location. That is, a tree structure entry has pointers to the location of the key or to the next index entry that might be checked (the logically preceding and following entries). Tree structures are described in greater detail in Section 6.3.3.

## 5.3  ADDRESS COMPUTATION

Rather than look up a key in a table or a nest of tables, it may be both faster and logically easier (to program) to compute the location as a function of the value of the key. Sometimes this can be trivial. For example, if there are 100 elements in a table, consisting of one computer word (or character, if that is the addressable unit) each, the address of the $i$th element is $t + i$, where $t$ is the address of the beginning of the table. If the table is a file of fixed-length records, the address is $t + i \cdot r$, where $r$ is the record length. If the table is stored on disk memory, the computation must take into account the blocking of records and the number of records or blocks per track and the number of tracks per cylinder. Still, the computation can be fairly precise and simple.

Now suppose the key is not the ordinal number of the record in sequence but a name or a serial number. In these cases the number of key values that actually occur in a file is vastly less than the number logically possible. That is, we will not find files with $26^{15}$ names, although that many combinations of 26 letters in a 15-character name field are possible. The system of nine-digit social security numbers allows for $10^9$ (one billion) people, but the Social Security Administration carries about $2 \times 10^8$ records. When a record is placed in sequence in a file based on such a key, there is no way to compute exactly where it will fall within the allocated memory space, but we can approximate the location.

For example, to find a name in an alphabetically ordered telephone book, one could convert the initial letter to a number ($A = 1$, $B = 2$, etc.). To look for a name beginning with, say, the letter $W$, the searcher would start 23/26 of the way from the top of the file. This method assumes that all letters have the same number of entries in the file (an unlikely situation), and it is equally likely to err in either direction. Furthermore, it finds only the beginning of a group of names having the same initial letter, it does not find a specific name. But the method is fast and simple, and less searching must be done than is required by a straight sequential search approach. Use of an index to find the beginning of each initial letter group will give more accurate information but at the cost of the extra time for the index search.

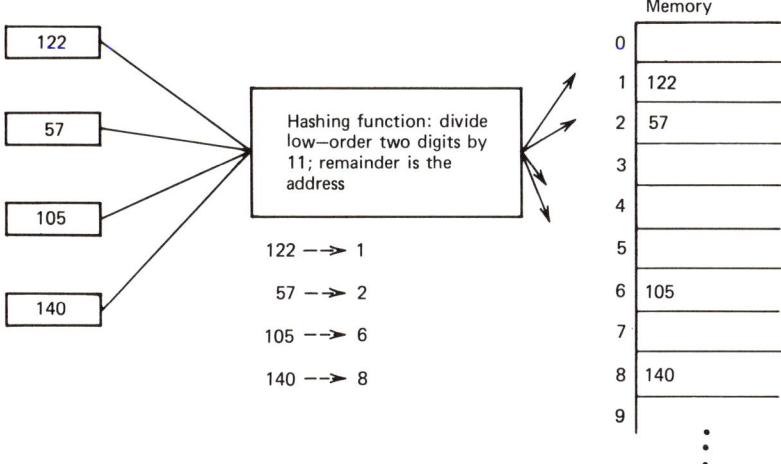

**Figure 5.9** Hashing, a randomizing computation to distribute records evenly in memory.

Another way to solve the location problem, called *hashing,* involves giving up the strict sequencing of records on key; thus the computation determines the storage address when a record is inserted into the file and again when the record is retrieved. This approach may also lead to more efficient allocation of storage space. A number of methods have been devised, and the name "hashing" is used because a file is "chopped up" and its pieces are evenly distributed throughout the space available for storage.

The essential idea is to compute a function of the record's key which will become the storage address. The function must be designed to give all addresses an approximately even chance of being used. In this way, records are evenly distributed, not bunched up in one part of memory where they might create overflow problems. In a typical method, the key is treated as a number (even if alphabetic), and not all the digits are necessarily used (Figure 5.9). Which characters are to be used depends on the key—we would not want to use the low-order (rightmost) five characters of a 15-character name field because they have a high probability of being blank, which means that a large number of names would yield the same storage address. The key, or portion thereof, might be divided by a prime number, say 97, and the remainder (a number between 0 and 96) is the address or is added to some base number to become the address. With a properly selected divisor and portion of the key, this method yields reasonably randomly distributed addresses.

It is immediately apparent that no matter how careful one is, more

114  *Aids to the Location of Information*

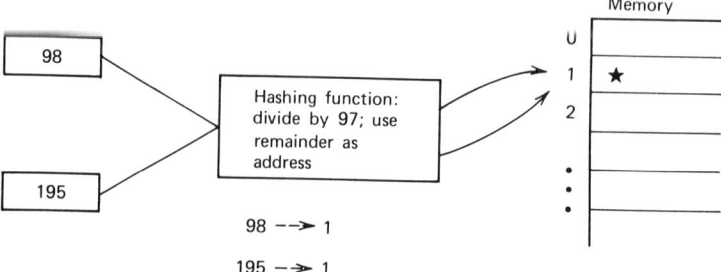

**Figure 5.10** A collision. Two records are assigned the same location, although their keys are different.

than one key can yield the same address in any such computational scheme. Both 98 and 195 yield the remainder 1 upon division by 97. When this happens we have a *collision* (Figure 5.10), or we say that the keys involved are *synonyms*. Since two records do not present themselves for storage simultaneously, the collision occurs when one has been stored and a second arrives and is directed by the computation to an address that is already occupied. The usual resolution is to place the new record in another portion of memory and set up a chain (Figure 5.11) from the first to the second record with synonymous keys. If a third synonym subsequently arrives, it is added

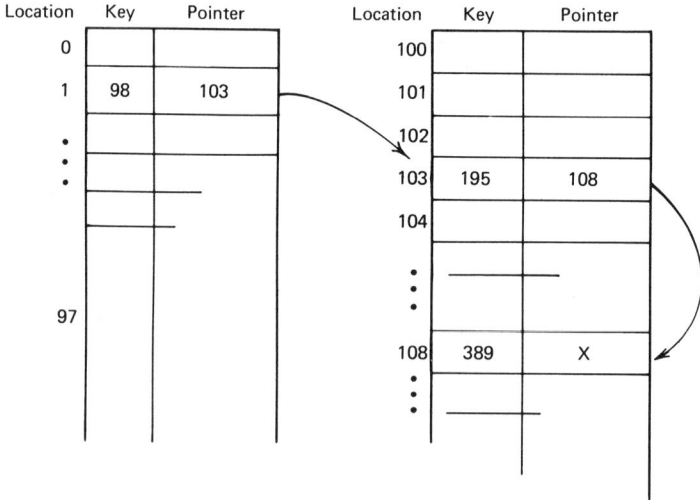

**Figure 5.11** A chain of synonyms. The keys 98, 195, and 389 all hash to the same location, causing a collision. A chain is set up, linking the synonyms.

to the chain. Remember that keys may be synonymous in this sense without being equal: there can be synonyms in a file that has unique (all different) record keys. In the previous example, there would be 97 memory locations to which records might be initially assigned. In effect, each would be a directory element pointing to other records in a chain of synonyms. A space-available program is obviously needed to assign space to new records and to recover space as records are deleted.

Hashing can be done in other ways. The key can be multiplied by some number and the low-order digits used as address. In Figure 5.11 the three keys 98, 195 and 389 might be multiplied by 97 and the low-order two characters used as an address. This would yield 06, 15, and 33, which are not synonyms under this transformation. On the other hand, multiplication by 97 makes synonyms of 95 and 195.

There are other variations, such as using digits other than the low-order ones after a computation. The method varies with the portion of the key used for the computation, the distribution of key values (e.g., names are not evenly distributed by initial letter), the divisor or multiplier, and the amount of memory available for storage.

## 5.4 COMBINATIONS

A multilist structure is an example of the use of a combination of methods of address location. One method serves for placement of records in the main data area and another for placement of entries in the directory area. In fact, hashing normally involves a combination of address location methods similar to those used in multilist. The hashing computation decides where in the directory or root area records will fall. Thereafter, the space management or space-available routine decides on how records chained to those in the root area will be placed.

In another variant, addresses may be computed only on input or only on search. If a file is maintained in order by key and is always searched sequentially, without benefit of an index, key-to-address transformation is used only on storage (if then). In other circumstances it might prove worthwhile to use an index when searching but to call on sequential access to insert a new record.

Sometimes no conversion of keys is used—null conversion. Consider a relatively short, frequently changing table, say, one listing the jobs currently being processed by a multiprogramming operating system. If there are relatively few elements in the table, it may be worth doing an exhaustive linear search each time the table is referenced and inserting new records wherever there is space available. This is conservative of memory and demands no time out for keeping indexes up to date. Since all searching is at main memory speeds, search time may be negligible. As a formality, we can consider null conversion a form of conversion. Then, regardless of the methods used, it is always necessary to convert a key to an address when a record is added or retrieved. The choice of a method involves an analysis of the economics of space in memory and time.

## RECOMMENDED READING

### Key to Address Transformation

Lefkovitz, David, *File Structures for On-Line Systems,* Spartan Books, Washington, D.C., 1967, pp. 82–125.

### Indexing

Meadow, Charles T., *The Analysis of Information Systems,* 2nd ed., Melville Publishing Co., Los Angeles, 1973, pp. 222–3, 319–30.

### Address Computation

Knuth, Donald E., *The Art of Computer Programming,* Vol. 3. *Sorting and Searching,* Addison-Wesley Publishing Co., Reading, Mass., 1973, pp. 506–49.

### Multilist

Lefkovitz, *op. cit.,* pp. 126–54.

*Chapter Six*

# Searching Techniques

## 6.1 INTRODUCTION TO SEARCHING

We define *searching* as a system, method, or algorithm for seeking information in storage by an iterative process of: determining an address, accessing the information stored at that location, testing the information against given criteria, and deciding whether to terminate the process or repeat the cycle starting at another address (Figure 6.1). Address determination may be explicit, by index or computation, or implicit, as in the case of a sequential file search in which the adjacent physical record is always the next one tested. A search is *successful* if the desired record or element is found; otherwise it is *unsuccessful*. A search is *resolved* when it can be decided whether it is successful or unsuccessful.

Success or nonsuccess of a search is programmers' terminology. For the user, being informed of the nonexistence of a record in a file may be as useful as finding the record. To him, success means getting information on his subject, and the certainty that it is *not* present in a file is information. For example, a police search of stolen car records that yields no result for a given vehicle registration number may be classified as successful by the police officer and surely will be so deemed by the driver of the car. To the programmer, though, the search is unsuccessful.

The particular method or algorithm used depends on the file organiza-

# 118 Searching Techniques

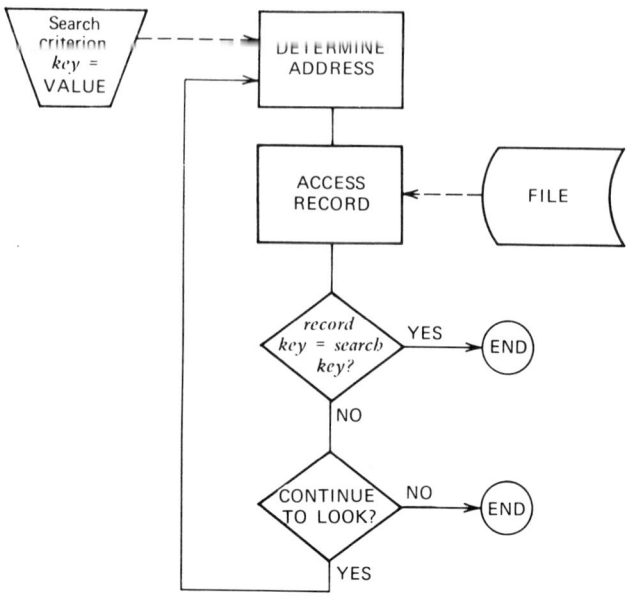

**Figure 6.1** Searching—a schematic diagram.

tion and the nature of the query or search criteria. A simple search consists of seeking an equality match for a single key against a similar key in the record, on the assumption that key values in stored records are unique. Because of the uniqueness assumption, we usually find the location at which the value would reside and resolve the search depending on whether it is actually there. But the user may want to search on the basis of more than one key value (*part number* = 1234 or 1235), more than one key (*subject* = QA 76.6 and *author* = WEINBERG), or inequality of key values (*date* ≥ 1973), or a combination of these, and he may have to deal with nonunique key values. The search algorithm must allow for these variations and for such structural variables as whether the file is sequential or list structured, the basis for ordering (sort key), and the nature of the storage medium.

This chapter explores basic search techniques for sequential files and for list structures, searches based on more than one key or key value or involving inequality matching, and multiple file searching in which information retrieved from one file aids in conducting a search of another. The ISAM and VSAM descriptions in Chapters 3 and 4 gave us examples of the search of sequential files with the use of an index.

## 6.2 SEARCHING SEQUENTIAL FILES

A sequential search is one in which the records are examined in order of their physical placement on the medium. A necessity for searching tape-stored files, the method is also used with direct access memories. Depending on the relationship of the search key to the sort key of the file, a search may be *exhaustive*—that is, each record of a file must be tested before the search can be resolved; or it may be *ordered,* when the search key is the sort key (the file is ordered on the basis of the search key) and the search can be resolved when the search key value is found or its logical position is found and the requested value is determined not to be present. There are other techniques that make use of knowledge of file organization by the search algorithm to reduce the number of records that must be acquired from memory and tested.

### 6.2.1 Exhaustive Search

An exhaustive search of a sequential file is required when (*a*) it is not known whether the search key has unique values *and* (*b*) the file is not ordered on the search key. Then there is no choice but to look at each record (Figure 6.2). Finding a match of search key and stored record key—a "hit"—does not necessarily terminate the search because there could be more than appropriate record, and if there is another, it will not necessarily be adjacent to the first. The number of record accessions and comparisons

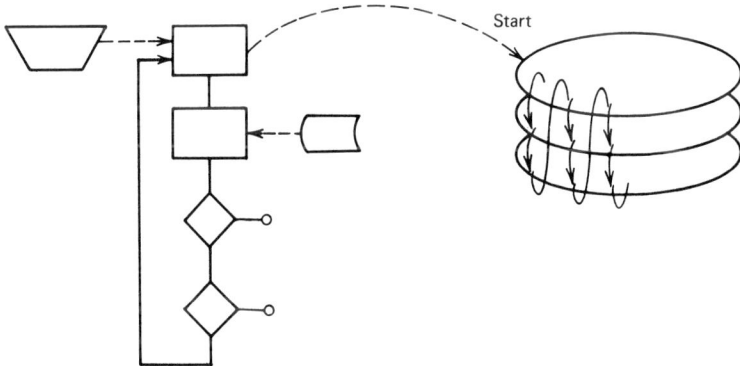

**Figure 6.2** Exhaustive search in cylinder storage mode. In this mode, only the starting address can be determined. The search program never knows until it reaches the end of the file whether it has seen all possible matching records.

for an exhaustive search of a file having nonunique keys is $n$, the number of records in the file. If the key is known to be unique, the search terminates successfully when the first equality is found. If no match is found, all $n$ records have to be examined. If the search is successful, the number of comparisons is, on average, $n/2$. Overall, the average number of comparisons will range between $n/2$ and $n$, depending on the probability of a search being successful. If half the searches are successful, the average number of accessions and comparisons is $3n/4$. Having unique keys, then, reduces the number of accessions, on the average, by $n/4$.

### 6.2.2 Ordered Search

An ordered search differs from an exhaustive one in that the file to be searched is ordered on the search key (Figure 6.3). An ordered search starts at the beginning of the file and proceeds sequentially until it is resolved; by a successful match, or when the next highest value is found, thereby verifying that the argument is *not* to be found. The search need not be exhaustive because the search key is the sort key. The average number of accessions is $n/2$. If keys are not unique, the search can be resolved as soon as a key higher than the search key is found; but the search continues after a match is found, since there could be more matches. The number of accessions is slightly larger than $n/2$, probably insignificantly so, depending on the average number of key value repetitions. The repeated values would, of course, be adjacent to the first occurrence.

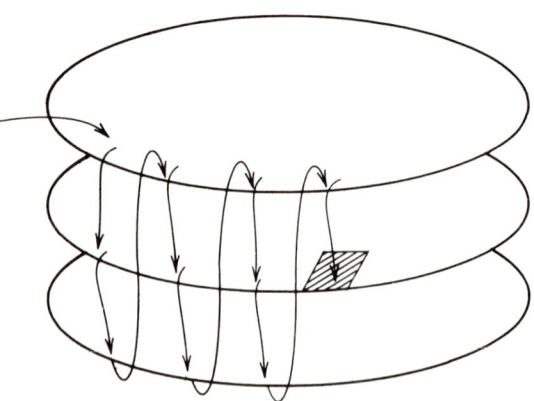

**Figure 6.3** Ordered search.

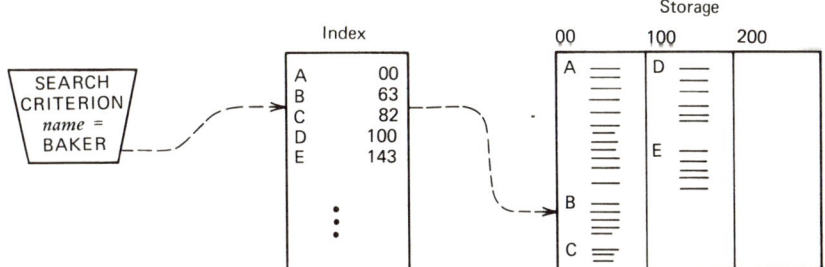

**Figure 6.4** Digital search. The index points to the location of the first record whose key value begins with the given character or digit. In this linear index, the subsequent search is ordered.

### 6.2.3 Techniques for Faster Searching

There is a number of ways to speed searching when the search key is the sort key, and an index or computation can be used to avoid many of the accessions and comparisons necessary to an ordered search. Of course, the memory medium must also permit direct access. Here are two examples.

*Digital Searching* The computer equivalent of the dictionary thumb-index method is digital searching [1], which involves use of an index or computation to compute the address of a major subdivision of a file, such as the first record beginning with the character B (Figure 6.4). An example is the location of the appropriate directory element in a multilist structure of limited string length. The number of comparisons is dependent on the specific file organization, key-to-address transformation method, and memory medium. In making direct accessions to a list-structured or chained file, timing is more important than mere number of accessions. It becomes important to know the distribution of records over cylinders and tracks, record blocking, and other physical organizational parameters. Roughly, the number of comparisons may be approximated as $1 + n/d$, where $d$ is the number of directory entries or other divisions of the file. For example, if the file has 10,000 records and 20 digital divisions, there will be one accession of the directory and about $10,000/20 = 500$ accessions of records in the chain, starting with the first one pointed to by the directory element. But a logically sequential search of the list (following pointers in key sequence) would take $n/2 = 5000$ accessions.

*Binary Searching* The first comparison, in any binary search [2] is made at the midpoint of the file (Figure 6.5). If the key of the "center" record is greater than the search key, the next comparison is made with the

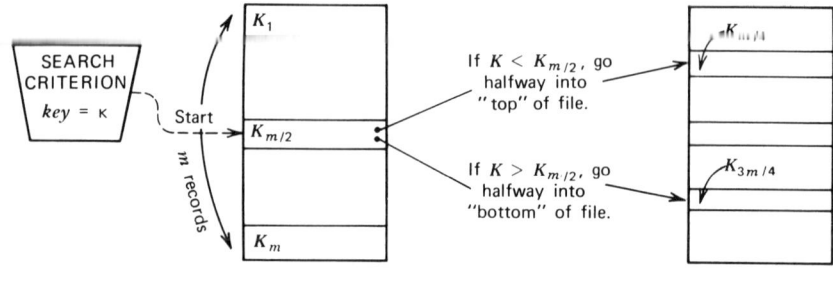

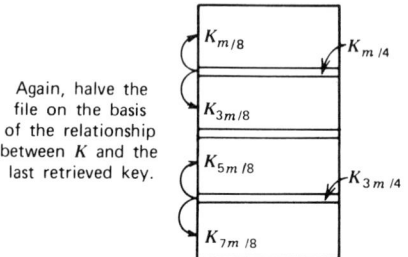

**Figure 6.5** Binary search.

record halfway from the start to the midpoint of the file. If the center record is smaller, the next comparison is made at three-fourths of the file length. If the two keys match, the search is resolved at once. In either of the unequal cases, after successive testing, the set of records potentially containing the search key is successively cut in half, until the search is resolved by finding a match or proving that none is possible.

If a file of $n$ records is successively cut in half $a$ times, until there remains only one record, then

$$2^a = n$$

or $a = \log_2 n$. Thus the number of *accessions* for comparison, or halvings of the file, is $\log_2 n$ or, if $n$ is not a perfect power of 2, $[\log_2 n] + 1$, where $[\log_2 n]$ is the largest integer in $\log_2 n$. In the 10,000-record file just referred to, whereas 501 accessions were required in a digital search, $[\log_2 10,000] + 1 = 14$ accessions would be needed in a binary search. For a sequential file, on the average, there is no faster search method in terms of number of accessions and comparisons. If the file is in direct access memory, the memory geometry may affect the comparative search speed because the time to perform all accessions is not uniform.

## 6.3 SEARCHING LIST STRUCTURES

The multiplicity of data structures based on chaining leads to a multiplicity of search techniques. List searching resembles sequential file searching in that the basis of logical ordering of records is fixed in advance and we are constrained to follow that ordering. One difference is that there may be more than one set of pointers in use within a list structure (a multilist), allowing the equivalent of an ordered search for more than one key.

Because logical and physical order is independent, or partially so, the economics of searching by a given method may be quite different from the analogous method applied to a sequential file. Records are randomly distributed in direct access storage; thus no time advantage accrues from looking at the next logical record, which may not be near the previous one.

### 6.3.1 Simple List Searching

In its simplest form, a list has only one pointer per element and searching consists of accessing the beginning of the list, then following this chain of pointers. If the basis for the pointers is the magnitude or alphanumeric precedence of a key field, the search will be resolved after an average of $n/2$, $3n/4$, or $n$ accessions, depending on whether the search argument is the ordering field, the search key is not the ordering field but has unique values in storage, or neither of these.

In the programming language SLIP, which is an extension of FORTRAN, the user is given a set of functions or subroutines for use in list searching [3]. One of these locates the beginning of any list, making its address available to other subroutines. A second finds the pointer in the last list cell retrieved and makes *its* address available. Thus one command initializes a search and another, one step at a time, follows pointers found in retrieved cells. SLIP uses both forward and backward pointers and has a pointer-following routine, called a *sequencer,* for each type of pointer.

### 6.3.2 Sublist Searching

During a simple search of a list, a cell might be encountered which points to a sublist as well as to a next list cell. To search the sublist requires logic similar to a simple list search, but in addition, it is necessary to "remember" the position (cell location) at which the search program diverged into the sublist, for it will be necessary to return to this point later, in order to resume searching the main list.

Not every cell will point to a sublist. A hospital patient record (Figure 6.6) might contain a sublist for *previous admissions*; but not all patients

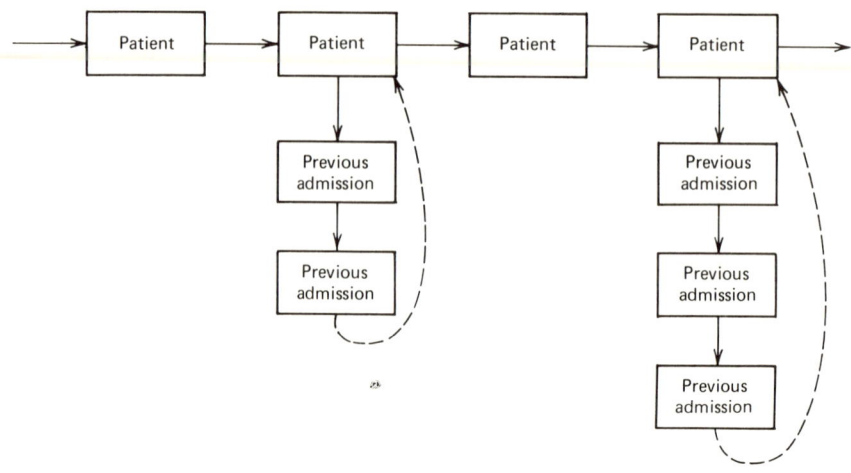

**Figure 6.6** Sublist search. To find patients previously admitted before 1970, follow the *patient* list. If there is a pointer to a *previous admission* sublist, follow that pointer through all the *previous admission* records, then back to the *patient* list again.

have a previous admission. To search for a patient who was previously admitted prior to 1970, we could search the main list, find any pointers to *previous admissions* sublists, then diverge to follow these pointers. Regardless of whether we find the appropriate data in the sublist, we would want to return to the main list and continue to search it until all patient records have been checked.

Searching a sublist adds no profound logical requirements, except that a record must be kept of the cell that pointed to the sublist. Complications arise, however, when sublists can have sublists, for we may then find a sublist search interrupted by a sublist search, and so on, inducing a sizable record-keeping requirement. A multiply sublisted structure is a *tree structure*.

### 6.3.3 Tree Searching

A *tree* is a list whose elements may be sublists, and the elements of these sublists may be sublists, and so on, without limit, except that of storage space (Figure 6.7). Or, a *tree* is a list whose elements may point to more than one next element (Figure 6.8). Like other structures, a tree may be searched on an exhaustive or an ordered basis, depending on the relationship between the search argument and the linkage between cells or records [4].

Searching List Structures    125

If there is no relationship between the search argument and the record-ordering key, we have the equivalent of searching a sequential file for an argument that is not the sort key. Every record must be accessed and tested. This requires a number of repetitions of the sublist search logic introduced earlier, and a roster must be kept of each interruption of a sublist by another. To find each instance of use of a particular pathology service in Figure 6.9, the entire list must be scanned because there is no direct entry to *pathology services*. When the lowest level sublist search has been completed, the search of the next-to-lowest is resumed. This may lead to new sublists, as in effect, the most distant branches of a tree are traced systematically from one end to the other. The roster of sublists encountered is in the inverse order of encounter, the first met being the last on the roster and the latest met being at the top of the roster. Search logic is to follow the sublist currently appearing at the top of the list. When the end of a sublist is reached, the searcher removes it from the roster and takes the new top one (Figure 6.10). This form of roster is called a *stack* or *push-down list*. Items are entered and then removed in the order last in, first out. Searching a tree exhaustively requires only that the stack be created and maintained as new sublists are encountered and their searches completed.

Another tree search of interest occurs when we have two or more forward pointers. Knuth [5] gives the following example in which we first build

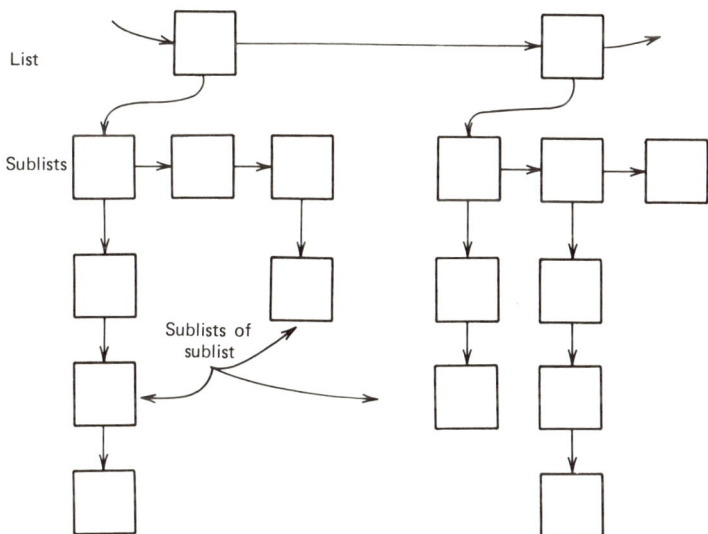

Figure 6.7    A tree of sublists.

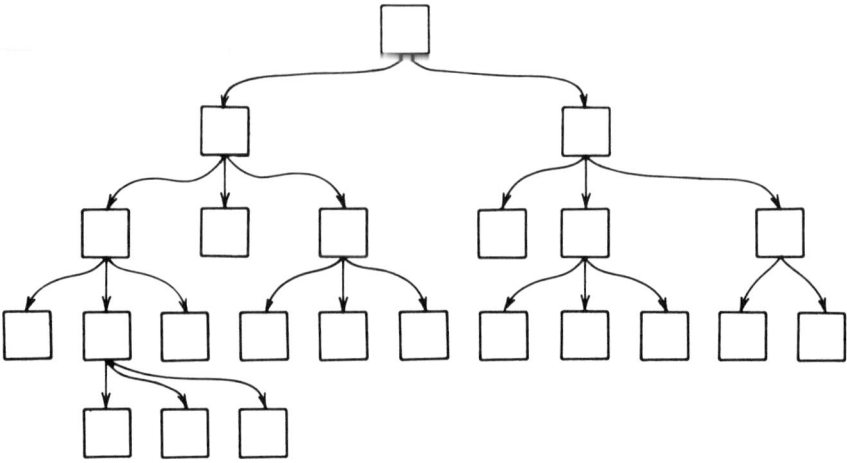

**Figure 6.8** A tree structure.

a tree, then show how to search it. We create a list of zodiac signs, entering them into the list in order of occurrence in the calendar and storing them in logically alphabetic sequence. Each symbol has two associated pointers, one to the next sign received that is alphabetically "less" than itself, and one to the next sign received that is "greater" than itself.

The tree starts with CAPRICORN and the next sign to occur in the calendar is AQUARIUS (Figure 6.11). Since AQUARIUS is alphabetically less than the first sign, CAPRICORN's *less than* pointer is set to AQUARIUS. PISCES is then added, which is alphabetically greater than CAPRICORN; hence a *greater than* pointer is set up from CAPRICORN to PISCES. Now ARIES is added. It is less than CAPRICORN, and we follow CAPRICORN's *less than* pointer to AQUARIUS. Since ARIES is greater than AQUARIUS, a *greater than* pointer goes from the latter to ARIES. Now add symbols the order: TAURUS, GEMINI, CANCER, LEO, VIRGO, LIBRA, and SCORPIO. Although the order of placing elements in the list is arrival order, their logical order in storage is alphabetic. The 11-element tree is illustrated in Figure 6.12.

To search this tree for SAGITTARIUS, the last symbol in calendar order, start at the "top" (in arrival order) with CAPRICORN and compare it with SAGITTARIUS. The latter is greater; hence follow the *greater than* pointer from CAPRICORN to PISCES. The same happens there, leading to TAURUS, from which we follow the *less than* pointer to SCORPIO and *its less than* pointer to the 8, which denotes a terminal position on the tree. Arrival at a terminal node without a match indicates an unsuccessful search. Let us now add SAGITTARIUS to the tree, at position 8 (Figure 6.13). If we were to search for a sign called SAGITTARIA, we would arrive at position 8*a* in Figure 6.13, an unsuccessful resolution.

### 6.3.4 Faster List Searching

Most of the techniques for speeding up list searching center on the use of more than the minimum number of pointers. This is analogous to the use of nested or inverted indexes for sequential files.

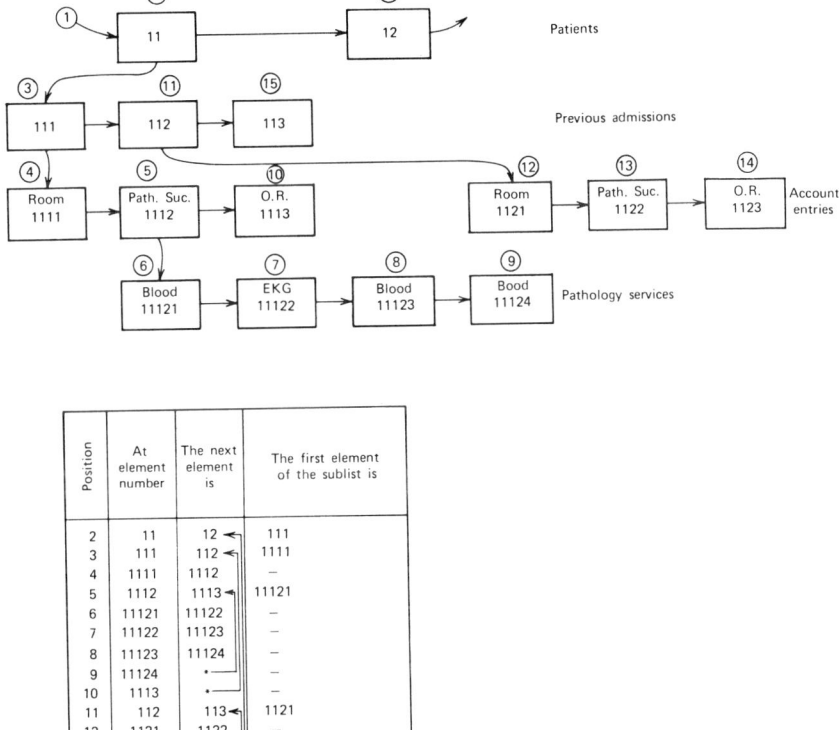

Figure 6.9  List searching. In this search a sublist is followed and, at its end, the next element to that which pointed to the sublist is followed. The table shows the order of record access.

| At position | PDL contents | Comments |
|---|---|---|
| 1 | 11 | Record 11 points to 111 (sublist) and 12 (next) |
| 2 | 111<br>12 | Delete 11 as it is accessed, insert 111 and 12 |
| 3 | 1111<br>112<br>12 | Delete 111 as it is accessed, insert 1111, 112 |
| 4 | 1112<br>112<br>12 | Delete 1111 as it is accessed, insert next record, 1112 |
| 5 | 11121<br>1113<br>112<br>12 | Delete 1112, insert sublist and next pointers to 11121, 1113 |
| 6 | . | Successively delete members of the sublist, replace them with next record key, finally deleting 11124 which has no successor. Then, list "pushes up" 1113. |
| 7 | . | |
| 8 | | |
| 9 | 1113<br>112<br>12 | |
| 10 | 112 | 1113 has no successor, 112 pushes up. |
| 11 | 1121<br>113<br>12 | 112 has a sublist and a successor. |
| . | | |
| . | | |
| . | | |

**Figure 6.10** Operation of a push-down list (PDL); figures at left indicate position on the tree of Figure 6.9.

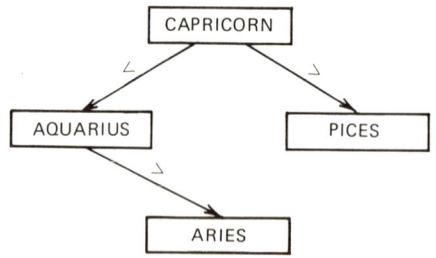

**Figure 6.11** Constructing a tree.

*128*

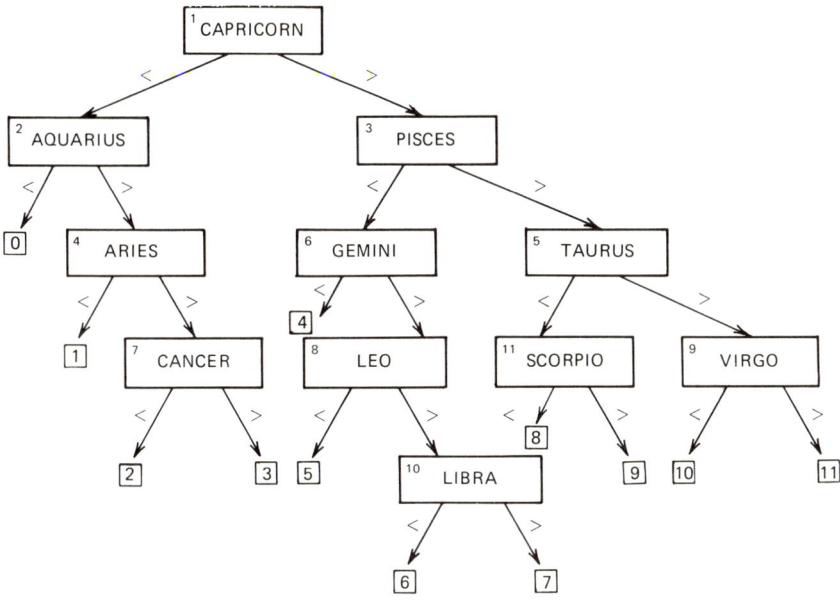

**Figure 6.12** Tree of zodiac signs. Terminal symbols (numbers in boxes) indicate pointers from tree elements that terminate the tree or resolve a search. For example, there is no element less than Aquarius (position 0), hence a search for such an element is resolved at position 0. Numbers inside boxes indicate order or occurrence of elements in the calendar. (After Knuth [5].)

***Rings*** In a conventional list, searching always starts at the top, and pointers are followed until the search is resolved. This is a *convention*, not a logical necessity. To start a search at some other point in the list, however, there must be a means of locating an appropriate starting point, which might be in an index or another pointer. In a ring structure (Section 3.4.2), the basic list is circular in that there is no first or last element. Each element points to the "next," and what might have otherwise been the last points to the first. The value of a ring structure is evident when there are several sets of pointers in use. Then each record is on several rings, and any record, in any ring, may point directly to any other record in any other ring, and that record may be directly accessed without starting at the beginning of its list (see Figure 3.23).

***Multilist*** The directory system used in multilist provides a form of rapid searching when there are multiple entries for each attribute. This occurs with the limited string length and cellular partitioning options (Section

## 130  Searching Techniques

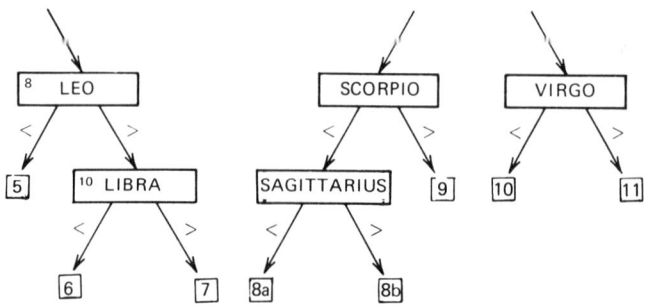

**Figure 6.13**  The completed zodiac tree.

3.4.2). The shorter threads make file searching faster at the cost of higher index search time.

### 6.4 MULTIPLE-KEY SEARCHING

Consider a search of a personnel file for an employee who is an accountant and speaks French. A file of employee records is unlikely to be sequenced on either *occupation* or *language spoken,* but there may be an inverted index for either field, or both. In the worst case, this query would require an exhaustive search.

If there is an inverted index for one field, say *occupation,* the search program could retrieve pointers to ACCOUNTANT records from the index, then access these records one at a time and test them for the attribute, *language spoken* = FRENCH (Figure 6.14). Similarly, in a multilist structure, one search of the directory retrieves a pointer to the chain of ACCOUNTANT records. Following this chain will produce the names of the accountants who speak French.

If there is an inverted index for both fields, all decision making can be done by working with sets of pointers in the indexes (Figure 6.15). We retrieve the pointers to ACCOUNTANT and those to FRENCH and select any pointers common to both lists. Only these are retrieved from the main file— at a considerable potential saving in memory access time over a search for the complete set of either FRENCH or ACCOUNTANT records. In multilist the savings are less dramatic because the index points only to a chain, not to each member of the chain. Then one of the chains must be searched, even if there is a directory entry for both attributes. However, some time can be saved by checking both directory entries and following only the shorter chain, since any record having both attributes must be on both chains.

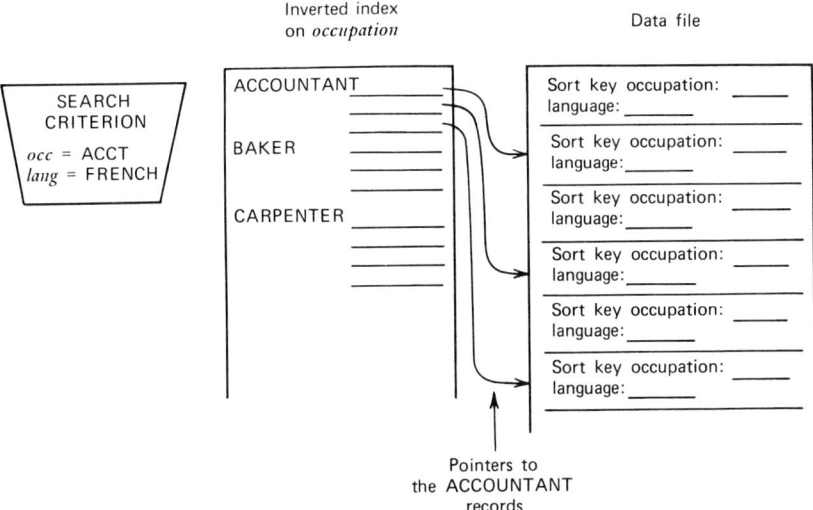

**Figure 6.14** Searching with an inverted index.

Each retrieval criterion (statement of the value of a field) implies a set of records that satisfy it. A combination of two or more criteria identifies another set defined in terms of the first two sets and the Boolean operators $\times, +, \sim$ (*and, or, not*). An inverted index explicitly denotes the members of

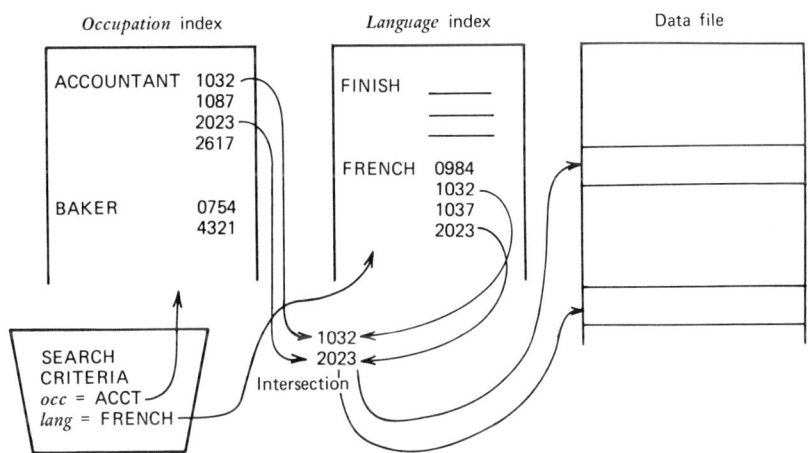

**Figure 6.15** Searching with two inverted indexes.

a set defined by a criterion of the form *name* = VALUE. The union, intersection, or negation of these sets can be computed by processing their pointers, without accession of the data records. If access to the data records is required, the index can be used to determine the smallest set that must be retrieved. Even with a sequential, nonindexed file structure, the concept that a search criterion defines a set has meaning. In some information retrieval systems, each set is given a name or number and new sets may be defined (i.e., new retrieval criteria may be specified) either by stating additional properties of fields in records or by combining existing fields properties. For example, a sequence of retrieval criteria or set definitions might be:

| | |
|---|---|
| *occupation* = ACCOUNTANT | (defines set 1) |
| *language* = FRENCH | (defines set 2) |
| 1 * 2 | (defines set 3, the intersection of sets 1 and 2, where * is the usual computer symbol for multiplication or set intersection) |
| *occupation* = LINGUIST | (defines set 4) |
| 1 * 2 + 4 | (defines set 5, calling for French-speaking accountants *or* linguists; note that an identical set is specified by 3 + 4) |

Another form of multiple-key searching features more than one possible value for any one key, as *occupation* = ACCOUNTANT or LINGUIST or INTERPRETER. Logically, this can be represented as a multiple-key query of the form:

*occupation* = ACCOUNTANT, LINGUIST, INTERPRETER

Another variant is the use of inequality relationships in search criteria, as *date* ≥ 1970 or *salary* between 10,000 and 15,000. Although not profoundly different from equality or multivalue criteria, this variant differs in that the actual values of fields that satisfy the criteria are not given explicitly. In the case of a sequential search, this matters not at all, since the same number of records are accessed and the time and logic to test for inequality of a field value are the same as for equality. When working with inverted indexes or multilist directories, however, an additional algorithm is required to search the index or directory for implicitly stated field values.

Multikey searching in any or a combination of its various forms is the information retrieval system user's likely choice for making queries. In usual programming practice, queries are broken down into a series of single-key statements of the form:

*field name*/relationship/VALUE

The manner of breaking the multikey query into individual one-key queries may be more important for total timing and efficiency purposes than is the method chosen for the individual searches. In our earlier example of the French-speaking accountant, suppose the query had been stated:

(*language* = FRENCH) * (*occupation* = ACCOUNTANT),

If there had been an inverted file on *occupation* but not one on *language*, the search program would examine each criterion to see whether there is an inverted index, and keep looking until it found one or concluded that there is none. If the search program first starts a sequential search of the data file, looking for the first French-speaking employee, and only then turns to the second criterion, for which an inverted index will be found to exist, it is too late. A large amount of time may already have been wasted beginning with the sequential search. Some query languages expect the user to be aware of this kind of problem and to order his placement of criteria accordingly.

## 6.5 MULTIFILE SEARCHING

Consider the search problem represented in Figure 6.16, File A contains a list of parts in use by our company. A record includes *part number* and *manufacturer*. File B contains data on manufacturers, including their ad-

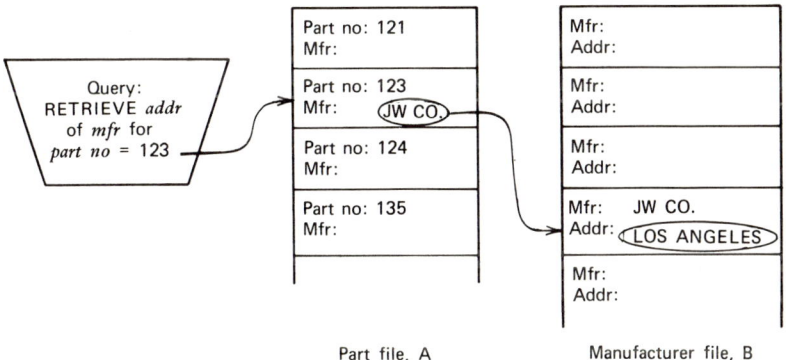

**Figure 6.16** A multifile search using two files.

## 134  Searching Techniques

dresses. To retrieve the address of the manufacturer of the part, *manufacturer* is retrieved from file A and used as a parameter in a search of file B. What initially seemed to be a straightforward search for a single field based on a single key value is complicated because the search key (*part number*) is not in the same file as the information sought (*address*). The information system that can respond to such a query must detect the multifile nature of the search and then work out a method of execution.

Let us now compound the problem. First, we add another file, a parts "explosion," which is a list of products the company makes, including the components of each, and for each component, its components, and so on, down to the level of a "part" that is not subdivisible (Figure 6.17). Each component or part has a part number that serves as the sort key of the file. Call this file C. Because of an impending strike by a supplier, we want to find all parts used in our product $x$, supplied by manufacturer $y$, at his plant location $z$, which is to be struck.

One approach is to go through file C, finding all parts used in product $x$ (Figure 6.18). This may take several runs through the file, because the

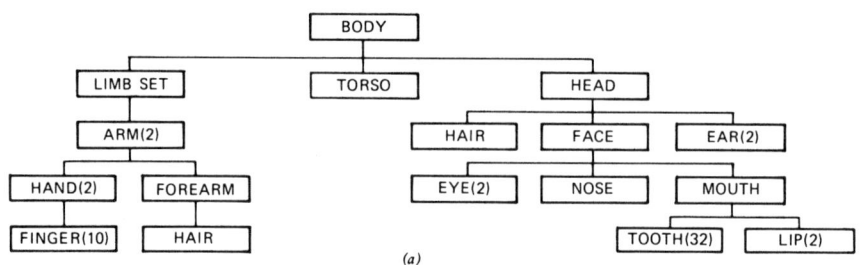

| Part | Number | Constituents | Contained in |
|---|---|---|---|
| ARM | 1 | FOREARM, HAND | LIMB SET |
| BODY | 1 | HAND, LIMB, TORSO | – |
| EAR | 2 | – | HEAD |
| EYE | 2 | – | FACE |
| FACE | 1 | EYE, MOUTH, NOSE | HEAD |

(b)

**Figure 6.17** Parts explosion. (*a*) List form, showing each component and its constituents; note that the same part, HAIR, can be part of more than one component. (*b*) Sequential form (of parts list).

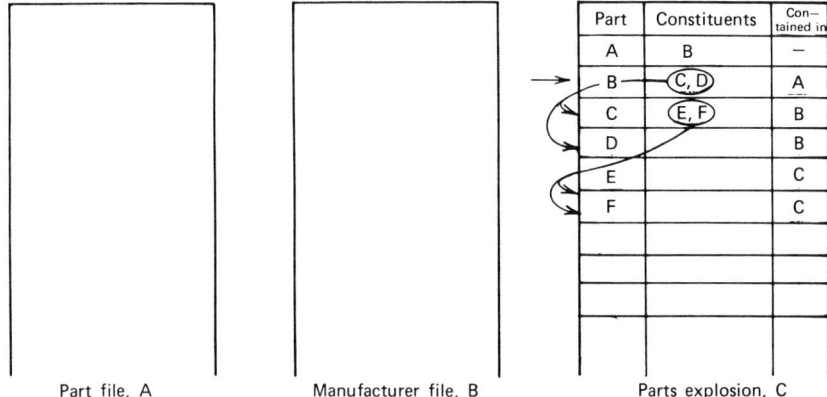

**Figure 6.18** To search a parts explosion, enter with B, a product name, retrieve its constituents C and D, then the components of C and D, and so on, until parts not containing other parts are reached, as in D, E, and F here.

order of listing of components is *part number,* rather than order of occurrence in the hierarchy of components. Thus we have to find product $x$, find its components (which may precede $x$ in the *part-number* ordered file), find their components, and so on. For a file in list form, each product would point directly to its components. For a file in sequential form, backing up might be necessary. We cannot know how many times we must scan up and down the file unless we know the structure and sequence and the average number of components and nested component levels.

Having found the list of parts, we search the parts list, file A, to retrieve the manufacturer of each (Figure 6.19). Each individual search of file B is straightforward, but there may be many searches. Among the numerous questions that arise is this: should the search program sort the retrieved part numbers before searching the parts file? If the parts file is in sequential form, sorting of search keys will reduce search time very considerably, because we can use a batch search, beginning the second part of the search with the first record after the first part, rather than going back to the top of the file. By the time we get to the last few parts, in numeric order, a substantial amount of search time may have been saved. For a file of one million records, if record access time is as little as 20 msec, the average time to search sequentially is $10^6 \times \frac{1}{2} \times 20$ msec or about 2.8 hr! If the number of parts sought is more than one or two, this becomes excessive. On the other hand, if the part numbers are sorted first, the maximum time to search is $10^6 \times 20$ msec or 5–6 hr, regardless of the number of parts sought.

If file A has an index permitting direct access to records by *part*

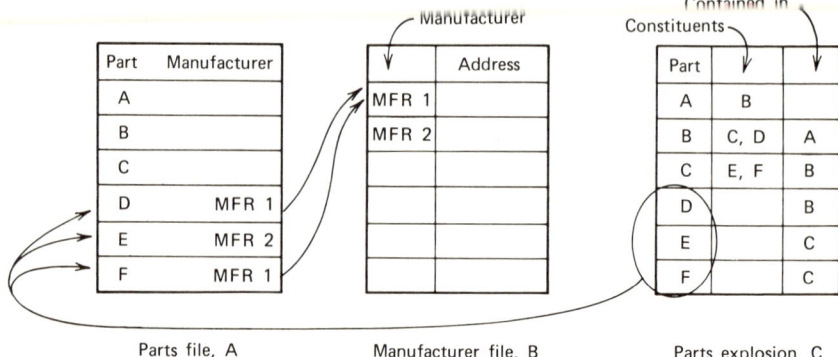

**Figure 6.19** In a multifile search part numbers retrieved from file C are used to search file A to check their manufacturer. Then the address of the manufacturer is verified in file B. Parts manufactured by the supplier at the location to be struck will be in short supply.

*number* or uses hashing to compute the storage address, the sorting operation is unnecessary, and search time, where $p$ is the number of parts sought, is $p \times 20$ msec $\times$ some additional factor for index search or hashing time. This factor, however, should be no greater than 2 or 3 (i.e., the index search should take no more than two or three accessions). For 10 parts, search time would be $10 \times 3 \times 20 = 600$ msec, whereas repetitive sequential searching for 10 parts could be 10 times our previous total of 2.8 hr, an enormous difference.

In summary, if file A is sequential and we search for each part number independently without sorting them, we must do an average of $n/2$ accessions for each of $p$ part numbers. If we sort the part numbers first, we do at most $n$ accessions. If file A is directly accessible, we can get by with $pk$ accessions, where $k$ is the number of accessions required to search the index or follow a pointer. If we know $n$ and $p$ we can quickly decide which method to choose. To decide, though, the program must know:

- whether the query can be fulfilled by a search of one file
- if not, which other files must be searched
- what the search key is in each search, and what fields are retrieved
- whether the search key retrieved from one file is the sort key of the next to be searched
- the organization, including sequence, each file searched
- how many search keys or values are retrieved from the search of this first file, to be turned into search criteria for the second file

There is another way to handle the search for manufacturers of parts used in given products. If the parts list is searched for all parts supplied by the manufacturer, these could be used to search the parts explosion file to find which parts belong in product $x$. Thus any decision process is accompanied by a formidable number of variables. The problem can be further complicated when we are interested in *address of manufacturer* rather than *name of manufacturer,* for this requires the search of a third file, and there are more options on the sequence in which files are searched.

## 6.6 SEARCH OUTPUT

To resolve a search by comparing search keys with stored values of the keys, it is necessary to retrieve at least part of an index, sometimes bringing complete data records into main memory to test them. But the user is not normally content to know that his query has found a record—he wants to see it, or some portion of it, or he wants to perform some process on the results. This means that the system user must have a means of telling the system what information he wants to recover and how that information is to be delivered to him.

Information retrieval languages commonly allow the user to retrieve the designation of the record elements separately from the designation of search keys and criteria. For example, we might find statements such as the following:

$$\boxed{\text{FOR } age > 40} \quad \text{PRINT } name$$

or $\boxed{\text{IF } key = 123}$ COPY RECORD TO FILEA

In both cases the search criterion is boxed, instructions for delivering retrieved output follow the boxed portion.

If there is no provision made for designating the items to be retrieved, a default assumption—probably that the entire logical record is wanted—is necessary. This is wasteful when only a few fields are needed and ambiguous when a program features multilist or ring structures that may obscure the definition of a logical record.

The designation of what is to be retrieved is relatively trivial in comparison with the designation of what is to be done with the information and the execution of the delivery request. The two most obvious choices are to print the information on the computer's high-speed printer and deliver it by mail, or to transmit the information to a remote terminal at which the user is working. Other possibilities include creating a new file and storing the retrieved information in the computer, or transmitting it to some other location or other computer. Some of these options may place a considerable strain on the computer programs. Printing locally or transmitting to the user's remote terminal are fairly standard options, but creating a new file, possibly in response to an on-line request calling for immediate action, may require reallocation of memory facilities (core, disk, tape) and may involve the operating system in a lengthy bookkeeping procedure. It is necessary to establish the new file's name, maximum space allocation, storage unit number, file index, and so on. These relatively simple requirements open the computer system to uncontrolled demands for resources and leaves the operating system to resolve conflicts. As a result, users ordinarily find their options for output delivery severely restricted.

An undesirable consequence of restricting output options is that the entire use of the computer is more stilted. Information transfer between systems or even between two programs operating in the same computer is inhibited. Nothing is more frustrating to a user than to be unable to feed a sophisticated information retrieval system directly from an equally sophisticated statistical analysis program. The trend is toward providing more options to users in terms of the information to be selected, the sequence of transfer, and the output or storage for transfer. To offer these options, user languages and their compilers must be more versatile. This will, in turn, require more experienced users. Some will resist the complexity, but others will appreciate the versatility. We can probably expect both languages and users gradually to mature together.

## REFERENCES

1. Donald E. Knuth, *The Art of Computer Programming*, Vol. 3. *Sorting and Searching*, Addison-Wesley Publishing Co., Reading, Mass., 1973, pp. 481 505.
2. *Ibid.*, pp. 406 14.
3. Douglas K. Smith, "An Introduction to the List-Processing Language SLIP." In *Programming Systems and Languages*, Saul Rosen, Ed , McGraw-Hill Book Co., New York, 1967, pp. 393 418.
4. Knuth, *op. cit.*, pp. 422 33.
5. *Ibid.*, p. 423.

## RECOMMENDED READING

Knuth [1].

Lefkovitz, David, *File Structures for On-Line Systems*, Spartan Books, Washington, D.C., 1967, pp. 92 154.

Lefkovitz, David, *Data Management for On-Line Systems*, Hayden Book Co., Rochelle Park, N.J., 1974.

Meadow, Charles T., *The Analysis of Information Systems*, 2nd ed., Melville Publishing Co., Los Angeles, 1973, pp. 269 83.

*Chapter Seven*

# File Maintenance

## 7.1 THE NATURE OF FILE MAINTENANCE

File maintenance is the process of changing the contents of a file. Its importance may overshadow retrieval, both in terms of value to users and the cost of computer and human resources committed to the process. In many information systems, such as a corporate financial management or accounting system, accuracy of data is generally deemed more important than speed of transmission or production of reports. News media and wartime intelligence-gathering operations are examples of information systems for which speed may be more important than accuracy. Changes can be made to a file's content or structure. Content changes modify the data values that describe some entity or the membership of the set of entities described. For example, an employee may be promoted, causing a change in the value of the *position* and *salary* data fields. Or, a new employee may be added to the set of those described by a personnel file—that is, a new employee record is inserted into the file.

Structural changes may be brought about by a change in the set of attributes of each entity to be described (changing the set of fields comprising a record, say, by adding a field to each record of a file to designate a security access code for that record), in the definition of any data element (say, an inflation-induced increase in the length of the *salary* field), or in the organization of the file (its sequence or index structure).

## 140  *File Maintenance*

In a file system having at least one data file and one index, any change to the data file, whether of content or structure, may be reflected in the index. As the index structure becomes elaborate, *its* maintenance may come to economically dominate the entire process.

## 7.2  TYPES OF MAINTENANCE TRANSACTIONS

In a typical information system there is a fairly constant stream of content changes leading to modifications of both the data files and their indexes. Structural changes are more rare and tend to be very expensive to implement.

### 7.2.1  Content Changes

There are three primary functions in content changing: *add* (or *insert*), *delete,* and *change* (Figure 7.1). Each may be applied to a record, a set of records, or some element within a record. In the simplest case, a record can be added or deleted by specifying which function is to be performed and providing the unique record key (and, in the case of *add,* the new record). *Change* denotes a combination of deleting an old record, element, or field value, and adding a new one. Again, the record or element to be changed must be identified.

If there is an element contained in a record that is to be changed, the record must be identified as well as the element within it. For example, we might:

- Change *name* in record having key *employee number* = 123456 to NEW NAME VALUE.
- Add NEW DEGREE to list of *degrees held* for record having key *employee number* = 123456.
- Delete EMPLOYEE NAME from list of *employees* in record having key *department number* = 1234.

In the first example a field (*name*) is changed in value in a record whose sort key is *employee number* and whose key value is 123456. In the second example, we are adding an element to an array contained within a record of the file, and in the third example we are deleting an element of an array within a record, leaving the record still in the file.

Changes can be ordered to a set of records with a single command, in effect making the change command conditional. An example is:

If *date of employment* < 1965
Change *rate of vacation* to 20

## Types of Maintenance Transactions

which alters the rate of vacation accrued for employees who have reached a certain seniority milestone.

Changes can also make use of existing values, such as:

Change *salary* to SALARY * 1.10

which awards all employees a 10% pay raise by multiplying the current value of *salary* by 1.10.

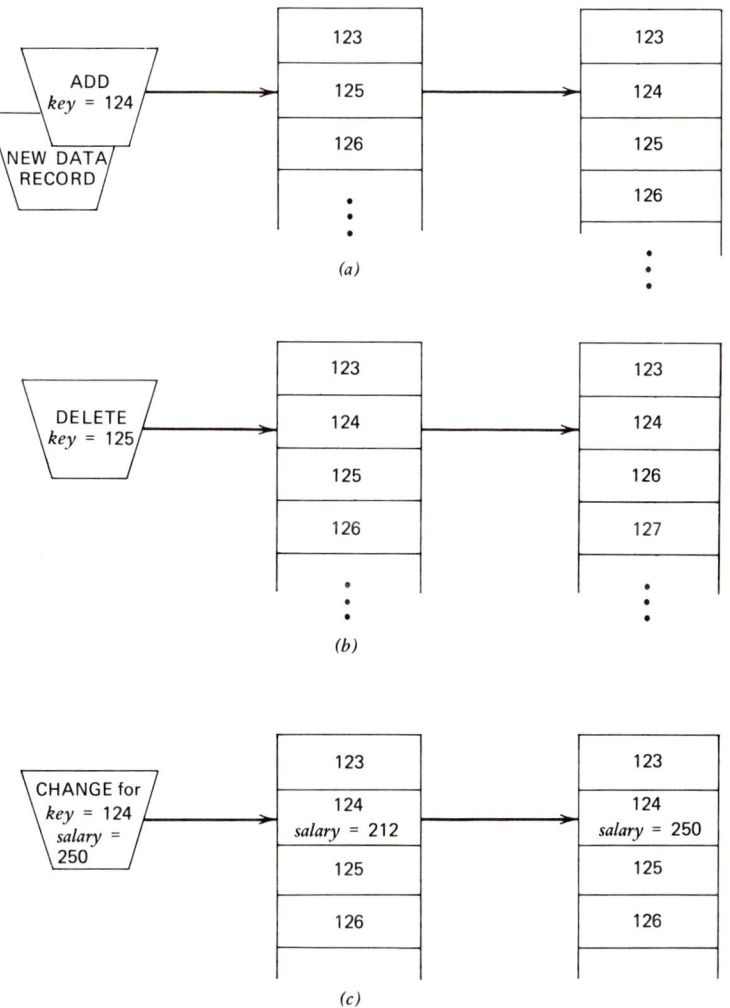

**Figure 7.1** Basic maintenance transactions. (*a*) Add or insert a record, (*b*) delete a record, (*c*) change a field, (*d*) add a field to an array, (*e*) delete a field from an array.

## 142  File Maintenance

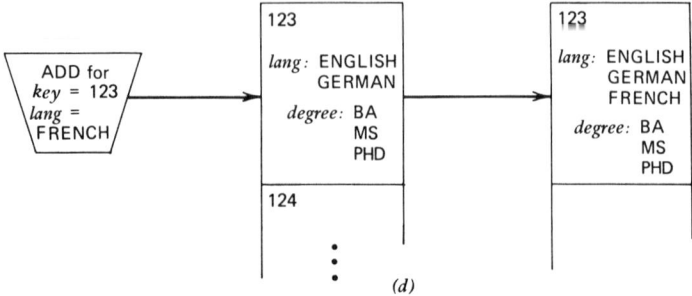

(d)

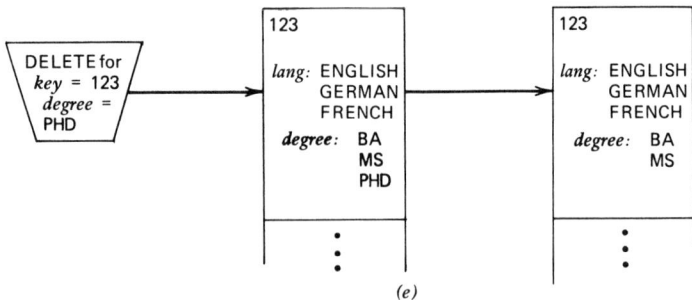

(e)

**Figure 7.1**  (Continued)

### 7.2.2  Structural Changes

Structural changes are alterations of the set of data elements to be stored, their number, sequence, or manner of indexing. If we assume that the entire structure of a file system is defined in another file (i.e., file A contains the complete physical description of file B), the process of ordering structural change is a file maintenance operation on the descriptive file (Figure 7.2). However, after we have changed the description, it is still necessary to implement the change. For example, we may change the record describing the amount of storage needed; but we must still, somehow, acquire the storage space.

Rarely is a file completely defined by a single additional file. Most modern programming languages and operating systems have not yet reached that level of sophistication. As a result, a programmer usually has to implement structural changes, starting with a careful analysis of all programs and file descriptions that might be affected. As a rule formal file definitions (as in COBOL or PL/I) must be augmented by additional definition to the operating system and by programmed checks on the validity of data values contained in applications programs. Sometimes each program using a file to be modified must be recompiled, and here we begin to see the possible cost of structural changes. In an instance in the author's experience, a change in specifications of a single field resulted in changing and recompiling some 200 programs that used the file containing the field—an extreme case of lack of data independence.

When we visualize a file description as the entity being changed, the change commands and functions are content-change functions. We can add or delete an element (in a list, say, of fields within a record), change a field specifying an attribute of a data element (e.g., length, composition), or

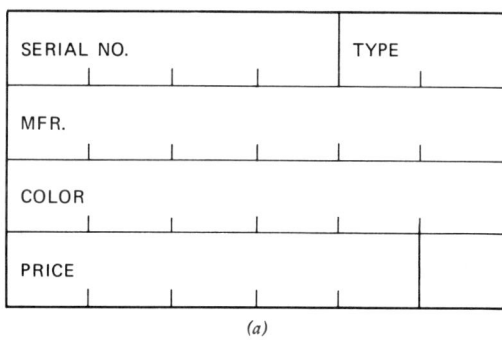

(a)

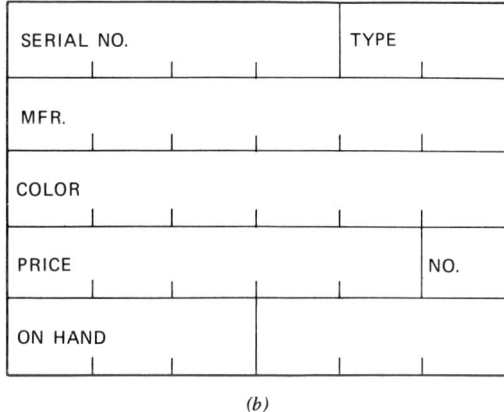

(b)

**Figure 7.2** Structural change. (a) Record in file A, (b) revised, expanded record in file A.

*144 File Maintenance*

change the field that names the sort key for the file or the number of cylinders of memory reserved for the file.

When a structural change is made to a sequential or indexed sequential file, recopying the entire file is likely to be necessary. Reorganizing an ISAM file when overflow areas are overloaded is a form of structural change. It temporarily changes a file that uses a combination of sequential and chain structures into a strictly sequential file, which then resumes its combination form when the next content change is made that causes an overflow.

One of the greatest advantages of list structures is that structural changes can be made with no or minimal recopying. For example, if a new element is to be added to a record, a pointer can be established from the existing record to a sublist containing the new elements.

**7.2.3 Validation of Changes**

Many, and perhaps the most effective, quality control procedures governing input to a computer-based information system, are performed by people—those who originate, transcribe, and check data on the way to the computer. But all people make mistakes, and it is unconscionable not to have the computer perform a programmed analysis of its input, even if the data have been visually checked. Although the functions performed in testing the validity of data entering a computer are limited only by the patience and ingenuity of the programmer, the following are the most commonly used:

*Single Value Specifications* An example: of a single value specification is simply: card column 5 must be blank. *Date* must be greater than 1960.

*Compound Value Specifications* Compound value specifications are shorthand notations for logical combinations of two or more statements, such as: *card type* = A, B, or C; 5,000 ≤ *salary* ≤ 10,000, which are equivalent to *card type* = A OR *card type* = B OR *card type* = C and salary ≤ 5000 AND *salary* ≤ 10,000, respectively.

*Composition or Alphabet Specifications* A field must be numeric (use only the characters 0, 1, 2, . . .) or alphabetic, or contain no embedded blanks.

*Membership in a List* Logically equivalent to a multiple equality of the form *card type* = A, B, or C, in this form the list of possible values would be stored in memory and referenced by name; for example, *card type* member of TYPELIST.

### Types of Maintenance Transactions

***Boolean Combinations of the First Four***   We might require:

> *date of birth* ≤ 1930
> or  *salary* ≥ 25,000
> or  *position* = DIRECTOR, VICE PRESIDENT
> or  *name* member of VIPLIST

A rather important distinction must be made between data values used in these validation statements and values stored either in the file to be modified or elsewhere (Figure 7.3). For example, if we are going to require any new employee's salary to lie between the limits $5000 and $20,000, we can store these limiting numbers with the validation statement. They become either constants stored "in" the computer program or part of a table always made available to that program in main memory. This is easy to provide. Another possible criterion for validity, say, of a salary change, is that the new value not exceed the old by more than 10%. To retrieve the old record, use the existing value of *salary* to validate the incoming data, and make the change, the validation and retrieval programs must be linked, and the usage may require the addition of many retrieval operations to the validation process. This added cost may be necessary if there is no other way to ensure that the new data are valid. The alternative is to test the validity of incoming data without reference to the current contents of the file. Cheaper and easier to implement, this approach lacks precision. For example, it is impossible to limit salary increases to 10% without looking at the current content of a record before posting a change. The result must be

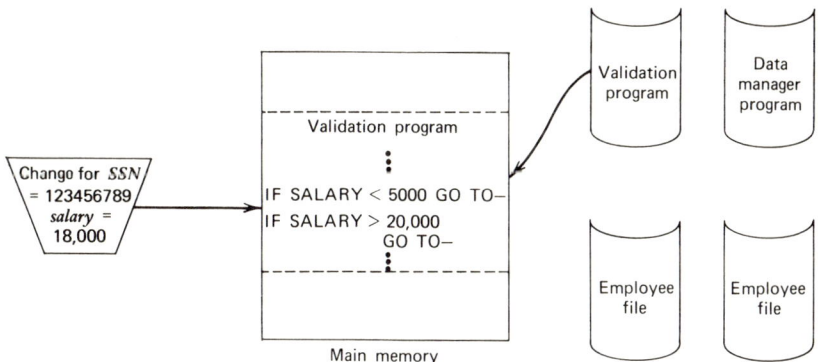

**Figure 7.3**  Availability of information for validation, I. Certain validation checks require only that the program and the input data be in main memory. To use information stored in the record that is to be modified, the data manager must be in memory and it must call the index to the *employee* file, then the data records. The number of input-output operations is much greater than if the input were accumulated into an economic batch.

## 146  File Maintenance

an approximation to the desired validation test and the consequent risk of error slipping through.

When file changes are to be made immediately, in response to commands entered from an on-line terminal, the random order of arrival precludes taking any advantage of file structure, such as ordering the change transactions in key sequence, making the validation-maintenance process more efficient in the use of computer time. But the value of continuously up-to-date files often makes this expense worth bearing.

Yet another order of complication is introduced when a file other than the one being changed must be consulted in order to validate (Figure 7.4). This could happen when the membership function names a table that must be retrieved from disk or tape when needed because it is not permanently stored in main memory. Obviously, all needed files must be available at the same time. If change data are being entered simultaneously by many people through remote terminals, the demand for memory, multiplied by the many simultaneous users, could overload the computer system.

The last example leads into another complication in file maintenance—namely, the need to prevent two or more programs from accessing the same logical record at the same time, when one of them may be changing the

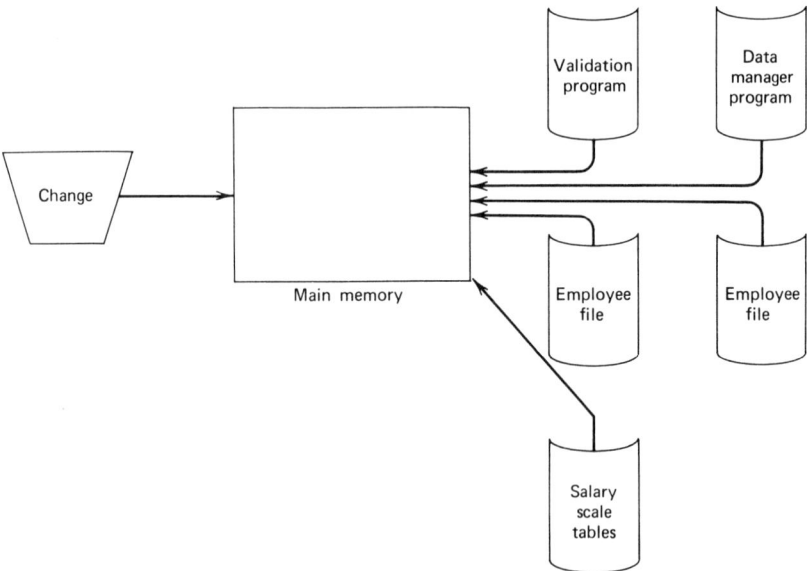

**Figure 7.4** Availability of information for validation, II. If the validation program requires the use of a table or file that is not part of the file being changed, the number of input-output operations is increased.

record. For example, suppose a logical record consists of more than one physical segment. In one segment is an employee's *salary* and in another his *rank* or *position*. When the employee is promoted, both fields change. If a retrieval program retrieves both segments during the brief interval after one segment has been changed but before the second has been changed, the output will be wrong. Worse than merely being old (reflecting the prepromotion information), it is contradictory, showing a new rank, perhaps, and a salary not compatible with that grade.

This form of conflict can be prevented by a software device known as *lockout* (Figure 7.5). Applied to a record, it means that as soon as the maintenance program begins to process a change to a logical record, it places that record's key on a list of locked records. All retrieval or maintenance programs must check the lockout list before accessing any record, and no program may access any record contained on it. When the maintenance transaction is complete, the record is unlocked by being taken off the list. Depending on usage patterns, lockout can be applied at the record level, as illustrated here, or at any level from individual field to complete file. The process is expensive, but it is necessary for an on-line system having multiple terminals and users able to either change or query the file at any time.

## 7.3 SOME MAINTENANCE EXAMPLES

Presented next are some examples of maintenance transactions for several different file organizations.

### 7.3.1 Sequential File

At one time the classic method of modifying files was as follows: have a *master file*—the original file to be changed—and a *transactions file,* which contains new data to be entered into the master file and commands or instructions for the maintenance functions. Both files are in sequence on the same key. Transactions probably arrive in random order and have to be sorted into this sequence. Each maintenance transaction must identify the unique record to which it is to be applied.

The master file is searched until the record matching the key of the first record in the transactions file is found. All records of the master file (*old master*) not matching a transaction record are simply written onto a new copy of the file (*new master*) (Figure 7.6). When a match is made, with both the master and transaction record in storage, the changes are made and the new version of the record written out. If the transaction is a dele-

**148** *File Maintenance*

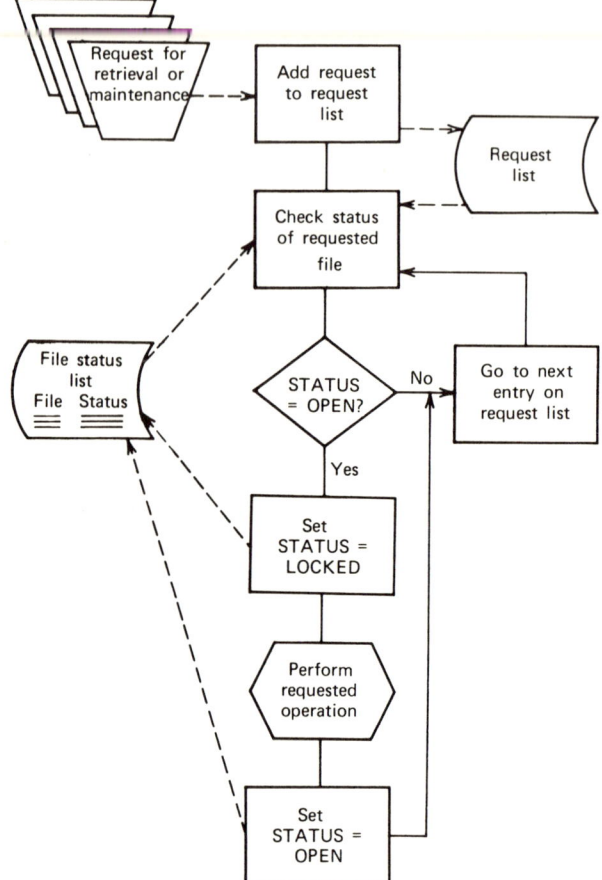

**Figure 7.5** File lockout. Requests for retrieval or modification stream continuously to the data manager and are queued and considered in order. A LOCKED or OPEN status is maintained for each file in use. The file is locked while a change is being made and is opened at completion. Since file transactions in a multiprogrammed computer are concurrent, a file must be locked while it is being changed, to prevent retrieval from it before the change is complete.

tion, the master record is not written, and the program proceeds to look for a match with the next transaction. If a new record is to be inserted, there will be no match for it (or should not be); but the new record is written out with the new copy of the master file at the appropriate point.

Any validity checking on input can conveniently be done as the transaction record comes up for consideration. When the matching master record is found, there is the added benefit of having "old" data available for use on validation, at no extra cost, since the record had to be retrieved anyway. But there is a disadvantage in this approach to validation. Waiting until the master file is being changed to verify the validity of the changes means that the resulting master file cannot be complete if any errors are found. The outputs of the process would be the old master, a new master only incompletely modified, and a listing of errors detected. These must be examined by a knowledgeable person, the error found, the transactions resubmitted, and the entire process repeated until it runs error-free. While these steps are being performed, the new master file is incomplete. This long delay accounts for much of the attraction of on-line entry of file maintenance data.

The time required for this maintenance method is almost identical to the time required to write the new master file or read the old (the number of records is usually about the same). The method is relatively insensitive to the number of maintenance transactions and to amount of validation programming, since this operation is performed in main memory, and all

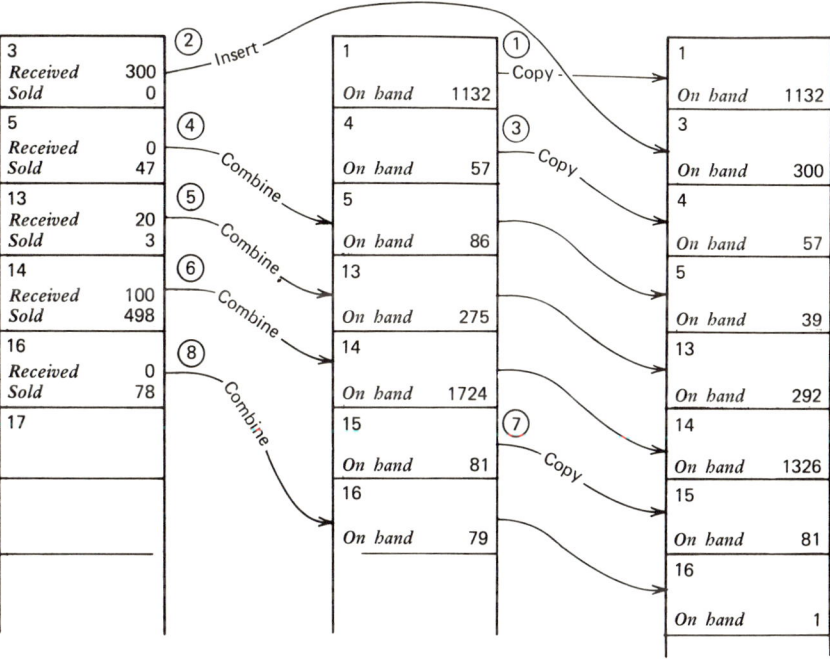

**Figure 7.6** To modify a sequential master file, records having no match in the transaction file are copied to the new master file. Matching records must be combined, computing *on hand* = *on hand* + *received* − *sold*. Records in the transaction file having no match in the master are inserted into the new master file, treating the existing value of *on hand* as zero.

*150*    *File Maintenance*

data needed are provided by the matching process. The insensitivity to number of transactions makes the method highly efficient when many changes are to be processed. Hence the larger the proportion of master records to be changed in any given maintenance "run," the more likely it is that sequential files should be used.

### 7.3.2 ISAM

In Section 3.4.4 we showed how records are inserted into and deleted from an ISAM file. A record that is to be changed must be retrieved, then rewritten into the same location from which it came, provided its size does not change. *Rewriting* a record into the original location, as opposed to *inserting* a record just retrieved, which looks for a new location, avoids the necessity for modifying an index or risking overflow. Of course, the one field that cannot be changed, in conjunction with a rewrite command, is the key, since that would change the location at which the record belongs.

It is not necessary to recopy an entire ISAM file when making changes. There is relatively little point in processing change transactions in key order, because the ISAM data manager goes through an index search each time, regardless of whether successive requests are for sequentially stored records. Thus when the percentage of records to be changed is not too high, ISAM is quicker at maintenance than sequential files. If errors are discovered in new data during a maintenance transaction, just as with sequential files, the resulting master file is only partially modified. Since the master file is the sole copy, it must be used with care until the changes can be corrected and reapplied. During the interval, when some but not necessarily all changes have been processed, the file may contain contradictions. For example, suppose that a hospital patient is discharged and a new patient is admitted and assigned the bed of the former patient. If the discharging record has an error that requires the time of a clerk to adjust, the master file may show two persons occupying the same bed at the same time.

Timing of ISAM processes is less certain than is sequential file timing. To make $n$ transactions, there must be at least $n$ file accessions. A change requires two accessions—one to retrieve the existing record and one to rewrite it. A deletion also requires two, since deletion is accomplished by tagging the record, making this a change transaction. An add requires only the store operation. Any of the functions, though, might require index maintenance, and such timing depends on where in the file the changed record happens to fall, whether an insertion becomes the new highest key in a cylinder, for example. Also, a search or retrieval time for a given key depends on the overflow situation at the time the retrieval is made; thus even two successive simple change operations on the same record can use different amounts of time.

### 7.3.3 Sequential File with Inverted Indexes

Whether the main data file is sequential or indexed sequential, direct changes to it are handled as described in the preceding section. When there are inverted indexes, however, each change to a data record may trigger a change to one or more inverted indexes.

Assume a file sequenced on *patient number* with inverted indexes for fields *physician, room number,* and *insurance carrier.* To add a new record to the file requires an insertion in the usual manner. Then the location of the new record must be inserted into the appropriate record of each of the inverted index files (Figure 7.7). Although the index files are usually much smaller than the main file, the number of memory accessions may be the same, or nearly so, to make the index changes. Hence inserting a new record into a file system of one data file and three inverted indexes requires about four times the maintenance cost that would be incurred for an unindexed file. A deletion uses similar logic. Not only is the record deleted or tagged as deleted, but each reference to it in an index must be deleted as well. It is possible to omit the index deletion, merely tagging the data record and waiting until the record is retrieved to discover that it was logically deleted. In instances of low rate of deletion of records from the files, this practice might be worthwhile. If the deletion rate is high, however, the approach would create clutter and possibly chaotic retrieval of large numbers of unwanted records.

A change to a file with inverted indexes involves the relatively low-cost

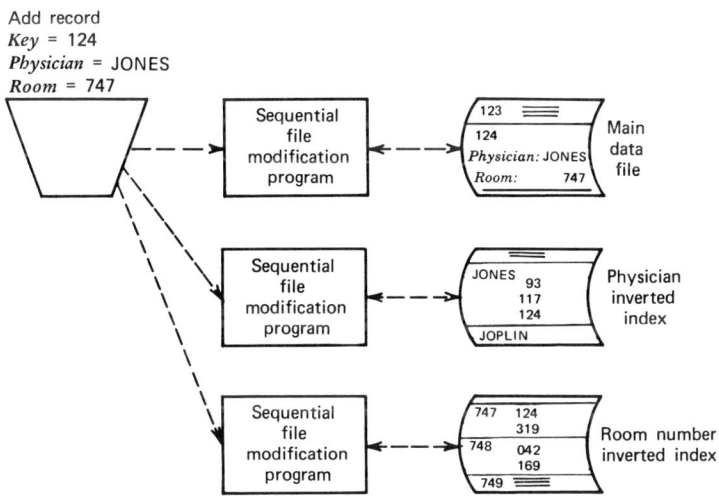

**Figure 7.7** Modifying an inverted file system.

process of deciding whether there is an index for each field changed. The average total cost of a change, then, depends primarily on the probability of the changed field being an index field.

Total timing depends on method of processing deletions, relative frequency of additions, deletions, or change transactions, and the probability that a field changed is an index field.

### 7.3.4 Multilist

Multilist maintenance is much like inverted file system maintenance. Adding or deleting a record is described in Section 3.4.2. Content changes can be handled "in place" by retrieving and modifying the record, then restoring it to the same location. An add or delete might require more than one record accession, because pointers to the affected record must be changed. If space is to be withdrawn from or returned to the space-available pool, one or more additional memory accessions may be involved. Directory elements must be changed in the same manner applied for inverted indexes.

Regarding the number of specific tasks involved, making changes to a multilist structure might be more expensive than doing the same to an inverted file system, because of the need to change pointers in the data records. It might be less expensive, however, if not every record is explicitly represented in a directory.


## 7.4 MAINTENANCE POLICY

To summarize the cost aspect of file maintenance, we can say that methods providing multiple access or speed of access to a file require that information about records be stored in some form of index. Changing the data means changing the index, and this necessarily adds to maintenance cost. When speed of direct access can be sacrificed, sequential file structures often offer the most efficient maintenance.

Some load balancing is possible. A brief example was given earlier of the idea of not deleting index references to deleted records at the time of record deletion, saving maintenance time but adding to retrieval time. A similar approach is possible in handling additions or changes (Figure 7.8). In an inverted file or multilist system, suppose that additions and changes are not posted immediately on receipt but are kept instead in a small auxiliary file. Any search must be directed to the main file as well as to this auxiliary file, clearly increasing search time. But if the auxiliary file is small enough, the increment of time added to retrieval may be less than the amount saved by delaying maintenance. The user would see no difference. Because data are split between two files and some records contradict others (i.e., there are new records and the unchanged versions of the old), programming purists and auditors might object. But an organization that opted for this method, or an analogous one for other file structures, might save money.

In setting maintenance policy for an information system, we must consider not only the cost of doing the maintenance but the cost of not doing it, or not being able to. All our examples in Section 7.3 were of content changes. In the context of structural changes, we often need to know whether we can modify a file for a reasonable cost, in a reasonable amount of time. Here are three examples, taken from actual experience, that bring out some of the problems.

*Example 1.* Company A has a liberal employee vacation policy. Management feels that a week or more of real vacation is desirable for each employee every year, rather than a series of single days off or long weekends. Hence longer vacations are encouraged and vacation leave cannot be taken less than one day at a time (i.e., no one-hour or half-day "vacations"). As a result, the payroll programs that keep track of vacation time accumulated and used treat *vacation used* as in integer variable—no fractional days or hours can be represented. One day there was a civic event of great importance and emotional concern. Since it was a nonrecurring occasion, there had been no previous plans for it, nor any apparent need to plan for another in the future. The company decided to release for a half-day employees who wished to attend the event, without taking vacation. Any employee who chose to attend could elect to return to work in the afternoon or take the afternoon off as vacation. But to be able to have the afternoon off, he had to take a full day of vacation.

To employees who understood file structure, the explanation for this curious situation was evident. There was no way to record a half-day of vacation. The company's options were to change the structure of the payroll file, making *vacation used* one or two digits longer to allow for fractional days off, or to grant a full day off to everyone. There was neither time nor inclination to change the payroll programs at this multisite company, where local autonomy was permitted in such matters as payroll program preparation. Changing policy would have been very expensive. The management announcement about the afternoon vacation was perceived as insensitive and discriminatory by employees not aware of its cause. Although the company was among the leaders in the data processing industry, no attempt was made to explain the logic of the decision in terms of file definition and the cost of structural file changes.

## 154    File Maintenance

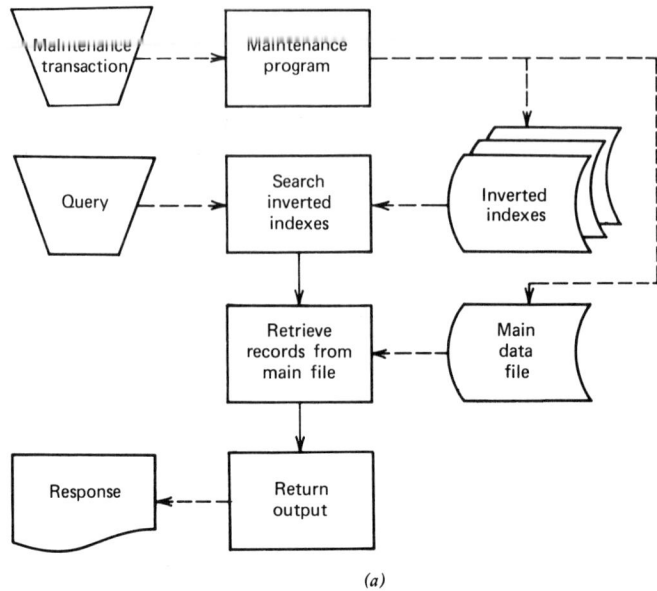

(a)

**Figure 7.8**  Load balancing by file organization. (*a*) Conventional search and maintenance of an inverted file system. (*b*) File changes go into an auxiliary holding file that like the main file system must be searched by search programs. Periodically the auxiliary file is merged into the main file.

*Example 2*  A department store permits applicants for new charge accounts to charge a limited number of purchases on the day the application is made. Records of these purchases, together with the applications, are forwarded to a central accounting office, where all data are entered into a computer and invoices are eventually produced. As a result of a keypunching error, the same customer's name and address were attached to two new charge accounts, and two invoices sent out, one valid, the other representing the purchases of another person. Protests to the company brought immediate understanding—everyone who looked at the evidence realized what had happened. But no paper record of the second customer was kept and apparently, even if one had been, the company had no established procedure for changing the identity of a customer. That is, one could change one's name, but the company was not prepared for the condition that the individual identified as responsible for the account is the wrong person. Thus protracted argument and threats and counterthreats concerning the unpaid bill preceded resolution. The problem here was a double one: no way to validate the keypunch operator's work, and no way to make a certain kind of

*Maintenance Policy* 155

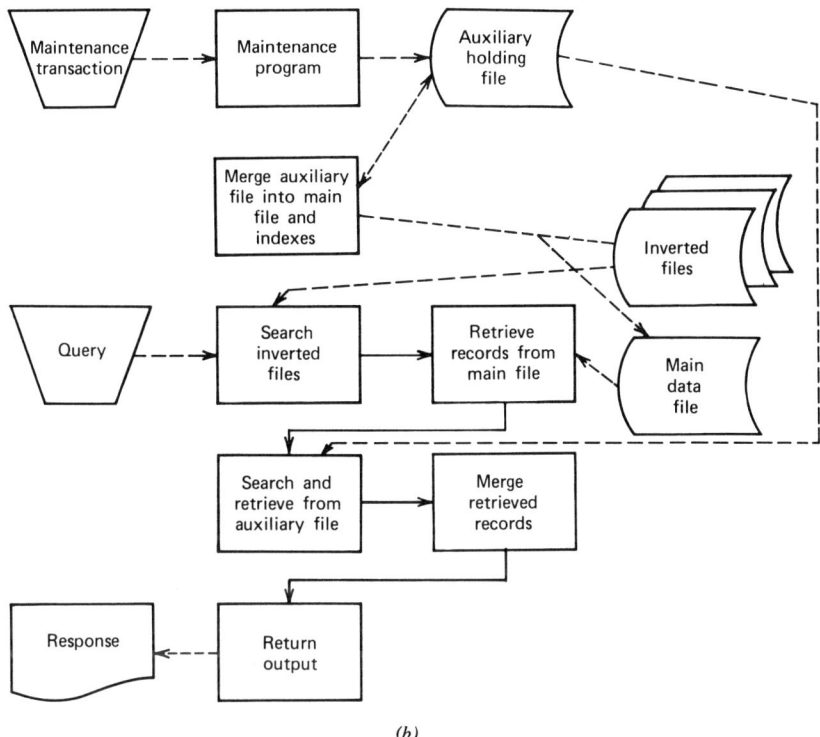

(b)

change, one so fundamental it never had been considered. The only way to handle this problem is to anticipate that such errors can occur, being prepared to ask customers to verify the accuracy of records and to track down errors that do occur, using a trained data processing person.

*Example 3* A physician subscribes to a data processing service that keeps track of bills, receipts, and overdue accounts. The physician's office assists patients in making insurance claims and is willing to await settlement of a claim before receiving payment. In some cases the insurance claim form provides a means of authorizing direct payment to the physician, and under this option the patient does not know when the claim is paid.

An insurance claim was filed and lost, and a subsequent replacement suffered the same fate. The program used by the physician's data processing service, routinely updating its files, discovered the patient to be in arrears. This condition first triggers a computer-printed dunning letter which, if necessary, is followed by assignment of the account to a credit bureau for collection; and of course, the patient's credit file acquires the notation "nonpayer." When the patient was dunned, there ensued a donnybrook similar to that in the department store case. All the *people* involved recognized what had happened: that the office had agreed to accept direct payment from the insurance company, which had lost the claim forms; but there was no provision for entering the facts of this situation into the information system. The individual physician does not operate the program, however, and does not meet this state of affairs often enough to decide to do anything about it. The data processing service gets no complaints, because only when the offended patient has a programming background does any participant recognize the cause of the problem and what can be done. Again, a structural change is called for, in this case adding new fields to permit more information to be collected on the patient's payment status.

These anecdotes involved organizations that probably considered themselves leaders in modern management practice. Large corporations and small private medical practices alike undoubtedly have clearly defined policies on insurance coverage for themselves, safety procedures, financial management, employee relations, and so on. The concept that a responsible firm should have a responsible file maintenance policy has not yet achieved currency. The passage of recent legislation in the United States, the Fair Credit Reporting Act [1] and the Privacy Act of 1974 [2], however, indicates that this situation may soon change for the better.

## REFERENCES

1. P.L. 91-508, 91st Congress, October 26, 1970.
2. P.L. 93-597, 93rd Congress, December 31, 1974.

## RECOMMENDED READING

Laden, H. N., and T. R. Gildersleeve, *Systems Design for Computer Applications,* John Wiley & Sons, New York, 1967, pp. 20–64.

Lefkovitz, David, *File Structure for On-Line Systems,* Spartan Books, Washington, D.C., 1967, pp. 155–80.

Meadow, Charles T. *The Analysis of Information Systems,* 2nd ed., Melville Publishing Co., Los Angeles, 1973, pp. 303–12, 329–30.

*Chapter Eight*

# Data Communications

## 8.1 BASIC COMMUNICATIONS CONCEPTS

*Data communications* is generally taken to mean communication between machines, computers, or computer components or peripheral equipment, in which the information is represented by digital codes [1]. There are, of course, other ways to transmit data: by talking over telephone or radio, by sending an ordinary letter or telegram, and by sending measurements in analog form (telemetry). Davenport stresses that "data communication [is] ... the movement of information in machine language" [2].

Claude E. Shannon, the founder of the modern mathematical theory of communication [3], defines communication as a process of information transfer involving five elements:

- *source,* where a message originates, such as a computer or teletype or other terminal
- *transmitter* that takes a message from the source and converts it to a form suitable for sending out through
- *channel* that carries the message (in data communication the channel might be a telephone line, a microwave system, or a coaxial cable); the channel delivers its message to
- *receiver,* which performs essentially the inverse role of the transmitter, converting a signal received from the channel into a form meaningful to
- *destination,* which might again be a computer or terminal.

For communication to take place, the destination must have the same understanding of a message as the source. Formal communication theory does not deal with meaning. If the source sends 040776 and the destination receives that string of numbers, we say that communication has taken place at the technical level. The communications engineer is not interested in knowing that these numbers can be interpreted as a date and that that date has special significance to Americans. Of course the ultimate purpose of most data communications is to deliver information to people who *are* interested in meaning, but we concentrate in this chapter on the technical aspects.

Modern data communications represents the marriage of two technologies that grew separately for many years. It is not surprising, therefore, that our computer equipment is not directly compatible with our major communications systems (such as the Bell Telephone System). Linking the two together requires conversion of signals and imposition of constraints on the use of communications facilities by computers. Once we connect the two to create data communications systems, however, we experience a major leap forward in the effective use of computers in business, libraries, schools, hospitals, hotels, transportation, and an almost endless list of other applications. Data communication enables the person or machine to use a computer for data entry, retrieval, or computation, wherever that computer may be.

Our emphasis here is on the softwave aspects of data communication used in conjunction with data management systems. In Chapter 12 we treat computer networks. We are primarily concerned with how one machine talks to another and we treat the following topics.

1. *Transmitters and receivers.* How the signal is prepared for transmission and for receipt at the destination. Mainly, preparation is accomplished at both ends by a device called a *modem*.
2. *Multiplexors and concentrators.* Without these devices for receiving signals from more than one source and transmitting them all over a single channel, much of data communication would be prohibitively expensive.
3. *Message switching.* Concentrating is a form of switching, but since there is more than one output channel, a decision must be made regarding which channel or set of channels should be used for transmission, and when the message should be sent.
4. *Computer message handling.* A computer receiving messages must go through the same kinds of processes that the communication system performed in bringing the messages to the computer. It must collect messages or fragments of messages (often from more than one source),

store them, and feed them to the appropriate processing programs. On output, the process is reversed. A message from any program is queued until a transmission facility is available; then it is sent, possibly in fragments.
5. *Applications of data communication.* Data communication has opened up a variety of ways of using computers remotely for data management.

## 8.2 PREPARING THE SIGNAL: MODEMS

Suppose a terminal produces the code 1000001 (A in ASCII). Electrically, the signal it transmits is a DC signal of varying voltage over time. It might resemble Figure 8.1 and it might travel at a rate of 300 bits/sec. It is expected to be sent out over a telephone line that was designed for sound input in the frequency range 300-3400 cycles per second or hertz (Hz). To send our relatively slow signal on this line, a carrier signal must be generated by the transmitter. The carrier signal is a uniform wave, at high frequency, as in Figure 8.2. To send our desired signal or a conventional voice signal, we *modulate* the carrier wave by the signal wave, adding a function of the signal to the carrier to produce the resultant wave pattern appearing in Figure 8.3.

The basic task of a modulator corresponds to the foregoing description. In addition, if the frequency of the carrier is high enough, it can speed up the rate of transmission of the original digital signal. The duration of a *one* bit, for example, need not be as long on the high-speed channel as it must be in an electromechanical printer terminal. When action of the modulator enables the channel to speed up a signal, there is an excess of channel capacity, which can be used to send other signals at a considerable saving in channel cost. The saving can be realized by interleaving parts of several messages, preserving the bit transmission rate of each, or by transmitting a message at a rate higher than its arrival rate, which requires storing the incoming message until it is complete, then retransmitting. Both methods are discussed in the next section.

At the receiving end, the signal must be converted back into a pulse train of the same type and speed originally characterizing it. (If communication is between digital machines that use different codes or operate at different speeds, the receiver's transformation may not be exactly the same,

**Figure 8.1** A coded signal made by varying voltage over time.

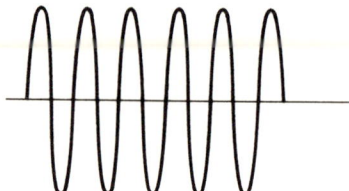

**Figure 8.2** A carrier wave.

but it will be of the same type.) This is the process of *demodulation*. If there is to be two-way communication between the machines, there must be a modulator and a demodulator at each end. Usually one machine does both jobs, hence the derivation of the term "modem," from *mo*dulator-*dem*odulator.

Modems have another task besides modulating and demodulating. When a call is initiated, say, from a terminal to a computer, there is a certain amount of setting up to be done, as well as verification that communication has indeed been established (i.e., that each end is clearly receiving the signals as sent by the other end). This process is roughly analogous to what happens when a business executive calls a colleague on the telephone. Most likely, the originator asks his secretary to place a call to the destination's secretary. Once communication has been established, the two principals come on the line. The calling secretary verifies that the destination executive is present and available to speak and also verifies (usually by the absence of any contrary indication) that the two parties can "read" each other's signals—that is, the line is not too noisy. Also involved is a certain amount of technical work: dialing the number, asking for an extension, and comprehending the meaning of the intermediate signals (e.g., the dial tone and the indication that the called telephone is ringing). The analogous operation in digital communication, not all done by the modem alone, is called "handshaking."

## 8.3 MULTIPLEXING AND CONCENTRATING

The transmission channel can be the most expensive part of a data communication system. For this reason, elaborate techniques have been devised to enable more than one source to transmit through a channel simultaneously. A clear example of the need for this is in transoceanic telephone cable, expensive to install, limited in capacity, and able to benefit from any technique that will increase message throughput without meaningful decrease in message quality.

A *multiplexor* is a device that has more than one input channel and a single, higher capacity, output channel. Using any of a variety of techniques, the multiplexor is able to transmit all its incoming messages simultaneously over the output channel. This rate of output is equal to the input rate in terms of symbols per unit time. In *frequency division multiplexing,* if a channel is capable of transmission of signals from 100 to 200 kilohertz (1 kilohertz, or kHz = 1000 Hz), it can be broken up into four bands of about 25 kHz each: 100–125, 125–150, 150–175, 175–200. Some of the available bandwidth (range of frequencies carried on a channel) must be set aside for separation of signals, perhaps making the actual bands 100–120, 125–145, 150–170, 175–190. In each band there can be a carrier signal, at 110, 135, 160, and 185 kHz, respectively. Each is modulated by an incoming signal, and the four resulting signals are sent simultaneously on the channel.

In time-division multiplexing each incoming signal is sampled in time, and the value sampled becomes the output signal; it has a shorter duration than it did on the incoming signal, however. We can see this in Figure 8.4, where there are four incoming signals and a sampling procedure that samples signal 1 at time 1, signal 2 at time 2, and so on, to produce the signal shown. At the receiving end the signal is resampled and the original reconstructed, as in Figure 8.5.

A *concentrator* is a form of multiplexor, but it may not actually modify signals and its output speed may be slower than its maximum rate of input. If messages are received on all input lines simultaneously, the concentrator must store some of the messages and forward them when channel capacity is available. A concentrator may send a message at a much higher rate of speed than the rate at which the message was received, thus achieving some reduction in channel use even without multiplexing.

Another device that performs a somewhat similar function is the *line control unit* or *transmission control unit,* which is used with *multidrop lines.* It is possible to link a set of terminals, each having a relatively low probability of being used at any given time, into a single, nonmultiplexed line to the computer. This "party line" arrangement, in which only one terminal may use the line at a time, is called a multidrop line (Figure 8.6). Since each incoming message must have an address in it, only the addressed unit gets the message. The line control unit, then, performs a relatively rudi-

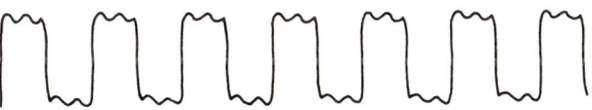

**Figure 8.3** A modulated signal.

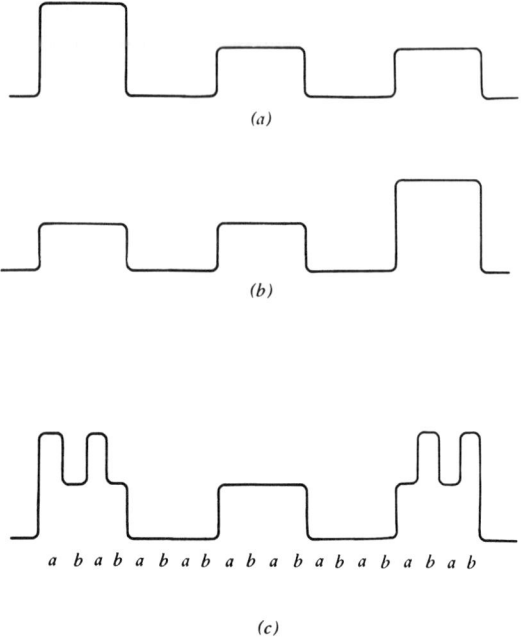

**Figure 8.4** In time-division multiplexing the two signals, (a) and (b) are alternately sampled to produce the resultant (c).

mentary form of switching that enables one class of user to economize on transmission lines.

## 8.4 SWITCHING

The case of switching more general than that just described involves making a choice of output channels and possibly order of transmission. A telephone switchboard is a form of switch, as the name implies. To reach any telephone extension connected to the switchboard, whether from an outside line or from another extension, a call goes through the switchboard, which connects it to the desired extension line. A telephone call from New York to Los Angeles, conveying voice or data, may involve several telephone company switching stations (Figure 8.7). Switches are used because it is impractical to directly connect every terminal with every other terminal or computer with which it may want to communicate. Just as multiplexing enables more than one message to use a channel at one time, switching enables more than one user to contend for access to a transmission channel

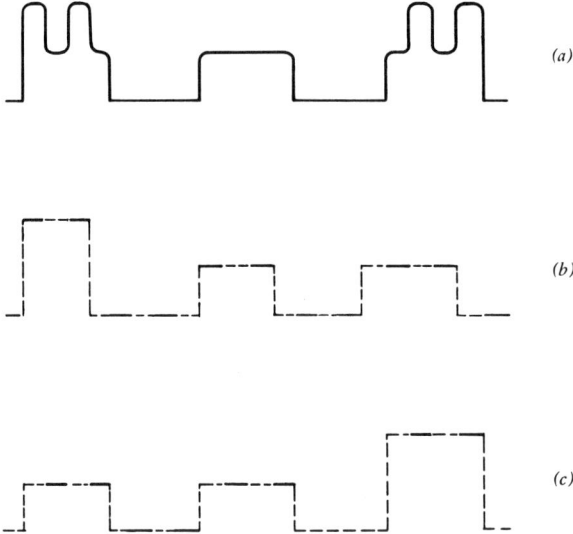

**Figure 8.5** Reconstructing signals from a multiplexed message. The incoming signal is sampled as indicated, and the two original signals are approximately reconstructed.

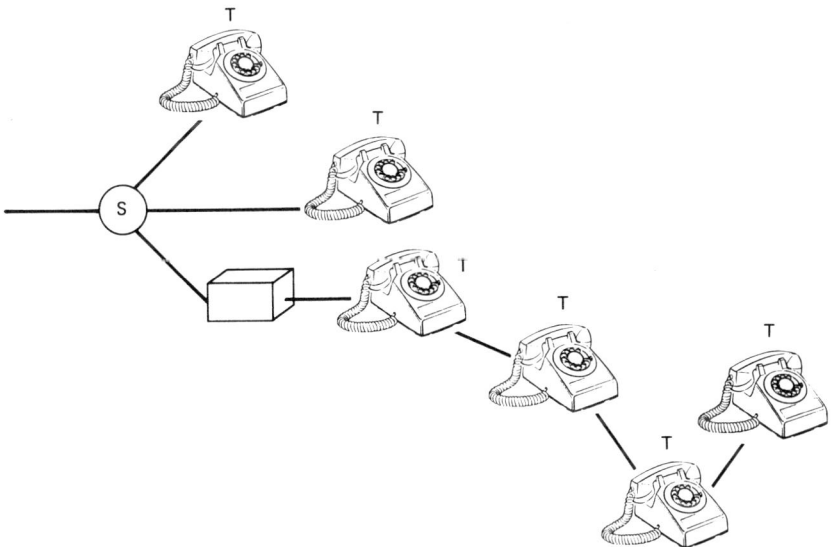

**Figure 8.6** A multidrop line: S = switching unit, T = terminal.

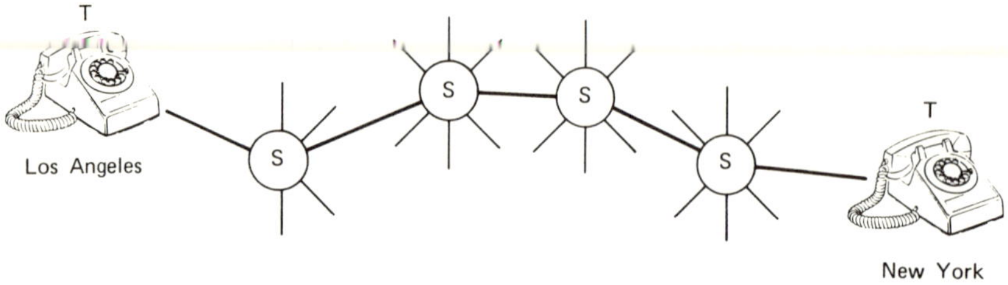

**Figure 8.7** Telephone call routed through a series of switches.

when the need arises. Switching systems carry the risk that no channel will be available when a transmitter wants to send a message.

There are two general kinds of switching, both applicable to data management. One is *line switching,* the other is *message switching.* Voice telephone is line switched. In this mode a given transmitter is assigned a channel for the duration of the transmission. (In high-priority cases, the assignment can be permanent.) When the call is completed, the channel reverts to the control of the switch and is available for assignment to another transmitter. If no channel is available when a transmitter has a message to send, the transmitter must wait. In voice telephone the caller would hear a busy signal or a recorded message such as "All circuits are busy. Please hang up and call again later." When more than one channel is available, the switch may attempt to find the most economical routing between source and destination.

Message switching is exemplified by a telegraph system or post office. The entire message is delivered at some input station, which then transmits it to its destination. Switching is involved because each input message has its own destination, and any input station accepts messages for any other station. The message may be sent to one or more intermediate locations where, again, a switching decision is made. It is not necessary to establish the complete route when the message is first accepted. Also, the message may be delayed in transmission. Once accepted, it is held until transmission facilities to its next destination (perhaps an intermediate switch) are available. On the other hand, there is rarely a delay in initial acceptance of an input. Message switching is probably more economical in most situations, since it uses a channel for a given message only as long as necessary to send that message, whereas a line-switched system must leave the line allocated to the transmitter until released, even if no message is being sent at any given time. Again, there are ways to override this rule. A long-distance call made from a pay telephone may be interrupted when the amount of money initially deposited has been used up.

To accomplish message switching, the message itself must contain an address and priority indication, as mail contains an address and some indication of class or type of service (e.g., airmail) being authorized. Collectively, this kind of information is called the message heading or *header*. In an automated switching system, a computer reads the header, extracts the needed information, surveys its available transmission and storage resources, and makes a decision whether to transmit or store, and if to transmit, over what channel. Message switching computers (described in Chapter 12) are among the units that may perform some error detection and correction functions.

Messages may be constrained to a maximum length in any given system. A message longer than the maximum must be broken into segments before sending. This process in itself causes no hardship, but since each message arriving at any switching computer separately enters the decision process that will determine whether to store or forward, message fragments that started out in one sequence may arrive in another. Even though segments may be required to be forwarded in the order in which received, selection of the best available route at any given time may send segment $i$ on a longer path than segment $i + 1$, which may depart later but arrive earlier. The switching computer that finally transmits the message segments to their destination terminal or computer should be required to reassemble the scattered fragments.

Whether messages are segmented or not segmented, it is common for any switch to keep a log of the messages arriving from each source, including other switches, and of the messages sent out. At the end of the day the various computers compare lists of messages sent and received to ensure that no traffic was lost. Any discrepancies can be made up by retransmitting a logged message.

## 8.5 COMPUTER MESSAGE PROCESSING

Until now we have viewed the computer (other than the switching computer) as just another terminal, the source or destination of messages. However, a modern teleprocessing (long-distance processing) computer may have many communication channels directly linked to it, unlike a true terminal, which links to only one line at a time. In effect, the computer serves as a switching system, transmitting messages back and forth between communication channels and the programs that are their ultimate sources or destinations. A program, of course, is not physically a source or destination—the computer operating that program is (the same computer that performs the switching function). To accomplish this internal switching, there is a control program (or *supervisory control program, I/O supervisor, communications supervisor,* or just *supervisor*) that may be part of the operating system or may run under the operating system as an application program. Both complex and critical to the success of teleprocessing systems, supervisor programs are now created and marketed separately from other software, although of course compatibility with standard operating systems is required. Individual systems vary in the work they perform, but the following functions are typical [4].

**Communications line control** The rate of transmission from computer or terminal to a computer tends to be much slower than is internal processing. The supervisor, therefore, may accept messages one character at a time, allowing some other functions to be performed between characters. (It takes 67 msec for a 15-character/sec transmission to send one character. During that time the computer can execute thousands of microsecond-duration commands. It takes only a few computer commands to read the character.) If there is more than one input line, the supervisor must take message fragments from all that are operating while still turning back to the operating system as much time as possible for other functions. Output is handled the same way. Outgoing messages may be sent one character at a time, there may be more than one line in use, and of course both input and output may be occurring simultaneously.

There are two general methods by which the supervisor reads incoming lines. It can scan the lines looking for one that is in process of delivering a character, read and store it, and go on to the next line. This is called *line polling*. Time must be taken to poll often enough to ensure that no input is lost. The other method is to let any input interrupt the computer, which then handles the line causing the interruption and returns to what it had been doing. In either method, an incoming message or fragment is usually placed in a *buffer storage* area until a decision is made regarding its disposition. The amount of memory that can be set aside for buffers can become a critical operating parameter of a data communications system. Similarly, buffers may be used to hold outbound messages between the time their channel has been selected and the time the transmission is complete.

**Message editing** Headers must be added to outgoing messages and stripped off incoming ones. Codes may have to be converted, errors detected (and, if so, retransmission requested), and a log of all traffic maintained, as done by the switch. All editing is communications oriented; it is not concerned with the content of the message.

**Scheduling and Queuing Messages** Since the timing of message arrival or departure and processing are not necessarily synchronized, messages may have to be queued while awaiting a free output line or output buffer, main memory space, or the availability of a processing program. Managing the queues entails entering messages awaiting some resource into a queue or withdrawing a message from a queue when a resource becomes available. Queue management is a supervisor function. Because of the priorities of either the programs or the messages, the sequence of removing messages from a queue may be different from the entry sequence.

*Calling Appropriate Programs* Once a message has been received, edited, and placed in a queue, the application program that will operate on it must be called into main memory (or found to be there already) and given the location of the newly arrived data. There are many ways of accomplishing this and many ways of dividing the program-calling function between the communications supervisor and the operating system. The programs that perform the functions described in the last three subsections can be viewed as application programs. In an interactive system the supervisor probably calls the programs, but in a batch mode system it may simply store data for later use and let the operating system take charge of bringing data and program together at another time.

*Interrupt Handling* Interrupt handling, too, may be a supervisor or operating system function. There are interrupts other than communications-related ones, such as completion of a tape or disk read operation.

*Recovery* The supervisor assists in restarting programs after a hardware failure. This is an intricate operation in a communications-oriented computer because there are so many messages in various states of assembly, disassembly, editing, queuing, and so on. Loss of computer power while examining a critical character in a message header could result in loss of the information and consequent misrouting of the message when power is restored.

## 8.6 APPLICATIONS OF DATA COMMUNICATIONS TO DATA MANAGEMENT

Our purpose here is to consider the types of services offered to users of data management through teleprocessing or data communications. In the chapters to follow, we give specific instructions for using the services. There are three rather traditional services, and several newer variants are beginning to appear. The basic three are on-line message processing, remote job entry, and time-sharing (with the implication of conversational processing—rapid exchange of messages). Cotton [5] adds to this list backup (the use of a remote computer as a temporary replacement for a local one), distributed multiprocessing (having more than one computer operate on data simultaneously), and teleconferencing (the use of a data communication system for sending individual messages, sometimes in a highly structured context).

### 8.6.1 On-Line Message Processing

We tend to use the term "on-line" today to mean *interactive,* but originally it meant merely that some piece of equipment was directly, electrically attached to a computer and under its control. For example, the first high-speed printers were not necessarily on-line. To save computer time, printing was done by connecting a free-standing tape unit to the printer and printing the contents of the tape independently of the computer. Multiprogramming made it more economical to put the printer on-line. Today we can have an on-line teletype that is used only as an input device, with no requirement at all for response back to that terminal. It is strictly a means for providing computer input. One can easily conceive of a network of these machines serving as nothing more than directly connected keypunches, sending data directly from source to computer. The computer could collect and store the data as they arrive and process them in the batch mode, according to a schedule, producing various reports on its printer. This method, which can be used for branch offices to report to a central location, has the advantage of reducing the number of manual operations performed on data, both speeding processing and reducing errors. An example is provided by a retail store chain whose branch managers place their orders for merchandise daily through a Touch-Tone telephone to a central ordering point but get no immediate feedback from the order [6]. In an air traffic control system, the radar inputs giving aircraft position are of this type. Radar data are fed into the computer for use as required. The fact that output goes to on-line display units for use by air traffic controllers is independent of the in-only nature of the radar data.

### 8.6.2 Remote Job Entry

Remote job entry (RJE) is a method by which a user sends his data or program, or both, to a computer and requests that a program (the one transmitted or one previously stored) be executed. The program is run is a normal multiprogrammed fashion (i.e., the request for the program is placed in a queue and serviced in turn). The output of the requested program may then be transmitted back to the user or it may be printed or stored locally in the computer center. A typical RJE terminal is not the desk-top variety; rather, it is a high-speed unit that includes a card reader and high-speed printer (high compared to teletype). It may include a magnetic type drive, a card punch, or a graphic plotter. However, if data and programs are stored at the computer center, they can be run in RJE mode from any low-speed typewriter or teletype-style terminal, since the data for input need not be transmitted—the terminal can get the run started simply by transmitting information about the run.

As with an on-line message processing system, the advantages of RJE to the user are speed of transmission, reduction of human handling, and making available of facilities to people who, because of distance, would otherwise have none. RJE is sometimes used by people in the same building that houses the computer center, to avoid the delay of internal mailing of input or output and the errors caused by repetitive human handling of card decks. Under appropriately low load conditions, turnaround time can be as low as 5 minutes, and this can begin to approximate interactive processing in some cases.

A data management user of RJE can enter data on-line, as in on-line message processing, and can request that reports be compiled and transmitted back to him. If these can be returned within 5–15 minutes, we have the approach to interactive information retrieval mentioned previously. This mode of operation is not particularly effective when the user is not certain what data he wants to see, or in what form, but it can be highly effective when he is asking for standard reports on a new batch of data.

### 8.6.3 Time-Sharing

There are several forms of time-sharing used with data management: (*a*) "true" time-sharing, involving the apparently simultaneous operation of unrestricted programs, (*b*) simultaneous use of a single program, operating in a dedicated computer, by multiple users, and (*c*) simultaneous use of a single program operating on a multiprogramming basis, possibly with other multiuser programs.

In time-sharing, each program being operated is independent of any other. If more than one user requests the same program, either separate copies of the program are given, or access to one program is written in reentrant code [7]. Reentrant code is a method of programming in which the program is never modified and any intermediate values computed are separately maintained for each different user. Hence one user can execute instructions 1–100 and be interrupted by the next user who operates instructions 50–150, yet the users will not interfere with each other. The main use of time-sharing is in program writing and debugging, where we may include queries in the term "program." Executing completed programs tends to be more efficient in RJE mode.

It is quite usual for an information retrieval program to be in operation for a long period, doing relatively little work for any one user per unit of time. The program must await human-rate input, human reading of output, and thinking by the user about what to do next. During these delays, the program's only duty, for that user, is to monitor the individual's input line to see if he has sent any new message. Therefore these programs are usually designed to service more than one user at a time; this is done not by time-sharing among different versions or writing in reentrant code but by having the program written to ensure that the application program distributes its attention over several user requests, giving the impression that it is working for all at once. In fact, sometimes it can work for several users at once, by batching requests or portions of them, perhaps by accumulating a small batch of requests for one file, then retrieving them in one file search. If an interactive information retrieval system such as this were to consume the entire capacity of a computer at one time, it would be called a *dedicated computer*.

Now faster computers and auxiliary memories, larger main memories, and better communications supervisory programs enable multiuser conversational programs to be multiprogrammed with other programs. Other programs, especially those of the mathematical variety that have low input-output requirements and long stretches of internal computing, can run during the frequent I/O delays of a multiuser information retrieval program, and there is little interference to either by the others. The load on the supervisor is high, although the functions of this component are the same as for a single application program. The overall system may show great fluctuation in the speed of response to individual users if a large number are contending for communication facilities. Nevertheless, time-sharing is becoming the normal mode of operation.

### 8.6.4 Backup

Since computers are necessities in many offices and laboratories, they require some form of reserve facility in case of failure. For a batch mode facility, arrangements can be made almost anywhere there is a compatible computer. But the backup facility for a communications-dependent computer must be part of the same network, or at least fully compatible with all the communications equipment, to ensure that it can be switched onto the network on short notice. In the event of a failure of one computer, users may not see much difference between the original and the replacement computer. Of course arrangements must be made beforehand to be sure that the backup computer has the same programs, including a fully compatible operating system, as the machine it replaces.

### 8.6.5 Distributed Multiprocessing

Distributed multiprocessing is the use of two or more computers to work on the same problem. *Multiprocessing,* as differentiated from *multiprogramming,* is the use of more than one central processing unit in a computer system. The purpose of the extra processors might be redundancy (one machine primarily to back up another, while both monitor the same problem and perhaps even execute the same programs, permitting either to take over full responsibility at any time), sharing of load, or distributing work between machines to take best advantage of the individual capabilities of each (e.g., one entirely devoted to communications supervision, the other to processing data from the communications computer). In distributed multiprocessing, the two (or more) computers need not be at the same location.

### 8.6.6 Teleconferencing

The ability to pass messages among users, or between users and an operator at a central location, was a feature of many early on-line systems. Gradually the message-passing capability was recognized as having a potential for conducting conferences through the medium of the data communications network. Messages could be routed from anyone to any one participant or any group of participants, and the computer could be programmed to ask for certain information from each participant, then disseminate it in processed form to others [8]. It is not necessary for all participants to be on-line at the same time. Messages can be stored and later retrieved and responded to by any participant.

The coupling of computers with communications networks may prove to be one of man's most significant technological achievements. In this chapter we have reviewed the elements of data communication. We now proceed to explore some broader aspects of data management, returning to the marriage of communications and data management in Chapter 12.

## REFERENCES

1. Edgar C. Gentle, Jr., *Data Communications in Business, An Introduction,* American Telephone & Telegraph Co., New York, 1965, p. 1.
2. William P. Davenport, *Modern Data Communication,* Hayden Book Co., New York, 1971, p. i.
3. Claude E. Shannon and Warren Weaver, *The Mathematical Theory of Communication,* University of Illinois Press, Urbana, 1959, p. 5.

4. James Martin, *Programming Real-Time Computer Systems,* Prentice-Hall, Englewood Cliffs, N.J., 1965, pp. 150-2.
5. Ira W. Cotton, "Computer Networks: Capabilities and Limitations." In *Structural Mechanics Computer Programs,* W. Pilkey, K. Saczalski, and H. Schaeffer, Eds., University Press of Virginia, Charlottesville, 1974.
6. Charles T. Meadow, *Man-Machine Communication,* Wiley-Interscience, New York, 1970, pp. 182, 187-8.
7. Anthony Ralston, *Introduction to Programming and Computer Science,* McGraw-Hill Book Co., New York, 1971, p. 452.
8. Murray Turoff, "Delphi and Its Potential Impact on Information Systems," *AFIPS Conference Proceedings,* Vol. 39, November 1971, pp. 317-26.

## RECOMMENDED READING

### Communications Concepts

Crowley, Thomas H., et al., *Modern Communications,* Columbia University Press, New York, 1962.

Martin, James, *Telecommunications and the Computer,* Prentice-Hall, Englewood Cliffs, N.J., 1969.

Pierce, J. R., *Symbols, Signals and Noise,* Harper & Row, New York, 1961.

### Signal and Message Processing

Abrams, Marshall D., "Remote Computing: The Administrative Side," *Computer Decisions,* October 1973, pp. 42-46.

Abramson, Norman, and Franklin F. Kuo, Eds., *Computer-Communication Networks,* Prentice-Hall, Englewood Cliffs, N.J., 1973.

Davey, J. R., "Modems," *Proceedings of the IEEE,* Vol. 60, No. 11, November 1972, pp. 1284-1301.

Martin [4].

### Applications

Cotton [5].

Katzan, Harry, Jr., *Operating Systems, A Pragmatic Approach,* Van Nostrand Reinhold, New York, 1973.

Lancaster, F. Wilfrid, and E. G. Fayen, *Information Retrieval On-Line,* Melville Publishing Co., Los Angeles, 1973.

Mader, Chris, and Robert Hagin, *Information Systems: Technology, Economic, Applications,* Science Research Associates, Chicago, 1974.

*Chapter Nine*

# Generalized Data Management Systems

## 9.1 THE CONCEPT OF A GENERALIZED DATA MANAGEMENT SYSTEM

*Generalized data management systems* (GDMS) have been developed to avoid requiring the end-user of an information system to deal with the intricate types of programs previously described so far and, aside from user convenience, to save on the cost of programming. A GDMS is a set of computer programs and languages that bring data into a computer, organize the data for storage, store and retrieve records, maintain files, process user queries and other commands to a system, and transmit or display retrieved data. These are the functions that are apparent to the user. In addition, there may be other supporting functions necessary to carry out the user-apparent functions. Although a GDMS performs a wide variety of functions, it does not incorporate all the file organizational techniques discussed earlier. A few offer a choice of method, some only one. The user must select the GDMS that best fits his particular problem needs.

There is little that is standard in data management. It is hard to provide a precise list of functions and insist that only programs performing these can qualify. The following three user-apparent functions, however, serve as a base of discussion.

1. *Data definition.* For describing the structure of data files, the GDMS normally provides a language that is simplified in comparison to a general-purpose programming language. This not only reduces the manpower cost of data definition but permits a nonexpert programmer to do the work, thereby moving the use of computers closer to the end-user of information.
2. *Retrieval specification.* The GDMS furnishes a problem-oriented language, tailored to a particular class of data processing programs—those primarily concerned with selecting information from files and organizing it for reports. As with data definition, simplification of this process reduces the cost of using the system and makes it available to other than professional programmers.
3. *Output specification.* The outputs are usually limited to terminal displays (on a CRT or print terminal) or printed reports. A "report" in this sense is a listing of a substantial number of records or portions thereof, as contrasted with printing or display of only a few items of information selected from a file. Most business systems are still centered around the report as the primary output of a computer.

These three functions may seem to be of less than earthshaking importance, but writing programs in a general-purpose language to create a file, select information from it, and print it can be a painstakingly slow and error-prone undertaking. Even more important, the hand-tailored programs have a tendency to be resistant to change. The programmer cannot foresee what the user is going to want to change, but he can be sure that changes will be made. He cannot write each program to allow any element in it to be changed easily. Yet the GDMS does, or attempts to do, just that. Initial programming using a GDMS is more economical, but it is in *reprogramming* that the real benefits are found.

Like other forms of high-order programming, a GDMS is often charged with being inefficient in the use of computer time. This is a difficult point to prove either way, because of the high cost of duplicating programming for test purposes. When first asked to work in a high-order language, a programmer often insists that he could write more efficient code than the compiler or the GDMS can. There are two points in rebuttal of this argument. First, the cost of computer time is not the sole component of system cost. It is necessary to consider how much more efficient one program is than the other, and how much the added efficiency costs. The trend for years has been for manpower costs to go up and computer costs to go down. Second, although *some* programmers can write more efficient code than a compiler can, it is not clear that all programmers, or even most, are so able. One must demand proof from the claimant that he can make good on his claim.

There is yet another reason for programmer resistance to the GDMS. Some feel that the simplified data definition, retrieval specification, and output specification of the GDMS are demeaning to the professional programmer, and they worry that conversion to it will cause them to lose their skills. They may be right on both counts, but management has the obligation to judge value by results, not by the application of skill.

A GDMS generally attempts to offer a particular class of users all the facilities they need to solve a particular class of problem. In other cases the GDMS answers only some of the known user needs and is built with the understanding that other software will have to provide the remaining facilities. The system that is complete in itself is called a *stand-alone* or *independent system*. It is not a component of another program. A program such as ISAM or a communications interface is not in itself a problem-solving program. To be used, it must be combined with other programs.

The stand-alone GDMS has its own language processor, the program that translates user commands and definitions into machine language commands, and its own means of linking to the computer's operating system. The dependent GDMS requires what is known as a *host language,* which implies both the programming language and its compiler. When used with a host language, the GDMS is addressed by commands recognizable and interpretable by the host language processor. It is far less expensive to produce a dependent GDMS because of some of the most difficult programming can be omitted and the functions performed by the host processor. Generally, a tie to a programming language makes the dependent GDMS less easy for the nonprogrammer to use.

In the preceding chapters we have considered component programs; now we address the complete system. Also in this chapter we bring out some of the differences between interactive and batch-mode systems, which may perform essentially the same functions from the user's point of view but nevertheless may operate in different ways and may have different program structures. In Chapter 10 we describe how systems appear to the user.

### 9.1.1 Examples of GDMS

There are many examples of GDMS commercially marketed under various names by computer manufacturers and independent software firms. They represent, perhaps, the fastest growing segment of the computer software market; indeed, a listing tends to become outdated within a year. For this reason, we restrict our coverage of specific systems to a few and reference lists and comparative analyses published elsewhere [1–4].

Two of our examples, Mark IV and S-2000, are well-known commercial systems. The other two are not even accepted as GDMS by all authorities. One of these is primarily an information retrieval system, intended to work mainly on files of literature citations—a bibliographic system. Its main difference from other GDMS is that it is not very flexible in the area of data definition. It is assumed that users will not vary much in file structure and that they will content themselves with retrieval, modifying files little and processing output only to format it. Users can modify files, but usually only in batch mode, while retrieval is on-line, and they can specify file structure but not in a particularly simple manner. The other nonstandard "GDMS" is a general-purpose programming language, which we include in our list for comparison purpose because it can do everything the GDMS can, except make itself readily useful to nonprogrammers.

*System 2000* Produced by MRI Systems Corporation, System 2000 can be used as a stand-alone GDMS or through a Procedural Language Feature, as a component of a COBOL or FORTRAN program. It has a language for users who are not programmers and it has a Report Writer Feature, which is a high-order language for generating lengthy or complex reports. Its Immediate Access Feature provides for interactive use of the system from remote terminals.

System 2000 has a data definition language rather similar to that of COBOL, although there are differences. Data elements in System 2000 are definable in a number of formats, such as *integer, name* (alphanumeric), or *date* (a numeric field containing three subfields and of the form *mmddyy* or *mmddyyyy*). Data can be defined hierarchically, there are the equivalent of groups and arrays, and portions of logical records can be split between direct and sequential memory, to economize on storage cost for record segments not often used.

The user can define one or more keys for a file, creating inverted indexes on as many fields as he wishes. The query language permits use of both key and nonkey fields in specifying retrieval criteria. The query language also includes commands for sequencing output and for limited computation on retrieved data.

File maintenance can be done on a batch basis or by immediate access from a terminal, giving the user a choice of the more machine-efficient approach or the more costly but often necessary immediate update [5].

*The Mark IV File Management System* Mark IV, produced by Informatics, Inc., is an older system, probably the first true commercial success in the field. This stand-alone system can accommodate COBOL subroutines when the user needs more complex selection or processing logic than its own language provides, but it may not be operated as a component of another program.

Mark IV uses a nonprocedural language. Basically, one *describes* selection criteria and output specifications, rather than telling *how* to select and format output, as with a procedural language. (Almost all the standard programming languages are procedural.) A set of forms is provided, one for each major function the system performs. These are filled out, and the contents are keypunched, then entered into the computer much like source language program statements. There are forms entitled *File Definition, Processing and Record Selection,* and *Output Content Specification.* Some numeric processing of selected data is possible, as is sequencing of output. File change data are submitted in a file, and another form governs their use in modifying files.

The system has been improved and added to many times since its inception. Users' confidence that this will continue to happen is one of the product's strengths in the marketplace. Like System 2000, Mark IV now has an interactive language capability for on-line use, and its selection and output specification forms correspond to the report-writing capability of the newer system.

One of the key differences between Mark IV and System 2000 is in the use of inverted indexes. Lacking this feature, Mark IV is severely limited in the economy of searching a file on any basis other than the value of its sort key [6].

*DIALOG* A product of Lockheed Missiles and Space Company, DIALOG is related to a system used by the National Aeronautics and Space Administration, called RECON. DIALOG is an interactive bibliographic information retrieval system. It is designed to be readily used by people having no training in programming, but data definition is not as generalized as retrieval and must be left to the professional programmer. Files can be updated only in batch mode, not at all from remote terminals.

Users can query files of literature citations or similar material, or a thesaurus. At file definition time the user specifies which fields are to appear in a thesaurus; this file lists all values of the specified field that occur and the number of occurrences, and points to other, semantically related field values. For example, the word COMPUTER may occur as a subject term. The thesaurus may list it, show the number of literature citations in which it occurred, tell how many semantically related terms, such as CALCULATOR, are in the thesaurus, and point to them.

The query language requires designation of the field name and a value. A set of records meeting that specification is created by setting up a list of pointers, not by actually copying the records. Sets may also be defined in terms of other sets. For example, set 1 may be defined by AU= SMITH, which designates the *author* field and a value for it. Set 2 may be defined by COMPUTER, the absence of a field name indicating a subject descriptor. Set

3 might be defined by the command COMBINE 1∗2, or create the intersection of sets 1 and 2. The user may have to define many sets before he has the combination he feels will best produce the results he wants. After each definition he is given a count of the number of records in the set and has an opportunity to have some or all of the citations referenced in the sets displayed on his terminal. Unlike the business user, the bibliographic searcher is rarely interested in all records that meet his formal specification. He will probably want to reduce the size of a set to a managable number because he is going to have to find the corresponding documents and, eventually, read them.

There are several options on format of output displays, but the user can select only from among a few predetermined ones. He cannot define his own format at the terminal. There is no capability to process output data.

DIALOG is representative of a class of highly specialized systems. To perform its specialized tasks using System 2000 or Mark IV would be more cumbersome and less efficient. However, DIALOG is clearly limited in its capabilities and is not appropriate for general-purpose business use [7].

*COBOL* By most definitions, COBOL or any other programming language is not a GDMS, but it is worth considering what the GDMS can do that COBOL cannot. Because it is general purpose and can link itself to the data management facilities of the operating system COBOL can provide the data definition, file organization, storage, and retrieval functions and output formatting of a GDMS. It does lack, in many implementations, the ability to communicate directly with terminal users. The general-purpose COBOL language has an advantage in that its formalities rarely limit what the user can do. The disadvantage of using a general-purpose language lies mainly in the amount of work that falls to the programmer, compared with the user of a GDMS. Use of COBOL is beyond the competence of the non-programmer. Therefore, not only does it involve extra work for data management, but there must be communication between the user of the information and the programmer, which offers much opportunity for misunderstanding and, eventually, greater cost. Thus systems such as System 2000 and Mark IV strike a balance between the generality of COBOL and the speciality of DIALOG. A large class of users want and need this particular balance.

### 9.1.2 Components of a GDMS

From the viewpoint of the end-user—the person whose interest in the system is presumably confined to the information it delivers to him—all generalized data management systems may appear very much alike. However, they may vary considerably in the way that basic functions are assigned to the various program components. Rarely is a GDMS so constructed that a user interested only in certain functions can readily find and separate the programs that perform those functions. Indeed, often the only real difference among competing products is that they have packaged the same ideas differently.

The following list of functions (not necessarily programs) that are usually performed by a GDMS goes into more detail than the list of three user-apparent functions introduced earlier.

- communications interface
- input checking and validation
- control of programs comprising the GDMS
- language processing (of query, formatting and maintenance commands)
- data definition
- data management
- restart and recovery
- utilities
- linkage to other program systems

We have already described communications interface (Chapter 8) and data management (Chapters 3–7). The remaining functions are described in the following sections of this chapter, roughly in the order of operation within a GDMS.

## 9.2. INPUT CHECKING AND VALIDATION

We may say dogmatically that data should be tested for validity upon entering a computer. There is no uniform standard indicating how to test or how intensively to test, at the least, however, data values that might prevent subsequent programs from operating correctly or efficiently should be detected. Failure to carry out tests may also lower the quality of files by permitting erroneous data to be stored in them—and possibly retrieved and used before anyone discovers the error. An example of the kind of item that should be tested is a field to be used for computing a storage address. An out-of-range value could produce miscalculation of an address from a key, resulting in a record being stored in an area reserved for another file or for programs. Thus a data change could modify a program and cause a major system malfunction.

Tests may be simple: verifying that all characters of a field are members of the correct alphabet or that a numeric field has a value within a stated range. More complex tests may involve conditional expressions (e.g.,

IF GRADE = 15 THEN 10,000 ≤ SALARY ≤ 25,000) or functions of fields (e.g., DUEDATE = TODAY + 30) or may compare old and new values of a field (e.g., SALARYINCREMENT ≤ .1∗SALARY).

The discovery of invalid fields calls for decisions regarding whether the entire record must be rejected, only the field rejected, or merely an annotation made on an error listing that will go to a data control clerk. Total rejection may be expensive and may introduce intolerable delays in entering information into files. Acceptance pending later revision may permit erroneous data to be retrieved and used before the correction is made. On the other hand, if the error is in the sort key, total rejection of the record may be necessary. Ignoring the problem of validation is a positive decision to permit erroneous data to accumulate and be used. The consequences of this decision were explored in Section 7.4.

## 9.3 CONTROL OF PROGRAMS COMPRISING THE GDMS

Program control is a function necessary in interactive data management systems and useful with batch-mode systems as well. It is a small, specialized version of an operating system that calls elements of the GDMS into play as needed. The level at which the larger operating systems work is seldom sufficiently detailed. What is needed is a program that looks at incoming commands and requests and calls for the data or programs needed to fulfill the input request. This involves making decisions based on input data, which is something operating systems normally do not do. To the operating system, the GDMS control program is an application program. To other GDMS component programs, the control program is the operating system. Thus individual GDMS components are relieved of the responsibility for resolving conflicts in requests for computer resources. A control program that is primarily responsive to user commands is often called a *command processor*.

Calling the appropriate data and program components into main memory and supervising the sequence of program operation can be a straightforward function, or it can be so complex as to be virtually a time-sharing operating system. For example, a control program might receive a command and oversee its complete execution before considering the next command. Or, the control program might accept commands from a number of users, then execute a small portion of each, in sequence, ensuring that execution of all pending commands is interleaved. This approach, which is a form of time-sharing, might yield greater machine efficiency and faster response to users, but at the cost of a more expensive, memory-consuming control program.

The control program may perform identification (i.e., verifying that a user's access to a file is authorized), execute high-order or *system commands* (which call a major GDMS component into play, perhaps a retrieval or report-generating function, as contrasted with commands that give an order to the component), and oversee the execution of the specific commands to store, retrieve, or process data by passing them to the appropriate GDMS components. A typical sequence of inputs might be identification of the user, request by him for a file update module of the GDMS (system command), entry of new data through the update module, request for a retrieval module (system command), entry of retrieval criteria, and sign-off (system command).

## 9.4 LANGUAGE PROCESSING

There are three major language needs of a GDMS user: (1) to specify the logic of a search and the information to be retrieved (query), (2) to specify what is to be done with output, both in terms of where to deliver it (terminal, printer, memory unit, etc.) and how to format it, and (3) to specify how files are to be changed—the file maintenance functions described in Chapter 7.

A GDMS usually has its own language for expressing these specifications, and it is usually a function of the GDMS to translate the statements in that language either into machine language or into some intermediary form. Some of the languages are described in Chapter 10. Suffice it to say that we are talking about programming functions, and a language for describing them is a programming language, however well disguised as natural language or tailored to particular applications. Languages are often disguised or tailored to simplify their use by nonprogrammers.

The language translation can be done in several ways. The GDMS can serve as its own compiler, translating high-order commands directly into machine language. Or, if a host language is used, the GDMS can pass the burden of language interpretation to the host language compiler, a far less expensive way to produce a GDMS. Finally, the GDMS can translate statements in its special-purpose language into high-order, general-purpose programming language statements and allow these to be compiled by the language's compiler. This approach, called a *generator,* differs from use of a host language because the user writes entirely in the GDMS language and may be unaware of the use of the general-purpose language. Interactive systems tend to require the first of these possibilities. The time required to call a general-purpose compiler into play may not be compatible with the response time requirements of such systems.

## 9.5 DATA DEFINITION

Data definition is the specification of the characteristics of files and data elements that a program works with. Different programs may need different kinds of information about the data they are to process. For example, a sequential access data manager needs only minimal information, since it can exercise only minimal options. It needs to know the location of a file (disk or tape unit), the identification of the storage unit (number of the disk pack or reel of tape), and record and block size. None of this relates to internal record structure or to the basis for file sequence. ISAM needs additional information: the value of the sequence key and the overflow structure in use. A COBOL compiler must know the complete details of record structure and specifications for each constituent group or field. In fact, all compilers need this type of information; hence all programming languages either have a set of statements for defining data attributes or assume the attributes. The original BASIC language, for example, recognized only floating point numeric variables and literal strings. A character string within a program statement enclosed in quotation marks, such as "A6," was assumed to be a literal; absence of quotation marks was taken to imply that the string was the name of a data element and A6 was therefore a data element name. FORTRAN assumes data elements whose names begin with I, J, K, L, M, or N are integer variables, and all others are floating point variables unless the programmer overrides these assumptions with an explicit definition.

COBOL has an elaborate data definition language to convey data attributes to the compiler. The *data division* of a COBOL program, which contains this information, is separate from the *procedure division,* which specifies how data are to be processed. FORTRAN and PL/I permit the programmer to embed data definition statements among the procedural statements. The advantage of a separate data definition is that all data specifications can be found easily if a change is to be made, and if a program is to process a record that has already been defined to an earlier program, a portion of the latter's data division can be copied into the new program, ensuring identical definitions. The advantage of embedding definitions among procedural statements is that a programmer can make a definition when he perceives the need for it and does not have to skip around in his own program to define a new element.

A long-range goal of many GDMS designers is to develop a data definition language, independent of the computer programming language used to process data, that can be "understood" by the compilers of COBOL, FORTRAN, or PL/I. This would mean that a file or record had to be defined only once, regardless of the number of different programs, programming languages, or computers that deal with the file. Currently, what to the user may seem to be the same file, can have different specifications as defined in the different programming languages, as organized under different file structures, or even if processed by different computers. A goal less ambitious than full interlanguage communication is to have a single data description for a data base such that each program using any part of the data base can draw on the same difinition; all programs would have to be written in the same language, however. If changes had to be made to any data elements, they would be made just once, and uniformly, regardless of the number of programs using the elements. This is by no means a trivial problem. Large information systems may contain hundreds of programs, and many of them refer to common files. If each program had its own complete data definitions finding and changing all references to the definition of any given item would become a formidable bookkeeping problem.

The Data Base Task Group of the Conference on Data Systems Languages (CODASYL), the organization responsible for the development of COBOL, has long been at work on the data definition problem. They have defined their purpose in this way [8]:

> Historically, control over data has gradually been relinquished by individual programmers in favor of a more centralized and coordinated control. This development has parallelled a change in the philosophy of processing away from the traditional approach where data is always accessed by one run-unit at a time. In such an environment files are frequently designed to optimize the processing of a run-unit; for other processing to be performed on the same data, the files are re-sorted or new files are created which redundantly include the same data. The traditional approach to data was thus to create process-oriented files. This is adequate in some circumstances, but is too costly or impractical in others. It is too costly in that today's storage devices permit a more integrated approach to be taken to data; one which permits multiple applications to use and share the same data without requiring redundancy. Since the quantities of data have a tendency to be large and ever expanding and since data acquisition and maintenance costs are high, this is an important consideration. The traditional approach is becoming increasingly impractical in that it is unsuitable for an environment where message processing is involved, especially when the data is used by more than one application or process. A point has now been reached where in designing systems capable of handling our current demands, it is essential to develop data bases that are available to and suitable for processing by multiple applications and that can be interfaced by multiple languages.

The Data Base Task Group's objective in developing these proposals was to make this possible by providing features which:

- allow data to be structured in the manner most suitable to each application, regardless of the fact that some or all of that data may be used by other applications—such flexibility to be achieved without requiring data redundancy

## 184 Generalized Data Management Systems

- allow more than one run-unit to concurrently retrieve or update the data in the database
- provide and permit the use of a variety of search strategies against an entire database or portions of a database
- provide protection of the database against unauthorized access of data and from untoward interaction of programs
- provide for centralized capability to control the physical placement of data
- provide device independence for programs
- allow the declaration of a variety of data structures ranging from those in which no connection exists between data-items to network structures
- allow the user to interact with the data while being relieved of the mechanics of maintaining the structural associations which have been declared
- allow programs to be as independent of the data as current techniques will permit
- provide for separate descriptions of the data in the database and of the data known to a program
- provide for a description of the database which is not restricted to any particular processing language
- provide an architecture which permits the description of the database, and the database itself, to be interfaced by multiple processing languages

## 9.6 RESTART AND RECOVERY

Restart is the rerunning of a computer program that has been interrupted for some reason, such as a hardware malfunction. When a malfunction occurs, restarting is not just a matter of resuming from the interrupted position. It is necessary to go through a recovery process, finding out what the status of the computer was when it quit, resetting to that status, and ensuring that all data are made available. One form of restart is simply to begin the interrupted program at the beginning, as if it had never been run before. Two problems are associated with this approach: (1) some programs take so long to run that to begin again is a major drain on computer time, and (2) if the program is maintaining an on-line file, that file has already been partially changed and it may not be possible to process the same set of changes against the now-changed file. For example, one form of change might be to increase an employee's salary by 10%. If, after this step has been done, the program is interrupted and then begun again from the start, the lucky employee would receive a raise of 21%.

By "restart," generally we mean restart from approximately the point of interrruption, giving due recognition to the problem of partially processed data. As an example of the difficulty involved, consider a search of a sequential file stored on tape. Suppose the computer is about to execute a GET NEXT command when it suddenly "goes down." While down, or while the computer operators are preparing to begin operation again, the tape is rewound. Now, the GET NEXT command no longer means what it originally meant, because the computer system is in a different state. The record that will be retrieved by GET NEXT now will not be the same as before. To restore the meaning of the command, the tape must be repositioned, and this requires information on what the position was when the malfunction occurred.

Not only is information needed on state of the system, but it must be accessible—it must be in a memory that can be successfully read after a power failure or even after replacement of a hardware component. To avoid having the computer completely taken up with recording its own status, status information is recorded at intervals, not continuously. This is sometimes called a *snapshot* (a picture of the whole) or a *checkpoint* (the recording of information needed to establish the status at a given time). In addition, all data entering the system are recorded on a log. Should the malfunction occur after the checkpoint has been taken, upon restart the computer begins processing again at the checkpoint and repeats whatever processing was done after that checkpoint but before the failure. Required for this are complete copies of the files, or at least the originals of the records modified as of the taking of the checkpoint, as well as a copy of all input data received.

As with any security or insurance plan, a balance must be reached between the desire for complete safety and the cost of providing it. Realistic checkpoint-recovery-restart plans involve some risk, at least the risk of having to go through an expensive process to restart a computer. Programs that run for only a few minutes and do not involve use of large data files may not need restart capability because it would be almost as economical to run them over from scratch as to resume from the point of interruption. But it is less easy to reinitiate data management systems, particularly on-line systems, that may be operating throughout the day, constantly bringing in new data and generating reports or responses to queries. An interactive system, for example, gets its input from terminals and returns messages to them. Even if a log is maintained of every input to a system, the program operation cannot be exactly duplicated without having messages sent and received as they were the first time. During restart, then, messages might be transmitted to terminals yet the inputs would be taken from a file of previous terminal-to-computer messages, rather than from the terminals, until the state immediately prior to the stoppage could be reestablished. Hence a system such as this must have an elaborate checkpoint-recovery-restart facility that saves system state information periodically and is able to reposition itself to resume processing at the checkpoint position.

## 9.7 UTILITIES

A data management system usually has associated with it a set of miscellaneous programs called *utilities*. These might include a sort program, a file reorganization program, file copying programs, print programs, and memory dumps. There is no reason for not performing these functions through regular processing commands (each then being considered a GDMS component), but often they are not packaged that way by the software producer. Instead, they may be invoked by system-level commands or as programs operated independently of the GDMS. In the latter case utilities are hierarchically equal to the data management system itself or to its major components. This is partly because GDMS rely on utilities provided with the operating system. Such reliance reduces the cost of the GDMS but changes the language for invoking utility functions from that of the GDMS to that of the operating system. Another typical attribute of utilities is that they are not interactive programs. Since they can be run in batch mode, the request language for an interactive system must recognize that their operation may be called for at a time remote from that in which it is requested.

## 9.8 LINKAGE TO OTHER SYSTEMS

No GDMS performs all possible data processing functions. Often it is desirable to retrieve data using a GDMS for passage to a standard mathematical program residing in a library, for example, where further processing would occur. Or, the processing program might be one that operates on input to the GDMS. At such times it would be convenient to ensure that the processing program and the GDMS are compatible in regard to data structures and definition. More likely than not, the processing program has its own rigid requirements for input and output and a conversion of format is necessary. Conversion can be achieved in a variety of ways. Ideally, the GDMS and the processing program would address a logical structure and would be unconcerned with the physical structure of the input or output files. Unfortunately, this is rarely possible. More likely, the GDMS takes the responsibility to reformat input to a processing program or to reformat its output when received by the GDMS. This calls for some versatility on the part of the GDMS, but more important, it requires that the file specifications of the processing program be made known to the GDMS. This, in turn, implies a programmer's intervention and limits the likelihood that a user could simply request, "run program $p$ on the output of the following query...."

## 9.9 SELECTION OF A GDMS

A large fraction of the total computer usage of many organizations involves a GDMS, and business files are all or mostly under its control. Thus the scrutiny given to the GDMS before purchase is far more careful than for any other program. An operating system may seem to be more critical, but once computer hardware is selected there is usually little choice of operating systems. Also, nonprogrammer users do not particularly relate to operating systems, but they can, or think they can, understand the requirements for and functions of data management systems. With GDMS, a potential buyer has a wide choice because the programs are produced and marketed by computer manufacturers and many independent software firms.

It has become common though not universal practice to draw up a lengthy feature list of GDMS requirements and compare candidates on many parameters, including number of levels of hierarchy permitted in a record structure or existence of the operator NOT in the query language. The best known feature list is that produced by CODASYL [4]. Often the items in a feature list are numerically weighted by the potential user organization. This is a valuable exercise. If nothing more, it forces the reviewers to examine competing products in great detail. However, this author has never seen a justification of the system of weights or a systematic way to consider how capabilities not directly provided for could be achieved. For example, if a language lacks the NOT operator, it may still be possible to accomplish the objective of the buying organization through the use of NOT EQUAL and comparable relationships. Lack of levels of hierarchy can be compensated for by segmenting records, and although this practice may appear to be limiting, the need for it is not always present. On the other hand, certain rather broad requirements, often hard to quantify, may be more important than some of the specific technical points. For example, is the product already in operation? How many users are there? Is there a user organization exerting serious influence on the producer? Where is the nearest maintenance office? What guarantees are provided of software reliability?

The appendix contains a feature list such as we have described, used by The Council of Great City Schools, Washington, D.C., for GDMS procurement. Bidders were asked to describe their product using the outline provided, and the list includes some of the broader features as well as the detailed technical ones.

The generalized data management system has become one of the most important software components of many large business data processing centers. Unlike selection of an operating system, which is normally an item of little or no choice once computer hardware has been chosen, the GDMS is separately procured. Thereafter it can dominate application system design and may deeply affect the attitudes of users and managers toward data processing. Generally, the flexibility of a GDMS—ability to change data structures and to implement new report programs quickly—has brought data processing to a new level of acceptance by management.

## REFERENCES

1. Ruth K. Anderson, *Index of Data Management Software Packages*, NBS Report 10-932, National Bureau of Standards, Washington, D.C., 1972.
2. Dennis W. Fife et al., *A Technical Index of Interactive Information Systems*, NBS Technical Note 819, National Bureau of Standards, Washington, D.C., 1974.
3. Thomas H. Martin, *A Feature Analysis of Interactive Retrieval Systems*, Report SU-COMM-ICR-74-1. Institute for Communication Research, Stanford University, Stanford, Calif., September 1974.
4. CODASYL Systems Committee, *Feature Analysis of Generalized Data Base Management Systems*, Association for Computing Machinery, New York, 1971.
5. *System 2000 General Information Manual*, MRI Systems Corp., Austin, Tex., 1972.
6. Informatics, Inc., *Mark IV File Management System Reference Manual*, Canoga Park, Calif., 1970.
7. Roger K. Summit, "DIALOG: An Operational On-Line Reference Retrieval System," *Proceedings of the 22nd National ACM Conference*, Washington, D.C., 1967, pp. 51-6.
8. Data Base Task Group, *CODASYL Data Base Task Group Report*, Conference on Data Systems Languages, Association for Computing Machinery, New York, 1971.

## RECOMMENDED READING

CODASYL Systems Committee [4].

House, William C., Ed., *Data Base Management*, Petrocelli Books, New York, 1974, pp. 233 322.

Jardine, Donald A., Ed., *Data Base Management Systems*, North-Holland American Elsevier, Amsterdam, 1974.

Mader, Chris and Robert Hagin, *Information Systems: Technology, Economics, Applications*, Science Research Associates, Chicago, 1974, Chapters 10 and 12.

Meadow, Charles T., *The Analysis of Information Systems*, 2nd ed., Melville Publishing Co., Los Angeles, 1973, pp. 396 412.

*Chapter Ten*

# User Interface

## 10.1 TYPES OF SYSTEM USERS

Almost any information system has a variety of kinds of users—some the true users for whom the system was created, others who use it in connection with their duties to supply it with information, write its programs, or maintain its data base. Because of their different backgrounds and interests, they may use the system in different ways, and system design may have to accommodate their dissimilar requirements. In this chapter we discuss who the users are and what kinds of requirements they have. In Chapter 11, we deal with an information system from the user's view point.

In this section we describe six classes of users: (1) the end-user, who is interested only in the content of an information system, not in the mechanics of operation or design; (2) a data entry operator, whose sole duty is to supply information to the system; (3) an analytic user, who may both supply information and use the system to retrieve information; (4) an application programmer, who uses the system or its components to develop a new information system or revise the existing one; (5) a data base administrator, who both controls and provides a service to application programmers; and (6) a systems programmer, who designs or modifies information systems. Not all user types are found in association with any given system and, as always, some people occupy more than one role.

### 10.1.1 End-Users

The end-users comprise the most obvious of the user groups. They may be direct users, or they may never communicate directly with the system, preferring to deal through intermediaries. Typically, they are not professional data processing people, and they tend to resist technically imposed limitations on what they can do or obligations to supply technical detail as part of a request. Examples of such users are management executives who employ computer systems through professional staffs, and research workers who themselves make direct use of the computer for bibliographic searching or mathematical programming. Because these groups are not necessarily skilled in computer use, special, simplified languages may be necessary.

### 10.1.2 Data Entry Operators

A data entry operator may be a clerk whose only duty is to transcribe information from paper forms into a computer system, say, orders to a warehouse or invoices. Here we may also place the keypunch operator and all modern variants: key-to-tape, key-to-disk, optical character recognition, and so on. At times this task is included in a professional job—for example, when library cataloguers directly enter information into a computer. Normally, the data entry operators are primarily machine operators, and in considering their needs for languages or other support, productivity and quality control are of primary importance.

### 10.1.3 Analytic Users

The first two user classes are often found in combination—people who enter data and also use the information system to recover information. A business manager, a parts buyer, an air traffic controller, a nurse, may all be personally involved in entering information that their speical training was required to obtain. Also, in the routine conduct of their business such persons need to retrieve information, often, for the purpose of ascertaining how to enter new information. Library cataloguing is the prime example of this need; cataloguers must strive for consistency, and knowing how other cataloguers handled similar books, how an author's name was previously spelled, or how many books are found in a given category may be critical in determining how to catalog a new item. We have called this class *analytic users*—people who use the system to solve a problem, who need the system's help to determine how to enter data, or who have to enter data to be able to retrive what is meaningful to them. This class is seldom composed of professional data processors, but its members must become familiar with the system's mechanics. They will know its limitations and how to circumvent them. They probably cannot design new program components, but they can communicate effectively with the system programmers who do.

### 10.1.4 Application Programmers

A related set of users are the application programmers and data base administrators. Application programmers design, implement, and modify end-user-oriented programs—budget analyses, accounts receivable, classroom scheduling, or library information retrieval. Some of their work may be original programming, in COBOL or FORTRAN or the like, but they also make maximum use of such general-purpose programs as a GDMS or some of its components. To them, an information system consists of more than a GDMS. It is also files and procedures. Even if the only computer program involved is a GDMS, there may still be a need for an applications programmer to see to it that files are properly defined, storage space allocated, data validation procedures worked out, and so on. The GDMS language may be oriented toward end-users, but there may be so much to arrange that a professional programmer must be engaged. Somtimes, only components of the GDMS are used, or perhaps the GDMS is to become incorporated into the application program. In this case communication with the GDMS is done in a programming language, not in an end-user language. This communication must be very precise because unlike the end-user, the programmer is concerned with data formats, file and record sizes, data storage devices, and response times. If a GDMS is being designed with both programmers and end-users in mind, these two constituencies probably will conflict in their demands for GDMS attributes.

### 10.1.5 Data Base Administrators

Related to the application programmer is the data base administrator (DBA), a relatively new formally defined job. The DBA is the person responsible for allocating storage space for files, maintaining data security and design standards, and consulting with users and programmers on how existing data bases can be used to satisfy the needs of a new application or how the data base might have to be redesigned. The function of the DBA generally is found in organizations that use very large files, large numbers of files, or integrated files. Integrated files (described in Section 11.3) are designed to contain all an organization's information without redundancy. Maintaining integrated files requires centralized control over the definition of every data element to ensure that none duplicates or conflicts with existing elements. The DBA knows who uses what information, who has authorized access to what information, and what the priorities of various programs and users are. When files are large or numerous, the DBA becomes involved in such matters as allocation of storage space, determination of time of day that the file may be kept on-line, number of backup copies of files to be kept, and standards of data documentation.

The DBA may also be in charge of recovery operations when a computer failure or a calamity—a fire, for example—has destroyed part of a data base. To handle all these tasks, the DBA must be able to query files, change their contents, change their storage assignment, and make extra copies of files. Clearly then, he must have a means for communicating his sometimes specialized requirements to the GDMS. Like the applications programmer, the DBA is a professional in data processing, and he communicates in precise terms about formats and structures. Unlike other classes of user, he represents a small group who may not be able to justify the cost of a language tailored to his own special requirements.

### 10.1.6 Systems Programmers

The final class of "user" is the systems programmer who designs, maintains, or modifies a GDMS. For debugging and diagnostic purposes he may play any of the other user roles, but his ultimate way of communicating is to write programs in a general-purpose programming language. Although systems are not traditionally designed with this class of user in mind, the increasing importance of providing maintenance services to packaged software owners and of writing software packages that can be modified to enable linkage to other packages indicate that systems programmers, too, should be considered in design.

## 10.2  USER LANGUAGES

Users of a GDMS perform the following functions, for which they need a language to communicate with the information system:

- entering data into a system and representing it in storage
- querying a system
- ordering a system to process data
- defining to the system the data it is to process
- specifying the processes a system is to perform (programming the system)

In many cases these roles are performed in a pure sense; the user occupies only the one role. Examples are a clerk transcribing sales transactions into an on-line data entry device (or a keypunch machine), a stockbroker whose terminal permits him to query a system only for price and sales volume information, or a system programmer writing a subroutine for the data manager. More often, though, any given user performs more than one role in accomplishing a task. Consider a bank teller entering data on a transaction into a computer and also querying it for validity of a customer's account number or bank balance, an airline reservation agent querying a system for space availability and also entering customer data and calculating the fare, and a person doing interactive programming who enters data (program statements), runs programs, and queries the system for values computed by the program and for segments of the program itself.

Each kind of user of the information system requires a language by which he sends or receives messages. Normally, the language is a programming like artificial language, but one having a vocabulary and a syntax that the user must master. The "language" may consist of a set of buttons, keys, or switches on a computer terminal (the vocabulary) and rules for their use (syntax). One can visualize the computer system as a "black box" whose internal functioning is unknown but which responds to inputs and produces outputs. The various languages are the means of conveying inputs and outputs. Each role or task to be performed requires the transmission of a different set of data elements, and the complexity of the language is determined by the number of elements, their relationships, and the amount of variability in statements. For example, the stock broker system may have only one form of input—a query based on a stock symbol. In this case there is no need to identify the message as a query or the data field entered as a stock symbol. An airline reservation system accepts queries of several kinds and data input records of several kinds. Not only are there more data in the message, but it is necessary to identify the types of input (query, etc.) and the individual fields (passenger's name, etc.). Recall also that it is the user language that determines the logical data structure in use. Information present in the physical structure but not representable in the language is not present, so far as the user is concerned. For example, the stored stock market record may contain a *time of transaction* field, but if the query language does not provide for its use, it may be nonexistent to the broker-user.

The technical requirements for the various languages differ, and they may be intended for use by people with very dissimilar backgrounds. In designing a language we must consider the functions to be performed (type messages to be conveyed), linkage with other language (as data entry and query), and computer sophistication and state of training of the language users.

One trend particularly beneficial to end-users is toward simplified language, giving the nontechnical user less to learn than if he were forced to handle a conventional programming language. To simplify the language that describes a process, the options available and the interconnections among components of the process must be restricted. Offer the user fewer options, and he can more easily master the language.

Another trend is toward natural language. The intent is to eliminate any specialized language training for users. Yet the functions to be performed remain as technical as ever, requiring precise specification. Natural language is not exact. Words and phrases have multiple meanings; the same concept can be expressed in multiple ways. Teaching a person to be precise when the language does not force him toward precision may be more difficult than teaching him a precise, artificial language.

As an example, suppose that an artificial, user-oriented language features a special data form (Figure 10.1) for writing a query, one that clearly indicates where information is to be placed, hence simplifies syntax. In the column designated, the user specifies the name of the search key, a relationship symbol, the field value, and the information desired to be retrieved from matching records. To ask the same question in natural language form, he might say

- for *date of birth* greater than 1945, retrieve *name* and *date of employment*

| IF FIELD $A^1$ | RELATION$^2$ | FIELD $B^3$ | ELEMENT $C^4$ | THEN RETRIEVE ELEMENT $D^4$ | ELEMENT $E^4$ |
|---|---|---|---|---|---|
| DATE OF BIRTH | > | 1945 | NAME | DATE OF EMPLOYMENT | |
| | | | | | |
| | | | | | |

Notes: 1. Must be a variable name.
2. Choice of $<, \leq, =, \neq, \geq, >$.
3. May be a variable or constant
4. May be name of variable or field, group, or record

**Figure 10.1** A simple query format.

- if *date of birth* is greater than 1945, retrieve *name* and *date of employment*
- print *name* and *date of employment* for *date of birth* > 1945
- retrieve *name, date of employment* for *age* < 30

The first three forms of the question all seem to be improvements on the constrained, artificial form of the query. To gain an idea of the difficulty of language translation, it is helpful to realize that there is no artificial, clear-cut way to distinguish between a word that is part of a field name or part of something else. Suppose there is a field named *today's date*. Then the language processor has to recognize that it is not this field but *date of birth* that is being referred to. An occasional typographical error makes the problem much worse.

A fourth example reveals a more insidious problem. The user is interested in people under age 30. Told that he may "speak" to the computer in natural language, he does so. But the computer does not store *age*, it stores *date of birth*, which does not change. The query as stated cannot be answered unless the information system programs are sufficiently powerful to discern what was meant and change the query accordingly. Otherwise the query must be rejected and the user indoctrinated into the realities of field names and definitions. Furthermore, even in the year 1975, *age* < 30, is not exactly equivalent to *date of birth* > 1945 unless the query is run on December 31.

As language processors improve, this type of difficulty will gradually disappear, precisely because the programs will gradually become able to recognize the kind of error illustrated and take remedial action. In today's technology, programs can be written to ask the user the meaning of the unrecognized word *age*, show him the list of acceptable variables and their definitions, and ask for a replacement. The user must still recognize that he has to change the logic of his statement. He does not want to require *date of birth* < 30, and the program is unlikely to be sophisticated enough to suggest this change to him.

The language chosen for any system should be that best fitted to the system, its budget, and its users. Factors to consider in selecting or designing a language are:

1. *Expressiveness.* Can the language represent the concepts and detail needed or desired?
2. *Ease of learning.* As a rule, the more expressive the language, the harder it is to learn, but this is not necessarily true for all people in all situations. A highly versatile programming language is needed to express all the selection and processing requirements of information system users. This may be beyond the learning capacity of many users, or beyond the economic value of learning for others.

3. *Error detection capability of the language processor.* To help overcome some learning difficulty, a language processor that can "skillfully" detect errors is helpful to the user.
4. *Default assumptions and error forgiveness.* One step beyond detecting an error is to do something constructive about it. Pointing out the error to the user, particularly in an interactive system, is useful. For the program to intelligently rectify the error and proceed may be even better, since this also permits the user to omit certain information, knowing the computer will supply it. Such program behavior is called a *default assumption,* the automatic assignment of a predetermined value to a variable not otherwise specified. For example, FORTRAN assumes by default that the variable I is an integer unless otherwise specified by the programmer. What this means is that the language processor assigned the value INTEGER to a field in a record used to compile the program. Information such as this, which is needed but not supplied, is called *implicit. Error forgiveness* is a more general term describing a program's ability to recognize the existence of an error, make some assumption of the correct value, and proceed accordingly.
5. *Availability of help.* When the user is unsure how to proceed or of the meaning of some computer-transmitted message, he would like the ability to query the system on these points, to ask for help.

### 10.2.1 Data Entry and Representation Languages

We should first draw distinctions among a *data representation* language, a *data description language,* and a *data entry language.* A data representation language is the one used to represent data stored in memory. The Dewey Decimal Classification is a language for representing the subjects of books. A mailing address is a multifaceted, syntactic term for representing a person's location to postal authorities; it usually consists of descriptors of *street number, street name, city, postal code,* and *state, province, county,* or *country,* and the order of listing has definite importance. A data definition language (DDL) describes attributes of the elements whose values are expressed in the language. A DDL might express the length of a term, its alphabet, or the number of elements in an array; it does not itself represent the data—a book's subject or a street name.

A data entry language conveys a message from a user to the system. The message transmits the value of one or more data elements and may contain a description of the elements being transmitted. In the simplest case, a message might be of the form FOR PATIENT NUMBER = 12345, ADD TO MISCELLANEOUS CHARGES, AMOUNT = .25, DESCRIPTION = LOCAL TELEPHONE CALL. A statement in a data entry language must *identify* one or more data elements and *provide a value* for each, although identification can be implicit. The language must be designed to express the logical data structure. For example, the statement SUBJECT = 629.138 82 implies that *subject* is a scalar variable, a single field. The statement is ambiguous if there can be more than one subject field in a record or subject array. In that case, the user is obliged to identify *which* subject he is entering. The patient record illustration (Figure 10.2) implies that patient number uniquely identifies a record, that *miscellaneous charges* is an array whose elements are groups of the scalar fields *amount* and *description*. No explicit statement is made telling what ordinal element in the array shall receive the new values. We want the language processor to assume that we mean the next available locations, and we want it to put the two new elements at the same relative positions, that is, both in the *n*th element of their respective arrays.

If an element of this array is to be changed, it would have to be identified by ordinal number or by content, as CHANGE MISCELLANEOUS CHARGES (3) or CHANGE MISCELLANEOUS CHARGE (.25, LOCAL TELEPHONE CALL). There is no unique key that orders the elements of this array. For this kind of transaction it becomes important for the language designer to know something about the people who will use the language. Will a notation such as MISCELLANEOUS CHARGE(3) bother them? Will they be facile enough in using a keyboard to enter a message such as the following, without mechanical error? FOR PATIENT NUMBER = 12345, ADD TO MISCELLANEOUS CHARGES, AMOUNT = .25, DESCRIPTION = LOCAL TELEPHONE CALL? Will they be sufficiently familiar with the data structure to know the components of data groups such as *miscellaneous charges*?

### 10.2.2 Query Language

In most information systems an information request, or query, defines the attributes of a subset of the file or data base to be searched. The command to search is often implicit. In some ways a query language can resemble a data entry language because values of fields are the usual bases for retrieval. Hence, just as in data entry, a user must identify a field and give a value.

The purpose of a query language is to convey to the information system the user's requirements for information to be retrieved. A query can be viewed as a command to isolate a subset of a file that meets specified criteria (Section 6.4) or as a conditional command to retrieve information *if* it meets the specified criteria.

Querying a file usually carries with it an element of uncertainty: has

198     User Interface

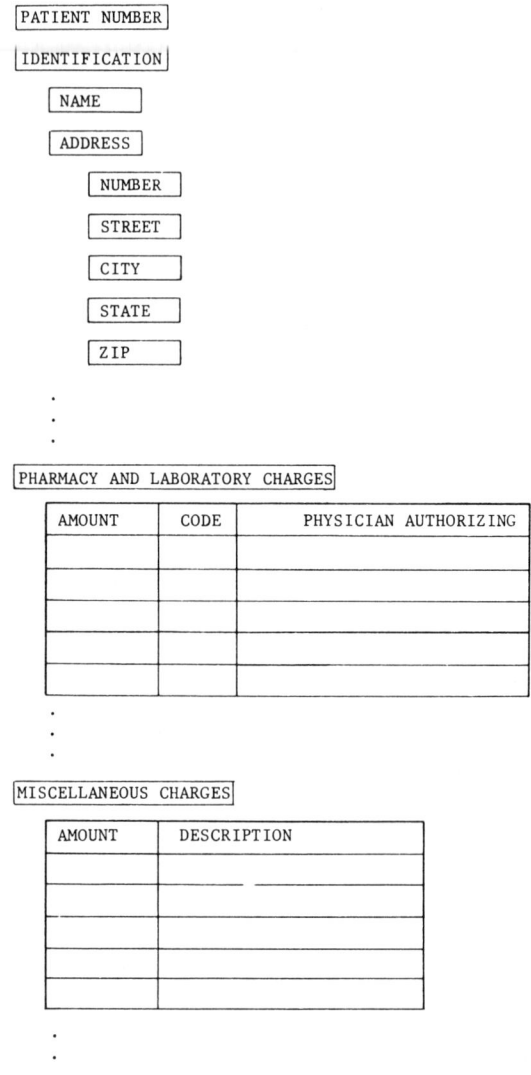

Figure 10.2   Portion of a hospital patient record.

the user correctly phrased his requirements, or does the data base contain the information he is seeking? For this reason, feedback is essential to the user. Procedural feedback assists him with the formalities of use of the language, and substantive feedback allows summaries of his retrieved information or presents suggestions about the existence of related information that was not retrieved.

### 10.2.3 Command Language

A query is really a command to search for and retrieve a particular subset of a file. There are a variety of other commands used to process retrieved data, but the retrieval command is so common and so potentially complex that it often has its own language. The very early information retrieval programs tended to offer a reasonably flexible query language but no processing options, hence no language with which to express processing requirements. Today it is generally recognized that users of information systems may want not only to retrieve data but to

- compute functions of retrieved data
- change the structure of retrieved records, to be able to display or further process them
- add other information to make human interpretation easier
- change the sequence of records
- store retrieved data for subsequent searching or processing
- insert new records or elements into existing files or records
- change the values of record elements
- delete information currently stored in a file

In addition to these functions performed on retrieved information, a user has the following needs to communicate to an information system on other subjects:

- to identify himself to the system and initiate a session of computer use.
- to identify the files to be searched or processed, to ensure that the required data are on the computer (e.g., tapes or disks mounted)
- to ask for system information, such as the meaning of a machine-generated error message or the names of programs or files available to the system
- to send messages to computer operators or to other users of the system
- to sign off or terminate a session of computer use

Although the command languages used to express these functions are not standardized, the following are typical of the kinds of commands used to perform the functions just listed.

***Computational Functions*** Typical commands are COUNT and SUM (Figure 10.3). The first asks for a count of the number of *information elements* meeting the stated criteria of a search, such as the number of records retrieved or the number of elements of an array.

The command SUM asks for the summation of the *contents* of a field

| name | dob | dedtype | dedamt |
|---|---|---|---|
| ADAMS | 1957 | INS | 12.50 |
|  |  | UGF | 7.00 |
|  |  |  |  |
| BECH | 1926 | INS | 18.70 |
|  |  |  |  |
|  |  |  |  |
| CARROLL | 1919 | UGF | 23.00 |
|  |  |  |  |
|  |  |  |  |
| DORIA | 1952 | UGF | 6.00 |
|  |  | INS | 12.50 |
|  |  |  |  |

Commands:

1. COUNT records with **dob** < 1930.
2. SUM dedamt for **dedtype** = UGF

Results:

1. COUNT = 1 + 1 = 2
2. SUM = 7.00 + 23.00 + 6.00 = 36.00

**Figure 10.3** The COUNT and SUM commands.

in all records of a subset. For example, to sum the number of parts on hand from a given manufacturer requires using the contents of a field (*number on hand*) rather than merely counting the number of parts records for which *manufacturer* has the specified value.

***Structure-Change Functions*** The command FORMAT might be followed, as in FORTRAN, by a description of field length, type, and relative positions, to be used in conjunction with an input or output command that names the fields to be transmitted. The example from FORTRAN

```
14   FORMAT (XX,A10,XXX,I5)
15   WRITE (3,14) NAME, SALARY
```

means: write on output unit 3 fields *name* and *salary*, using the format description of statement 14. This says that two blanks (XX) are to be followed by *name*, which consists of 10 alphabetic characters (A10). *Salary* is to be five integers (I5), following three blanks. This kind of notation is quite independent of the structure of the records in which *name* and *salary* were found originally.

Mark IV uses a special data form to present the information on output formats in nonprocedural form. Included in the output format specifications are indications of how and when titles, page numbers, line numbers, or the like are to be added to data retrieved from the files for inclusion in reports or displays.

*Addition of Data to Retrieved Information* The information added may be only the most simple parameters, but it is information that was not in the data base being searched. The computational functions described previously are one means of creating such data. For example, a user might wish to retrieve all records containing a value of *salary* greater than the average of all *salary* fields in a file. This could be done using a SUM and a COUNT command followed by a division of the resulting sum by the count to determine the average. Another search based on the computed value would yield the desired result. Other forms of information supplied by the user at the time of an information request are page numbers for reports, class intervals to be used for statistical presentations, and cutoff dates for reports.

*Sequence-Changing Functions* The SORT command permits to COBOL users to resequence an existing file according to parameters provided in the command. Thus a user can retrieve a set of records from a file and resequence them, or create a set of records and change their sequence. Mark IV permits users to request a sort by making a few entries in a table descriptive of output format. Most GDMS have provisions for output sorting.

*Storage Functions* Illustrative of a command that orders a data set to be placed on a memory device or at a location designated in conjunction with the command and reserved for this purpose, is STORE. For example, the results of a query may be designated *set 1*, stored in a predetermined location, and thereafter searched or processed in the same manner as any other system file. It is required that both the name of the file and the address be predetermined.

The command CREATE represents a type found only rarely in practice. It establishes a completely new file. It is related to STORE but is limited to asking the system to recognize a new file and to allocate space for it: STORE does not necessarily involve creating a new file; it may refer to an existing file into which new data are to be placed. The command CREATE calls for the operating system to recognize a new entity.

*Insertion Functions* We can say that ADD is an illustrative command calling for the insertion of a record into a file or an element into an array. The element must be identified in a manner similar to that used in queries; its key or storage position must be given. Also the command must be accompanied by the data to be inserted or the location at which the data will be found. When this command is implemented in a language, it is usually assumed that the information to be added does not already exist—that there is no record having the key of that to be inserted. Should there already be such a record, an error message is sent to the user or to the computer program that issued the ADD command.

*Change Functions* To replace an existing value with a new one, we use CHANGE. The specific information element must be identified, and it is assumed to exist. The command can be conditional or made to apply to a set, as CHANGE, FOR *date* < 1940, *status* = INACTIVE. This command sets the value of field *status* to INACTIVE in all records for which the field *date* has value less than 1940.

*Deletion Functions* The command DELETE asks for the logical removal of a record from a file or an element from an array. Deletion of a scalar field is accomplished simply by setting its value to blank or zero. The DELETE command is needed when only one of many values is being deleted. Therefore, the specific element must be identified. As with CHANGE, the identification may apply to a set of records, for example: DELETE ALL RECORDS FOR *date* < 1940. The assumption is made that the information to be deleted is present. If a unique key is identified but cannot be found and deleted, there is an error indication.

The complement of CREATE is REMOVE. It asks that the control program or operating system no longer recognize a given file and requests it to make any space used by that file available for other purposes.

*User Identification Functions* The command SIGN ON is used with on-line or interactive information systems. It is equivalent to dialing a telephone switchboard operator to indicate that the user is on the line and is ready to proceed to use the system. Identification of what is to be done is the next step. Almost all on-line systems require users to identify themselves by a password or by testing whether a user's name appears on a list of approved names. This check both denies use of the computer to unauthorized people and ensures that costs of use are properly allocated. When the user's *bona fides* is established, the starting time of his use of the computer is noted and he may proceed. In batch-mode systems, identifying the user may be a simple matter of filling in a few fields on a data form giving the user's name, job number, and so on. Identification of the user as the first step in using the computer has become a standard practice.

*Data Identification* There is a difference between the data identification used in a query language and that which signifies to the system and its human operator what files are to be used. The latter is a general notification of intent that ensures that the appropriate files—tapes or disks—are physically loaded onto the computer and are recognized and located by the operating system. At this level, the logic of a command such as SELECT FILE is simple. The files need only be named, but no combinatorial logic is involved. The command differs from STORE or CREATE in that SELECT FILE identifies a previously created file that is required in this session. It does not store data or create new files.

*System Interrogation* Another command that is becoming common for on-line systems is HELP. When the machine transmits a message the user does not understand, he enters the response HELP, which is interpreted as a request for a display of a prestored message explaining or elaborating on the last machine-to-man message.

*Transmitting to Other Users* The SEND command permits a terminal operator to transmit a message through the computer to another terminal, designated in the command. A distinction may be made between a master terminal to which anyone may send a message and other terminals for which there may be limitations on traffic. In computer-assisted instruction, for example, a number of students may be using a computer simultaneously. Any of them may send to the instructor in charge, who may also send to any student, but students may be barred from transmitting to one another.

*Sign-off* The command SIGN OFF is used with on-line systems to release computer facilities and establish the time of completion of a session for cost computation purposes. No similar command is needed for batch-mode systems because it is the termination of the job that signifies the release of facilities for the next job. In on-line systems, in the absence of a sign-off command, the computer might continue to reserve space for messages from the terminal in use or even stand idle while waiting for the next message.

### 10.2.4 Data Definition Language and Data Independence

The need for formal data definition was described in Section 9.4. It is the file designer's communication to the programs that will process his files, providing them with information on data structure and representation. This specialized form of communication calls for a special language. Reference was made earlier to the work of CODASYL toward a single data definition language appropriate for all programming languages. Until this goal is achieved, data definition is considered part of the programming process, and the definition statements are part of the programming language.

Perhaps the best description of a DDL can be given by comparing how three different languages would describe the same information. We assume

## 204 User Interface

a data record (Figure 10.4) consisting of the elements *name, address, number of dependents,* and *names of children. Name* and *address* are groups consisting of several dissimilar fields each. *Number of dependents* is a single numeric field, and *names of children* is an array of alphabetic fields.

A COBOL definition of this record appears in Figure 10.5. COBOL has two divisions of a program devoted to data definition. There is the *environment* division and the *data* division. Roughly speaking, the environment division is concerned with information about the file and the data division with information at the record level and below. Although our illustration concentrates on the data division, a small amount of file information is given. The notation RECORDING MODE F specifies fixed-length records, and the absence of any notation about blocking factors indicates unblocked records, or a blocking factor of 1. There can be more than one record type in a file, and each must be named. In this file we have only one, and the name of the record is DATA_RECORD. (COBOL does not permit blanks in a data name. The _ character is often used instead.)

Within the record, we begin by identifying the record being described (redundant here, but not in a file containing multiple record types). Level numbers indicate subordination. If the record is level 1, the first data element under it is level 2. At that level we find *name,* which is a group containing other elements. *ZIP* in the *address* group is a numeric field of five characters.

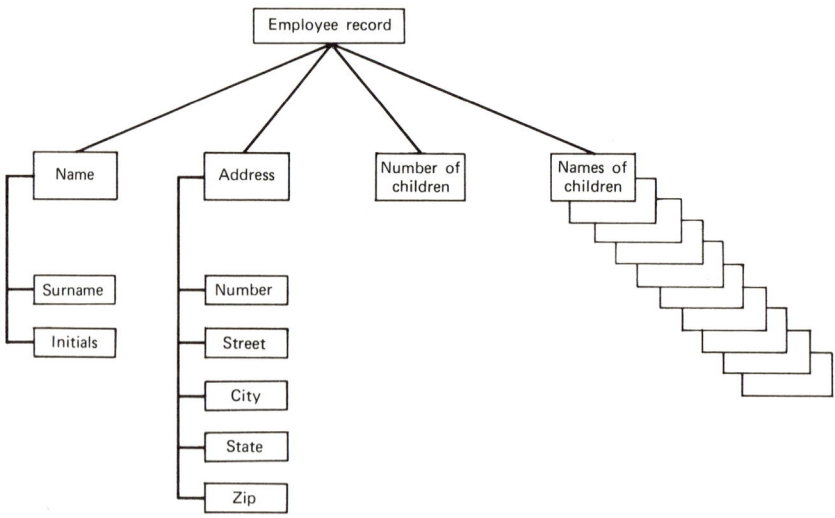

**Figure 10.4** Illustrative employee record.

```
01  EMPLOYER_REC
    02  NAME
        03  SURNAME      PICTURE  X(15)
        03  INITIALS     PICTURE  X(2)
    02  ADDRESS
        03  NUMBER       PICTURE  X(5)
        03  STREET       PICTURE  X(12)
        03  CITY         PICTURE  X(2)
        03  STATE        PICTURE  X(2)
        03  ZIP          PICTURE  9(5)
    02  NOCHILD          PICTURE  9(2)
    02  CHILNAME         PICTURE  X(15)  OCCURS 10 TIMES
```

The notation X(15) denotes a 15-character alphanumeric field.

The notation 9(5) denotes a 5-character numeric field.

NUMBER is coded alphanumeric because house numbers sometimes have letters included in them.

CHILNAME is set up as a 10-element array and space is reserved for this many elements even though not all employees have ten children.

**Figure 10.5**  Part of a COBOL record definition.

*Number of dependents* is also a numeric field, but we have added the notation USAGE IS COMPUTATIONAL, since some computers (such as the IBM 360s and 370s) can represent integers in several ways. By indicating that we want *primarily* (not exclusively) to use this field for computational purposes, we ensure that the field will be stored in a compact form. Had we indicated USAGE IS DISPLAY (the default assumption if no usage is specified), the form of representation would have been less compact but more compatible with the form in which display units of the computer are able to accept data.

*Name of dependent* is an array element. Space will be reserved in the record for 10 occurrences of the field. Note that since there was a name of the *address* group, there is no name of the array separate from the name of the element of the array.

The PL/I version of the record definition is very close to the COBOL definition (Figure 10.6). Although both languages feature a variety of ways to describe the record, PL/I the data definition is not separated from the procedural portion of a program; hence there is an explicit command DECLARE that indicates the nature of the information to follow. A number of data elements can be defined with a single DECLARE statement; the end of this definition is indicated by the semicolon following the *name of dependents* line. The DECLARE statement can occur anywhere in the program, provided only that it precedes any reference to any of the defined data elements in the procedural statements. The notation is similar to that of COBOL: CHARACTER (2) has the same meaning as PICTURE 'XX', and these equate to COBOL's PICTURE XX.

PL/I offers more variety of numeric representations. For example, FIXED DECIMAL (5) indicates a five-character integer.

The array *name of dependents* has 10 elements, each a 15-character field, as in the COBOL version.

Much of Mark IV's prescribed form for recording record structure (Figure 10.7) contains information used for purposes other than structure-

```
DECLARE
    01   EMPLOYEE_REC
         02   NAME
              03   SURNAME   CHARACTER(15)   VARYING   *
              03   INITIALS  CHARACTER(2)
         02   ADDRESS
              03   NUMBER    CHARACTER(5)
              03   STREET    CHARACTER(12)
              03   CITY      CHARACTER(12)
              03   STATE     CHARACTER(2)
              03   ZIP       FIXED(5)
         02   NOCHILD   FIXED(2)
         02   CHILNAME(10)   CHARACTER(15)   VARYING;
```

\* The attribute VARYING results in the field not being filled with blanks if the particular name is less than 15 characters in length. The advantage is that, when printed, a short name does not use up the full 15 characters on the printed page. In most other ways, this definition is much like the COBOL one.

**Figure 10.6** Record definition in PL/I.

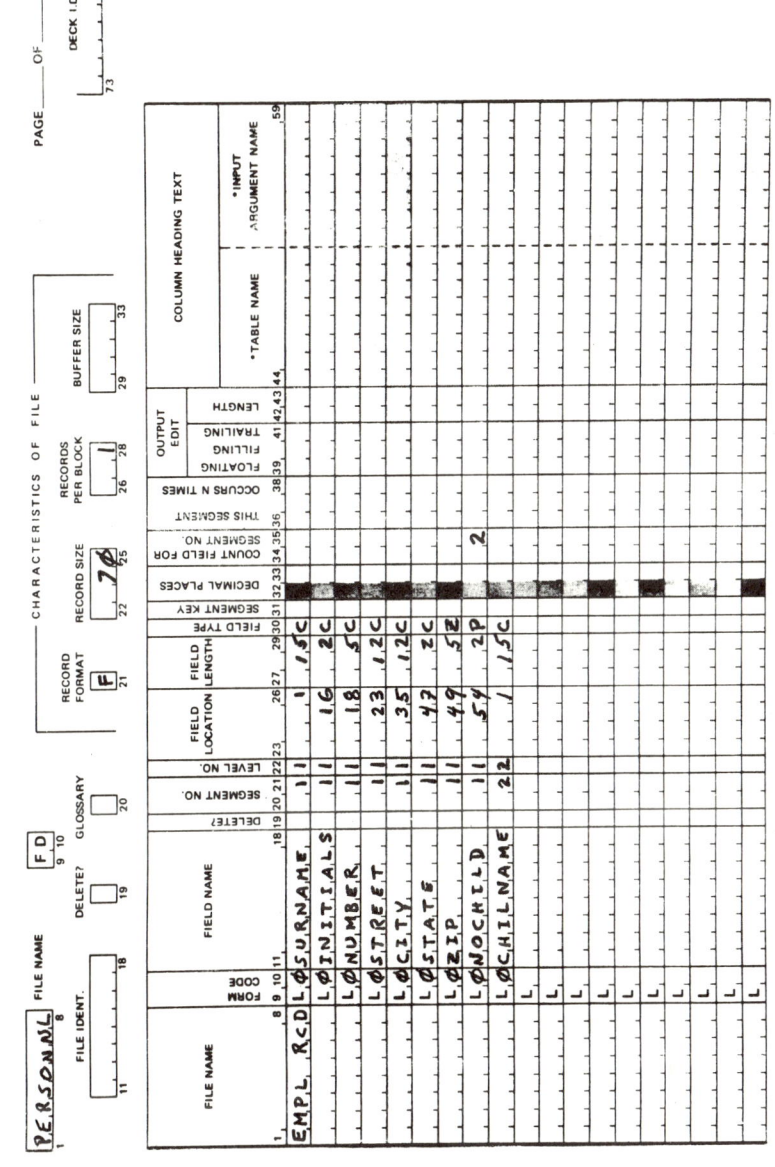

Figure 10.7 A Mark IV record description.

and representation- defining, hence it may appear more complex than it actually is. The file name is entered in the upper left-hand corner. Thereafter, the file name appears on each line that conveys information about a field or segment. Also in the heading is an indication of *record format* (21) and *record size* (22–25). The format indicated here is F for fixed record size and the number of characters in the record is 70.

In the body of the form, *line number* indicates a type of line, not a sequence number. A line numbered L0 defines a field. Other numbers would be used in conjunction with the *column heading text* group, which has to do with printed reports listing the field. The array of dependents' names in Mark IV must be a segment separate from the rest of the record. Hence we enter name data in segment 1 (columns 20,21). Since Mark IV does not permit us to name a group of fields unless we declare them to be a separate segment, a physical separation, there is no name of the *name* or *address* groups because these groups are in the same segment.

The array of dependent's names is in a separate segment, segment 2, which is subordinated to the name and address data in segment 1. Segment 1 is then considered to be at level 1 and segment 2 at level 2. This is similar to the PL/I and COBOL level numbers.

The column headed *field location* contains the character position in which the field begins, and the column headed *field length* contains the number of characters in the field.

*Field type* is also similar to its PL/I and COBOL counterparts. The C indicates a character field, the P a packed decimal field (COBOL's computational usage), and the Z a zoned decimal (COBOL's display usage).

The *segment key* identifies the sort field for the segments. This is not present in the COBOL environment division. Finally, the field *this segment occurs n times* identifies the length of an array.

A Mark IV array requires a field containing the number of entries actually present, as opposed to the maximum number of occurrences. This is the field *nochild* in the higher level segment. Neither of the other languages has a requirement for this information to be an explicit part of the record.

The proponents of these languages argue the superiority of their respective choices. Impartial analysis reveals that for a record as simple as the one we have illustrated, there is not much difference. There would be greater difference as the record and its containing file increase in complexity.

Data independence (Section 4.5) is one of the benefits of a versatile data definition language. True data independence exists if a user (program or person interrogating a system) can address a logical data structure without regard for the physical arrangement of the data in memory. Data independence frees users from having to address data in terms of machine addresses and access commands, which many nontechnical users are incapable of doing. In its ideal form, data independence permits each user to address data in terms most meaningful to him.

Data independence can exist at various levels. The user of ISAM need not be concerned with actual location of a record or the organization of its contents, because he can address or store the record entirely by use of its unique key. But he must be aware that it is an ISAM record, and its storage, deletion, or retrieval must be in the approved ISAM manner, which begins to involve technicalities not known to all users. The user of a sequential or direct access method addresses only a relative or absolute position and, since the position may have no correlation with record content or key, this may be even more obscure to the nontechnical user. In all three cases, to examine a field within a record, the using programmer (end-users do not address data managers) needs information not available to or supplied by the data manager—namely, knowledge of where the field is within the record. The data manager does not provide data independence at that level.

Information about the location of fields within a record is available from the data definition portion of a high-order program. A high-order source program can refer to a data item, (e.g., call for it to be printed or added to another item) without direct reference to the definition. Should the definition later change, say, by extending the length of a field, the source program need not be changed. The data definition must be changed, and the program recompiled. The machine-language object program is *not* independent of the physical structure, but the high-order source language program is. Thus we change the data definition in the high-order program and, by recompiling, change the procedural part of the object program. This is another illustration of how a high-order programming language is primarily a vehicle giving users a means to address data independently of physical structure.

Another level of data independence is found in the concept of the *schema* and *subschema* as defined in the CODASYL Data Base Task Group report [1]. A schema is the definition of a data structure. A subschema is a definition of a logical substructure that may have no separate physical existence. For example, the structure may include two files containing record types A and B. Type A contains fields $A_1$, $A_2$, and $A_3$ and is sorted on $A_2$ as the key. Record type B contains fields $B_1$, $B_2$, and $B_3$ and is sorted on $B_1$. A subschema C might define a record consisting of $A_2$ and $B_3$, in logical sequence on $B_3$, and the user might write a program that used C just as if it were a separate physical file. If the schema described the entire data base available to an organization, subschema could be defined for any subset, and any programmer or GDMS user could address only the data he wanted in the logical form most convenient for him in each instance of usage.

The *virtual file* represents another form of data independence. This form of representation frees the user from considering record access at all by allowing him to treat each record as if it were stored in main memory. He must still be concerned with identifying the record he wants, and he may choose to search a file sequentially or by binary search, but he does not have to know the command (or its equivalent) to get a record from auxiliary storage and he is not responsible for the time it takes to access the records. Before the designer of the information system elects to use a virtual memory computer, however, he must be sure its response characteristics are in keeping with his users' requirements.

*Content addressing* is an old concept embodied in some data management systems. ISAM, for example, permits its users to address a record by means of an attribute of the record. Multilist and other multikey retrieval systems do the same but offer the user a greater choice of attributes for addressing. The high-order, end-user-oriented query languages of many GDMS in effect permit data to be addressed by combinations of attributes, all without regard to physical structure or location.

### 10.2.5 Programming Language

There is no need here for a detailed definition of "computer programming language." A programming language builds the data management system or, when the user is a skilled programmer, the programming language processor can perform most of the functions of a data management system. The advantage of a GDMS, to most users, is to eliminate the technically difficult and error-prone process of writing a program in a general-purpose programming language.

The language processor of the generalized data management system sets the limits on what the GDMS can do, and how. This program determines what query or command language statements will be possible and what logical data structures will be recognized. Queries, commands, or data definitions are, in fact, nothing more than raw input data to the GDMS's language processor.

If a user needs to perform a function not allowed for in the design of the GDMS, or to ask a query or define a data structure, a change must be made to the GDMS at the programming language level. The amount of time required for a change in the system, compared to the time required to carry out a system function, is very large—possibly weeks or months, compared to minutes or hours for the latter function. Thus changes to a GDMS cannot be carried out casually; they tie up resources and may interfere with usual system operation. For these reasons, users are often well advised to change their requirements to fit the availability of software, rather than changing the software to accommodate the problem. Although this dictum is seldom questioned in regard to hardware (users tend to accept the lack of equipment as an excuse not to perform a function, and certainly individual users rarely take upon themselves the modification of complex hardware), it is less widely accepted as it applies to software. Probably this is because so many users cannot visualize the complete cost of a major software modification, but they can visualize the nature of the change. This does not imply that software development should be permitted to stagnate or that users should forever be satisfied with what is now available. However, true cost and need should be evaluated against the probability of future commercial availability of the software at a lower price.

## 10.3 MAN–MACHINE INTERACTION

The term "interaction" has come to mean not just any interaction between a man and a computer, such as entering a deck of cards containing a program, but a special form of conversational communication. This has been described as involving dialogue, exchange of information, bargaining, or man-machine symbiosis. *Symbiosis* is used by Licklider [2] by analogy to denote two dissimilar organisms in a condition of mutual dependence and, in this case, sharing a common goal. We have a human and a computer, and the human user deals with the computer through a communications terminal. The user wants to solve a problem—say, solve a mathematical equation or retrieve some information—and he will use the computer as a tool, but a tool having virtually the status of a partner. The user can ask questions or issue commands. The computer can answer, carry out a command, or ask its own questions if the man's input has been incomplete, wrong, or ambiguous. Elsewhere [3] I have said:

> Interactive communication is two-way communication, each party providing feedback to the other, usually each indicating whether the last utterance of the other was understood and supplying results, or progress indications, for any action that was requested. . . . Man-machine communication . . . is goal-oriented—aimed toward the accomplishment of a specific objective—and . . . both parties contribute a necessary function. Each performs a role of which the other is not capable. Usually the man provides creativity and originality, makes decisions, or analyzes complex patterns or arrays of data. The computer's main contribution tends to be fast and accurate storage and retrieval of large quantities of information and extremely rapid calculation.

## 212  User Interface

This kind of computing, or use of a computer, is usually contrasted with batch processing, but the two do not exhaust the possibilities. Computers can be operated in a mode in which data are submitted in increments, some processing done to assure validity, but most of the data stored for later processing in the batch mode. Even in preinteractive days, batch programs were often written to type out a message to the computer operator when error conditions were detected, and work did not proceed until the operator had intervened.

### 10.3.1  Examples of Interactive Systems

Bibliographic information retrieval is one of the common applications of the interactive systems technique. In these systems there is typically a large file of records that approximate library catalog cards, often with an abstract added. Indexing—the entering of subject and other searchable terms into the catalog record—is richer than in a conventional library, there being far more descriptors of subject and such other attributes as the affiliation of the author. The searcher has more information available to him than in a conventional library, but he may be overwhelmed by the amount of output; hence he must select carefully. He exerts care by browsing: making a request, viewing the output of the request on his computer terminal, deciding that he may want to revise the request, entering the changes, and so on. He may wish to consult a thesaurus, which is a list of descriptors indicating the relationship of the descriptors to one another. The user of a system such as this faces uncertainty about exactly what information is in the files or how that information is structured, a large volume of data to sift through, and the need to change his mind about what he says he wants if his sampling of the files fails to produce the desired results. Because of the high probability that he will have to change his initial request, an interactive approach is indicated. The immediate user of a bibliographic system may be the ultimate consumer or a professional intermediary, a librarian.

Airline and theater ticket reservations systems are also common interactive computer applications. Searching files for available flights or seats is part of the problem, but the user (in this case a professional intermediary representing the seller of the space) must change the files as well as search them. At the least, he orders space to be sold and must change the file to show this. He may also enter a description of the purchaser: name, address, and so on. When a seat is sold, that fact must be immediately noted in the file to prevent another agent from selling the same seat. The customer of course wants immediate confirmation of the sale, to be sure he actually has a seat. Hence an interactive system is used to satisfy the customer and to permit the space vendor to sell his space more efficiently because he does not have to allocate blocks of tickets to agents who are not in communication with one another.

Many stock brokerage firms help their account representatives ascertain the latest price and sales volume of a stock by means of remote inquiry to computers. Here the selection is quite straightforward. Prices fluctuate during the trading day and day-old or even hours-old information may not be acceptable. If the broker does not have current information, he might as well use the daily newspaper, whose stock price information may be from 3 to 24 hours old. Querying a file of stock prices and sales volume information is a new development in what may otherwise be the oldest online information retrieval system in existence. Telegraphs were used for stock market information before Edison developed his printing telegraph or stock ticker in 1871. The stock ticker transmits records of sales containing volume and price, but it is not interactive; it cannot be queried except by scanning the accumulation of paper tape.

The most complex interactive systems are those used for such tasks as air traffic control or space flight control. These are characterized by a large amount of input data steadily flowing into the system from a variety of sensing devices, such as radar, a great deal of mathematical processing to relate individual radar returns with established tracks and to predict future position of the vehicle being tracked, and a complex situation to be displayed to a human controller. Speed is essential, not only to process automatic input but to act on the controller's input, which may be in the form of requests for information or commands to be passed to the vehicle. In these systems many programs operate on rapidly changing data. The user is involved, even absorbed, in a complex decision-making process. The number of variables or items of information that any one user may look at is generally kept relatively small, partly to simplify the mechanical aspects of the job and not add difficult computer usage decisions to an already complex task.

### 10.3.2 Benefits of Interactive Systems

One of the benefits of interactive computing is that the user gets results quickly. This is clearly a requirement in a reservations or brokerage system, where delays in retrieving information can result in loss of business. It is often asked whether high response speed is worth the price in such applications as bibliographic retrieval or management information systems, and this question is valid in connection with the design of any system. It cannot be answered in general; the value of interaction depends on the particular case. We can, however, state some of the general benefits of interaction, and these must then be examined for their relevance in individual applications.

*Speed* The most obvious and often the most meaningful benefit of speed is well illustrated by the cases of ticket reservations systems or air traffic control, in which in adequate response speed would render the systems ineffectual. Speed of response enables the user to maintain continuity of thought when working on a complex problem.

*Output Content Control* In such applications as on-line computer programming or bibliographic information retrieval, users enter program commands or retrieval requests with the expectation that the desired results will not appear on the first try. Some trial and error is necessary, and quick interaction allows for such experimentation. The user can determine rapidly whether his program or query is the correct one for the particular problem. Sometimes final results are not received through the interactive terminal: query results may be printed in the computer center, or a program, once debugged and compiled, may be run in batch mode in the evening. But when the user leaves final instructions for these remote-in-time events, he knows he is going to get the results he expects. In these cases, it is possible to work entirely in the batch mode, but the consensus of experienced people is that both time and money can be saved by using interactive techniques.

*Input Quality Control* Errors are always possible when entering data into a computer. There are mechanical or typographical errors caused by inadvertently striking the wrong keys, and content errors such as selecting the wrong classification code or unit of measure for an item. Not all errors can be detected by a computer program, but with diligent programming many can be spotted. An interactive computer system can immediately feed back information about an error that has been detected. In many cases, the operator who receives the feedback—a nurse, clerk, library cataloguer, or purchasing agent—is the person best qualified to make the correction, and the best time to make it is while the information is still fresh in his mind. This can save the time that would be needed subsequently to recover source documents from files, if the feedback did not come until, say, a day later. Some system designers feel that errors should not be fed back immediately to operators because this slows their rate of production (i.e., rate of data entry) and that the machine operator may not be the best person to make the correction. These criticisms are particularly applicable when the operator serves only to transcribe data from one form to another (e.g., paper to computer memory) and plays no intellectual part in composing or coding the information.

### 10.3.3 Programming Style

Writing an interactive computer program is different from ordinary programming in two fundamental ways: (1) most data items are processed fully before another item is considered, rather than being stored at some stage for later consideration, and (2) the programmer must be concerned with how the user interacts with the program as well as with how the program interacts with data and other programs.

***Input Processing*** In batch processing machine efficiency is most often the guiding principle of programming, the object being to minimize program execution time or storage requirements. Optimization of one of these variables usually occurs at the expense of the other. The interactive program designer has a less clear-cut situation. Memory and time saving are still important, but the programmer must heed his response time constraints, often at the price of seemingly wasteful memory use. He must also remember that the response time restriction is in terms of elapsed time to the user, not CPU seconds, and in time-shared or multiprogrammed systems much of the elapsed time is not under his control. Thus the single greatest time-saving technique, accumulating an economical batch size before processing data, is not available to him. He must process data items in arrival sequence even if this imposes severe penalties in file access delay. Also, the programmer must take his input element all the way through the process to some resolution (updating a file, answering a question, or rejecting the item because of error), but he cannot ignore even a defective data element. This often leads to the frustrating circumstance that far more time is spent programming the handling of deviant cases than of conventional or acceptable cases. One consequence of this, in turn, is that programmers of interactive systems need to know more about the overall system of which their program is a part than do their batch-processing brethren, since they must be aware of all the error conditions that other programs can detect or cause. A somewhat far-reaching analogy is the craftsman who makes a complete object, compared to the specialist who performs one operation on all objects on an assembly line.

***Conversation with the User*** Fortunately there is an abundance of literature on the very broad subject of conversation with the user, and much of it is not computer-related but concerned with programmed instruction, a pedagogical form in which short presentations (in print, on film, from a computer terminal) are followed by questions. The student's answer to the question determines what presentation-question or "frame" is taken up next [4]. In addition, Martin [5], Meadow [6], and Lancaster [7] discuss a number of conversational procedures.

Basically the programmer is obliged to put himself in the position of the user and to visualize how the interactive system appears from the user's side of the terminal. For a simple example, the programmer wants to ask the user a true-false question. He plans for what steps he will take in the event of either response. But what if the user's response is 1, or the misspelling TRVE, or no response at all? A reasonable number of high-probability invalid answers can be anticipated, and TRVE may be one of them. But not all combinations can be anticipated. Therefore, the programmer must plan for three contingencies: (*a*) an invalid answer that could be anticipated, such as a misspelling, (*b*) an unrecognizable answer, and (*c*) no answer.

The programmer will probably know what to do in case *a*: forgive and ignore the error, tell the user exactly what he did and ask him to try again, or simply reject the input and ask for another. In case *b* he cannot tell the user what went wrong, only that something did. In case *c,* if he has a timing mechanism available, he can treat a period without response as an anticipated answer and ask for some user action or disconnect the terminal.

Another order of problem occurs when the user repeatedly makes errors. Then the programmer is likely to want to know if it is the same error, or if there is any discernible pattern, and he must decide how many times he is willing to have his program respond to erroneous inputs before he simply turns off the terminal.

One way to cut down on operator error is to ask for information item by item, with detailed instructions, to say

    _____ (instructional material)

    _____

    ANSWER T FOR TRUE, F FOR FALSE

rather than

    ANSWER TRUE OR FALSE

    _____ (instructional material)

    _____

(The second alternative allows the user to forget how he is supposed to reply because response instructions come first and seem to require the full word TRUE or FALSE, rather than a single character.)

With a CRT terminal, where writing speeds are high, it costs little to provide detailed information for each data item being elicited from the operator. For print terminals, when the user must watch messages being typed at a rate of 10–30 characters per second, excessive or repetitive instruction can be nerve-racking.

The programmer, often with little background qualification, is responsible for achieving *conversational fluency,* the smooth passage of information back and forth between man and machine. Failure to achieve fluency results in inefficient, perhaps ineffective use of the computer *and its operator,* possibly a far more serious problem than inefficient use of the computer. Again making a broad analogy, the responsibility for a smooth interview of the type so often seen on television talk shows lies with the interviewer. Like the guest, he must know the subject, but ability to ask questions that bring out the best in the interviewee is a skill altogether different from display of subject-matter knowledge.

**Continuity** A requirement deriving both from the design of the processing programs and of the man-machine conversation is that the conversation cannot abruptly cease. The data item must be brought to some resolution (stored, rejected, etc.), and the operator must be aware of what is happening if he is to continue to do his job. Fortunately in some of the most troublesome cases the programmer can rely on the operator to help him by informing the user of the situation and presenting alternative choices for action. In this way, when the user helps the program resolve errors, true symbiosis is achieved. For example, suppose that a user has just entered a new record for insertion into a file. After all the validity checks are made, the program tries to store the record, only to find that the data manager rejects it because there is already a record having this key. Simply rejecting the record is expensive—the user has spent considerable time keying the data in, and that work should be conserved. On the other hand, the program cannot tell whether the user meant to change the existing record or simply used a seemingly valid, but erroneous key. At this point, it is well to consult the user, inform him of the situation and the alternatives, and let him make the decision.

### 10.3.4 Design Implications of Interactive Systems

As we have pointed out, an interactive information system is as different from its batch-mode counterpart as dialogue between two people is from a book written by one of them. The author of a book presents his ideas in a continuous stream. He gets no feedback from the reader while the book is in use (i.e., being read). The author must carefully plan the readership he is aiming at. He assumes the background he feels a reader should have, may omit information from the book that he feels the reader should already know, and explains material he does not expect to be familiar. Any book will be too difficult for some readers, too elementary for others. Human dialogue, on the other hand, involves short messages with feedback in several forms (oral, gesture, expression) to show level of comprehension or acceptance by the partner in dialogue.

A batch-mode computer program expects certain input data and may have certain validity tests to perform on input. But omissions or errors tend to cause rejection of input and possibly abortion of the program. The program cannot modify the input, just as the author cannot modify his book for individual readers as they come to difficult passages. Interactive systems are programmed to look for omissions or errors in data, inform an operator of the condition, possibly suggest the next step, and await new input. In carrying out the dialogue between machine and man on the subject of input errors, the computer is much more anxious to learn what is wrong than to merely confirm that something is amiss. The program should be written to provide the operator with all the information he needs to take the next step, and to be prepared to answer the operator's requests for more information.

We may consider the design implications of interactive systems from two points of view: the *user* (how he will work with the system and how his work will be changed by it) and *interface languages*.

*User Impact*   The user of the computer is a part of an information system. When given an interactive system, he may expect to exercise more control over programs, to receive faster turn around on any processing, to have more information available to him, and to be faced with more decisions about how to handle unexpected situations. This shifts much of the burden for direct responsibility for operating an information system to the user or to a professional staff assigned to serve users. As a result, users or user support personnel must become more familiar with the data and the machinery than ever before. This, in turn, implies possibly different personnel selection criteria and certainly more technical training on the job.

*System Languages*   Interaction can result in simplifying all user languages because it is not necessary to enter long, complex statements at any time. Conversational systems permit users to enter small increments of information or commands, thereby doing away with the elaborate syntax of less direct forms of communication, just as any single statement in a dialogue between people is liable to be both shorter and grammatically simpler than a written paragraph. Here is an example of the difference between a query to a batch information retrieval system and one to a conversational system, using hypothetical languages. In the batch system, we might ask for

$$(age > 40) \,\&\, (occupation = \text{MATHEMATICIAN} \,|\, \text{STATISTICIAN}) \,\&\, (employment\ date < 1959)$$

where & is the symbol for *and* and | is the symbol for *or*. An interactive system user might ask for the same information in the conversation illustrated in Figure 10.8, where, each line shows a multilpart conversation. The computer, "knowing" the user wants to retrieve, asks him to define the first set by asking

SET 1:

This message both informs the user of the set number and implicitly asks him to provide the next element of information, which is a choice of a selection criterion or a combination of previously defined sets. Here the user responds S, stating that he wants to provide a selection criterion.

The computer asks for the name of the data item, which the user gives as AGE. Then the computer asks for the relationship between the field value in a record and the value about to be entered; the user replies >. The value is requested and given as 40. This is followed by the symbol ▼ to indicate the end of selection criteria for this set. A common alternative way to signal the end is for the computer to ask whether there is another criterion, the user replying yes or no; but this is an example of a tediously repetitive question.

Although this way of entering data into a computer uses far more characters than the compact form given before, the burden on the user to remember and apply syntactic rules is substantially lessened. The set 2 conversation of Figure 10.8 furnishes an example of what may happen when the user ignores a grammatical rule—in this case that alphabetic fields have no defined magnitude, hence there is no meaning to ≥ in connection with the *occupation* field.

Rather than accept the ≥ symbol and go on to request a value, the program rejects it with the message INVALID SYMBOL and gives an explana-

```
SET 1:  S  DATA ITEM:  AGE  REL:  >  VALUE:  40▼

SET 2:  S  DATA ITEM:  OCCUPATION  REL:  ≥  INVALID SYMBOL

OCCUPATION IS AN ALPHABETICAL FIELD.  REL:  =  VALUE:  MATHEMATICIAN

ALTERNATE VALUE:  STATISTICIAN▼

SET 3:  S  DATA ITEM:  EMPLOYMENT DATE  REL:  ≤  VALUE:  1959

SET 4:  C  SET NO:  1  LINK:  *  SET NO:  2  LINK:  *  SET NO:  3▼
```

**Figure 10.8** Portion of an information retrieval conversation. Messages that are shaded are sent by computer, others by the user.

tion of the error. The user may then try again, and he does so with =, which is acceptable. This time two possible values of the field are given before the criteria conversation is ended.

The error illustrated here was immediately made known and explained to the operator, who could easily correct it. But this involves an assumption by the system that the field name was correct and the relationship symbol in error. Suppose the field name had consisted of a single character, say O, making it much easier to accidentally enter it incorrectly without the operator noticing it. Then the error message could have been misleading because the program would have had to assume either that the name was wrong or that the relationship was wrong. Once the presence of an error is detected in any syntactic language, there may be ambiguity in locating the source of error. Assuming the source, and being wrong about it, is misleading. Failing to supply whatever information is available may be costly in the long run. Providing all known possibilities may be confusing, as well. The programmer must base his choice on what he knows about the users.

When the language of communication is as simple as that illustrated, the language processor does not need to build and maintain a set of tables descriptive of the input statements and their syntactic interconnections as elaborate as would be needed if the processor had to keep track of where each symbol fit or might fit into a larger syntactic unit. The information the language processor extracts to execute the request or compile another program to do so is the same regardless of whether the input is conversational. The difference is user convenience and the complexity of the program needed to parse any given input statement. For this reason, many interactive systems tend to use rather simple languages.

The net effect of a transition to interactive systems is higher investment in computer hardware and software, greater dependence on the mechanical system (hence raising the criticality of its reliability), and greater productivity of users. Not all these effects are found in all systems. The individual designer must determine their applicability in each instance.

## 10.4 STRATEGY IN THE USE OF DATA MANAGEMENT SYSTEMS

We are concerned here with using a data management system to retrieve information, whether a single item or a lengthy report or subfile. In many retrieval situations, and those we principally discuss here, there is an element of uncertainty in what will happen and an element of risk in that use of the system bears costs, mainly in money and time. The uncertainty comes about because the user has a problem to solve, wants information to help him, and cannot always be sure what information is there—what records, what they will tell him, or what the content of those records is. Thus he knows at the start that he is going to have to ask a question, receive a response, decide what to do next, based at least partially on that response, and so on. Each iteration costs time and money. Each, hopefully, contributes to a solution of the problem, although not necessarily in a positive way, for complete failure to find what is sought is always a possibility.

The user should have in mind if not in writing a statement of his objective. What, ideally, is he looking for? Knowing that he may not achieve a perfect response, the user should also have some feel for what he will settle for and how much time and money he is willing to devote to the effort. For example, a user might be about to query a bibliographic information system for some precise information about a new scientific development. He knows the name of the subject, probably knows the principal authors in the field, but does not know how the subject is catalogued in this particular system or how much information he will find. He recognizes, therefore, that part of his effort must be devoted to browsing to find how to identify the subject, and he recognizes that the data base he is searching may not have all the information he wants. Thus he knows that he may have to decide to quit searching before reaching his ultimate objective, but only after he has become convinced the desired information is not there.

Or, suppose that a business executive planning his long-term investment strategy wants information about how particular products are selling and on classes of products, on regional buying habits, price trends in raw materials, performance of salesmen, manufacturing costs of his company, transportation costs, and population trends in the country at large. He faces the same problem as the bibliographic searcher in that he may not find what he wants; but in addition, the whole course of his search may be changed by what he finds. If the national trend is away from buying buggy whips, he not only loses interest in buggy whip raw materials and transportation facilities but begins to look not at how to invest in buggy whips but how to dismantle this portion of his business. Although a single person seldom undertakes so wide-ranging a search for information in one sitting at his computer terminal, there is no time limit on strategic concerns, and an individual's use of information retrieval strategy applies as much to the larger information system, which is his corporate staff, as it does to his computer system. In either case a user must have knowledge of the kinds of information in his data base, knowledge or understanding of the limitations of the particular records stored in the system (e.g., the system has bibliographic citations of publications on research in biochemistry, but not necessarily all publications, and none published within the last two months), and good knowledge of the user's language, to enable him to probe the material that is there.

Information retrieval strategy, let us emphasize, is not something unique to information retrieval. This form of thinking—facing an uncertain situation, using trial and error probes that consume some resource of value, needing to recognize that total victory may not be possible and, if not, determining the best path to follow—is precisely what the businessman, soldier, or football coach does routinely in his own field. No matter how clever the computer language, there remains the task of using it well to achieve an objective, and this requires the same degree of skill and judgment that must be exerted in most professional activities.

## REFERENCES

1. Data Base Task Group, *CODASYL Data Base Task Group Report*, Conference on Data Systems Language, Association for Computing Machinery, New York, 1971.
2. J. C. R. Licklider, "Man-Computer Symbiosis," *IRE Transactions on Human Factors in Electronics*, Vol. HFE-1 (March 1960), pp. 4–11.
3. Charles T. Meadow, *Man-Machine Communication*, Wiley-Interscience, New York, 1970, pp. 3–4.
4. J. L. Hughes, *Programmed Instruction for Schools and Industry*, Science Research Associates, Chicago, 1962.
5. James Martin, *Design of Man-Computer Dialogues*, Prentice-Hall, Englewood Cliffs, N.J., 1973.
6. Meadow, *op. cit.*
7. F. Wilfrid Lancaster and E. G. Fayen, *Information Retrieval On-Line*, Melville Publishing Co., Los Angeles, 1973

## RECOMMENDED READING

### *Interactive Systems*

Lancaster [7], Licklider [2], and Meadow [3].

Meadow, Charles T. and M. B. Henderson, Eds., *Interactive Bibliographic Systems*, CONF-711010, U.S. Atomic Energy Commission, Washington, D.C., 1973.

Martin, Thomas H., "The User Interface in Interactive Systems." In *Annual Review of Information Science and Technology*, Vol. 8, C. A. Cuadra and A. Luke, Eds., American Society for Information Science, Washington, D.C., 1973, pp. 203–20.

### *Languages*

Barnett, E. H., "Learn to 'Think' Like the Computer," *Programming Time-Shared Computers in BASIC*, Wiley-Interscience, New York, 1972, pp. 100–3.

Pirtle, M. W., "Help." In *Conversational Computers*, W. D. Orr, Ed., John Wiley & Sons, New York, 1968, pp. 96–101.

*Chapter Eleven*

# Information Systems

## 11.1 THE NATURE OF INFORMATION SYSTEMS

The users of information, for whom information systems are designed, begin their quest for a new system because of the existence of a problem having to do with the acquisition, processing, retrieval, or delivery of information. Users are primarily concerned with solving their own problems, not with the information technology used in a solution. Their scope of interest is broad. How is the information created or acquired? What people contribute to it? What has to be done to make the information more useful? What information is needed by the organization or the clientele served?

    A computer system consisting of hardware and software is merely a component of the total information system needed to serve users. The process of determining user requirements and using them to derive complete system specifications is in the realm of *systems analysis,* which is not the subject of this book. This chapter sets the broad framework in which computer systems are conceived and designed. An information system, in this context, comprises data, people, and procedures as well as machines. It is as important to identify the purposes and objectives of a system and to evaluate performance toward them as to evaluate internal functioning.

### 11.1.1 The Nature of Information

A system to collect, store, and process information cannot be designed in the absence of some understanding of what information is and a definition of "information system." Most machines, at least complex ones, are information systems in that the various components pass messages to one another, such as a thermometer reporting a temperature to a thermostat, which uses this information to pass a message to the heater or air conditioner. Communications engineers have a precise mathematical definition of information, but their concern is solely with the transmission of messages *not with their meaning*. In data management, information retrieval, and management information systems, we are very much concerned with the communication of meaning. Meaning, in turn, is highly dependent on human interpretation. That is why the human aspects of information systems are so important.

Some theorists define information as an input to a decision-making process. In this sense, a message contains information only if used to formulate a decision. This is a useful distinction in many technical processes (weather prediction, control of continuous chemical processes, etc.), but it does not seem well suited to one traditionally recognized information system—the library. Rather than passing judgment on the use of information, libraries react to the demand for it. If a library were to elect to acquire and store only material that would be of pragmatic, decision-making value to its users, it would be obliged to develop a system for measuring the utility of information to users instead of being satisfied with fulfilling user requests. Thus how we define information can affect how we design systems.

Another poorly defined area that can affect system design is reflected in the difference between data and information. *Information,* to many users, is the result of analysis or processing; it is a useful entity. On the other hand, there is a tendency to view *data* as unprocessed or unevaluated symbols. Some users insist that they want only information from a system, not data that must be processed or evaluated. That is, they want reliable information in a particular, useful, and valuable form. Yet each user may assign a different meaning to "useful" or "reliable" or "evaluated," and any one person may change his views over time. Furthermore, data to one person may be information to another. The department store clerk who carefully records and reports his total sales for the day believes that he is providing information, for the report is a processed, evaluated summary of his day's activities. To the store's long-range planner, the information constitutes raw data, useful in planning only in conjunction with other data and when processed by the appropriate sales forecasting models. The user whose meaning of "information" is narrowly defined in contradistinction to data, may be very demanding of his information system, possibly requesting the impossible. The more flexible user who recognizes that the transformation of data into information is a highly subjective and temporal matter, may be satisfied with a broader based system that provides the informational raw material for his needs.

Without trying to resolve the philosophical issues underlying the various meanings of "data" and "information," it is convenient to have a vocabulary with which to describe the various interpretations, because all have some importance. The problem is simply that we cannot use the same term, "information," for many different concepts.

Our preference is to designate by "information" the lowest common element in the many meanings—the meaning often used for data—a string of characters or symbols. If this is information, we must recognize that there are other concepts descriptive of information before or after processing, refinement, or selection, including the following.

1. *Raw data or information* consists of symbols collected and stored but not evaluated relative to a particular user's point of view.
2. *Evaluated information* is a set of symbols ascribed some value or credibility, but usually at one point in time and for one evaluator. Often people forget the temporal nature of this evaluation or that others do not share the value judgment.
3. *Transmitted information.* In formal communication theory a transmission implies a message received as well as one sent; unless both events occur, we cannot say that transmission has taken place. Information is that which is transmitted.
4. *Decision input* is information selected for use in making a decision.
5. *Reference information* is about other information and descriptive of the location or content of an element or set of information.
6. *Derived information* is produced by induction, deduction, or mathematical processing from an existing set of information (input). The validity of the derivation is as transitory as the evaluation of the input.

### 11.1.2 The Composition of an Information System

An information system consists of the computer languages, programs, and hardware that we have already described, but it also includes the people who use, operate, or manage portions of the system, the procedures under which they operate, and the data stored or processed. The design of any component must be in the context of the whole, and the objectives of the system must be set in terms of the overall system not individual components. The most common instance of failure to meet these goals is the technology-driven system, in which the main force is determination to implement a computer system or other technological innovation rather than desire for achieving a particular level of performance.

*Procedures* Procedures are the rules under which a system operates: rules of air navigation govern the design of an air traffic control system; rules of library cataloguing determine the manner in which books are processed in a library; the accounting rules of a firm determine how its financial transactions are conducted. These kinds of procedures tend to be established independently of the mechanical part of the system that carries them out.

*People* Whenever procedures are subject to interpretation, people tend to dominate the system. It is the people who decide how to implement procedures. For example, people classify books in a library, direct aircraft, and enter data into a computer-based invoicing system. Failures or imperfections in these manual operations may negate the value of the remainder of an information system.

*Data* The data form the heart of an information system, its reason for being. All the other components are present to process or store data. We have a tendency to speak interchangeably of the system-including-its-data, and the system-apart-from-its-data, and this leads to confusion and inaccuracy in setting or measuring performance objectives. We recognize that a data base may be characterized by quality or freedom from error; *timeliness*, a relative concept concerned with the speed by which data elements are updated to reflect a change in real-world conditions; and *completeness*, which has two dimensions, *breadth* and *depth*—roughly, how many entities are reported in the data base and how much information there is on each. A complementary characteristic to completeness is *selectivity*, a measure of how well a subset of a totality of information is selected for a particular purpose (e.g., how books are selected for a library from the population of books available).

The design specification of an information system must encompass all these components *and* must state the nature of their interaction. Thus it should not only identify new procedures but account for how procedural changes are to be brought about, such as through employee training, hiring of new staff, or contracting the new work to a service organization. Similarly, the design of a data base must encompass the collection and quality control of data, not just its organization in storage.

### 11.1.3 Categories of Systems

The usual categorizations of information systems depend on the kind of information processed. Since the nature and definition of information are not generally agreed on, precision of definition is questionable. The following are the traditionally recognized types of information systems.

1. *Document retrieval system*—a library; an information system whose principal output is documents that have been stored within but were not composed by the system.
2. *Reference system*—an information system whose principal data base consists of references to documents or other external entities (e.g., photographs, people) but does not store or retrieve the documents or other referents themselves.
3. *Bibliographic systems*—a generic term, generally applied to document retrieval systems, reference systems, or a combination of these.
4. *Fact retrieval system*—named in reaction to some of the inadequacies of bibliographic systems; providers of *answers,* rather than references or documents potentially containing answers. But in fact, most business applications of computers fit this category, and their use predated the use of this term. The nature of "fact" is problematical and it is hairsplitting to debate the difference between a *reference,* which gives facts about a document, and a *stored fact,* which is not a reference to something.
5. *Data retrieval system*—generally has about the same meaning as *fact retrieval* but avoids use of the controversial term. It is intended to distinguish between a system that retrieves symbols stored within it and processable by it (e.g., a field within a file stored on magnetic tape) and a system that retrieves only documents it cannot process.
6. *Deductive or question-answering systems*—typically, the data sets are not complete, and in addition to retrieving information the system is able to make deductions or draw conclusions from the fragmentary data elements provided. The systems are thereby capable of composing their own answers to some questions. Hence they supply direct answers to questions rather than merely providing references or documents or even recovering facts that were indexed in the manner requested by a searcher. Whether the response to a question deduced by the system is a fact must be determined by the user.
7. *Data base management or generalized data management systems*—tends to be a programmer's term rather than a user's term. It refers to a program able to carry out data management functions, more or less without regard for the nature of the data and usually offering wide variation in permissible data structures.

228     *Information Systems*

If a system user were interested in the value of butter exported from Denmark during 1973, he would ask a document retrieval system for documents pertaining to his subject or to a broader subject. If he used a reference system, he would have to be content with references to documents, but if he were an experienced researcher and good library facilities were available, the references could be invaluable. In other words, a reference system is used in conjunction with a document retrieval system and together, in many circumstances, they provide all the service needed. Put to a fact or data retrieval system, this question should yield an answer—an amount of money. If the user had sufficient confidence in the system, this might satisfy him completely. If he had any doubt, he might have preferred a document or a reference to one that would furnish supporting evidence or some means of evaluating the quality of the information given him. A question-answering system might deduce the amount from other "facts" in its store if the precise information were not explicitly available. For example, it might retrieve the 1971 and 1972 figures and assume that the 1973 value is an average of them. The weakness of such a system is that the user may not know the logical chain of reasoning by which the result is determined. A data base management system would not answer the question at all, it would merely provide the computer software upon which one of the categories of information system would be built. With the probable exception of question-answering systems, the software underlying these different system types may be the same or at least similar. The differences tend to be in the definition of data elements within a system and the expectations of the users.

## 11.2  FUNCTIONS AND PARAMETERS OF INFORMATION SYSTEMS

There is no accepted set of parameters or measurable variables that can be specified to determine the design of an information system. Therefore, few mathematical models of information systems can be used to predict performance and thereby to probe assumptions made during design. By contrast, in the design of a physical structure, say, a bridge or an airplane, the various properties of components and the forces acting on them are fairly well known, are measurable, have predictable behavior, and have known interactions. Therefore, we can predict the performance of an assumed structure from a mathematical model of it before the real version is built.

There is often a tendency to make computer algorithms, such as a data manager, the kernel of information systems design. Such algorithms are, of course, important, as emphasized in Chapters 2–8. At this point, however, we wish to address some data- and people-related variables and processes and point out that their impact on information systems may be as great as that of the data manager.

### 11.2.1 Acquisition

The origin of data (or information), how it is selected, how it enters a system, and the timing of its collection and entry are of critical importance for they affect the reliability and general utility of information. For example, a stock market system that is complete and accurate but three hours behind the market is of little more use to a trader than a daily newspaper. Any information acquisition system picks up a certain amount of "noise" or spurious signals. A common example is the entry of information into an automobile repair shop's manually operated information system. The man in the white coat, who greets the customer with a set of forms attached to a clipboard, tends to be a highly distortive information acquisition system. He often oversimplifies or misrepresents the problem as identified by the customer, with the result that the entire servicing process goes awry. A battlefield intelligence observer is another example. He sees only a limited part of a complex, dynamic situation and his reports are often misleading, but they are all the commander has to go on. Clearly the net performance of an information system is affected by how well the acquisition subsystem functions in its various dimensions of completeness, selectivity, accuracy, and timeliness.

### 11.2.2 Data Preparation

Often seen only by the professional, data preparation concerns the human processing of collected information before it is passed into a mechanical processor or to storage. A prime example is a library cataloguer, who is not concerned with acquisition of books or in searching them on behalf of users; instead, this individual composes the record that becomes the basis for organization in storage and for searching—the catalog card. The telephone switchboard operator or receptionist for a large organization also performs such a function, for when a stranger first contacts the organization, this employee "classifies" the caller and determines who shall talk with him. An error here can waste time, affect public relations, or lose a sale. Yet the operator is an imperfect classifier of these messages because he rarely knows the firm or its products well enough to refer the call unerringly to the correct person. Another example is the newpaper editor, sometimes known as a "gatekeeper," who selects the stories to be used from among the many available on the press association wires.

Any error or ambiguity introduced by the preparer is added to that of the originator or acquisition subsystem. On the other hand, the preparer may detect and correct acquisition errors and can cope with inconsistency. The use of human data preparation personnel rather than a mechanized subsystem is not inherently good or bad but depends on the judicious selection of people and functions.

### 11.2.3 Transcription

In typical business or bibliographic information systems, most of the information stored in a computer is entered by means of some key stroking operation, whether keypunching data into punched cards or entering data through a remote CRT terminal or teletype. There are, of course, automatic acquisition devices such as radar or optical character readers (OCR). Many business uses of OCR merely recycle information previously key stroked, as when a document is typed, then read into a computer by OCR, or when a computer prints an invoice to be mailed to a customer, then reads it when the customer returns it with his payment.

Transcription, the rendering of information into machine-readable form, is expensive and it introduces errors into a system, since no transcriber is perfectly accurate. There are countermeasures, such as proofreading or verifying. (The latter consists of repetition of the keystroking process in such a way that the differences between the two transcriptions are flagged. If one transcriber punches ABC and another punches ABD, the conflict is noted by the machine.) But at best these techniques only detect errors; they do not correct them, and they add materially to the cost of data preparation. Correction must be performed by a human operator.

For any data stream entering a computer (or other storage or processing component), the cost, time, and errors introduced by the transcription function must be taken into account. More than one information system has failed or aborted because the required input rates could not be humanly achieved.

### 11.2.4 Validation

As discussed in Section 7.2, validation is the testing of the content of input data. Content errors may occur in the acquisition, preparation, or transcription stages. Validation in some form is necessary: the alternative is chaos in the system files.

In using validation, one must recognize that while detection of errors may be at rapid, computer speed, correction tends to be a human process in which a person is informed of the error, collects background information needed to correct it, and proceeds again through the data preparation and transcription steps.

The cost of validation can be deceptively high. Validating computer programs are not particularly difficult to write, but it is time-consuming and tedious to record in algorithmic form all the validation criteria for the elements of a record. An even more taxing problem is changing the programs to keep up with changes in criteria, such as wage scales, course offerings at a university, or the classification codes in use by a library. All such variables are subject to change, and modification, in turn, subjects validation criteria to change.

### 11.2.5 Data and Transaction Characteristics

A possibly apocryphal story is told of the airline reservation system in which the ticket agent's terminal had a special key whose label denoted "cancel my last transmission." During periods of heavy loading on the system, when response from the computer was slow, agents often cancelled requests for information that was desirable but not actually necessary. Getting no acknowledgment of the *cancel* message, the agents struck the key repeatedly, as if trying to attract a telephone operator's attention. However, each jiggle was sending another *cancel* message, and all but the first had no real "last message" to refer to. The result was to choke an already belabored system. The intriguing point is that the final, choking condition came about only because the system was already overloaded. Regardless of the truth of the story, it illustrates the problems that may arise when a system designer does not know the distribution of arrival time of messages and the factors that affect arrival rate.

For another example, assume an on-line system for which $x$ uses a day are expected and $y$ seconds of computer time are required, where $xy = 24$ hours. If the arrival rate is evenly distributed throughout the day, the load can be handled. But if $x/2$ uses arrive during an 8-hour interval, a variation from the mean value of only one-sixth during one-third of the normal business day, there may be a serious overloading problem. Thus time of day of arrival of input may be an important design characteristic.

Also important is the content distribution of input. Suppose, for example, that 50% of change transactions to an ISAM file are directed to the middle third of the file in alphabetic sequence. This might overload the cylinder overflow areas and push the system near the danger point of losing data. Knowing that this is the distribution may lead to a different choice of data manager, primary sort key, or overflow strategy. Failing to anticipate the distribution may result in unacceptable system performance.

We cannot list all relevant characteristics of data. These few examples indicate that implicit assumptions about data characteristics can be disastrous. When data characteristics are unknown, we cannot validly assume they will be convenient.

### 11.2.6 Response Time

Response time is the time required to react to a user's input to an information system—to answer a query, for example, or to confirm or otherwise reply to a file change message. Deciding on the necessary response time or the economically optimum response time is often no more subject to quantitative analysis than are data characteristics. Given the choice between batch-mode transactions, remote job entry (RJE), and truly interactive approaches to man-machine communication, often involving large cost differentials, a designer may be hard pressed to justify his selection among those methods, even though it will be the major determinant of response time.

Load conditions and the computer's system of handling priorities may slow an interactive system below the performance level of an RJE mode. Once again, to choose between them, a system designer must know the specific requirements of his users, which may vary from application to application. At times a researcher, for example, may wish to interact conversationally with an information retrieval system, but occasionally he may willingly settle for overnight service, at far lower cost.

## 11.3 INTEGRATED SYSTEMS

Within any large organization using computers, the move toward mechanization of information handling typically proceeds in piecemeal fashion. In a business system the payroll function may come first, followed by inventory control, customer billing, and budget planning. Gradually, as the individual systems grow and new ones are added, the combined data bases begin to show some of the following characteristics.

1. *Redundancy*—essentially the same data elements are found in more than one file (e.g., an employee's home address in both the personnel and payroll files, a description of a part in the inventory file, the purchasing file and the file listing components of products produced).
2. *Intercommunication*—information is passed from file to file (e.g., from

the personnel to the payroll file as an employee is hired or promoted, from the engineering listing of components of products to inventory and purchasing files on design of a new product or change in an existing design).
3. *Data conflict*—data elements bearing essentially the same label may contain different values (e.g, the project manager's budget may differ from the controller's budget because even having started from the same point, these officers use different means of updating and different definitions of obligation and expenditure of funds). Or, long-range predictions of sales or income may vary depending on the assumptions used by the estimators—the marketing, engineering and finance departments may all produce different estimates. We cannot blindly interchange these estimates, even if they happen to have the same name and formal data definition. It is necessary to know exactly what the item *means,* and this is not normally an element in data definition languages. In the examples just given, estimates of future income by different estimators may be based on amount planned to be spent plus a profit margin, on amount committed to by a manager as a sales quota, or on the amount estimated to be received on sales of as yet undeveloped products in terms of future, inflated currency. It is unlikely these varying concepts will be mistakenly interchanged in conversation, but an information system user or programmer browsing through a file definition might well interpret them all as equivalent.

Even with identically defined fields, differences can exist in the ways the organizations that use the file update it. Simple differences in reporting times and deadlines can affect meaning. What is a patient's condition? A customer's credit balance? The score of a football game (when there is a critical difference in meaning depending on whether the score is final or the game is still in progress)?

As a result of these kinds of communication problems, the idea of an *integrated data base* or *integrated information system* has arisen. The fundamental idea is to eliminate redundant storage of information by entering each data element only once for the entire organizational data base, thereby saving storage space, the cost of redundant processing, and the cost of having to deal with conflicting data.

Multilist and network concepts have facilitated the evolution of software that enables many individual users or local information systems to use part of a computer data base as a subschema, without duplication of information. Attempts to build such systems having this characteristic gave rise in the organization to a new type of job called *data base administrator* (Section 10.1.5). This employee designs and maintains a data base that serves disparate users, and he assists individual users in arranging to use it. In effect, this is a centralized information service for the information system, an essential form of control when many people are entering and retrieving data with respect to a common data base.

Integrated systems are a technical ideal, still not common in practice; the difficulties in their implementation lie perhaps more in the human than the mechanical sphere. A successfully integrated system requires coordination among many people who often have honest reasons for defending a parochial point of view. The investment in time to coordinate definitions, data base maintenance schedules, and validation rules may be more than the cost of the duplicate information under the older concept. Although this state of affairs seems clearly inefficient to data processing professionals, the politics of competing groups within an organization do not always yield to rational analysis.

At its worst, the integrated system is an example of the technological imperative—taking an action because it is technically feasible (because, as the mountain climber says, it is there), without due regard for the effects of the action on the social feasibility. Designers must recognize that people change their habits slowly, whereas programs can be changed overnight. On the other hand, to ignore the clearly apparent problems and costs of nonintegrated files is foolhardy. Each separate instance of communication from one file to another, without prior agreement on definition of fields, priority of maintenance, timeliness of reporting requirements, access restrictions, and so on, requires tedious and expensive bargaining among using groups and reprogramming of computers that can be eliminated by the integrated system. The system designer must select his strategy of integration in full awareness of the costs and benefits of either extreme position and try to find the approach best suited to his organization. It is, of course, possible to integrate slowly, to make a move in this direction each time a major program or file is modified. The extreme positions are represented by high cost of full integration and high cost of no integration.

## 11.4 PERFORMANCE

In weighing the merits of any design pending a decision to proceed, once it seems that the proposed system can produce the desired results, the key question is: what measure of performance will be achieved per unit of investment? Since objectives are stated broadly, there is often more than one system that can meet them. Then as the question suggests, the problem becomes not necessarily to find the best in terms of performance but to determine the best in terms of performance per cost unit. Unfortunately, in information systems we are almost without meaningful measures of performance and may even be hard pressed to define cost units. Let us consider these conditions separately.

### 11.4.1 Specification of Performance

The ideal first step in the design of anything is to decide what it should do, and the only way to determine whether objectives have been met is to devise a way of quantifying performance requirements and to measure actual performance against these requirements. Having set up a structure of objectives, requirements, and measures for the system as a whole, it is then possible to do the same for each of the major components, for the components of the major components, and so on.

In real life, particularly when working with systems involving people, there is no neat, logical progression from higher objectives and requirements to lower ones, and often no means of measuring performance at any but the lowest component level. For example, the objective of a business is not simply to maximize profit. It might be to maximize the probability of continued profitability. In other words, no reputable company wants to make enormous profits in one year if this policy will jeopardize its continued existence. Thus the company's objective becomes a compromise of goals: profits plus the goodwill of its customers, its employees, the government, and the community in which it is located, for all these relationships can affect future prosperity. But how does one specify the performance of a company in achieving good customer relations? How can management decide whether a low profit year, due to an investment in pollution control equipment, was fully justified by long-term community goodwill?

When we consider government or nonprofit organizations, the specification and measurement of performance is even more difficult. Is the best police department the one that makes the most arrests or the one that reports the least crime in its area of responsibility? How do we tell how well a library performs?

Difficult as the overall goals may be to set, it is sometimes fairly easy to specify component objectives and to measure their performances. For example, regardless of the aim of a business, we might be able to set precise performance objectives for a machine or production unit and to measure output precisely. Regardless of why the library exists, we can specify and measure the performance of the bindery, circulation, and microfilm units. What is important is to avoid confusing the whole and the part, a logical systems analysis error that has been likened [1] to *synecdoche,* the name of a figure of speech in which a part is substituted for the whole (*sail* for *ship,* or *hand* for *sailor*). It is relatively easy but often fallacious to evaluate an information system according to the *efficiency* of its computer programs or the percentage of relevant records it can retrieve in response to a query. Their *effectiveness* in aiding the achievement of some objective is really more significant, but harder to measure.

As we have said, often in real life we must specify component performance without specifying overall system performance, and we are frequently obliged to measure the performance of parts when we cannot measure the performance of the whole. So long as information systems design remains an inexact science, we must continue in this fashion. The main objection to the practice involves the possibility of mistaking one for the other—not recognizing that measuring computer performance is different from measuring system performance, or conversely, claiming that because the overall system seems to work well, the computer operation must be efficient.

### 11.4.2 Measurement of Performance

To set a goal whose achievement cannot be unequivocably demonstrated may be meaningless. It is desirable to be able to measure performance against requirements. The possibilities are endless. We shall concentrate on six: cost, speed, throughput, efficiency, quality, and effectiveness.

*Cost*  Cost is the one measure that is usually applicable to any system and gives the most reliable basis for comparison of one system against another. Yet cost is not represented as a single number. There is cost to develop and cost to operate a system. The most obvious cost is financial, but each use of a resource represents a cost, and often such resources as people and building space are as critical as money cost.

Standard accounting principles can be used to compute the cost of developing and operating an information system. The critical problem is accuracy of estimate. Because the information field is still relatively primitive compared to a field such as civil engineering, estimates are often low. Thus in selecting systems on the basis of estimated cost, another factor is the probability that the estimated cost is accurate. Truly probabilistic cost estimating, in which it is fully recognized that each element of cost is represented by a probability distribution of possible values, is rarely done. To introduce such complications would confound legal contracting and corporate or governmental budgeting procedures. Insisting that costs are known and fixed in advance is unrealistic, although commonplace.

*Speed* How quickly an information system responds to its users is another usually measurable parameter, but again one that does not consist of a single number. Response time is likely to vary on a number of factors: type of request, time of day, system load, or specific type of service requested (e.g., full interactive or remote batch). Reasonable speed of response is almost always a necessity, although users have a tendency to invoke the technological imperative and exaggerate their requirements. Nonetheless, it is important to specify the approximate speed of response as a system requirement and to monitor carefully its actual performance.

*Throughput* The amount of work or number of transactions the system can handle in a given amount of time may be among the most significant factors in the evaluation of computer performance or that of any other production component. At higher levels of abstraction, throughput can be misleading. The author has encountered at least one bibliographic system that measured its productivity in terms of number of references retrieved, even going so far as to count repeated references on the same response (which can happen if more than one search criterion retrieves the same record) and to count as additional references carbon copies of the computer listing! This is like paying a taxi driver for gasoline consumed rather than miles driven. Fuel consumption, or production of redundant references, does not necessarily contribute to an objective, even though achievement of the objective may require these activities. A poor information system may generate many transactions and much output. Along with any analysis of throughput must go consideration of how much is desirable and the value of the transactions put through.

*Efficiency* Efficiency is a measure of output per unit of input or of work performed per unit of cost. Like the specification of performance, the measurement of efficiency often suffers because of conflicts between efficiency of the part and of the whole. A typical example is in use of the computer. Computer programmers and operators object to procedures that "waste" computer time or use the machine inefficiently. System designers, on the other hand, argue that it is worth wasting some machine time to achieve the important goal, namely, user service. Since the "wastage" of machine time can be measured but "service to the user" often cannot be quantified, this conflict cannot be resolved mathematically. An efficiency measure of an overall system can be approximated by considering alternative approaches to design, holding performance requirements constant. By carefully estimating the cost of each alternative, an impression, more than a measure, or efficiency can be gained. If system throughput can be measured, cost efficiency (i.e., throughput or output per unit cost) can be measured. We must remember that there are other forms of efficiency, such as output per unit of energy (say, staff manhours) or output per unit of time.

*Quality* Another factor rarely applied in any measurable sense at the overall system level is quality. Typists are measured in terms of words typed per minute, and there is a correction factor for errors. Data transcription errors may be counted and used as an organizational quality control guide. But the quality of output of an information system is not a measurable entity. Attempts to arrive at an artificial measure, say, by questionnaires addressed to users, may backfire. Asking a user to rate service may or may not elicit his true feelings about the service used, and his objectively stated feelings may or may not reflect the "true" quality of the system. Users (of information or other services) have a general tendency to rate in the *fair* to *very good* interval, regardless of what they are assessing. Thus they may be equally supportive of a "good" system and a "bad" one.

*Effectiveness* The ultimate objective of an information system is often effectiveness. Achieving lower cost may be a goal, but the accomplishment of new objectives or improvement in an operation is more commonly desired. We have already pointed out some of the difficulties of measuring effectiveness. For lack of a direct measure we often substitute accomplishment of objectives in the terms listed earlier (cost, speed, etc.). A mark of the skill of the system designer is how meaningfully he converts his performance objectives into the more specific objectives.

### 11.4.3 Guidelines for Performance Evaluation

So long as the world remains without precise measures of information system cost and performance, the designer or manager of a system must rely heavily on intuition and experience. A rough guide to evaluation is given below.

1. *State objectives clearly.* Often it is at least possible to determine whether a proposed course of action will affect the objective, even if one cannot measure the degree. Be careful not to mistake the objective for the technological means of achieving or fulfilling it. An objective of an organization is rarely to provide interactive information retrieval. A more likely goal is to improve the employees' knowledge or access to knowledge of a subject.
2. *Differentiate specific requirements from goals.* An objective is a goal, not necessarily fully achievable, such as profitability, good community mental health, or peace. A requirement is a specific, achievable

milestone along the path toward the objective, such as achieve a production cost of $1.00 per unit, provide an outpatient psychiatric unit, establish a communications link between capitals of major powers to help lessen international tensions. Various authors use different terms for these concepts, but most recognize the difference between a general goal and a reachable milestone.

3. *Enumerate constraints.* A constraint is a limit, a negative prescription: do not exceed a cost of $x$ dollars, complete the system before year $y$, do not use more than $z$ people to operate the system.
4. *Enumerate assumptions.* The design of a system is usually based on an unstated assumption. Some examples are as follows: there will be no change in copyright legislation (critical to many library systems), there will be no change in privacy legislation affecting personal data files (critical to many businesses that maintain files on employees, customers, investigatees, etc.), software will be developed within $n$ years to solve a particular data management problem.
5. *Develop multiple solutions.* Goals, objectives, constraints, and assumptions tend to change and, however well articulated, they are subject to different interpretations by different people. By developing a set of designs rather than a single one, we can protect against the financial and psychic cost of redesign that accompanies a change.
6. *Use the experiences of others.* "Ask the man who owns one" is an old automobile advertising slogan that has much validity for information systems. Knowing how another organization beset with similar problems solved them (or failed to) is invaluable.
7. *Understand users.* Notwithstanding the difficulty of translating the desires of potential users into design parameters, users' opinions on the nature of a proposed system are essential, as is their support during and after implementation.
8. *Measure components.* We have pointed out the fallacy of substituting component measurement for system measurement, but in the absence of the total measure, use what is available.
9. *Reevaluate costs, objectives, requirements, and constraints.* Expect these variables to change; cope with the changes when they occur.

In the early days of the concept of designing a complete information system rather than a specific data management algorithm, there was a tendency to promise the world and deliver little. Over enthusiastic software production estimates were the rule. Hardware often was not fast enough or reliable enough to do the job. Gradually we are becoming both more realistic and more productive. Today reliable system design can be expected in every case when managers and system designers are willing to face their problems directly, evaluate the hardware and software available for the job, and recognize the need to prepare users and operators for the new system.

## REFERENCES

1. Frank Marzocco, *Proceedings of the NATO Advanced Study Institute in Information Science,* Aberystwyth, Wales, August 1973, Anthony Debons and William Cameron, Eds., Noordhoff International Publishers, Amsterdam, 1974.

## RECOMMENDED READING

Heany, Donald F. *Development of Information Systems, What Management Needs to Know,* Ronald Press, New York, 1968, pp. 3–146.

Marzocco [1].

Rosove, Perry, E., *Developing Computer-Based Information Systems,* John Wiley & Sons, New York, 1968.

Sackman, Harold, *Computers, System Science, and Evolving Science,* John Wiley & Sons, New York, 1967.

Senko, Michael E., "Information Storage and Retrieval Systems." In *Advances in Information Systems Science,* Julius T. Tou, Ed., Plenum Press, New York, 1969, pp. 229–82.

### Components and Types of Information Systems

Couger, J. Daniel, and Robert W. Knapp, Eds., *Systems Analysis Techniques,* John Wiley & Sons, New York, 1974.

Head, Robert V., *Manager's Guide to MIS,* Prentice-Hall, Englewood Cliffs, N.J., 1972.

Senko, Michael E., et al., "Data Structures and Accessing in Data-Base Systems, I. Evolution of Information Systems," *IBM Systems Journal,* Vol. 12, No. 1 (1972), pp. 30–44.

Robert F. Simmons, "Natural Language Question-Answering Systems," *Communications of the ACM,* Vol. 13, No. 1 (January 1970), pp. 15–30.

### Performance Analysis

Drucker, Peter F., *Management, Tasks, Responsibilities, Practices,* Harper & Row, New York, 1973, pp. 130–66 (concerning management of service institutions).

King, Donald W., and Edward C. Bryant, *The Evaluation of Information Services and Products,* Information Resources Press, Washington, D.C., 1971.

Lancaster, F. Wilfrid, *Information Retrieval Systems,* John Wiley & Sons, New York, 1968.

*Chapter Twelve*

# Network-Based Data Management

## 12.1 COMMUNICATIONS NETWORKS

A network is a connected set of transmitting and receiving mechanisms. A card reader communicating in one direction only with a computer is a rudimentary network. At the other end of the scale, most of the world's telephones are members of a network that allows any two instruments to be in two-way communication, almost without regard to their respective locations. By linking the telephone system to other networks, it was made possible for telephone messages to reach the astronauts on the moon. More specific to data management are communications networks consisting of one or more computers and one or more user terminals. Such networks allow users to enter data into a computer and query the machine from afar. In addition, computers can exchange information and a remote user can direct his computer to query another computer.

Although as we have pointed out, a modern computer with its complex of peripheral equipment constitutes a communications network in itself, we are primarily concerned with communication between a computer and other computers and terminals located outside the installation, beyond cable distance. (Some computer components and user terminals can be as far as about 2000 feet from a computer, directly connected by means of a cable, and making no use of telephone or other networks.) Computers have been adapted to the traditional telephone and telegraph (or teletype) networks that were in use long before computers appeared on the scene. It remains true today that the simplest way to build a network is to attach computers and users to one of the existing networks, leaving it to the telephone or other communications company to handle installation, switching, and maintenance.

### 12.1.1 Growth in Data Communications

The growth in usage of telephone lines for data communications has been little short of phenomenal. Figure 12.1 plots the growth of data communications terminals used in connection with the telephone network in terms of cost, in millions, of terminals in use. The measure itself is of less importance than the shape of the curve. The prediction illustrated was done by Baran and Lipinski [1] for the Institute for the Future, and it covers the years 1970–1995. Since the authors estimated a 50% growth during the period 1965–1970, we can add one more data point for the earlier year, and this helps us see the start of the period of sharpest growth. Prior to 1965 data communication was not a major industry; if the Baran-Lipinski figures are accurate, however, it will be a highly significant one before 1995, by which time it will have passed its period of most rapid growth. Overall, a fiftyfold increase is predicted from 1965 to 1995.

Richard L. Gehring of Sperry Univac has estimated [2] that 43% of computers used terminals (not all connected via the telephone system) in 1973 and that by 1980 this will rise to 70%. Presumably it will edge toward 100% by the 1995 leveling off predicted by Baran-Lipinski. The number of terminals per computer was estimated by Gehring to be 23 in 1973 and was projected as 36 in 1980. Thus there is growth not only in the number of computers that are able to communicate with terminals but also in the number that each communicates with.

Clearly data communication, both computer-to-computer and man-to-computer, has arrived as a major factor in data processing and is going to remain. Our discussion in this chapter focuses on how its use affects data management, and vice versa.

### 12.1.2 Basic Network Concepts

Some terminology will be helpful in our discussion of networks to follow. A point in a network capable of communicating with two or more other points is called a *node*. A point capable of communicating with only

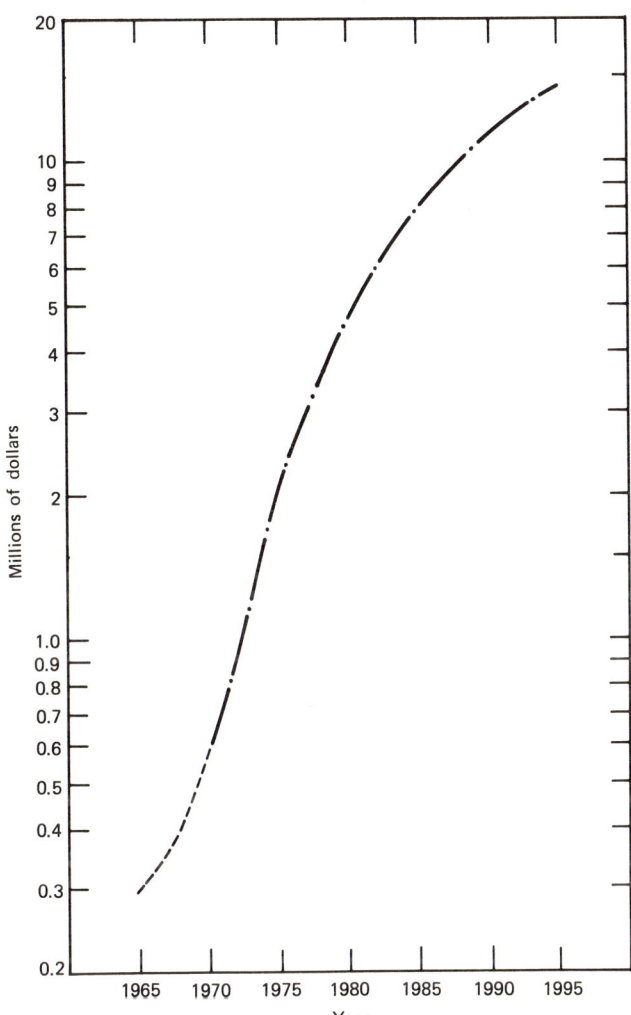

**Figure 12.1** Growth of data terminals, 1970–1995. Source: Baran and Lipinski [1].

one other point is called a *terminal* (the, or an, end of the network). In normal usage, a telephone is a terminal, and there are many nodes between a caller's telephone and the instrument of his destination. At each of these nodes, the call may be switched to the appropriate outgoing line. Connections between nodes or between nodes and terminals are called *links*.

Between any two points of a network the transmission may be *simplex, half-duplex,* or *full duplex* (Figure 12.2). Simplex transmission is strictly

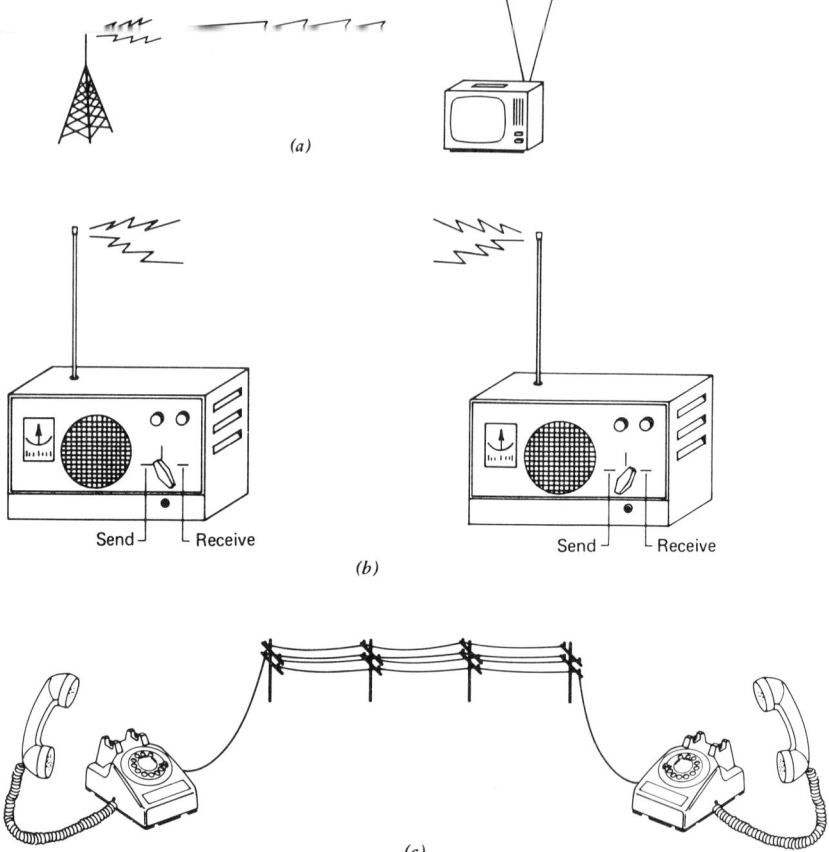

**Figure 12.2** Transmission modes. (*a*) Simplex (one direction only), (*b*) half-duplex (either direction, but only one at a time), (*c*) full duplex (both directions simultaneously).

unidirectional. One station may only send, and another only receive, on a simplex line. Communication between a card reader and a computer is simplex; information goes always from the reader to the computer. A half-duplex line permits traffic to flow in either direction but only one way at a time. The communication between a computer and a magnetic tape unit is half-duplex—the computer can read from or write on the tape but cannot do both simultaneously. Full duplex transmission permits simultaneous two-way communication. Voice telephone is such a mode. Two parties in direct communication can talk at the same time.

The most familiar communications networks are *star networks* (Figure 12.3), so named because the network has the shape of a star: there is a

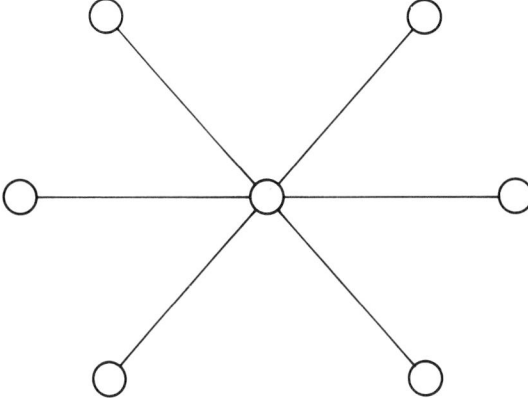

**Figure 12.3** A star network. The links may be simplex, half-duplex, or full duplex, but each transmission must be between the central station and an outlying station.

central station, and all communication is done between outlying stations and central. Communication between two outlying stations must be done by way of central. Any given link can be simplex (radio or television broadcasting has this configuration) or full or half-duplex. In one variation on this form a network has outlying stations that are themselves network nodes (Figure 12.4). An example is the telephone system of Figure 8.7. The central station may be a central switching office, located in a large city and having a number of exchanges connected to it. A line from an exchange may be to a single telephone or to another, smaller network within an of-

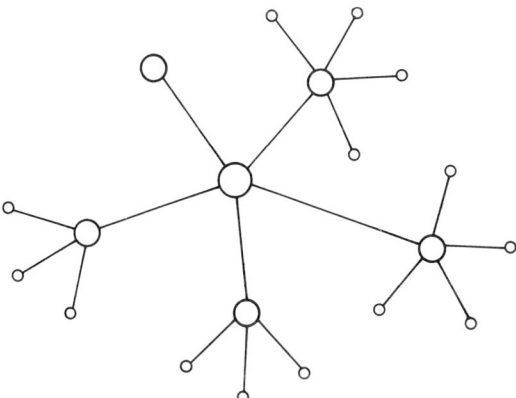

**Figure 12.4** Variation on a star network. An outlying station may control its own star network.

fice, such as the *private branch exchange* (PBX) used for switching calls within one organization's many branch lines when all incoming calls use the same telephone number. Another variant is to permit direct links between outlying stations of a star network (Figure 12.5). Extrapolating from this, we have *distributed networks,* featuring many possible links between any two points and no requirement that all communication go through a central node (Figure 12.6). This configuration offers an advantage in that when any link is down or busy, there is another possibility for routing transmissions. The disadvantage is that each time any two nodes wish to communicate, a decision must be made on the best path through the network for their transmissions. Making such a decision requires data on the current status of lines, and it takes time. This is a technical communications meaning of the term "distributed network." In data management, a distributed network (Section 12.2) is one in which a data base is distributed, part residing in each of several computers linked by communications facilities. Finally, a *ring network* (Figure 12.7) has no control station and only one path from any node to any other node.

Returning to telephone networks, we have shown a hierarchy of networks, from central office to exchange office to private branch exchange. It is also possible, on any given individual line, to have more than one instrument, whether telephone or remote printer. These are multidrop lines (Section 8.3), which are useful when there are many potential users of a system, each having a low probability of use at any given time. The alternative may be heavy investment in unused direct lines.

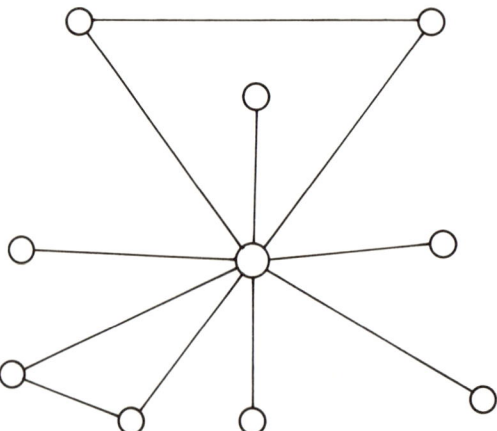

**Figure 12.5** Variation on a star network. Some outlying stations have direct links among themselves and can communicate without going through central.

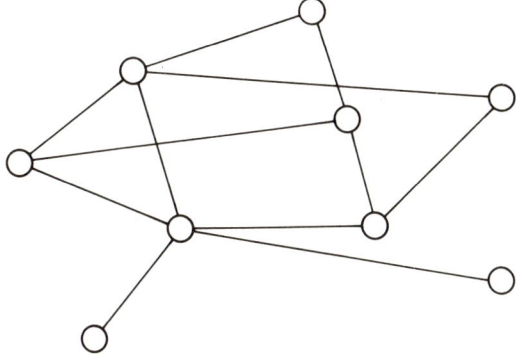

**Figure 12.6** A distributed network does not necessarily have a central station, and there may be more than one path from any node to any other node.

Individual terminals tend to be slow-speed devices, but because there may be many of them trying to communicate with the same distant node, high-speed links from the vicinity of the terminals to that of the nodes are used. This feature presupposes a way to convert multiple incoming messages, enabling them to travel out on a single, high-speed output link. The multiplexors and concentrators described in Section 8.3 are the devices that accomplish this.

There are several ways of carrying messages when points $a$ and $b$ in a data communications network want to communicate. We introduced earlier the concepts of line and message switching. One form of message switching is *packet switching,* in which the unit of transmission is a uniform size

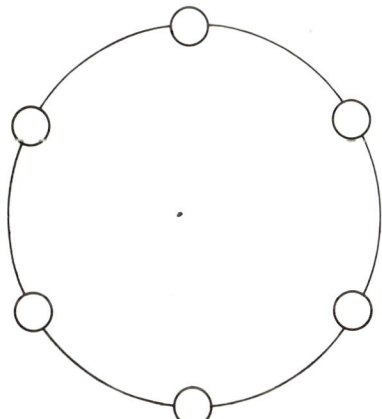

**Figure 12.7** A ring network.

message, and several units may be needed to convey the original message. Thus if $a$ wishes to send $b$ a long message, and $b$ wishes to respond, we might have $a$ sending out message units $a_1$, $a_2$, and $a_3$, and $b$ responding with $b_1$. Each of $a$'s units might be routed differently, since each is treated independently of any previous units. The recipient would then have to reassemble the original message.

The use of multiplexors, packet switching, and distributed networks having more than one path from point to point all lead to the requirement for control over the network. Some control unit must be aware that $a$ wishes to send to $b$ and to find an available path. Switching (Section 8.4) is one function of control, but we introduce other functions of *network control* as we proceed, and we find that regardless of whether it is centralized or involved in all transmissions, the function must be performed.

### 12.1.3 Common Carrier Facilities

A *common carrier* in communications is a company authorized by a government regulatory agency to provide communications services for all customers on an equal basis. This is an outgrowth of the use of the same term to describe passenger and freight carriers. Generally a communications common carrier is given at least a limited monopoly and is then regulated by a local or federal government agency. Some of the facilities available through the Bell System, the largest of the common carriers in this country, are described in the remainder of this section [3].

**Data-Phone Services** The data phone is a modem that converts computer-generated, digital signals into sound-coded signals for transmission over regular voice telephone lines. At the receiving end, the code is reconverted by another data-phone (Figure 12.8). This device permits a computer to reach or be reached by anyone with access to the Bell System, which includes other telephone companies. The specific network of users need not be set up in advance, although security, economy, and overload considerations may make this advisable. A telephone call involving data transmission through a data-phone is called a *data call*.

**Leased Lines** A user may lease a communication channel from the telephone company when he has enough traffic to justify it or must have direct access to a remote point without the delay that may be experienced when the "public" lines are busy. Leased lines bypass much of the switching equipment that is used by the conventional, switchable lines and is responsible for introducing a certain amount of noise into a line. Leased lines, on the other hand, may be *conditioned* by the telephone company to eliminate much of the noise, thus improving the data transmission capability of the lines.

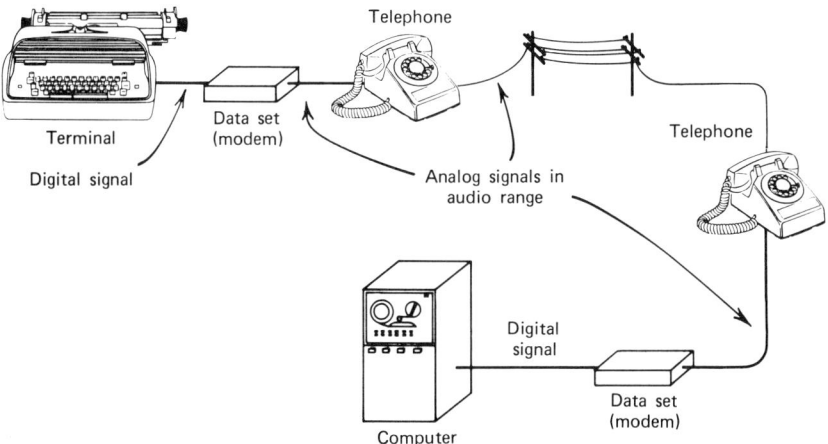

**Figure 12.8** Use of a data-phone or modem.

*Wide-Area Telephone Service (WATS)* WATS is a *service* not a device, and it has many uses not related to computers. A WATS user contracts with the telephone company for a degree of service and pays a fixed fee. Briefly, he buys the rights to an unlimited number of long-distance messages, although he may be limited with respect to the time of day when he may use the services. Subscribers may select the geographic area of concern—for example, some are interested only in talking to nearby states, others want the service to include the entire continental United States. Service may be inward only, outward only, or both.

*Telpak Service* A telpak is a set of telephone channels leased at quantity discount rates. A telpak may consist of 12, 24, 60, or 240 voice channels. A company having major divisions in New York and Chicago may find itself making so many calls between these cities that a wholesale rate is indicated. Like WATS, the user agrees to pay a fee regardless of the number of calls actually made, but unlike WATS, the telpak links two specific locations.

*Teleprinter Networks* Western Union operates the Telex teleprinter network and has recently purchased from the Bell System the Teletypewriter Exchange Service (TWX). Both are dial-up systems for sending digital codes from one teleprinter to another. A computer input/output channel may perform the same communications functions as a teleprinter, permitting the computer to become a direct user of one of these networks.

Besides these services, others have become available in recent years.

Some are services provided to common carriers, some are competing with the established common carriers, and some make use of the carriers' facilities, the so-called *value-added networks*. This is an area of rapid change, and we give only a few examples.

**Satellite Communications**  Satellites are now commonplace in intercontinental communications. From the user's point of view they are extensions of existing facilities, providing for greater channel capacity than was previously available through submarine cables. Within the United States, plans are being made for domestic satellites. An interesting side benefit is that the ground distance traversed, a factor in transmission cost when messages must travel through wire or over the surface, is no longer significant. In time, domestic satellites may dramatically reduce the cost of long-distance communication.

**Specialized Data Communication Services**  To use a regular telephone line for data, the data codes that emanate from a computer or terminal must be converted (by a modem) into tones for transmission by voice telephone facilities. If lines were dedicated solely to data transmission, more efficient coding could be used, and greater transmission rates and lower costs would result. A number of independent (i.e., independent of AT&T and Western Union) carriers have attempted to compete for this market. In 1963 Microwave Communications, Inc., petitioned the Federal Communications Commission for permission to set up a specialized microwave data link between Chicago and St. Louis. Other services have since been proposed by other carriers. A precedent has been established that carriers other than AT&T and Western Union can legally enter those interstate markets, and we may expect many more participants in years to come [4]. The network designer, then, may have more than one carrier and type of service to choose from in assembling a new network.

**Value-Added Networks**  The value-added networks are built using the basic facilities of common carriers to which the developers have added their own computers, concentrators, and control services. The network operator leases facilities in bulk, and it may be economical for a user to deal with a computer 3000 miles distant because the communications costs are low, whereas the same user could not afford the computer services if he had to pay full rates for a data call, reserving a link for his sole use. The network operator may sell computer services as well as communications services.

TYMNET, operated by Tymshare, Inc., is an example of a value-added network [5]. Originated in 1970, it continues to evolve as user requirements change. In 1973 it connected 54 cities, used more than 40,000 miles of leased telephone lines, and had 37 large computers linked to it. A typical TYMNET user might use the network to access one of Tymshare's time-shared computers. He ties into the network by connecting his terminal, which might be a 30-character/second print terminal (such as a Model 35 Teletype), to a *Tymsat,* a satellite computer. One Tymsat is located in each city in which the network operates, and each user terminal or computer operates through a Tymsat, both for sending and receiving. Since the Tymsat performs such functions as speed and code conversion (the network may transmit the terminal's 30-character/sec messages at a much higher rate), a variety of different terminals may be used on the network. A modem is still required to link the terminal into the telephone system that leads to the Tymsat. When a user first comes on the network, he is put in communication with a network control computer that logs him in, verifies that he is a valid network user, determines what computer he wants to link to, and sets up the necessary communications links. It is left to the computer to determine if the user is appropriately authorized—TYMNET does not perform this function. (In Chapter 13 we discuss authorization procedures.)

The satellite computer continues to perform code and speed conversion once the link is established and also checks for transmission errors. The receiving Tymsat acknowledges each message it receives in which no error is detected. Failure to acknowledge results in automatic retransmission by the sending Tymsat. The complete error-handling system results in an undetected error rate of only one bit in $4 \times 10^9$ bits transmitted. The common carrier's system permits up to one error in $10^5$ bits; thus TYMNET improves on this by a factor of 40,000.

TYMNET uses line switching to set up the shortest available link between user and computer and then permits direct communication from user to sending location Tymsat to receiving area Tymsat to computer (Figure 12.9). The network control computer is involved only initially, in logging in and selecting a route. Among the advantages of this arrangement is that if the controller goes down, an alternate can take its place without disrupting user transmissions.

The unit of transmission in TYMNET is a block containing between 12 and 66 characters, to which is affixed various check sums to be used in error detection. Long messages must be broken up to meet this length restriction, and one of the functions of the Tymsat is to prepare such messages for transmission.

TYMNET is an example of a distributed network. Not all transmissions need go through a central control point, and there may be more than one path between any two nodes.

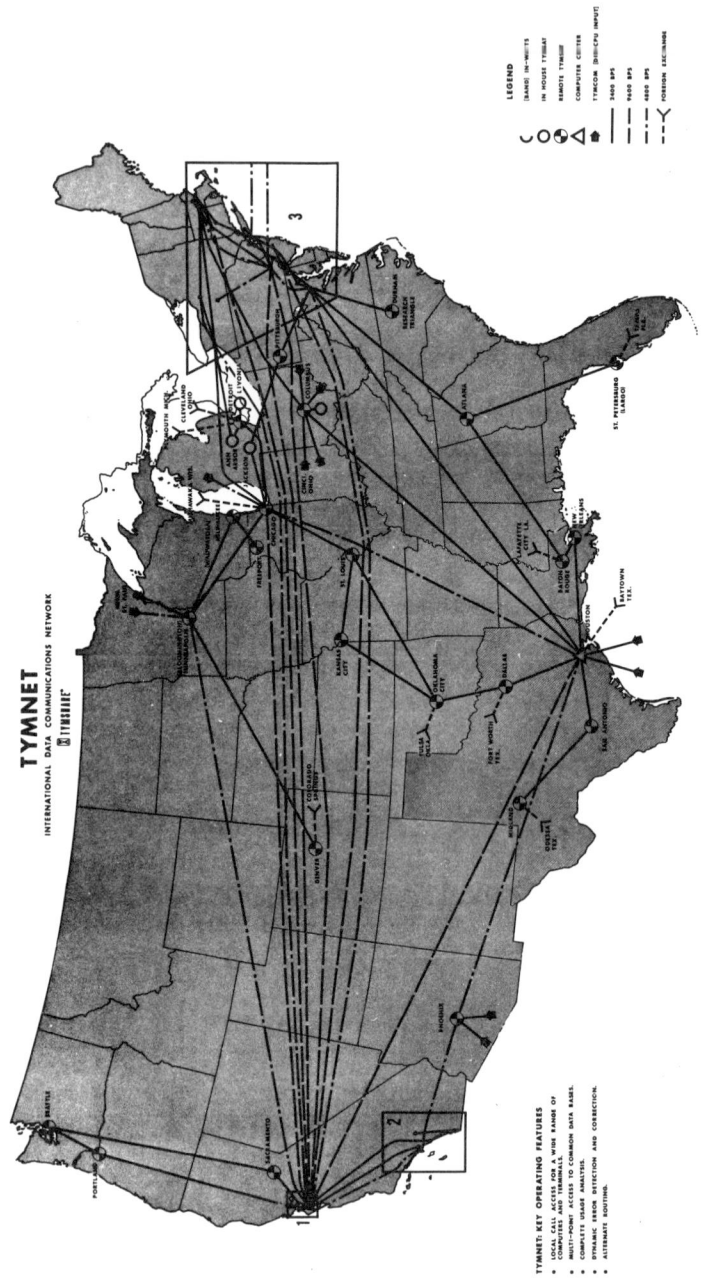

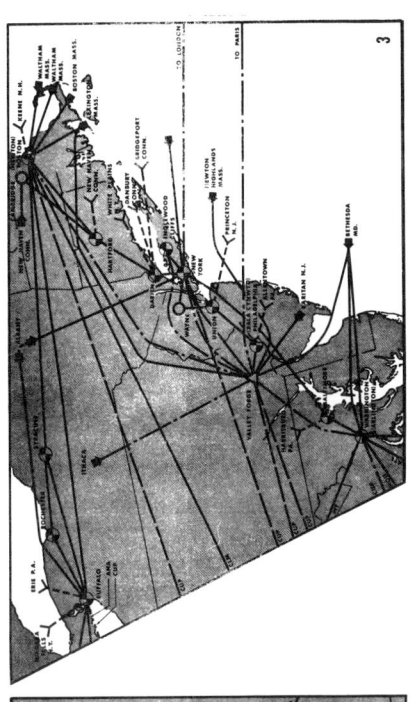
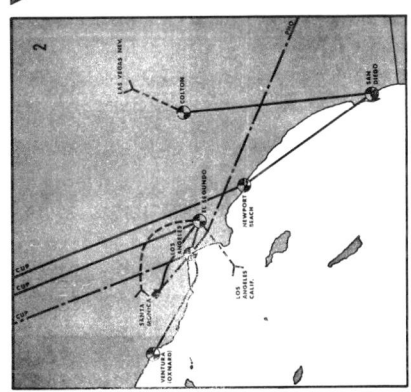
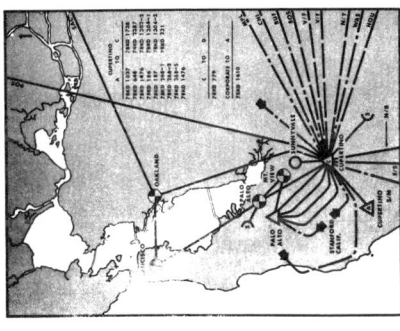

**Figure 12.9** The TYMNET network: users link to it through satellite computers at many locations. Courtesy Tymshare Corp.

253

### 12.1.4 Linking the Computer to the Network

The specifics of computer interaction with communications systems were covered in Chapter 8. The minimum requirements are that codes and transmission speeds be compatible between components and that the requisite software be available to poll input or output lines or handle interrupts, to queue messages, and to detect errors.

It is difficult to estimate exact hardware requirements because so much depends on users' patterns. For example, the response time of a multiprogrammed computer to a particular user query, although obviously dependent on the amount of machine time needed to carry out the search, is dominated by the number of other demands placed on the computer during the time of the search. This, in turn, depends on how many other users there are at the moment, the nature of their commands, and the amount of memory devoted to each user. Smaller allocations of memory to application programs generate more I/O requests to bring in program segments, adding to the demands for time. Larger allocations tend to solve time problems but raise the cost.

In any given instance of use of a terminal to communicate with a computer, some information must be supplied by the user before productive work can begin. Mere self-identification may be sufficient, or there may be a lengthy conversation in which the user identifies himself to the network, asks the network to link him to a given computer, then asks the computer for a particular program. Sometimes the program reached offers so many options to the user that it, too, must have a conversation with him to determine what services he wants.

The procedure that links a terminal with a computer is called a *protocol*. Most network protocols involve essentially the same kind of information, but they tend to differ in detail. The actions taken in establishing a link, in general, were summarized by Neumann [6] approximately as follows (the author has slightly modified the presentation from Neumann's original work).

1. *Initiation of access.* Terminal equipment is turned on and various options, varying with the type terminal, are selected. An example is transmission speed, and some terminals offer a choice.
2. *Establishment of a communication channel.* The terminal is linked to a network entry point, such as a TYMNET Tymsat. Establishing a channel may require a telephone data call to the entry point, it brings the user into the network but not yet to his desired computer.
3. *User identification.* The user is identified to the network, both to control who has access and for accounting purposes.
4. *Authorization.* A means by which the system verifies that the user is, in

fact, authorized to use the system is a number or word known only to authorized users. The authorization serves as a security control (Chapter 13).
5. *Presentation of network status.* Various aspects of the network may change from time to time, such as the set of nodes that are operative or the load on the system. Some networks provide this information to the user, either automatically or on demand.
6. *Computer selection.* Once the network has been linked to the user and has accepted him, attention focuses on determining what computer he wants to reach and establishing a link to that computer.
7. *Computer log in.* A somewhat similar procedure is required to log in, or log on, to the computer. The data involved are about the same as those described in items 2–6, for logging in to a network. All data may not need to be retransmitted by the user, however, once given to the network control system.
8. *Log out.* At the end of a session of computer use, the user goes through an approximate reversal of the foregoing sequence of steps, disengaging himself from program, computer, and network. Normally, he is given some accounting data from the system telling how long he used the computer or network.

As an example of a protocol, we show one instance of linking a user with a computer through the ARPANET, a computer communications system sponsored by the Advanced Research Projects Agency (ARPA) of the U.S. Department of Defense [7]. In 1970 it linked 15 computer science research centers whose work was supported by ARPA, and now more than 40 facilities are linked. The objective of the network is to encourage researchers to use computing facilities at each other's sites rather than duplicate expensive hardware and software. The computers at the users' locations do not need to be identical in hardware and software. Each computer is linked to the communications network through a small intermediary computer called an *interface message processor* (IMP). The IMP assures compatible message formats, transmissions speeds, and protocol among dissimilar computers. The lines connecting IMPs are high-capacity leased telephone lines. Through ARPANET, a user at one location can make use of a program resident at another location, transmit his data to that computer, and receive his results in his own computer.

After the basic ARPANET had been constructed, a second form of interface processor was added to permit more users access to the network. The *terminal interface processor* (TIP), a modification of an IMP, permits users equipped with a terminal, but not necessarily a computer, to use computers on the network. The user's terminal communicates by telephone line to a nearby TIP and from there to whatever computer the user identifies. Of course in this as in all cases, it is the user's responsibility to gain approval to use a computer and to correctly identify himself for billing purposes. The TIP performs a function similar to TYMNET's Tymsat.

Here is an abbreviated example of how a user accesses a computer through ARPANET. The protocol is for working through a TIP to reach a computer at the Stanford Research Institute (SRI) in which resides an operating system called *Tenex*. The first step is to dial the TIP and link the terminal to it. Thereafter, the conversation is

| | |
|---|---|
| USER: e[ LF ] | LF stands for a single character—*Line Feed*—on a teletype that advances the carriage one line. *Carriage return* is a separate function. The letter e is used by the TIP to determine the transmission speed of the terminal and adjust itself accordingly. |
| TIP: HELLO 306 | The TIP replies, confirming that contact has been established. The number of the version of the operating system in the TIP is 306. |
| USER: @ L2[ LF ] | @ indicates that a command to the TIP follows. L is for LOGON—the user is ordering the TIP to begin the log on process. The SRI computer being requested is number 2 in the network. |
| TIP: LOGGER<br>R OPEN T OPEN | The TIP confirms that it has logged in the user and has established a communication link to the computer; R is the receiving line, T the transmit line; communication is one way on each. |
| COMPUTER: TENEX 1.31.20<br>ARC/NIC EXEC 1.50 | The SRI computer provides some status information about itself. TENEX is the operating system in the computer, ARC/NIC is the site designation of the computer. EXEC 1.50 denotes the currently operational version of the operating system. |

| | |
|---|---|
| COMPUTER: @ | An example of nonstandardization. The same character that previously denoted a user message to the TIP here serves as the computer's code to ask for input by the user. It is a go-ahead command to him. |
| USER: log [CR] | The user asks to be logged on to the computer. The *carriage return* character [CR] ends his message. |
|    john q user [CR] | User's identity |
|    secret [CR] | User's password |
|    1234 [CR] | User's account number |
| COMPUTER: JOB 5 ON TTY 43<br>          7-JUL-74 15:54 | The computer assigns a number to the user's job and to his terminal and gives the date and time the job begins. |
| COMPUTER: @ | Logging is complete. The computer now wants to know what program the user wants. |
| USER: nic [CR] | This is the name of an application program, which then takes over the conversation. The network is now transparent to the user. |
|    .<br>   .<br>   . | The user converses with the program. |
| COMPUTER: @ | The computer and user interact as long as necessary. Eventually, the user finishes his task. When the computer asks for its next command |
| USER: logout [CR] | the user replies, asking to be logged out. |
| COMPUTER: TERMINATED JOB 5,<br>          USER JOHN Q USER,<br>          ACCT 1234, TTY 43,<br>          AT 7-JUL-74 16:08<br>          USED 0: 0:39<br>          IN 0:14:28 | The computer provides confirmation of termination and gives time of quitting, computer CPU time used, and total time connected to the computer. |

| | |
|---|---|
| USER: @ c⌐LF⌐ | The user addresses the TIP and asks to be disconnected (c). |
| TIP: T R CLOSED | The TIP closes out the receive and transmit connections. |

## 12.2 DATA MANAGEMENT NETWORKS

Our primary purpose in this chapter is to investigate the effect of the use of a communications network on data management. Our discussion concentrates on the user and how such parameters as frequency of use might affect a system. We distinguish among three kinds of network-based data management systems. The first is a *centralized system* with remote users—one computer, one data base, many users who may be located anywhere, in a star configuration, so long as they can attach a terminal into the telephone network (or other common carrier network). The second is called a *distributed system*—a usage based on the concept of a distributed network and referring to a data management system making use of more than one computer and data base. Any user, within the bounds of security, financial, and administrative controls, can select any of the computers and use it in any fashion the computer is programmed to permit. Both these network forms exist today and examples are given below. The third type of data management network, which we call a *distributed intelligence system*, is a combination of the first two and, if existent, is not yet commonplace. It consists of a network of computers having a data base distributed among them. Some files may be at one location, some at another; some may be duplicated, having copies stored at more than one location. The totality is available to widely dispersed users.

### 12.2.1 Centralized Networks

The most common form of network-based data management system puts a data base in a centralized computer (or a set of computers appearing as one to the user) and permits remote users to access it for retrieval purposes and perhaps also for file maintenance. Among the early successful examples of centralized networks were bibliographic systems in which the remote user was permitted only to search, and file maintenance was done locally at the central facility, usually not on-line. Time-sharing systems offering general-purpose computer services to remote users were also based on centralized networks but were not data management systems. Airlines reservation systems were early examples of systems in which both query and maintenance functions could be performed remotely, and today systems offering these capabilities are common in banks, utilities, and credit bureaus to keep track of individuals' accounts and to quickly answer queries, especially those of the form, "should I cash this check?"

As we described in Chapter 10, users' behavior can be profoundly changed by a centralized network system. Before the advent of on-line systems, some computer users had to go through a tedious and time-consuming process of preparing data forms for keypunching and batch processing; these users access a computer at will, normally with only minor delays of a few seconds to a few minutes. The typical result is that their usage rate goes up and their tolerance for error or delay goes down. In business systems, immediate access to data is likely to lead to demand for more timely updating of the data base. Users become intolerant of delays caused by the communications subsystem. Also, once users come to depend on direct access they become addicted, and reversion to manual operation is most unpalatable. For these reasons, there is relentless pressure for expanding facilities and increasing their reliability.

Correlative with this drive for expansion and reliability improvement is an insistence that the data base be up to date. Particularly remote users, whose previous access to a computer may have been only by scheduled runs or by unscheduled jobs taking days to set up, find it frustrating to achieve instant access to data only to learn that the information may be unreliable and that it takes as long to make the on-line data base reliable as the same procedure formerly took through batch processing. This dissatisfaction is likely to arise when system designers concentrate on on-line query of data bases without giving any thought to the processes of building and maintaining a data base. Organizations contemplating remote access computer systems may discover, and ought to search out beforehand, bottlenecks in their data handling. For example, suppose the west coast division of a company can access the data base at its east coast headquarters at any time, but its own personnel data simply are never up to date in the eastern computer. This may be because the collection of personnel data follows a pattern established prior to the introduction of the on-line remote system—for example, information collected once or twice a month, sent by mail on paper forms to headquarters, proofread, keypunched, and entered into the computer, then validated and invalid items rejected, reprocessed, and reentered. The same pattern can easily develop in departments such as accounting when collection of data follows a pre-on-line schedule that produces instant access, today, to data 2 to 4 weeks old, hence invalid as descriptors of current fiscal status.

The lessons to be learned from this kind of behavior are that: (1)

improved access alone may not benefit users if information is not kept up to date, and (2) given a new technical capability—namely, on-line search—users will inevitably press for technical improvement (shorter access time and fewer periods on "down time") and for concurrent improvement in data input services. Attempting change in the last of these points, data input, may induce more profound changes than did data retrieval, because more people and more individual, manual operations are affected.

An example of a centralized data management network is MEDLINE, a bibliographic information service of the National Library of Medicine [8]. In 1973 its data base contained more than 400,000 citations from biomedical literature and it linked 120 using installations, employing more than 200 terminals. The communication system used is TYMNET. The computer is located at the National Library of Medicine. Users may view the system logically as a star network, since all users contact the central computer. (Consideration was given to decentralizing the network, using a number of computers, each having a copy of the data base.) In its 1973 form, MEDLINE users saw the system as a centralized one, even though other users of TYMNET gave a different configuration to the network.

Had MEDLINE developed its own data network, it might have ranked among the world's larger independent systems. It is the first major data management system to place its communications needs totally in the hands of an existing data communication network, and this is probably an indicator of future developments in the field.

### 12.2.2 Distributed Systems

A distributed system links individual computers and users through a network. Any user may access any computer if that computer is programmed to accept him. The distributed system is a facility for sharing data processing resources: hardware, software, and data. Individual users and suppliers of the capabilities may make their own rules for its use.

As pointed out in the description of the ARPANET, which was the first outstanding example of such a network, users of a distributed system have access to programs and data at remote locations, which saves them the cost and time of developing and maintaining their own programs and files. Success opens up the possibility of using such a system within a single, decentralized organization, with assigned rules of access and distribution of responsibilities for providing programs and data to other authorized users. ARPANET does not assign any user the responsibility for supplying some particular kind of data processing service. When a single corporate entity so organizes its data management, we have what is termed *distributed intelligence*.

### 12.2.3 Distributed Intelligence

Consider a large, multidivisional, geographically dispersed corporation or government agency. It probably needs computers at each of its major locations and likely employs some form of decentralized management, extending at least partially to procurement. Furthermore each location is unique in its information problems, its mix of mathematical, business, and bibliographical systems, its response time requirements for local users, the familiarity of its staff with different brands of computers, and the investment in software written for particular computers. In short, there are compelling reasons for *not* having identical computers at each location and for not converting to a single, unified software system throughout the company.

On the other hand, there is a considerable flow of information among locations, such as:

- orders from sales offices to warehouses
- warehouse replenishment requirements to manufacturing locations
- engineering test data from laboratories to factories
- personnel and accounting data from all locations up through channels of command to corporate headquarters
- budget data in both directions (up and down the hierarchy): requests for budgets, modifications to budget drafts initiated at either end of the hierarchy, and finally approved budgets
- reports to various government agencies on spending, overseas investments, use of critical materials, minority hiring, occupational safety, air pollution, and so on

Not atypically, a location other than headquarters is best qualified to coordinate the company's air pollution reports to the government, and another to maintain records of all corporate purchases. Headquarters will be interested in all persons employed by the company, but they might not wish to maintain a central personnel file if they can have occasional access to all personnel records to respond to corporate planning needs, answer government reporting requirements, or the like. In establishing a management information system in which files are built and maintained at the location that has the data or is in best position to collect, maintain, and validate data, the company is using a distributed intelligence network. This network is many networks, and there is more than one "center." File maintenance information continually flows from installation to installation and frequently a need arises for any one installation to retrieve data from the files of one or more others. In this situation it is not feasible to allow each installation to develop its programs and file structures completely independently, yet the decentralization policy would make it a practical impossibility to impose a common standard on all computers, programs, and files.

The communications solution can be handled by a network of the type of ARPANET or TYMNET. If a compatible file structure could be achieved, the need for standardized programming would be lessened or eliminated. A solution might be reside in a software equivalent of the ARPA IMP, which would convert any data record (within some broad limits) retrieved from any file to a standard interchange format for transmission. In addition, each independent location would have to agree to provide some means of translating queries in a standard language into its own information retrieval query language. The latter step would involve some program modification and probably some diminution of logical capability, but long-range benefits for each using location within the organization might be obtained.

The Library of Congress has developed an interchange file structure called *Machine Readable Catalog* (MARC) for disseminating bibliographic information to other libraries [9]. Like the ASCII character format, there is no suggestion that the interchange format be used internally in any computer system, only that all intercomputer communications be carried out by translating internal file formats into this format, then translating again into the format of the receiving computer. Since the same format is used by intermediate processing centers that prepare Library of Congress data for use by individual libraries, it is not just the format chosen by one library but a standard among libraries.

Returning to our hypothetical company, even if it could solve the software compatibility and data exchange problems, there would remain quality control and scheduling problems. Is each location performing the same validation checks on its contribution to a given file? Are they all, for example, checking accounting reports uniformly before transmitting them to headquarters? If not, the headquarters or other receiving computer system might have to repeat validation on all data, at considerable cost, since the recipient might not have the facilities to correct errors once detected. Even the scheduling of file changes can be a problem calling for careful coordination. If all files are modified on-line and kept as continuously up to date as possible, any query across the whole system will retrieve current and valid data. If, however, some files are updated in batches (e.g., accounting files brought up to date only at the end of an accounting period ranging from a week to a month), each location might operate on a different schedule. Grossly misleading information might be retrieved if a query were addressed to the entire system at a time when some local files had been updated and some had not. One of the penalties each location in a network of this kind must pay for membership (which, in a corporation, is not optional) is a much higher degree of coordination in the logic and timing of file maintenance, previously a matter for local autonomy. It will come as no surprise, then, that increasing interlocation communication decreases local autonomy. The same process has been going on for years as telegraph and mail communication gave way to leased telephone lines, and train travel was superseded by jet aircraft.

Many of the difficulties of implementing and operating distributed intelligence systems are the same as those of integrated file systems. Although "integrated files" may be a collection of data at one location, integrated and distributed systems are much the same kind of thing. The people who build, maintain, and use these files must develop a new order of consciousness about communications and file maintenance, to make either system successful. Neither form can be decreed into existence.

This discussion is not intended to suggest that distributed intelligence networks are impossible or even undesirable. Examples are already reported in the literature [10]. However, creating such a network is not merely a matter of leasing communication lines and installing modems. Software must be considered as well as hardware, and manual data handling procedures must be coordinated as well as computers. Since changes in procedures involve the basic ways in which people do their jobs, and the relationships among people and corporate subdivisions, the latter changes are the more likely to be overlooked or resisted.

## REFERENCES

1. Paul Baran and Andrew J. Lipinski, *The Future of the Telephone Industry,* Report R-20, Institute for the Future, Menlo Park, Calif., September 1971, pp. 145–6.
2. Richard L. Gehring, "The Future in Data Communications," *Data Management,* Vol. 12, No. 9, (September 1974), pp. 43–5.
3. Edgar C. Gentle, Jr., *Data Communications in Business, An Introduction,* American Telephone & Telegraph Co., New York, 1965.
4. Edgar A. Grabhorn, "Specialized Communications Common Carriers 1973–1974," *Datamation,* August 1973, pp. 44–48.
5. Bill Combs, "TYMNET: A Distributed Network," *Datamation,* July 1973, pp. 40–43.
6. A. J. Neumann, *User Procedures Standardization for Network Access,* NBS Technical Note 799, National Bureau of Standards, Washington, D.C., 1973, pp. 2–5.
7. L. C. Roberts and B. D. Wessler, "Computer Network Development to Achieve Resource Sharing," *AFIPS Conference Proceedings,* Vol. 36 (May 1970), pp. 543–9.
8. Davis B. McCarn and Joseph Leiter, "On-Line Service in Medicine and Beyond," *Science,* Vol. 181, No. 27 (July 1973), pp. 318–24.
9. *Books, A MARC Format,* 5th ed., MARC Development Office, Library of Congress, Washington, D.C., 1972.
10. Joseph C. Marshall, "Distributed Processing on Wall Street," *Datamation,* July 1973, pp. 44–46.

## RECOMMENDED READING

### Networks, General

Crowley, Thomas H., et al., *Modern Communications,* Columbia University Press, New York, 1962.

Martin, James, *Telecommunications and the Computer,* Prentice-Hall, Englewood Cliffs, N.J., 1969.

Neumann, A. J., *A Guide to Networking Terminology,* NBS Technical Note 803, National Bureau of Standards, Washington, D.C., 1974.

Pierce, John R., *Symbols, Signals and Noise,* Harper & Row, New York, 1961.

Pyke, Thomas N., Jr. and R. P. Blanc, "Computer Networking Technology—A State of the Art Review," *Computer,* August 1973, pp. 13–19 (includes bibliography).

### Data Management Networks

Abramson, Norman, and Franklin F. Kuo, Eds., *Computer-Communication Networks,* Prentice-Hall, Englewood Cliffs, N.J., 1973.

Cotton, Ira W., *Network Management Survey,* NBS Technical Note 805, National Bureau of Standards, Washington, D.C., 1974.

Cox, J. E., "Western Union Digital Services," *Proceedings of the IEEE,* Vol. 60, No. 11 (November 1972), pp. 1350–57.

James, R. T., "AT&T Facilities and Services," *Proceedings of the IEEE,* Vol. 60, No. 11 (November 1972), 1342–49.

Martin, James, *Design of Real-Time Computer Systems,* Prentice-Hall, Englewood Cliffs, N.J., 1967.

Meadow, Charles T., *Man-Machine Communication,* Wiley-Interscience, New York, 1970.

Roberts and Wessler [7].

*Chapter Thirteen*

# Privacy, Protection, and Security

## 13.1 PRIVACY AS A COMPUTER PROBLEM

At one time poor communication and the lack of centralized records were a real form of protection to some people. It was possible to commit a crime, go into dept, or become involved in a paternity suit and then move away, establish a new identity, and live peacefully and honorably thereafter. Today this is nearly impossible. There are central fingerprint files, well-guarded international borders, social security numbers, national crime information systems, nationwide credit investigating firms, all making anonymity hard to achieve. In many cases these systems embarrass innocent people and prevent the once guilty from joining society as fully accepted members.

The trend toward centralized files and communications among the holders of different files to track down people or to expand a searcher's base of information about a subject seems natural. Equally natural is the reaction of people who do not want their lives to be an open book and who fear the misuse of centralized files maintained, searched, and interpreted by fallible people who shoulder no responsibility for their own errors or misdeeds in regard to the handling of sensitive information.

As computers have been brought into the collection, maintenance, and search of files of information about people, the sheer size of the data bases managed has intensified the problem. The impact of this use of computers is altering the relation between individual spontaneity and social control in our society in a way so profound we are only barely aware of it. As computers have made possible the collection, storage, manipulation, and use of information at quite low prices and through operations done at incredible speeds, our society has become the greatest data collector in human history [1].

Government agencies, corporations, universities, and other organizations now collect many times the amount of information about their members, customers, or clients than they ever did before. Many organizations exchange this information. Centralized systems are growing up to collect information according to certain functional aspects of individual life, such as educational records, security clearance records, and medical records. Pressure is mounting to move from our present cash and check economy to a moneyless transaction system, based on computerized flow of credits and debits to bank accounts for each individual. Such a system would interconnect, in one information system, data on bank accounts, credit status, and buying habits. All these systems are vulnerable to misrepresentation and mischief.

During the last several years, issues and problems of privacy and protection involved in the operation of computers have been brought to public notice through Congressional hearings and investigations of the privacy aspects of large data banks maintained by governmental and nongovernmental institutions, and through newspaper accounts of computer bandits. The problems of controlling access to and retrieval from computer data banks have gained more and more attention from concerned citizens. People are beginning to recognize the issues and are demanding that some protective measures be provided to ensure their rights of privacy.

We are becoming increasingly aware that the problem is many faceted and is not simply a matter of protecting one's own privacy. For example, the United States has a highly credit-oriented economy. We are also a nation of movers. As people move from city to city, they expect to reestablish personal credit immediately. For this, information is needed, and the very credit information systems that seemed so abusive before a move become the means for quickly establishing credit afterward. The credit system could change, of course, by relaxing its standards—that is, by requiring less information to establish credit. This would inevitably raise credit costs through increased defaults and, although it might be worth the price, the approach does not seem very likely today. The police information systems that can harm the reputation of a person who committed a single, minor offense years ago, can aid society by helping to apprehend true criminals and to find and restore stolen property. In the face of rising crime rates and increasing use of technology by criminals, police information systems are growing in importance. It is cheaper for a business to put its market research information into a commercial time-sharing computer, to save money on storage and processing, than to buy its own computer. But the firm incurs the risk that other users of the same computer can find and steal the information.

Preventing the storage of sensitive information is no real solution to the discomfort occasioned in some people by the misuse of data. Such information is needed, often for the individual's well-being, or perhaps as statistical input to government or commercial decision making. We all like adequate mail service in our new housing areas, schools for growing families, and nearby markets. Planning for these institutions requires information about family growth, spending, and moving patterns. What is needed is a more careful, reasoned approach to the collection, storage, and use of the data. A *Washington Post* editorial [2] stated

> Computers have indeed eroded man's ability to control who knows how much about a person's private life and how such knowledge is used. But the basic problem is less the capability of machines than the curiosity of man, particularly the curiosity of those in power over the lives of their fellow citizens.

### 13.1.1 A Historical Perspective

Technology-based threats to privacy and freedom are not new. In the fourth century B.C. prisoners of Dionysius, the Tyrant of Syracuse, were placed in a prison cell formed from a cave shaped somewhat like a human ear. Guards could easily overhear conversations, even though the prisoners were deep in the cave. This may have been the first form of "bugging." Some later activities were described by David Kahn in his book *The Code Breakers* [3].

Regular intercity postal service began in Europe around 1650. Soon thereafter, so-called *black chamber* operations were organized by governments to intercept mail messages. The efficiently run black chamber in Vienna was typical. Bags of mail arrived in the city daily at 7 A.M., the seals on letters were melted with the flame from a candle, and the letters were opened and read by a staff fluent in many languages. Important information was retained by dictation to stenographers. By 9:30, letters had been resealed and were delivered as addressed. Afterward the transcriptions of intercepted correspondence were analyzed and, if necessary, deciphered.

In 1850 the telegraph was introduced. Government-operated black chambers again appeared. In France, messages from the Italian and

German military attachés to their respective governments were intercepted and deciphered and were eventually critical in clearing the famous Captain Dreyfus. Unlike mail, telegrams did not need to be diverted to be intercepted; hence the recipient had no way of knowing if someone had had prior access to his message.

Radio came into use in 1895 as wireless telegraphy. Again governments undertook operations to intercept information, and again interception could be accomplished without the recipient's knowledge. During World War I radio communications were widely intercepted. France alone operated eight intercept stations. Prior to World War II the United States, using intercepted information, broke both the Japanese and German military codes.

In modern times we have learned of telephone bugging, tiny microphones that can be hidden in an office or hotel room, and voice-actuated tape recorders in the White House. Here are summaries of three privacy-related activities of the United States government.

In 1965 a committee of the Social Sciences Research Council recommended the establishment of a Federal Data Center (FDC), to be organizationally located in the then Bureau of the Budget (part of the Executive Office of the President) and to serve the purpose of bringing together diverse information in files of the federal government related to economics, population, housing, and other matters. The desire for such an organization was based on the need by scholars and government planners alike for reliable data about the nation's economy and population [4]. The initial recommendation triggered several reactions. A further study commissioned by the Bureau of the Budget supported the idea (now called the National Data Service Center) [5]. Reaction in Congress tended to be negative, and Representative Cornelius E. Gallagher began hearings into the possible threat to privacy of the proposed system. Yet another committee, under Dr. Carl Kaysen, supported the idea, while recommending various safeguards [6]. Concern for privacy seems to have won this battle—the FDC never came about.

The center's desirability is still debated: it would close gaps in knowledge, one data set might help validate or explain another, duplication in data collection might be reduced, it might become easier for planners to test ideas for their effects on a broad spectrum of variables, using simulation. It was feared that even a benignly planned system would evolve into a national collection of dossiers on individuals, and the potential for harm would be enormous.

The Fair Credit Reporting Act of 1970 recognized that "there is a need to insure that consumer reporting agencies exercise their grave responsibilities with fairness, impartiality, and a respect for the individual right to privacy" [7]. The purpose of the act was to "enable persons to protect themselves against the dissemination of inaccurate or misleading information bearing on their credit worthiness, insurability, or employability by requiring that all consumer reporting agencies adopt reasonable procedures ... meeting the needs of commerce ... in a manner which is fair and equitable to the individual" [8]. The law permits an individual to examine his file in a credit agency and specifies procedures by which an individual may rectify or challenge a disputed entry. There are still weaknesses, but the act is a landmark in protecting individual rights from corporate error or exploitation.

The National Crime Information Center (NCIC) is operated by the Federal Bureau of Investigation and was implemented in 1967 [9]. Its original purpose was to provide a central index of wanted persons and stolen property. It contained physical descriptions of wanted people and identified the offenses of which each was accused and the agency issuing a warrant. Property items were entered only if uniquely identified by a serial number. Police in the United States and Canada can use the system by contacting an NCIC remote terminal and querying the file on a specific key—*name* or *serial number*. The restriction on types of records maintained minimized the chance of erroneous identification. The FBI has been quoted as attributing to NCIC a jump from 20 to 43% of recoveries of vehicles stolen in interstate automobile thefts, seemingly a clear enough social benefit.

In 1970 the FBI added to NCIC an index to criminal history files, to provide a reference to criminal history records stored at participating state agencies. This introduced a data problem. The FBI could not control the file maintenance—seeing to it that records were updated when a case was resolved, particularly when an accused person was acquitted or charges were dropped. Also, the FBI could not physically control access to the history records, hence could not ensure that they were used only by law enforcement personnel as part of their official duties. Standards for control of files have been devised, but the system remains the center of controversy—an apparently effective tool against crime that apparently affords insufficient protection to innocent people caught up in criminal investigations. In 1974 the U.S. Court of Appeals for the District of Columbia ruled that the FBI was responsible for the accuracy of its records and instructed a lower court to "... enter an order directing appellees [the Attorney General and the FBI Director] to remove appellant's record from their criminal files" [10].

### 13.1.2 Basic Concepts

Let us consider why the computer has become so important and what the related concepts *privacy, security,* and *protection* mean.

*Privacy* is a social concept—the extent to which a person keeps information about himself to himself, or advises only a limited number of people and organizations pledged to honor the sanctity of his information. Or, it can be the assumed right of a person to this degree of self-containment. As a right, the notion is ill defined. Westin [11] says

> Privacy—the "right to be left alone"—has been called by Justice Louis Brandeis the "right most valued by civilized men." While there is no doubt that claims to individual and group privacy have been part of the American civil-liberty tradition throughout our history, legal definition of our right to privacy has been less firmly developed than [that of] due process. At the constitutional level, the Bill of Rights contains no mention of the term "privacy." However, in the course of protecting some explicitly stated constitutional rights, the Supreme Court has given protection over the past decades to many important "components" of the right to privacy.

*Security* may be defined as the extent to which we achieve the privacy of information, property, or person.

*Protection* is a process—how we go about providing a measure of security. Whereas privacy is largely a social matter, protection resides largely in the technical domain. Society at large, not computer people, decides what degree of security is one's right, but technical people take the lead in working out new methods of protection to achieve security and in identifying weaknesses in existing methods.

Computers are looked on with dread as a threat to personal privacy and are regarded as a threat to corporate security for several reasons: one is sheer size. It is unquestionably easier to steal a personal file or a sales prospect list from a company's safe than from the company's computer. But theft from a computer often goes undetected because the information is still there; hence countermeasures may not be taken. Also, since it is nearly as easy to steal an entire file from a computer as a single record, the magnitude of the loss or embarrassing disclosure can be great. Error is yet another form of threat. Errors in records are as old as records. Computers do not often cause errors. But there is a tendency for small errors to propagate massively through an information system, and correcting them and eliminating their cause may involve more expense than system operators care to assume.

In the next section we deal with the computer, the technical threat to it, and the controls and protective measures that can provide security.

## 13.2 PROTECTION OF COMPUTER SYSTEMS

A *threat* to a computer system is any potential damage, error, theft, or other action that might cause harm to the system, its data, or the user of its data. Threats may be malicious (theft or arson), or they may be accidental (storm damage, communication line failure) or the result of error (by a computer operator, a data collector, or a person responsible for judicious release of information).

Deliberate attempts to damage a computer system are called *attacks*. One purpose of attack is to deny use of a facility, and under this category come the more brutal crimes of bombing, burning, or software sabotage (causing an operating system to malfunction). The objective of *penetration*, a more subtle form of attack, may be to steal information or programs or to alter stored information without otherwise disrupting the system, perhaps avoiding detection of the crime. These are the computer versions of "white collar" crime.

Both attacks and protection come in many forms and can involve many different aspects of a computer. Let us first examine the computer environment in which protective measures operate.

### 13.2.1 The Computer Environment and Threats

Although we are primarily concerned in this book with computer software, we must consider all aspects of computers in the security problem. We define the environment of consideration as consisting of five principal components.

*The Computer Installation* The installation is the premises in which a computer, tape or disk library, communication equipment, or the like is stored. At one time protection of information was almost synonymous with protecting the physical premises in which the information was stored, and that protection was afforded by limiting the number of persons having access to the facility. As computers have grown more expensive and their users more dependent on them, environmental protection has become more important. We often find elaborate measures taken against fire, dust, power failure or surges, and water leakage. We now recognize that theft is possible by persons accessing the computer through electrically connected remote terminals. Moreover, it is possible for a programmer to steal information from a file without being present in the computer installation: he simply writes a program that accesses and copies the file.

*Personnel* If all personnel who have access to a computer, directly or through communication channels, could be fully trusted to be honest, competent, and sensitive to the importance of information they might acquire, there would be no security problem. Since this is rarely the case, and since bribery of an employee is always an alternative to direct theft, personal clearances are required for anyone who has contact with a computer or file needing protection. Such personnel problems are not germane to this book.

***Computer Hardware*** When it is the object of an attacker to deny use of a facility rather than to steal information, the hardware is the most vulnerable component and must be protected against all kinds of threats from man and the natural environment: dust, self-generated heat, fire, water, and explosion. Another way to attack hardware is to monitor the electromagnetic radiation emanating from any electrical machinery and to learn to convert these signals into meaningful information. Since electromechanical components generally radiate the most, a device such as a printer is a good target. A printer is even more inviting because the information it handles has been arranged for human interpretation and it is only necessary for the attacker to recognize the character codes in his intercepted messages. Radiation from within the CPU would tell what commands are being executed or what information is being transferred between computer components; but it is no small job to deduce from, say, the stream of data into a program control element or command decoder, the content of a file or the purpose of the program being executed. Radiation protection can be provided by shielding the computer with a metal screen in three dimensions—walls, ceilings, and floors—or by intentionally transmitting a broad spectrum of electromagnetic noise to interfere with any monitoring equipment. An attacker can work through the computer by *encroachment*. Using an application program to read or modify files that the program was not supposed to have access to can be done by having the application program modify the operating system's tables temporarily, changing the access restrictions. Accidental encroachment, which can have as much impact as the intentional variety, is particularly likely when new programs are being debugged on the same machine used to store sensitive files and execute production programs.

***Computer Software*** Prior to the advent of multiprogrammed computers, any one user had complete control of a computer at any one time, and there were no files or programs in or attached to the computer for him to copy or encroach on. With multiprogramming came permanently on-line files, present while any number of programs are operating and potentially vulnerable to being read or changed by those programs. This form of breach of security is the more threatening because it may go undiscovered for some time. *Most computer protection activities are directed toward this problem.*

***Files*** The ultimate objective of any penetration of a computer installation for theft is the files, whether of data or programs. Files can be improperly removed by physically taking the recording medium, by intercepting electromagnetic radiation, or by having a program make a copy to be removed along with that program's legitimate output. Files are also subject to malicious or accidental modification.

### 13.2.2 The Nature of Security Controls

Threats to security in the areas just described can be neutralized by setting up protective controls of the following types: physical access control, hardware protection against one program encroaching on another or on unauthorized files, authorization procedures for users of multiprogrammed systems, particularly remote users, and content control on data.

***Physical Access Control*** Physical barriers, limiting access to people whose backgrounds have been checked, escorting visitors, and so on, are not data management controls. In a sense, radiation protection also falls into the physical access category.

***Hardware Encroachment Protection*** The problem of encroachment is caused when a program addresses an area of memory it was not intended to address. The simplest explanation is a programming error, but the phenomenon can also occur when addresses are being computed and one or more of the data elements used in the computation has value outside the permissible range. In the latter case we might say that a strategic programming error was made in not validating all input variables; but in the event of a logical error in programming, little can be done at the moment. The result is that a program retrieves data at a location that was not intended, and this almost certainly means that what is stored there is not what is expected; hence any use of such data will lead to further error. If the errant program writes in the wrong place, it will overwrite someone else's data or even a program, conceivably even the operating system, with completely chaotic results. Encroachment can be intentional when a programmer intends theft of data or sabotage to the system.

One form of protection is called *fetch* or *storage protection*. As implemented in IBM computers, main memory is divided into blocks, much like pages, of 2048 characters. A code number or *protection key* is assigned to each block. Similar keys are assigned to programs (by the operating system) that will use the memory blocks (Figure 13.1). If a program attempting to store or retrieve a command does not have a key that matches the store or fetch protection key on the data, the computer refuses to carry out the command. In this event, the program is interrupted and the operating system resumes control of the computer [12].

Similar controls are possible on auxiliary memory. Each program that uses a file must be accompanied by instructions in job control language (or the similar language for non-IBM computers) informing the operating system which files are to be used. Files must be separately defined to the operating system, and the file description includes a statement of what program may use it. Files may be shared by several programs or restricted to use by a single one [13].

274  Privacy, Protection, and Security

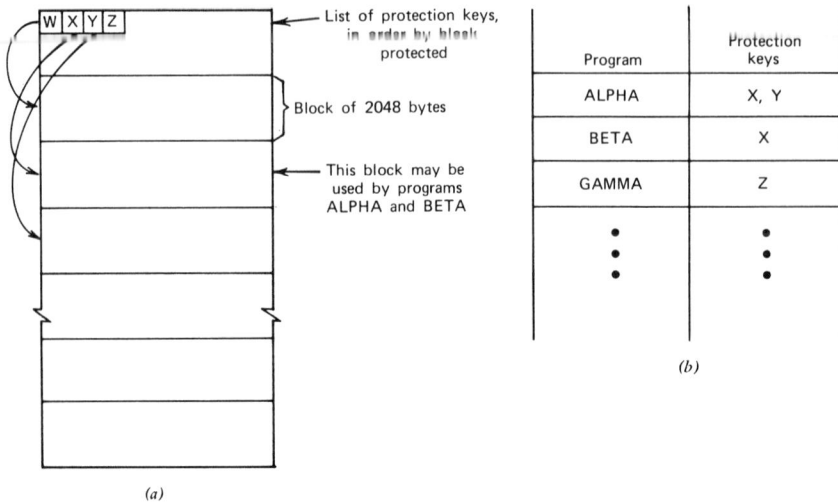

**Figure 13.1** Storage protection keys. (*a*) Main storage, (*b*) table maintained by operating system.

***Authorization of Users*** Authorization is the giving and checking of passwords of various kinds from a user to a computer, the use of personal identification devices, such as fingerprinting or voice printing, or keys to open locked doors or pieces of equipment. A password may be an organization code, mainly intended to ensure proper billing of the computer time and, presumably, available only to authorized users within the organization. The organization code may be coupled with individual user codes, to facilitate adding or dropping individuals as authorized users within an organization. Authorization codes are illustrated in Figure 13.2.

Variable passwords, a form of either individual or organizational identification, are changed often, and users are required to know the currently valid ones. Passwords may be multifaceted, that is, the machine asks a question, receives a password response, asks another question based on that response, and so on. The more protection provided, the greater the cost of the associated software, and the greater the probability of innocent error. The user's responses may be items of personal information, random numbers previously generated by the computer for this use, or randomly selected words (Figure 13.3).

Another aspect of authorization is the practice of varying what is being authorized. The authorization conversation is between the user and the computer's operating system. The access granted can be to any or all

| Authorization Code | | User No. |
|---|---|---|
| 2 | QAZ | 4 |
| 3 | WSK | 2 |
| 4 | EDC | 1 |
| 5 | RFV | 5 |
| 6 | TGB | 2 |
| 7 | YHN | 3 |
| 8 | UJM | 2 |
| | | |

| User No. | Address |
|---|---|
| 1 | |
| 2 | |
| 3 | |
| 4 | |
| 5 | |
| 6 | |
| . | |

a. Authorization code is used to retrieve user number.

b. User number is used to locate those blocks that a given user is authorized to access.

Sample interactive conversation concerning authorization codes:

COMPUTER: AUTH CODE?

USER: 2gaz

COMPUTER: INVALID

AUTH CODE?

USER: 2qaz

**Figure 13.2** Authorization codes. The code may be a random alphanumeric string. More than one user may have the same code.

| Name | Mother's Maiden Name | Date of Birth | Random Word | Random Number |
|---|---|---|---|---|
| A B JONES | LEWIS | 12/16/47 | BUICK | 53804 |
| C D KING | JOHNSON | 5/31/38 | ASTER | 21433 |
| C F LILLY | OLSON | 2/17/40 | PAPER | 19104 |

Sample interactive conversation concerning variable passwords:

**COMPUTER:** NAME?

USER: a.b. jones

COMPUTER: DATE OF BIRTH?

USER: 12/16/47

COMPUTER: NUMBER?

USER: 53804

**Figure 13.3** Variable passwords. This technique enables the user first to identify himself, then respond to questions calling for personal or previously supplied random data. There may be more than one question, and a different sequence of questions may be presented each time.

components that are controllable by the operating system. For example

1. Users may be authorized only to use certain terminals, and there may be restrictions on what files may be displayed on the terminals. Thus "classified" information may be prohibited from being displayed on certain terminals or may be sent to these terminals only when authorized people are using them (Figure 13.4).
2. Users may be restricted to certain files, certain programs, or certain areas of main memory (Figure 13.5).
3. Users may be restricted to operating during certain hours of the day, at which times sensitive information is kept off the computer.

*Authorization of Programs* Program authorization is a form of high-order application of some of the ideas of hardware encroachment protection. It is not sufficient to limit access of programs to the files specifically denoted in job control statements. It is also necessary to guarantee that no programmer is allowed to claim access to an unauthorized file. Otherwise a programmer might declare the payroll file available to his unrelated program and use this access to raise his own salary. To protect against such accessions, each program used on a given computer has an entry for it in a

| User | Terminal |
|---|---|
| A B JONES | 1,2,3,4,10 |
| C D KING | 1,3 |
| C F LILLY | 9 |
| | |

| Terminal | Files Authorized |
|---|---|
| 1 | LIBRARY |
| 2 | ANY |
| 3 | INVENTORY |
| 4 | SALARY |

Sample interactive conversation concerning use of terminal control:

```
COMPUTER:  NAME?
USER:   a b jones
COMPUTER:  FILE?
USER:   salary
COMPUTER:  YOU ARE NOT AUTHORIZED
           ACCESS TO THIS FILE AT
           THIS LOCATION.
```

**Figure 13.4** Terminal control. A user may be allowed to use any of a designated set of terminals, but there may be restrictions on the information that can be sent to any given terminal. Here the terminal (presumably because of its public location) rather than the user is denied access to the salary file.

## Protection of Computer Systems   277

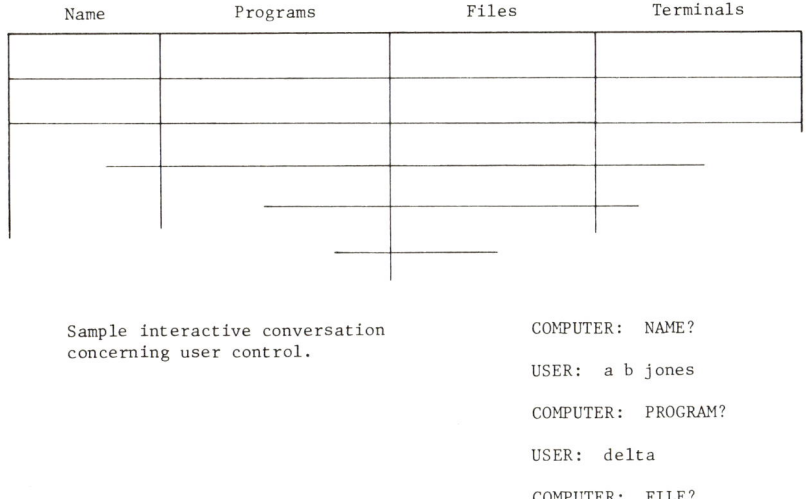

**Figure 13.5** User control. Storing information defining each user's access privileges permits closer control. The user would be expected to provide full information about which files he will use with which program.

security table, available only to the operating system or to a highly protected applications program. The table explicitly lists the file to which a program may have access, and input must come from a high authority in the computer installation. Under these conditions, no programmer can self-declare his authority to see any given file.

***Content Control*** Possibly the only way to guarantee the security of sensitive information is to prevent it from being stored in an accessible place. This is done to some extent in the domain of military security, where documents are given a specific classification denoting the degree of protection they must be afforded and are stored only in locations deemed to be adequately protected for a given level of sensitivity. Thus a top secret document can be stored only in a place (say, a safe within a building) specifically authorized for top secret and providing the requisite physical protection. Only people who are specifically authorized to work with information at the security level named may have access to the storage place. Lesser levels of sensitivity are assigned lesser degrees of control.

Classifying information in this sense works only when the documents, their storage places, and the people who have access are all part of a coordinated system that recognizes well-defined levels of security and sensitivity and screens and limits the individuals involved. It is an expensive process that has been effective, although not perfectly, in protecting military information. Thus control of content goes hand in hand with control of users. Both forms of control are necessary: only selected information is put into a safe, and only selected people are authorized access.

Security classification can be applied to an entire file, to individual records, or to a single field within a record. For example, a payroll file might be totally denied to all except the payroll department. In some companies, though, a manager may see the payroll records of his employees and prospective transfers into his department, making for variable clearance to see certain records. Finally, certain personnel data in the file might be generally released, but salary-related fields of all records (*salary, tax deduction,* etc.) would be denied to everyone outside the payroll department.

Similarly, certain types of information may be barred from a system because access cannot be controlled adequately, given the sensitivity of the information. Criminal justice files are an example. Police officials tend to want all the information they can get on a criminal suspect, including record of prior convictions and arrests. But arrest alone implies no wrongdoing if there was no conviction, and many argue that no record should be kept of arrests because this information cannot be made inaccessible to the police or others who might misuse or misunderstand it.

Short of keeping whole classes of information out of an information system, another form of protection is to limit the manner in which one file is linked to another, the most common form of link being a common record key. For example, automobile insurance companies like to know the traffic violation records of their policyholders. Some states use the driver's social security number as the key to a driving record file. When this key is known, the insurance company can easily check the records of any person. To protect the individual against both a form of spying and possible misinterpretation of information (only one side of an issue is in most files), it has been argued that states should not use the social security number which gives the company this master key to files.

It is certainly true that use of a standard key facilitates multifile searching. On the other hand, absence of the standard key does not guarantee against multifile searching, and energy expended in protecting the sanctity of the social security number may be wasted. Searching can be done using a combination of *name, date of birth,* and *address.* Each of these is somewhat unreliable in itself. A man may write his name one time as JOHN JONES and another as J. JONES. He may forget or lie about his age (even when he might never lie about anything else), and he may both move often and vary the spelling of his address just as he does that of his name. Nonetheless, by allowing some variation in matching terms (as *date of birth* = 1935 or 1936, or *name* = J# JONES, where # means any symbol or symbols will be accepted), paying more for a search as a result, and being willing to tolerate some degree of error, the information obtainable with a social security number can be found without it. The amount of error that a commercial firm is willing to accept in this form of searching may be more odious to the consumer than having all information available and being more nearly sure that the correct person is always identified. In general, though, it is a principle of security that if penetration is made too expensive, it can be deterred.

## 13.3 THE FUTURE

The future of computer security is hard to predict because it is dependent on people's attitudes as well as on technology. Concern about the security of computer-stored files began after the development of control programs and operating systems, which represented heavy investments by computer manufacturers. By the time it was found that they did not offer adequate degrees of protection, it was not economically possible to change them. Hence today's operating systems are weak links in the protection chain. In the future, operating systems must provide for control of

- *people,* who use or operate the computer or its remote terminals
- *resources* or computer components requested by users
- *programs* requested by users
- *data* requested directly by a user or by a program called by a user
- *mode of operation*—for example, whether a user is cleared merely to see information or also to change it

New generations of software must be proof against tampering by repeated entering of a password, by systematic attempts to find an acceptable one, by system programmers who fraudulently change passwords, or file memory allocations, and by other methods.

There are other, nontechnical solutions to some of the most vexing of privacy problems. Legal obligations can be imposed on owners of data bases or operators of information services, requiring them to take responsibility for accuracy of content and authorized release. This is not unlike requiring a manufacturer to be responsible for the safe performance of his product in the hands of the consumer. Mechanically simpler, but socially more difficult, is to change people's attitudes. The need for vigorously protecting credit or arrest files is largely due to fear that a person's early indiscretions, or even recent errors not likely to be repeated, will be forever held against him. The fear is not irrational. Rather than build protective measures to prevent disclosure, however, society might learn to be more understanding. It would help if people began to realize that a single teen-age arrest does not make the adult a criminal, or that a single bad credit incident does not mean that the "guilty" person is unreliable. In fact, it might well be we hold these incidents against people because incomplete record keeping, not angelic behavior, prevents similar items from showing on the records of the rest of us.

## REFERENCES

1. Alan F. Westin and Michael A. Baker, *Databanks in a Free Society,* Quadrangle Books, New York, 1972, pp. 13-14.
2. "Controlling the Data Banks," Editorial in *The Washington Post,* Washington, D.C., February 4, 1974.
3. David Kahn, *The Code Breakers; The Story of Secret Writing,* Macmillan, New York, 1967.
4. Robert L. Chartrand and Louise G. Becker, *The Federal Data Center: Proposals and Reactions,* TK 6565 C SP 137(rev), Congressional Research Service, Library of Congress, Washington, D.C., June 14, 1968.
5. Edgar S. Dunn, Jr., *Review of Proposal for a National Data Center,* Office of Statistical Standards, Bureau of the Budget, Washington, D.C., 1965.
6. Task Force on the Storage of and Access to Government Statistics, *Report of the Task Force to the Bureau of the Budget,* Carl Kaysen, Chairman, Washington, D.C., 1966.
7. Title VI of the Consumer Credit Protection Act, PL 91-508, 91st Congress, 2nd Session, October 26, 1970.
8. *Ibid.*
9. Westin and Baker, *op. cit.,* pp. 47-64.
10. United States District Court for the District of Columbia Circuit, No. 71-1768, *Dale B. Menard, Appellant* v. *William B. Saxbe, Attorney General of the United States, and Clarence M. Kelley,* decided April 23, 1974.
11. Westin and Baker, *op. cit.,* pp. 17, 18.
12. Harry Katzan, Jr., *Operating Systems, A Pragmatic Approach,* Van Nostrand Reinhold, New York, 1973, p. 52.
13. Gary Deward Brown, *System/360 Job Control Language,* John Wiley & Sons, New York, 1970, pp. 101-12.

## RECOMMENDED READING

### General Works on Computers and Privacy

Miller, Arthur, *The Assault on Privacy: Computers, Data Banks, and Dossiers,* University of Michigan Press, Ann Arbor, 1971.

Westin and Baker [1].

Martin, James, and Adrian R. D. Norman, *The Computerized Society,* Prentice-Hall, Englewood Cliffs, N.J., 1970.

## Legislation, Legislative Hearings, and Legal Aspects

Committee on Scientific and Technical Information, Federal Council on Science and Technology, *Legal Aspects of Computerized Information Systems,* COSATI Report No. 73-1, National Technical Information Service, Washington, D.C., PB-223 496/1, September 1972.

PL 93-579, *The Privacy Act of 1974,* 93rd Congress, December 31, 1974.

U.S. Congress, House Committee on Government Operations, Special Subcommittee on the Invasion of Privacy, *The Computer Invasion of Privacy,* Hearings before the Special Subcommittee, 89th Congress, 1st Session, July 26–28, 1966, Washington, D.C., 1966.

U.S. Congress, Senate Committee on the Judiciary, Subcommittee on Administrative Practices and Procedures, *Computer Privacy,* Hearings Before the Subcommittee, 90th Congress, 1st Session, March 14–15, 1967, Washington, D.C., 1967.

U.S. Congress, Senate Committee on Banking and Currency, Subcommittee on Financial Institutions, *Fair Credit Reporting,* Hearings Before the Subcommittee, 91st Congress, 1st Session, May 19–27, 1969, Washington, D.C., 1969.

## Technical Aspects of Computer Security and Bibliographies

Hart, M. Kathleen, and Rein Turn, *Privacy and Security in Data Bank Systems: An Annotated Bibliography, 1970–73,* R-1361-NSF, RAND Corp., Santa Monica, Calif., March 1974.

*Data Security and Data Processing*
    Vol. 1   *Introduction and Overview*
    Vol. 2   *Study Summary*
    Vol. 3   Part 1, *State of Illinois: Executive Overview*
            Part 2, *Study Results: State of Illinois*
    Vol. 4   *Study Results, Massachusetts Institute of Technology*
    Vol. 5   *Study Results, TRW Systems, Inc.*
    Vol. 6   *Evaluations and Installation Experiences: Resource Security System*

G320-1375-0, IBM Corp., White Plains, N.Y., 1974. This series of documents contains an extensive bibliography on the subject in Vol. 4, pages 238–300.

*Appendix*

# Feature analysis of a generalized data management system used by the Council of Great City Schools for solicitation of bids on a GDMS.

## 1. System Highlights

Indicate briefly, one or two lines for each point, how your system addresses the eighteen points contained in Table 1. The Highlights should adequately describe your system. This section should be limited to three or four pages if possible.

## 2. Status and Planned Extensions

The development status of this system (effective May, 1971) is to be given. Planned extensions to the system should be identified and described here

*Table 1   Highlights for Section 1*

1. System Name
2. First Operational Date
3. Number of present installations
4. Number of Versions Available
5. Number of Versions Bid
6. Ancestry of System
7. Data Structure
    a. Class (e.g. single level, multi-level, hierarchical structure)
    b. Security Available (e.g. file protection, data element protection, read-only access, etc.)
    c. Limitations
        - Number of files
        - Number of Records per file
        - Number of characters per record
        - Number of fields per record
        - Data Base size (characters)
        - Number of data bases supported simultaneously
8. General Processes Provided (e.g., file definition, creation, updating, interrogation, data editing and validation on input, etc.)
9. Language Type, Form Characteristics (e.g. Procedural, non-procedural, tabulor, string, etc.)
10. Report Capability (e.g. Multifile, destination choice, generation procedures, etc.)
11. Storage Structure (e.g. Inverted, free, multi-list, user controlled, oriented to retrieval or up-dating, etc.)
12. Modes of Use (e.g. Batch, on-line, etc.)
13. Hardware Environment (CPUs, Terminals, etc.)
14. File Media (e.g. Disk, tape, etc.)
15. Operating System Environment (e.g., O.S., DOSD, Multi-programming Computable, etc.)
16. Source Language of Data Management System (e.g. COBOL, FORTRAN, BAL, ALGOL, etc.)
17. Maintenance Agreements (e.g. Length, levels, etc.)
18. Documentation (e.g. System manuals, user manuals, Source code listings, flow charts, etc.)

and referenced in other sections of the text. The extensions should be detailed as to: (1) implementation date, and (2) type, i.e., major characteristics as described in 4. below.

## 3. Background

Indicate the origin of the system, its predecessors, its time frame of development, and other information that will fully convey its history and evolution.

## 4. Major Characteristics

These items may be answered through references to or extracts from existing manuals, if these references are clear.

### 4.1 DATA STRUCTURE

This section should describe the data as it is seen by the user of the system, without regard for any transformation that the data may undergo prior to storage in a *storage structure*. In some cases, the storage structure is identical to the data structure, in which case the description should be given here rather than in the section on storage structure.

The following definitions are terms used in the data structure description. When these terms are used to indicate specific values rather than parts of the structure description, in order to avoid confusion, they may be preceded by the phrases "instance(s) of" or "occurrence(s) of." The terms defined are limited to describing tree structures.

ITEM  The term applied to the structural element which cannot be structurally subdivided and which may be associated with occurrences of values.

GROUP  An association of zero or more items and/or zero or more groups. This implies that groups may be nested.

ENTRY  The group at the apex of the tree structure. All other groups and items are included within the entry. (An occurrence of this is sometimes called a record, a term we avoid in order to forestall the confusion between "physical records" and "logical records.")

FILE  The set of occurrences of the entry. Some systems permit multiple entry types in a single file.

### 4.1.1 Items

***Item Naming*** Describe the system's facility for designating items, e.g., by character position within a group, by user specified name, etc. Also include facilities for assigning synonyms and column headings for printed output.

***Item Data Types*** Items may have values in one of a number of data types, such as alphnumeric, integer, date, etc. Describe the separate types provided by the system. Also include facilities provided for different internal and external representations for a given item, e.g., coded items.

***Data Variability*** This is the ability of the system to handle characteristics of an item, such as length, which may vary from one instance to another.

***Multiple-Valued Items*** If a system has the ability for an item to have multiple values (apart from a facility for repeating groups or for it to have no value (null) or non-existant value), it is described here.

***Subitems*** Some systems permit an item to be divided into sub-items, sub-items into sub sub-items, and so on. In a hierarchical system which allows this, a sub-item is not considered to be at a separate level in the hierarchy.

### 4.1.2 Groups

The concept of group is introduced to deal with the following situations:

*a.* An association of items is considered as constituting a single logical entity, often with a name or other identification of its own. Such an entity is called a non-repeating group. For example, "number," "street," "city," and "state" might make up the group "address."
*b.* In many cases, an association of item values may occur more than once, e.g., the association "education" may consist of items "college," "degree," and "year," and each person may have several "educations." Such an association is called a repeating group. As a special case, a repeating group may contain just a single item, in which case it affords an alternative way of handling multiple-valued items (see 4.1.1).
*c.* The hierarchical relating of items in a entry may be accomplished by "group-nesting," i.e., by permitting groups to contain other groups as constituents. Thus, the group "background A" might consist of the items "birthdate" and "birthplace," and the group "education." Alternatively, group constituents may be limited to items, and relating of

items achieved by defining superior-inferior relationships between groups. E.G., in a different system, the group "background B," consisting of items "birthdate" and "birthplace," might be declared superior to the group "education". A reference to "background A" will generally mean a reference to the items in background A *and* in its included groups, whereas a reference to "background B" will include only the items in "background B" and not those in its subordinate groups.

*Group Structure*   Describe any limitation on the number of groups, and detail the method used to distinguish different groups.

*Group Relationships*   Describe the ability of the user to define relationships among groups, e.g., hierarchical relationships. In hierarchies, significant parameters are the number of levels permitted and the number of different groups permitted at each level. The description may include a graph-like diagram, for example, one in which the nodes represent groups and the directed arcs represent the relationships among groups, e.g., "is superior to."

*Group Identification*   For retrieval and updating purposes, each occurrence of a group may be required to contain an item or set of items which is unique within some set of such occurrences. Any such restrictions should be described here.

*Types of Groups*   In some systems, there are several fundamentally different types of groups which are treated differently. Any such characteristics should be described here.

### 4.1.3   Entries

*Entry Types*   Files may be composed of entries of a single type or of entries of multiple types; transaction files are a good example. Describe the system's capability for accommodating files with multiple entry types; the method used to distinguish entry types; and limitations on number of types that can be accommodated.

*Entry Identification*   For updating and retrieval purposes, entries often must contain an item or set of items which have a different value in each entry. Any such requirements, constraints, or options are described here. Also, indicate any limiting factor on the number of entries in a file.

### 4.1.4   Files

*File Types*   Some systems provide only a single type of file for all processing, while others provide a number of types which differ with respect to logical organization, or use within the system. For example, a system may have "master" files which collectively constitute the data base, and "transaction" files which are used to update the master files. The different types should be identified here for ease of reference later on.

*File Identification* Describe the convention for identifying individual files within a multifile system. Also, indicate the limiting factors on the number of files that can be accommodated in the system.

### 4.1.5 Data Structure Generalization

Describe any features provided by the system for accommodating data structures more general than those implied by the foregoing paragraphs. For example, a system may provide the data type "pointer" so that the user may establish explicit relationships among entries of the same or different files. Other systems permit the user to define such relationships but keep the pointers hidden from the user. The conventional procedure of using a normal item value from one file to locate a second item in another file is not considered to be a data structure feature.

### 4.1.6 Data Security

Many systems permit the user to define levels of security. These may be on a file entry, group, or item level and may be classified in terms of interrogation security and update security. Describe these here and amplify with examples how security is implemented.

### 4.1.7 Other Data Structure Features

Any other features of data structure as opposed to the process of defining data structure, are covered here.

## 4.2 FUNCTIONS

### 4.2.1 Language Form

Regardless of the functions performed by the language, it must have a form. Some systems have highly tabular languages, others are free form within an 80 character limit and others are completely free form but use linguistic elements such as specific characters or words to terminate a specification. Some languages use a mixture of all techniques. Describe yours here, presenting a complete syntax of the language and the necessary explanations.

### 4.2.2 Data Structure Definition

Describe how the user defines the data structure of the system. Cover features discussed in section 4.1. Mention any restrictions on the way in which these definitions are made—especially the sequence in which the various levels are handled.

Specifically, procedures for defining the following items should be given:

- data item types
- data item length limitations
- multiple-value items
- groups
- entries and entry types
- files and file types
- general data structures
- data security and levels applicable
- data content validation
- data definition revision

### 4.2.3 Interrogation

In non-procedural self-contained systems, the function of interrogation is one most frequently automated. Interrogation typically consists of two parts, one to express a condition on the data in the file and the other to define which data must be copied out of the file into printed reports or mechanized files. Indicate how interrogation is handled. How it is programmed in a conventional programming language or how it is automated in the framework of a non-procedural language should be described here. Emphasis should be placed on two areas, interrogation verbs, and methods or techniques of qualification. The verbs should be listed and defined. The qualification techniques should be fully amplified to illustrate how they might assist users in the areas indicated in the Introduction section of this RFP. All computational and statistical capabilities that are in the system should be defined and illustrated.

### 4.2.4 Report Capability

Although this is really part of the previous section, its importance ... requires that it be dealt with separately. [we] require two types of report capability. First, the conventional type, i.e., "paper," and secondly, magnetic, i.e., disk or tape for use as input for other programs or computerized models. Points to be addressed in each are listed below:

### Conventional

- content lines
- titles
- heading lines and footing lines
- user specified text
- editing and formating
- derived data

### Magnetic

- use with FORTRAN
- use with COBOL
- use with APL
- user formating options

Although not specifically related to either conventional or magnetic, some systems have the capability to store frequently used report-generations routines comprising selection criterion and extraction specification, with the file. This Report-Generating Routine may then be invoked either in its stored form or with explicit or implicit modification of its parts. Any such facilities should be described here both in terms of how and when the Report-Generating Routing is stored and how and when it may be invoked.

Finally, if a user wishes to control a Report-Generating Routine, options such as abortion, continuance, or batching, etc., that will allow this should be fully discussed here.

### 4.2.5 Update

Update is the process of changing the value content of the file or data base in accordance with the receipt of input messages frequently referred to as transactions. Such input messages may be messages requiring analysis by the system to determine the selection criteria to be applied. Discussed here should be the selection criteria or languages that are used for update. The levels of updates that are allowed should also be discussed. These include:

- entry
- group
- item
- intraitem

Also discussed here should be the procedures necessary for validation of the update. Finally, if there is an *Audit Trail* facility, it should be fully addressed.

### 4.2.6 File Creation

The file creation process, namely that of producing the initial instance of the file may be handled by updating a null file or it may be handled as an appendage to the file definition process as described in 4.1.

Some systems do not have a process of file creation explicitly conceived. They operate only on files which are already in mechanized form and which can be defined. How initial file creation is achieved should be described in this section. If the system has explicit facilities for reading data entries to be input to the system, then the restrictions in the input form are to be described.

### 4.2.7 Own Code

Any ability or necessity for a user to enter a procedural language (or code generated by its processors) should be covered in this section along with any assembly language interface requirements.

### 4.2.8 Multiple Files

Indicate how your system would handle a requirement to extract (4.2.3) and report (4.2.4) data from more than one file.

### 4.3. STORAGE STRUCTURE

The storage structure capabilities vary extensively among different systems. Some generalized systems consist of nothing more than facilities to define and operate on sophisticated storage structures feasible only in a direct access device. In other systems, the user of the system need have no knowledge of the storage structure, which usually implies that he has no control over it. Storage structures can be described on at least two levels. The organization of the data within a stored entry, of entries within a file and files within a multifile system are examples of levels. Typical storage structure techniques may include the use of primary and secondary indexes, pointers, chains, etc.

### 4.3.1 Item Level Storage Representation

Include the internal representation of discrete values (including null where appropriate) and also the storage of multiple occurrence items.

### 4.3.2 Entry and Group Level Storage Structure

The organization of values and possibly links, intra-entry indexes or separators within the stored representation of the entry should be described here.

### 4.3.3 File Level Storage Structure

Within the stored representation of a file, entries may be stored sequentially as is necessary on a sequential medium, such as magnetic tape. On a direct access device more intricate file level storage structures are not only feasible, but also necessary to take advantage of the capabilities of the medium. Various indexing and chaining techniques should be described here.

### 4.3.4 Multiple File Storage Structure

The representation of file linkage and indexes to files within a multifile system should be described here.

### 4.3.5 Logical-Physical Structure Relationship

Make explicit the relationship between logical and physical file organization. This discussion should describe physical storage structures and allocation resulting from file creation and modification commands.

### 4.3.6 Other Storage Structure Features

Any other features of storage structures not covered in the preceding sections should be described here.

## 4.4 OPERATIONAL ENVIRONMENT

This section should be used to fully discuss the hardware and software environments.

### 4.4.1 Hardware Parameters

Indicate generally the following items as they apply to your DMS:

- minimum basic system
- storage media
- terminal equipment
- hardware transferability

*Table 2*

Given a file of 200 entries with 10 items in each entry that are named A, B, C, D, E, F, G, H, I, and J, explain the procedures and statements required to:

1. Count occurrences of positive numeric values in item A.
2. Print a report (list) of field A that is sorted by item values in item B and C and D.
3. Print the minimum, maximum, and average values in item A.
4. Print standard deviation of values in A.
5. Print a report of minimum, maximum average, and standard deviation of values in A for each value of item B equal to 5.
6. Print the same report as 5 above except that the entry must satisfy the following requirements for item B (each condition should be considered as a separate "screen").
   a. Zero
   b. 1, 2, or 3
   c. Odd
   d. Even
   e. Zero or odd
   f. Greater than 100
   g. From 5 to (inc) 50

Given two files constructed as in the tables below, answer how your system would be able to handle this problem:

| File #1 | | File #2 | |
|---|---|---|---|
| Item | Contents | Item | Contents |
| 1 | Name | 1 | Social Security No. |
| 2 | Code (1–10) | 2 | Address |
| 3 | Social Security Number | | |
| Last | | Last | |

Print the addresses where name is Jones and Code is equal to 8.

### 4.4.2 Operating System Parameters

Indicate generally what operating systems your DMS uses and whether it can operate in a multi-programming environment.

### 4.4.3 Restart and Recovery Capability

Indicate the procedures available for restarting or recovering the DMS from a hardware system failure.

### 4.4.4 System Operation Reports

This section should be used to indicate any reports that the DMS may be able to produce about itself in terms of efficiency or operation.

## 4.5 SAMPLE PROBLEMS

This section contains typical types of problems that are anticipated. The Council would like to see how your DMS would handle these problems. It is not required that you "crank-up" your system and include the print-out. The Council would like the steps necessary for solution listed as if they were to be coded. The problems are contained in Table 2.

## 5. Relevant Applications

This section should include typical examples of your DMS in operation. Special interest will be paid to any applications that are obviously close to [our needs.]

# Index

Abrams, Marshall D., 172
Abramson, Norman, 172, 264
Access control, 273
   to data sets in VSAM, 96-97
   method, 54
   time, 35
Acquisition of data, 229
Address, 107
   computation of, 112-115
Alphabet, 4, 5, 15-17
Alphabetic order, 5
American Standard Code for Information Interchange, 15-17, 262
Anderson, Ruth K., 188
Argument, 107
ARPANET, 255-258, 260, 262
Array, 21, 55
ASCII, see American Standard Code for Information Interchange
Ashby, W. Ross, 12
Authorization, of programs, 276-277
   of users, 274-276

Bachman, C. W., 80
Backup, 170
Baker, Michael A., 280
Baran, Paul, 242, 263
Barnett, E. H., 222
BASIC, 182
Becker, Louise, 280
Berryman, Jeffrey A., 93, 101
Bibliographic information systems, 212, 227
Binary-coded decimal number representation, 17
Binary number, 17
Black chamber, 267
Blanc, R. P., 264

Brown, Gary Deward, 12, 13, 280
Bryant, Edward C., 240
Byte, 18

Cellular partitioning, 3, 62
Chain, 51
   structures, 75-76
Chapin, Ned, 103
Chartrand, Robert L., 280
Checkpoint, 185
Cherry, Colin, 33
COBOL, 178, 182-184, 204
CODASYL, see Committee on Data Systems Languages
Code, 15
Codes as identifiers, 19-20
Collision, 114
Combs, Bill, 263
Command language, 199-203
   processor, 180-181
Committee on Data Systems Languages, 93, 103, 183, 187, 203, 209, 222
Common carrier facilities, 248-251
Communication, 8
   between computers, 15
   data, 157-172, 242
   elements of, 157
   line control, 166
   supervisor programs, 165-166
Comptre Corp., 12, 13
Computer, environment of, 271-272
   protection of, 270-279
   threats to, 271-272
Concentrating of signals, 160-162
Content-addressable structures, 89-90
Content changes to file, 139-141
Content, control of, 277-279
Context of language elements, 15

*295*

296    Index

Control area, 94
  interval, 94
Cotton, Ira W., 167, 172, 264
Couger, J. Daniel, 240
Cox, J. E., 264
Crowley, Thomas H., 172, 264
Cylinder concept of disk storage, 40
  of data, 40
  mode, 40

Data, as a component of an information system, 226
  acquisition, 229
  characteristics, 231-232
  communication, 157-172
  communication applied to data, management, 167-171
  definition, 174, 182-184
  definition language, 196, 203-210
  entry, 190
  entry language, 196
  independence, 83, 100-101, 203-210
  management, 4-7
  management support systems, 54
  management systems, generalized, 173-188
    strategy for, 220-222
    manager, 53-54
  organization, 20-28, 49
  preparation, 229-230
  representation, 14-20
  representation language, 196-197
  retrieval, 227
  set, 25
  storage, 34-80
  structure, 4, 20-28
  transcription, 230
  validation, 230-231
Data base administrator, 191, 223
Data-phone, 248
Datum, 56
Davenport, William P., 171
Davey, J. R., 172
DDL, see Data, Definition Language
Detail records in IDS, 75
DIALOG, 90, 177-178
Direct access, to inverted files, 67
  structures, 64-68
Directory of a list, 60
Distributed intelligence, 261-263

  systems, 260
Document retrieval system, 227
Dodd, George G., 12, 80, 103
Drucker, Peter F., 240
Dunn, Edgar S., Jr., 280

EBCDIC, see Extended Binary Coded Decimal Interchange Code
Effectiveness of information systems, 238
Efficiency of information systems, 237-238
Encroachment protection, 273
Extended Binary Coded Decimal Interchange Code, 16-18
Extent of a file, 62

Fact retrieval system, 227
Fair Credit Reporting Act, 156, 268
Fairthorne, R. A., 14, 32
Fayen, E. G., 172
Federal Bureau of Investigation, 269
Federal Data Center, 268
Fetch protection, 273
Field, 23
Fife, Dennis W., 188
File, 11-12
  logical structure of, 81-102
  maintenance of, 139-156
  modification of, 5
  organization of, 25-28
    ordered, 41
    sequential, 55
Flight control system, 213
Floating decimal number representation, 18
Floating point number representation, 18
Flores, Ivan, 12, 33, 80, 103
FORTRAN, 182
Fowler, F. G., 12
Fowler, H. W., 12
Free space, in VSAM, 96
  management of, 98-99

Gallagher, Cornelius E., 268
Garbage collection, 51
Garbassi, U., 33
GDMS, see Generalized Data Management System
Gehring, Richard L., 242, 263
Generalized data management system, 173-188, 227
  components of, 178-179

selection of, 187-188
Generic search in VSAM, 97-98
Gentle, Edgar C., Jr., 171, 263
Gildersleeve, T. R., 12, 156
Gottlieb, C. C., 33
Grabhorn, Edgar A., 263
Group, 23-25

Hagin, Robert, 172, 188
Hart, M. Kathleen, 281
Hash coding, 65
Hashing, 65, 113
Head, Robert V., 240
Heany, Donald F., 240
Hierarchical structure, 88
Host language, 175
House, William C., 12, 188
Hughes, J. L., 222

IDS, see Integrated Data Store
Indexed random structure, 67-68
Indexed sequential access method, 69-75
 files, 69-75
  maintenance of, 150
Indexes, 48, 55, 107-112
 full, 67
 in VSAM, 95-96
  inverted, 109
  linear, 107
  nested, 111
Information element, 3
 nature of, 92-93
 networks, 4
Information systems, 1-4, 223-240
 categories of, 227-228
 characteristics of, 2-4
 composition of, 225-226
 functions of, 228-232
 nature of, 224-225
Input/output operations, 9
Input validation, 179-181
Integrated data base, 75
 Data Store, 75-80
 files, 75
 systems, 232-234
Interactive systems, 211-220
 benefits of, 213-214
 design of, 217-218
 programming of, 215-216
Interrupt handling, 167

Inverted file structures, 63-64
 indexes, 89
  maintenance of, 151-152
ISAM, see Indexed Sequential Access Method

James, R. T., 264
Jardine, Donald A., 103, 188
Job control and monitoring, 9-10
 initiation, 8-9
Job Control Language, 12

Kahn, David, 267, 280
Katzan, Harry, Jr., 13, 172, 280
Keehn, D. G., 103
Kent, Allen, 12
Key-direct structure, 89
 access in VSAM, 97
Key sequential access in VSAM, 97
Key to address transformation, 104-107
King, Donald W., 240
Knapp, Robert W., 240
Knotted lists, see Multilist
Knuth, Donald E., 33, 80, 116, 125, 138
Kuo, Franklin F., 172, 264

Lacy, J. O., 103
Laden, H. N., 12, 156
Lancaster, F. W., 172, 215, 222, 240
Language, command, 199-203
 data definition, 196
 for GDMS, 195-196
 processing, 10, 11, 181
 query, 197-198
 system, 218-220
Leased communication lines, 248
Lefkovitz, 12, 80, 103, 116, 138, 156
Leiter, Joseph, 263
Licklider, J. C. R., 222
Line control unit, 161
Linkage of programs, 10, 11, 186
Lipinski, Andrew J., 242, 263
List, 51
 structure, 31, 51-53, 56-64
Location of information, aids to, 104-116
 relative, 2
 physical, 49
 symbolic, 49
Lockout, 147
Logical file structure, 81-103
 types of, 87-91

298    Index

Machine readable catalog (MARC), 262
Mader, Chris, 172, 188
Maintenance of files, 139-156
  policy on, 152-156
  types of transactions, 140-147
Man-machine interaction, 211-220
Mark IV file management system, 175-177, 206
Marshall, Joseph C., 263
Martin, James, 12, 80, 172, 215, 222, 264, 280
Martin, Thomas H., 188, 222
Marzocco, Frank, 240
Master records in IDS, 75
Match, 47
McCarn, Davis B., 263
McCracken, D. D., 33
Meadow, Charles T., 13, 116, 138, 156, 172, 188, 215, 222, 264
Meaning of messages, 224
MEDLINE, 260
Memory geometry, 5, 34-39
Merging, 42
Message processing, 165-167, 168
  editing, 166
  scheduling and queuing, 166-167
Miller, Arthur, 180
Minker, Jack, 12
Modem, 159-160
Modification of files, 5
Modulation of signals, 159-160
Mooers, C. N., 12
Mooers' Law, 6
Multidrop lines, 161
Multilist, 59-63, 129-130
  maintenance of, 152
Multiplexing signals, 160-162
Multiprocessing, 171
Multiprogramming, 8

Name of a list, 56
National Crime Information Center, 269
National Data Service Center, 268
Natural language, 194
Network-based data management, 241-264
Networks, basic concepts of, 242-248
  centralized, 258
  communications, 242-258
  data management, 258-263
  distributed, 261-263

information, 6
  linking computer to, 254-258
  types of, 243-248
Neuman, A. J., 254, 263, 264
Node of a network, 242
Norman, Adrian R. D., 280

Operating systems, 7-12
  programming of, 11-12
Order of data elements, 5
Ordered file, 41
Ordering of records, 41-49
Output specification, 174
Overflow area, 69, 71
  independent, 73

Packaged software, 6
Packed decimal number representation, 18
Packet switching, 247-248
Paging, 91-93, 101-102
Performance, of information systems, 234-240
  evaluation of, 238-240
  measurement of, 236-238
  specification of, 235-236
Pierce, J. R., 33, 172, 264
Pirtle, M. W., 222
PL/I, 182, 205-206
Pointers, 29-31
  backward, 57
  explicit, 31
Pollack, S. V., 33
Position of information elements, 28-32
  logical, 28
  physical, 28
Positionally addressed structure, 87
Precedence, 17
Privacy, 6, 265-281
  as a computer problem, 265-270
  definition of, 269-270
Privacy Act of 1974, 156
Program libraries, 11
Programmers, 191, 192
Programming an operating system, 11-12
  of interactive systems, 215-217
  language, 210-211
Protection of data management systems, 265-279
  of computer systems, 270-279
  definition of, 270

Protocol, communications, 254-255
Push-down list, 125
Pyke, Thomas N., Jr., 264

Quality of information systems, 238
Question answering systems, 227

Ralston, Anthony, 172
Randomizing, 65-67
Random structure, 49-50, 65-67
Record, logical, 21
  order, 78-79
  organization, 23-25
  physical, 21
  storage, 79-80
  unit, 21
Recovery, 167, 184-185
Reference information system, 227
Referent file, 107
Relative byte address, 94
Remote job entry, 168-169
Reorganization of files, 74
Repetition of data elements, 20
Response time, 232, 237
Restart, 184-185
Retrieval specifications, 174
Ring structure, 57-59, 129
Rivest, R. L., 80
Roberts, L. C., 263-264
Rosove, Perry E., 12, 240

S-2000, 176
Sackman, Harold, 1, 12, 240
Satellite communications, 250
Schema, 209
Search, batch, 83
  binary, 48, 121-122
  criteria, 47
  digital, 121
  exhaustive, 48, 119-120
  field, 47
  key, 47
  of list structure, 123-130
  multifile, 133-137
  multiple key, 130-133
  ordered, 119-120
  output, 137-138
  resolution of, 117
  sequential, 48
  sublist, 123-124

successful, 117
techniques, 117-138
tree, 124-127
unsuccessful, 117
Security controls, 273-279
  of data management systems, 265-279
  definition of, 270
Semantics, 14
Senko, Michael E., 240
Sequence of information elements, 28-32
Sequence set, 95
Sequential files, 55
  files, maintenance of, 147-150, 151-152
  searching of, 119-122
  methods of organization, 55
  structure, 50-51
Shannon, Claude E., 157, 171
Simmons, Robert F., 240
Smith, Douglas K., 138
Social Security Administration, 19
Social security number, 19
Software, packaged, 6
Sort field, 41-42
  key, 41
Sorting, 29, 41-47
  bubble, 43-45
  exchange, 43-45
  external, 43
  internal, 43
Space-available list, 57
Stack, 125
Sterling, T. D., 33
Storage mechanisms, 34-40
  media, 5, 34
  protection, 273
  structure, 49-80
Structure changes to files, 139, 142-144
Subfields, 25
Sublists, 56
Subschema, 209
Summit, Roger K., 103, 188
Supervisor program, 165-166
Switching, 162-165
  line, 164
  message, 164
Symbol, as a unit of transmission, 14
  representation, 17-19
Synonym, 66, 114
Syntax, 15, 193
System, definition of, 1

Table, 55
Teleconferencing, 171
Teleprinter networks, 249-250
Telpak service, 249
Terminal of a network, 243
Thrashing, 92
Threaded lists, *see* Multilist
Throughput of an information system, 237
Ticket reservation systems, 212
Time-sharing, 8, 169-170
Transaction characteristics, 231-232
Transmission control unit, 161
Transmission, modes of, 243-248
  of messages, 224
Transparent computer features, 81
Tree structure, 111
Turn, Rein, 281
Turoff, Murray, 172
TYMNET, 250-256, 260, 262

UNIVAC File Computer, 46
User, analytic, 190-191
  end, 190
  impact of information system on, 218
  interface, 189-222
  language, 192-211
  types of, 189-192
Utility programs, 11, 186

Validation of data, 230-231
  of file changes, 144-147
  of input, 179-180
Value-added networks, 250-251
Vector, 20
Virtual file, 210
  memory, 90-101
  sequential access method, 93-101
Vocabulary of user language, 193
VSAM, *see* Virtual sequential access method

Weaver, Warren, 171
Weizenbaum, J., 80
Wessler, B. D., 4, 263
Westin, Alan F., 280
Wide-area telephone service, 249
Williams, S. B., 80